POLITICAL LIBERALIZATION IN THE PERSIAN GULF

For my daughters

" ישימך אלהים כשרה, רבקה, רחל ולאה..."

JOSHUA TEITELBAUM

editor

Political Liberalization in the Persian Gulf

Columbia University Press
New York

Columbia University Press
Publishers Since 1893
New York   Chichester, West Sussex

Copyright © 2009 Joshua Teitelbaum
All rights reserved

Library of Congress Cataloging-in-Publication Data

Political liberalization in the Persian Gulf / Joshua Teitelbaum, editor.
   p. cm.
Includes bibliographical references and index.
ISBN 978-0-231-70086-3 (cloth : alk. paper)
   1. Persian Gulf Region—Politics and government—21st century. 2. Free trade—Persian Gulf Region. I.
Teitelbaum, Joshua. II. Title.

DS326.P65 2008
953.6—dc22

                          2008048756

♾

Columbia University Press books are printed on permanent and durable acid-free paper.
This book is printed on paper with recycled content.
Printed in India

c 10 9 8 7 6 5 4 3 2 1

References to Internet Web sites (URLs) were accurate at the time of writing. Neither the author nor Columbia
University Press is responsible for URLs that may have expired or changed since the manuscript was prepared.

POWER AND POLITICS IN THE GULF

Christopher Davidson and Dirk Vanderwalle (editors)

After decades of sitting on the sidelines of the international system, the
energy-exporting traditional monarchies of the Arab Gulf (Saudi Arabia, the United Arab Emirates, Kuwait, Bahrain, Qatar and Oman) are
gradually transforming themselves into regional, and potentially global,
economic powerhouses. This series aims to examine this trend while
also bringing a consistent focus to the much wider range of other social, political, and economic issues currently facing Arab Gulf societies.
Quality research monographs,country case studies, and comprehensive
edited volumes have been carefully selected by the series editors in an effort to assemble the most rigorous collection of work on the region.

CONTENTS

CONTRIBUTORS

Muhammad al-Atawneh is Lecturer in the Department of Middle Eastern Studies, Ben-Gurion University of the Negev. He has been a Visiting Researcher in Harvard University's Islamic Legal Studies Program, and has published articles on Islamic law in Saudi Arabia. His book *Fatwas and Ifta' in Saudi Arabia: A History of Islamic Thought, 1971-2000* is in preparation.

Ofra Bengio is Senior Fellow at the Moshe Dayan Center for Middle Eastern and African Studies and Professor, Department of Middle Eastern and African History, Tel Aviv University. She is the author of several books and articles on Iraq, and most recently of *The Turkish-Israeli Relationship: Changing Ties of Middle Eastern Outsiders.*

Jill Crystal is Professor in the Department of Political Science at Auburn University. She is the author of *Oil and Politics in the Gulf: Rulers and Merchants in Kuwait and Qatar*, and *Kuwait: The Transformation of an Oil State.*

Christopher M. Davidson is a Fellow of the Institute for Middle Eastern and Islamic Studies at Durham University. He is a former Assistant Professor of Political Science at Sheikh Zayed University in Abu Dhabi and Dubai, and is the author of *The United Arab Emirates: A Study in Survival* and *Dubai: The Vulnerability of Success.*

Michael Herb is Associate Professor in the Department of Political Science, Georgia State University. He is the author of *All in the Family: Absolutism, Revolution and Democracy in the Middle Eastern Monarchies.*

Joseph Kostiner is Senior Fellow at the Moshe Dayan Center for Middle Eastern and African Studies, and Associate Professor, Department of

Middle Eastern and African History, Tel Aviv University. He is the author of *The Struggle for South Yemen*; *South Yemen's Revolutionary Strategy*; and *From Chieftaincy to Monarchical State: The Making of Saudi Arabia 1916-1936*. He is co-editor (with P.S. Khoury) of *Tribes and State Formation in the Middle East*.

Meir Litvak is Senior Lecturer in the Department of Middle Eastern and African History, and Senior Fellow at the Moshe Dayan Center for Middle Eastern and African Studies and the Center for Iranian Studies, at Tel Aviv University. He is author of *Shi'i Scholars of Nineteenth Century Iraq: The 'Ulama' of Najaf and Karbala'*, and co-author of *From Empathy to Denial: Arab Responses to the Holocaust*.

J.E. Peterson is a historian and political scientist specializing in the Arabian Peninsula and the Gulf. Until 1999, he served in the Office of the Deputy Prime Minister for Security and Defence in Muscat, Sultanate of Oman. He is the author of a dozen books on the Arabian Peninsula and the Gulf.

Uzi Rabi is Senior Lecturer in the Department of Middle Eastern and African History, Senior Researcher at the Center for Iranian Studies, and Research Fellow at the Moshe Dayan Center for Middle Eastern and African Studies, Tel Aviv University. He is the author of *The Emergence of States in a Tribal Society: Oman under Sa'id bin Taymur, 1932–1970*.

Elisheva Rosman-Stollman teaches political science and conflict studies at Bar Ilan University and Ashkelon Academic College. Her articles have appeared in *Middle Eastern Studies* and *Armed Forces & Society*.

Joshua Teitelbaum is Senior Fellow at the Moshe Dayan Center for Middle Eastern and African Studies, Tel Aviv University. He is also Visiting Associate Professor, Center on Democracy, Development, and the Rule of Law, Department of Political Science, and W. Glenn Campbell and Rita Ricardo Campbell National Fellow, Hoover Institution, Stanford University. He is the author of *The Rise and Fall of the Hashemite Kingdom of Arabia* and *Holier than Thou: Saudi Arabia's Islamic Opposition*.

Mary Ann Tétreault is the Una Chapman Cox Distinguished Professor of International Affairs at Trinity University in San Antonio, Texas, where she teaches courses in world politics, the Middle East, and feminist theory. Her most recent monographs are *Stories of Democracy: Politics and Society in Contemporary Kuwait*, and *The Kuwait Petroleum Corporation and the Economics of the New World Order*.

Onn Winckler is Senior Lecturer in the Department of the History of the Middle East at Haifa University. He is the author of *Modern Syria: From Ottoman Rule to Pivotal Role in the Middle East*, and co-editor (with Elie Podeh) of *Rethinking Nasserism: Revolution and Historical Memory in Modern Egypt*.

UNDERSTANDING POLITICAL LIBERALIZATION IN THE GULF: AN INTRODUCTION

Joshua Teitelbaum

Our world has changed tremendously since terror struck US shores. Nearly 3,000 people died on September 11, 2001 in a series of terrorist attacks carried out by nineteen Arabs, seventeen of whom were from Gulf[1] countries (fifteen from Saudi Arabia and two from the United Arab Emirates; the remaining two were Egyptian and Lebanese). The toll was greater than the losses incurred on December 7, 1941, following the Japanese attack at Pearl Harbor. Americans should be greatly concerned with what happens in the Gulf, not the least because 21 percent of US oil imports come from there,[2] but also because Americans have been and are currently in harm's way as a result of events in that turbulent region.

The main goal of any government is to provide for the security of its citizens. Providing for the security of Americans has often been linked to democracy promotion overseas, the belief being that if other countries shared what are perceived as American values, they would be less likely to do it harm. This book provides needed context and perspective for both practitioners and scholars concerned with the Gulf.

---

[1]   Iranians prefer the term Persian Gulf (*khalij-e fars*), while Arabs use the term Arab Gulf (*al-khalij al-'arabi*). We have entitled our book *Political Liberalization in the Persian Gulf* since in the West this body of water is most commonly termed in this manner. But in our discussion we have chosen to use the neutral term, Gulf, as is the practice in the leading scholarly forum on the Gulf, the Columbia University-based Gulf 2000.

[2]   Statistics are for January to June 2006. "Crude Oil Imports from Persian Gulf 2006," US Energy Information Administration, August 28, 2006, http://www.eia.doe.gov/pub/oil_gas/petroleum/data_publications/company_level_imports/current/summary2006.html.

It is worth briefly recalling some of the cultural and ideological foundations of the US response to 9/11, for they have an impact on how America pursued its post-9/11 policy in the Gulf and the Middle East as a whole.[3] As the US administration set about seeking explanations, and ways to respond that went beyond a military response, it drew on some deeply held ideas about America's role in the world. These ideas were derived from the very stuff that has made America what it is: the idea that America has a mission in the world, one that has often been carried out with religious zeal. George Kennan once remarked that US foreign policy has been periodically affected by periods of "evangelical idealism" dating from America's Puritan heritage.[4] One of the ideas brought about by the Puritan heritage was "Manifest Destiny." First coined by politicians of the 1840s as America expanded across the continent (although with earlier roots), the notion developed that the United States has a mission to settle North America, an idea not unlike the British "white man's burden" or the French *mission civilisatrice*. Indeed, most nations often have a sense of national destiny or purpose that guides foreign—and sometimes domestic—policy.

Preparing America for war in his "War Message" of April 2, 1917, President Woodrow Wilson waxed evangelical, stating that "America is privileged to spend her blood and her might for the principles that gave her birth and happiness and the peace which she has treasured. God helping her, she can do no other." "The world must be made safe for democracy," he most famously stated.[5] In post-9/11 America, the idea developed that America could best defend itself against terrorism by fostering democracy in the Middle East. And just as Manifest Destiny was often conceived in missionary, religious terms, so were the US democracy efforts in the Middle East not bereft of the same powerful religious symbolism. President George W. Bush, in his January 2003 State of the Union address, noted: "Americans are a free people, who know that freedom is the right of every person and the future of every nation. The liberty we prize is not America's

---

3   For a full discussion, see Tony Smith, *America's Mission: The United States and the Worldwide Struggle for Democracy in the Twentieth Century* (Princeton University Press, 1994); Ernest Lee Tuveson, *Redeemer Nation: The Idea of America's Millenial Role* (University of Chicago Press, 1968); Walter MacDougall, *Promised Land, Crusader State: The American Encounter with the World since 1776* (New York: Houghton Mifflin, 1997).

4   John Judis, "Some Mideast Realism, Please," *American Prospect*, Vol. 13, No. 24 (January 2003), http://www.prospect.org/print/V13/24/judis-j.html.

5   http://www.lib.byu.edu/~rdh/wwi/1917/wilswarm.html. The Kennan and Wilson remarks were brought to my attention by Reuven Pedatzur's article in *Haaretz*, December 19, 2006.

gift to the world, it is God's gift to humanity."[6] He repeated the refrain in his November 2003 speech on democracy in the Middle East: "Liberty is… the plan of Heaven for humanity."[7]

Various influential neo-conservatives supported this idea, and Bush himself remarked that he was particularly moved by the former Soviet refusenik and Israeli minister Natan Sharansky's book, *The Case For Democracy: The Power of Freedom to Overcome Tyranny and Terror*. In this book, Sharansky argued that it was in the nature of democracies not to be belligerent, and it followed that if countries that had populations which did not like the US could be made democratic, they would cease to be enemies of America. Bush said that the book summarized "how I feel," and urged people to read it.[8]

The 9/11 hijackers were Arabs and Muslims, and therefore "democracy promotion," drawing on a deep reserve of American sentiment, became the cornerstone of US policy toward the Muslim and Arab world. Nearly 90 percent of the hijackers were from the Gulf states profiled in this book, countries that were allies of the US.

For both policy and scholarly reasons, it is therefore important to know where the Gulf countries really stand when considering the general debate over American democracy promotion in the Middle East and the Islamic world at large. Failures in Egypt, the Palestinian territories and, most notably, Iraq have raised serious questions about this policy. Those in the field of democracy promotion have argued that the policy itself is not wrong, but that it has not been followed through—when elections have been supported before democratic institutions could be established—or else that the policy was carried out at gunpoint.[9] They persist in their opposition to the idea that the Arabs might be exceptional in not being prepared for democracy. Elie Kedourie probably put forward the most forthright case for Arab exceptionalism to democracy; he wrote that Arab political traditions held nothing "which might make familiar, or indeed intelligible, the organization ideas of constitutional and representative government," and concluded: "Those who say that democracy is the only remedy for the Arab

---

6   State of the Union address, January 28, 2003, http://www.whitehouse.gov/news/releases/2003/01/20030128-19.html.

7   Remarks by the President at the 20th Anniversary of the National Endowment for Democracy, http://www.whitehouse.gov/news/releases/2003/11/20031106-2.html.

8   "Bush's New Book for a New Term," news.bbc.co.uk, January 21, 2005.

9   Martin Kramer, "Democracy Promotion in the Middle East: Time for a Plan B?", Washington Institute for Near East Policy event, December 4, 2006.

world disregard a long experience which clearly shows that democracy has been tried in many countries and uniformly failed."[10]

The time seems ripe for a sober assessment of the possibility for, if not democratization, then liberalization in the Gulf states. "If they were more like us, would they like us?" is the question on the minds of many. The seemingly endless war in Iraq and the skyrocketing price of oil after 9/11 further focus policy and public imagination on this region. If these states liberalized, so went the argument, they would be more likely to be stable and to support the US agenda.

Those who follow the Middle East cannot but notice that with all the speeches made and the ink spilled about democracy and political liberalization in the region, there is only one area in which some progress has been made: the Gulf. More space has been made in the Gulf for political activity, beginning in the period following Iraq's invasion of Kuwait in August 1990. That war was a catalyst for liberalization most notably in Kuwait, but also throughout the Gulf. And this presents researchers with an interesting phenomenon. While these countries are usually perceived as more "traditional" (or patriarchical, neopatriarchal, patrimonial or neopatrimonial) despite the region's long history of monarchy and other forms of autocracy, Kuwait and Bahrain have received the designation "Partly Free" by Freedom House's 2007 report, a designation it shared with two other Middle Eastern monarchies, Jordan and Morocco (along with Lebanon and Mauritania).[11]

The Iraqi invasion of Kuwait in 1990 created "new realities" such as demands for change and the huge expenses of the war.[12] Gulf populations began openly to question both the large regional footprint of the United States and the inability of the leaders to protect them from invaders, both Western and Iraqi.[13] The "demonstration effect" of the fall of the Soviet Union added its influence as well, adding to a series of liberalization measures that were defensive in nature, ways for the regimes to cope with some popular demands and to cater to the West.

---

10   Elie Kedourie, *Democracy and Arab Political Culture*, quoted by Kramer, "Democracy Promotion in the Middle East: Time for a Plan B?", Washington Institute for Near East Policy event, December 4, 2006.

11   Freedom House, "Freedom in the World 2007," www.freedomhouse.org.

12   Anoushiravan Ehteshami, "Reform from Above: The Politics of Participation in the Oil Monarchies," *International Affairs*, Vol. 79, No. 1 (2003), pp. 53-75.

13   See the chapters on the Gulf countries by Joshua Teitelbaum in *Middle East Contemporary Survey*.

This book is the first to address the question of political liberalization of all the Gulf littoral countries. We have chosen to concentrate on political liberalization and not democratization, since democracy, probably most succinctly defined as the freely and regularly practiced replacing of leaders by universal suffrage,[14] does not exist in the Gulf, nor is it expected to in the foreseeable future. Yet there is no doubt that an opening—or liberalization—of the political space has taken place, whether in the restricted elections held in 2005 for just half of the seats in Saudi Arabia's essentially powerless municipal councils, or in Kuwait's vigorous parliament which can interpellate ministers.

While this book focuses on the Gulf, developments there are of course not divorced from the Middle East as a whole, where the scholarly community as well as the policy community have been focusing for many years on what has been called the "democracy deficit" or "democracy gap." Attention has been drawn famously to this in the series of UN-sponsored *Arab Human Development Reports* written by Arab scholars and issued since 2002. The report for 2002 noted that there "is a substantial lag between Arab countries and other regions in terms of participatory governance." In the 1990s, continued the report, the Arab states had the lowest freedom score out of the world's seven regions.[15] The *Arab Human Development Report 2004* was equally devastating, noting that despite "variations from country to country, rights and freedoms enjoyed in the Arab world remain poor." It went on to stress that while most Arab countries had elected parliaments, their election "was little more than a ritual, representing a purely

---

14   It will be clear that I prefer the electoral-procedural definition of democracy, as advanced by Robert Dahl. Dahl sets six criteria, two of which emphasize elections: elected officials; free, fair, and frequent elections; freedom of expression; access to alternative, independent sources of information; autonomous associations; and inclusive citizenship. See Robert Dahl: *Dilemmas of Pluralist Democracy* (New Haven: Yale University Press, 1982); *Polyarchy: Participation and Opposition* (New Haven: Yale University Press, 1971); "Democracy," *International Encyclopedia of the Social and Behavior Sciences*, Vol. 5 (Amsterdam: Elsevier, 2001), pp. 3405-8. While it is also recognized that definitions of democracy change over time, these criteria constitute how modern democracy should be conceived. In the Gulf, perhaps only one of these criteria obtains, and that is access to alternative, independent sources of information. This is due, however, mostly to the internet. In Kuwait, one may say that there are free and frequent elections, but questions remain how fair they are, and officials are not elected. Dahl essentially sees true democracy as liberal democracy, and therefore does not limit it to free, fair, and frequent elections. Larry Diamond parses out the variations of democracy and rightly cautions against viewing electoral authoritarian regimes as democratic. See Larry Diamond, *Developing Democracy: Toward Consolidation* (Baltimore: Johns Hopkins University Press, 1999), and Larry Diamond, "Thinking about Hybrid Regimes," *Journal of Democracy*, Vol. 13, No. 2 (April 2002), pp. 21-35.

15   *The Arab Human Development Report for 2002: Creating Opportunities for Future Generations* (New York: United Nations, 2002), pp. 2, 27.

formal application of a constitutional entitlement." The modern Arab state, notes the report, is a "black hole" state "which converts its surrounding social environment into a setting in which nothing moves and from which nothing escapes."[16]

Civil society

Scholars have been looking at the issue of political development in the Middle East for quite a long time.[17] Taking a cue from the disintegration of the Soviet Union and the fall of communist rule in its satellites, in the 1990s study of liberalization and democratization in the region focused on "civil society," that is, on the theory that voluntary social, political, and religious groups and institutions that were not part of the state were essential for formation of a space to work toward democracy, and would eventually challenge the state and bring about positive political change.[18] This effort resulted in a monumental, two-volume study of the issue, which argued that civil society, deemed by many as a *sine qua non* for liberalization and democratization properly conceived, did exist in the Middle East, and that therefore the region did indeed have some of the necessary prerequisites for positive change.[19] But the civil society approach had its limitations. First, it was difficult to assert that civil society actually existed in the Middle East, and in many cases the strongest "civil society" organizations were actually Islamist ones, which seemed committed to democracy and liberalization

---

16   *Arab Human Development Report 2004; Towards Freedom in the Arab World* (New York: United Nations, 2005), pp. 8, 9, 15.

17   During the post-colonial decade or so following World War II, Western scholars of the Middle East waxed hopeful about political development, particularly in Iraq, Syria, and Egypt. See, for example: Elizabeth Fernea and Robert Fernea, *The Arab World: Personal Encounters* (Garden City, NY: Anchor Press, 1985), pp. 204, 210; Roger Owen, "State and Society in the Middle East," *Items*, Vol. 44, No. 1 (March 1990), p. 10; Michael Hudson, "Arab Integration: An Overview," in Michael Hudson (ed.), *Middle East Dilemma: the Politics and Economics of Arab Integration* (New York: Columbia University Press, 1999), pp. 7-9, all cited in Kramer. Modernization was just around the corner and traditional society was thing of the past, as the title of Daniel Lerner's *The Passing of Traditional Society: Modernizing the Middle East* so famously claimed.

18   It was Alexis de Tocqueville who was the first to draw attention to the importance of civil society for American democracy. See Omar Encarnación, "Beyond Civil Society: Promoting Democracy after September 11," *Orbis* (Fall 2003), pp. 705-20.

19   Augustus Norton (ed.), *Civil Society in the Middle East*, 2 Vols (Leiden: Brill, 1995-96). A few years later liberalization and democratization were again the subject of a major study. See Rex Brynen, Bahjat Korany and Paul Noble (eds), *Political Liberalization and Democratization in the Arab World: Theoretical Perspectives*, Vol 1 (Boulder, CO: Lynne Rienner Publisher, 1995), and Bahjat Korany, Rex Brynen, and Paul Noble (eds), *Political Liberalization and Democratization in the Arab World: Comparative Experiences*, Vol 2 (Boulder: Lynne Reinner Publishers, 1998).

not as a value, but simply as the best way to seize power:[20] a case of "one man, one vote—once." Secondly, scholars also began to question the efficacy of the theory: "Contrary to popular opinion," wrote Omar Encarnación, "a vibrant and robust civil society is not a requirement or precondition for a successful democracy." It could actually undermine democracy, particularly if surrounded by failed or illegitimate institutions.[21] And the opposite could also be true: Rex Brynen notes that Romania was a country without civil society, but which did develop into a democratic country.[22]

Other scholars wanted to keep the theory, but simply change it a bit to fit the Middle East. Gerd Nonneman challenges us to think that civil society needs to be conceived differently where the Middle East is concerned, and takes one of his examples from the Gulf. When civil society is usually conceived as "modern, legal, formal activity or organization, aimed at the whole polity," it is often contrasted with the "primordialism, parochialism, and tradition which are seen as diametrically opposed to these ideals." Relying on the research by Sheila Carapico and Mary Ann Tétrault (see also Tétrault's contribution to this volume), he argues that in Yemen and Kuwait civil society is very much alive. In resource poor, highly tribalized Yemen, civil society expanded and then contracted with the repression of the state, which in the end had to take civil society demands into account. In resource-rich Kuwait, political space has expanded. Shifting the focus from civil society as traditionally conceived, Nonneman stresses that Tétrault looks more at "agency," which she defines as "the capacity of human beings to act, speak, convince and mobilize one another to do something together." It is in this space that a liberalization of politics can occur.[23] And it has indeed in several Persian Gulf countries, as several essays in this book demonstrate. This, of course, calls into question the utility of the entire civil society paradigm, and that is a good thing, as it has perhaps outlived its usefulness.

---

20   On the exploitation of civil society by Islamists, see Sheri Berman, "Islamism, Revolution, and Civil Society," *Perspectives on Politics*, Vol. 1, No. 2 (June 2003), pp. 13-26.

21   Encarnación, p. 706.

22   Rex Brynen, "Democratic Dominoes?," lecture and presentation delivered at the Moshe Dayan Center, Tel Aviv University, May 17, 2005, www.dayan.org/commentary/dominoes-brynen.pdf.

23   Gerd Nonneman, "State of the Art: Rentiers and Autocrats, Monarchs and Democrats, State and Society – The Middle East between Globalization, Human 'Agency', and Europe," *International Affairs*, Vol. 77, No. 1 (2001), pp. 141-62.

Culture and society

Recently, scholars of the Middle East have also looked, gingerly, at issues of political culture to explain the liberalization and/or the lack thereof. Fearing that examining "culture" might brand them racist or even worse— "Orientalist"[24]—they have only recently returned to the concept and acknowledged some of its explanatory power.[25] Still, they are wary. Korany, Brynen and Noble are clearly uncomfortable with the idea, and put the concept in quotation marks. Under the sub-heading "Contextualizing 'Political Culture'," they write: "Certainly, attitudes seem to play some role in shaping political outcomes. Yet there is clearly not some timeless and overarching Arab-Islamic political 'culture' that determines the politics of the region. If this were true, one would expect political homogeneity rather than the heterogeneous group of political systems that characterize the Arab world today."[26] Perhaps, but there is indeed some political homogeneity in the lack of freedom and democracy.

While Middle East area specialists are extremely wary of cultural explanations, comparativists and actual Middle Easterners are not. As explained by Samuel Huntington in his and Lawrence Harrison's *Culture Matters*, culture is a "large part of the explanation" of why some societies develop economically and politically, while others do not.[27] Far from being deterministic and racist, Huntington drives home the point that cultural values can change, as happened in Germany and Japan after World War II, and in Spain, which was widely assumed to have an authoritarian culture.[28] Culture, like other aspects of a society, can adjust as a result of historical

24   On the effect of Edward Said's theory of "Orientalism" on the academy, see Joshua Teitelbaum and Meir Litvak, "Students, Teachers, and Edward Said: Taking Stock of Orientalism," *Middle East Review of International Affairs* (March 2006), pp. 23-43.

25   Michael Hudson, "The Political Culture Approach to Arab Democratization: The Case for Bringing it Back in, Carefully," in Brynen, Korany and Noble, vol. 1, pp. 61-76.

26   Korany, Brynen, and Noble, vol. 2, p. 267.

27   Samuel Huntington, "Foreword," in Lawrence Harrison and Samuel Huntington (eds), *Culture Matters: How Values Shape Human Progress* (New York: Basic Books, 2000), p. xiii. See also Ronald Ingelhart, "The Renaissance of Political Culture," *American Political Science Review*, Vol. 82, No. 4 (December 1988), pp. 1203-30; Pippa Norris and Ronald Ingelhart, "Cultural Obstacles to Equal Representation," *Journal of Democracy*, Vol. 12, No. 3 (July 2001), pp. 126-40.

28   Huntington, p. xv. This idea forms the central argument in Lawrence Harrison's new complementary volume, *The Central Liberal Truth: How Politics Can Change a Culture and Save It from Itself* (New York: Oxford University Press, 2006).

and political circumstances. Catholic countries, where the church was once widely seen as an impediment to democracy, are a case in point.[29]

Middle Easterners writing about the difficulties of democratic development and liberalization do not hesitate to look at cultural and social explanations. In fact, self-criticism in the Arab world has increased to the point where "had it come from any other pens, [it] would have been dismissed as stereotypical Orientalism."[30] First, there is the nature of much of Arab society itself, perhaps even a cultural flaw according to the analysis of the late Hisham Sharabi, a Palestinian scholar formerly at Georgetown University. He described Arab society as being afflicted by "neopatriarchy," whereby modernization has been harnessed to strengthen rather than change traditional patriarchical society. This kind of society, writes Sharabi, is dominated by a patriarch, who is the center around which the nation as well as the family are organized. There exists only a vertical relationship between the ruler and the ruled, the father and the child, and the paternal will is the absolute will. The internal security apparatus, the *mukhabarat*, is the most advanced and functional aspect of the neopatriarchical state. "Thus in social practice ordinary citizens are not only arbitrarily deprived of some of their basic rights, but are the virtual prisoners of the state, the objects of its capricious and ever-present violence, much as citizens were under the classical or Ottoman sultanate." The neopatriarchical state is no more than a modernized version of the traditional patriarchical sultanate.[31]

As for civil society (he terms it civil space), writes Sharabi, where one would hope to find shelter from the state or from family, clan or religious sect, this too is similarly affected by authority and violence. "Thus whatever the outward ('modern') forms – material, legal, aesthetic – of the contem-

---

29   Rex Brynen, "Democratic Dominoes?" Larry Diamond, citing Huntington, credits changes within the Catholic Church as contributing to the "Third Wave" of democratization which swept many Catholic countries in Europe and South America. The church moved from supporting oppressive ruling establishments to the forefront of the struggle against authoritarian rule. Larry Diamond, "Can the Whole World Become Democratic? Democracy, Development, and International Policies," April 17, 2003, *Center for the Study of Democracy*, Paper 03-05, http://repositories.cdlib.org/csd/03-05. But it is worth mentioning that Islam has no hierarchy approaching that of Catholicism, and therefore there is no Islamic "Church" to initiate and carry out such a policy.

30   John Waterbury, "Democracy without Democrats?: The Potential for Political Liberalization in the Middle East," in Ghassan Salamé (ed.), *Democracy without Democrats: The Renewal of Politics in the Muslim World* (London: I.B. Tauris, 1994), pp. 23-47 (quote on pp. 30-1).

31   Hisham Sharabi, *Neopatriarchy: A Theory of Distorted Change in Arab Society* (New York: Oxford University Press, 1988), p. 7.

porary neopatriarchical family and society, their internal structures remain rooted in the patriarchical values and social relations of kinship, clan, and religious and ethnic groups."[32]

Arab writers writing in Arabic have not shied away from cultural explanations for the lack of political development in their region. A huge selection of this kind of writing, translated into English, has been assembled by MEMRI, as part of its "Reform in the Arab and Muslim World" project.[33] While proclaiming that "the real flaw behind the failure of democracy is not cultural in origin," the Arab authors of the 2004 *Arab Human Development Report* do not pull punches when criticizing Arab society. They blame what they call the "chain that stifles individual freedom," which they specify, much like Sharabi, as the Arab family and "clannism." These structures implant submission and are the enemy of personal independence, say the authors.[34]

Alfred Stepan (with Graeme Robertson) tried to isolate the Islamic variable from the Arab one by looking at electoral competitiveness as a measure of democracy, noting that of the 47 Muslim-majority countries, the sixteen Arab countries noticeably "underachieve," while the thirty-one other non-Arab Muslim-majority countries "greatly overachieve." This means, he writes, that "Islam" cannot be the main cultural factor preventing democracy. Despite liberalization in the Gulf countries, Stepan notes correctly that in none of them "have the most important and powerful political offices actually been filled by way of free and fair elections."[35] On the other hand, M. Steven Fish's analysis of the level of democracy in Muslim societies concludes that Muslim countries "are markedly more authoritarian than non-Muslim societies, even when one controls for other potentially influential factors."[36]

---

32   Sharabi, p. 8.

33   MEMRI, Reform in the Arab and Muslim World, http://www.memri.org/reform.html. Arabic-language websites such as www.elaph.com and www.metransparent.com (in English as well) also carry on such a dialogue.

34   *Arab Human Development Report 2004*, p. 17.

35   Alfred Stepan with Graeme Robertson, "An 'Arab' More than a Muslim Electoral Gap," *Journal of Democracy*, Vol. 14, no. 3 (July 2003), pp. 30-44. Stepan's data only go up to the year 2000, and might have changed slightly with the enfranchisement of women in Kuwait in and other liberalization efforts, but probably not altered his overall conclusions.

36   M. Steven Fish, "Islam and Authoritarianism," *World Politics*, Vol. 55, No. 1 (October 2002), pp. 4-37 (quote on p. 37).

Vali Nasr looks hopefully at "Muslim Democrats"—not simply Islamist parties which admit the democratic process. Whereas the latter, he argues, do not view democracy as legitimate but rather only as a tool to gain power and establish an Islamic state, the former do not wish to "enshrine Islam in politics, though they do wish to harness its potential to help them win votes."[37] Nasr's examples (Bangladesh, Indonesia, Turkey, Malaysia, and Pakistan until the 1999 military coup) are, however, admittedly taken from non-Arab Islamic countries.

Bernard Lewis is more cautious. He notes that since Islam is not just a religion but a civilization, adopting extra-civilizational world-views is more difficult, particularly with respect to political theory, where Islam has a long and venerated tradition. This tradition is not necessarily incompatible with liberal democracy, as it contains within it liberal ideas, such as disapproval of arbitrary rule and an emphasis on dignity and humility.[38] In practice, however, Muslim leaders often did not adhere to these ideas, which was, of course, the reason for their formulation by Islamic jurists. The ideal ruler was Muhammad, who was both a prophet and a ruler. Islam was interpenetrated by "cult and power, religion and the state." While historically Islamic scholars have produced copious volumes on nearly every aspect of the state, there was little discussion of the distinction between temporal and religious powers. Arabic had no intrinsic word for citizen, democracy, or freedom.[39]

In "The Impossible Imperative? Conjuring Arab Democracy," Adam Garfinkle maintains that the Arab countries lack "certain dispositional pre-requisites" for democracy, including the notion that society itself is the source of state authority, and the concept of majority rule. In Western-style democracies, legitimacy stems from the people, while in Islam it stems from God. With respect to the idea of majority rule, Arab societies have sanctified consensus, where the idea, simply put, of a leader being chosen by only 51 percent of the people is a hard sell. Agreeing with Huntington's

---

37   Vali Nasr, "The Rise of 'Muslim Democracy,'" *Journal of Democracy*, Vol. 16, No. 2 (April 2005), pp. 13-27 (p. 14 quoted).

38   Bernard Lewis, "Islam and Liberal Democracy: A Historical Overview," *Journal of Democracy*, Vol. 7, No. 2 (1996), pp. 52-63.

39   Lewis. On the word "democracy" in Arabic, see also Ofra Bengio's chapter in this volume. Freedom, usually translated into Arabic as *hurriya*, originally meant the opposite of being a slave. It later came to mean freedom from foreign occupation, and has only recently assumed the meaning of freedom of oppression by the individual from his own government.

general observation on culture, Garfinkle concludes that, like other societies, Arab societies can change as well.[40]

Garfinkle's arguments are supported by one of the Arab world's most famous poets and social critics, 'Ali Ahmad Sa'id, known as Adonis. Like Garfinkle, he conflates Islam and Arab society, stressing that the two together prevent the emergence of democracy: "If we want to be democratic, we must be so by ourselves. But the *preconditions for democracy do not exist in Arab society*, and cannot exist unless religion is reexamined in a new and accurate way, and unless religion becomes a personal and spiritual experience, which must be respected." He adds: "The Arab individual is no less smart, no less a genius, than anyone else in the world. *He can excel - but only outside his society*."[41] On another occasion Adonis stressed, like Lewis, that in the case of the Arabs, political rule was based on religion. And like Sharabi, he argues culturally and socially that the "Arab individual does not elect from among people of different opinions who represent different currents. The Arab is accustomed to voting according to pre-determined concepts. Whoever represents this pre-determined concept...The nationalist will vote for a nationalist, and the communist will vote for a communist. These are all types of religious sects. The tribal and sectarian structure has not disintegrated, and has not melted down into the new structure of democracy and the democratic option."[42]

The assessment of several researchers and leading Middle East intellectuals is that Islam and Middle Eastern culture act together in ways that "do not auger well for democracy."[43] In Frederic Pryor's recent statistical analysis of studies on Islam and democracy, including several mentioned here, he stresses that in "all but the poorest countries, Islam is associated with fewer political rights." Countries with an Arab culture were found to have an even lower level of political rights than other Muslim countries.[44]

40   Adam Garfinkle, "The Impossible Imperative? Conjuring Arab Democracy," *The National Interest*, Fall 2002, pp. 156-63 (p. 162 quoted).

41   "Renowned Syrian Poet 'Adonis': The Arabs are Extinct," Dubai TV, March 11, 2006, translated by MEMRI, Special Dispatch Series, No. 1121, March 21, 2006. Emphasis mine.

42   "Renowned Syrian Poet 'Adonis': 'We, in Arab Society, Do Not Understand the Meaning of Freedom,'" ANB TV, November 26, 2006, MEMRI, Special Dispatch Series, No. 1393, December 15, 2006.

43   Waterbury, p. 33.

44   Frederic Pryor, "Are Muslim Countries Less Democratic?" *Middle East Quarterly*, Vol. 14, No. 4 (Fall 2007). A more detailed and technical version of the Pryor article can be found at www.swarthmore.edu/SocSci/Economics/fpryor1/Islam%20and%20Democracy.pdf.

It is very important to add, however, that when asked, Arabs express support for democracy. Moreover, research demonstrates that Islam should not be reified and that even those with strong Islamic attachments support democracy.[45] Pryor concludes hopefully that since several Muslim countries have good political freedom ratings, there is the possibility that "this deficit may not be a permanent condition."[46]

The rentier state

The "rentier" mode of production, according to the 2004 *Arab Human Development Report*, is directly responsible for perpetuating authoritarian governance.[47] A rentier state is a state that gains most of its revenues from natural resources ("rent")—in the case of the Gulf states covered in this book, oil. This can theoretically make the state autonomous over a long period of time, since such a state does not need to rely on society for revenue, usually in the form of taxation. Moreover, as Giacomo Luciani writes,

a state that economically supports society and is the main source of private revenues through government expenditures, while in turn is supported by revenue accruing from abroad, does not need to respond to society. On the contrary, a state that is supported by society, through taxes levied in one form or another, will in the final analysis be obliged to respond to societal pressure.[48]

According to rentier theory, since these countries do not need to tax their citizens, they do not need to demonstrate accountability either, nor to grant representation. Instead, governments provide for their citizens and demand no taxes in return. The citizens, so goes the theory, do not demand representation.

---

45   Mark Tessler, "Islam and Democracy in the Middle East: The Impact of Religious Orientations on Attitudes toward Democracy in Four Arab Countries," *Comparative Politics*, Vol. 34, No. 3 (April 2002), pp. 337-54; Mark Tessler and Eleanor Gao, "Gauging Arab Support for Democracy," *Journal of Democracy*, Vol. 16, No. 3 (July 2005), pp. 83-97.

46   Pryor.

47   *Arab Human Development Report 2004*, pp. 151-3. This theory is also advanced by Jill Crystal, *Oil and Politics in the Gulf: Rulers and Merchants in Kuwait and Qatar* (Cambridge University Press, 1995); Giacomo Luciani, "Allocation vs. Production States: A Theoretical Framework," in Giacomo Luciani (ed.), *The Arab State* (Berkeley: University of California Press, 1990); and Lisa Anderson, "The State in the Middle East and North Africa," *Comparative Politics* 20 (October 1987), pp. 1-18.

48   Giacomo Luciani, "Resources, Revenues, and Authoritarianism in the Arab World: Beyond the Rentier State," in Brynen, Korany and Noble, Vol. 1, pp. 211-22. The classic statement of rentier theory is Hazim Beblawi and Giacomo Luciani (eds), *The Rentier State* (London: Croom Helm, 1987).

Michael Ross probably makes the best case for a strong causal link between rentier states and authoritarianism, and states forthrightly that oil income hinders democracy building. Rentier states effectively buy off the opposition, in what Ross calls "fiscal pacification."[49]

Rentier theory has come in for its fair share of criticism. John Waterbury argues convincingly that taxation in the Middle East has traditionally produced revolts, not representation.[50] In fact, there is little direct taxation anywhere in the Middle East, so rentierism might not be the explanation for the survival of authoritarianism in the Gulf. Michael Herb also calls into question the causal relationship between rentierism and authoritarian rule. Using different data sets and methods than those used by Ross, he does not find a causal link between rentierism and democracy scores. Authoritarianism, he concludes, is more likely found in regional factors, although he does not elaborate on them.[51] Most likely these factors are some of the others discussed here, such as culture, society, and the lack of civil society.

In the early 1990s Saddam's invasion of Kuwait was the catalyst for movements for greater representation in Saudi Arabia, Kuwait, and Bahrain. Among the issues raised was how rent was distributed. Gwenn Okruhlik argues that even if at times the state can buy off the opposition, "in Saudi Arabia, Kuwait, and Bahrain opposition has arisen and with it a discrepancy between the expectations derived from the rentier framework and empirical reality. Not the simple receipt of oil revenue, but the choices made on how to spend it shape development."[52] While Okhrulik maintains that there has always been opposition in Saudi Arabia based on regional (Najdi vs. Hijazis) or religious divisions (minority Shiites vs. majority Sunnis), I would add that this opposition, including the opposition of the 1990s, has never been particularly effective or widespread, although it did elicit some symbolic changes in Saudi Arabia, such as the creation of a non-elected consultative council. In Kuwait and Bahrain, on the other hand, opposition has been effective, and had led to more representation. It

---

49   Michael Ross, "Does Oil Hinder Democracy?" *World Politics*, Vol. 53 (April 2001), pp. 325-61.

50   Waterbury.

51   Michael Herb, "No Representation without Taxation? Rents, Development, and Democracy," *Comparative Politics*, Vol. 37, No. 3 (April 2005), pp. 297-316.

52   Gwenn Okruhlik, "Rentier Wealth, Unruly Law, and the Rise of Opposition: The Political Economy of Oil State," *Comparative Politics*, Vol. 31, No. 3 (April 1999), pp. 295-315.

is much harder in those countries to buy off the opposition, so the rentier model may apply less there than in Saudi Arabia.

Half empty or half full: the record of liberalization in the Gulf

It has become axiomatic in political science that with an increase in economic freedom and the rise in the level of socio-economic status (SES), a middle class will develop and demand accountability, eventually leading to democracy.[53] Yet the Middle East has shown itself quite resistant to that paradigm.

The Middle East, writes John Waterbury, has "an environment singularly inhospitable to legal pluralism and democracy." Armed conflict (which enables the state to oppress its citizens) and an oppressive and pervasive military and intelligence apparatus (sometimes called the *mukhabarat* state) are certainly factors that impede democratization. Waterbury also adds another critical factor, what he terms "the ambivalent middle class." Whereas in many countries the middle class supports democratization as it develops its own priorities that are not always in line with those of the state, in the Middle East in general, and the Gulf in particular, a huge portion of the middle class is often made up of bureaucrats who are employed by and are dependent on the state. Even members of the private sector are often beholden to the state for contracts and access, in what has been termed an "alliance for profits." Finally, Waterbury echoes what we have written, notably that Islam and patriarchy, which constitute Middle Eastern culture, inhibit democratization.[54]

As demonstrated in this book, some combination of the factors discussed above works throughout the Middle East and in the Gulf to inhibit democratization. But in the Gulf, rising SES, while not facilitating democratization, has facilitated a degree of liberalization, particularly, but not only, in Kuwait, Bahrain, and Qatar. There are more demands for accountability, and nearly everywhere in the region the regimes have responded to varying degrees by institutionalizing some forms of liberalization, all of which are discussed by the authors of the chapters in this book. Certainly the

---

53   On the association between democracy and indicators of national wealth, communication, industrialization, urbanization and education, see Seymour Lipset, *Political Man: On the Social Bases of Politics*, new and updated edition (Baltimore: The Johns Hopkins University Press, 1981), and Marsha Pripstein Posusney, "Enduring Authoritarianism: Middle East Lessons for Comparative Theory," *Comparative Politics*, Vol. 36, No. 2 (January 2004), pp. 127-38.

54   Waterbury.

tight relationship between the bureaucratic and private sector middle class has limited demands for democratization. These elites know that they can make the government more responsive, but they are not all that enthusiastic about real elections, since they are not organized enough to protect their interests and they fear the Islamists, who have a good chance of winning.

The governments of the Gulf have learned how to respond skillfully to calls for liberalization. To a great extent, these are "liberalized autocracies," to use Daniel Brumberg's term.[55] They know how to maneuver, how to give just enough and take just enough, in order to remain in power. So these systems work to the benefit of the rulers. They are not committed ideologically to democracy, and their programs of liberalization are simply instrumental, sophisticated ways of remaining in power.

In a way they have little choice, and here we can lay the blame at the foot of globalization and its harbinger, the new media. Once, it was possible for Gulf regimes to control the access to information. The government controlled the press and the airwaves as well. This system reached its apex in Saudi Arabia. The local press was semi-official, and to a great extent still is. Television and radio were entirely government controlled, and consisted primarily of religious speeches, Qur'an readings, and the comings and goings of the royal family. The main satellite channels, MBC and Orbit, were Saudi-owned, as were the two main pan-Arab newspapers, *al-Sharq al-Awsat* and *al-Hayat*.[56]

But since the mid-1990s, this has become increasingly more difficult. The advent of the Al-Jazeera Satellite Channel is only the most obvious of these new developments. Even the local media have had to make themselves more interesting to compete with satellite channels, and newspapers are now allowed to discuss previously taboo issues such as the status of women, the religious establishment, and corruption. Criticism of the Saudi family, however, remains out of bounds. Even though Saudi Arabia tries to filter the internet, it knows that it is only partially successful, so that all kinds of new information are flooding the country. Without a monopoly on the flow of information, controlled liberalization becomes a necessity.[57]

55   Daniel Brumberg, "The Trap of Liberalized Autocracy," *Journal of Democracy*, Vol. 10, No. 4 (October 2002), pp. 56-68.

56   Joshua Teitelbaum, "If You Can't Beat 'Em, Buy 'Em," *The Jerusalem Report*, November 16, 1995, p. 48.

57   Joshua Teitelbaum, "Dueling for Da`wa: State vs. Society on the Saudi Internet," *Middle East Journal*, Vol. 56 (Spring 2002), pp. 222-39.

One distinguishing feature of political and social life in at least the Arab Gulf states has received scant attention in the literature. This is the role of tribalistic patterns of politics and their influence on liberalization. The demand for liberalization, not to speak of democracy, may be attenuated because citizens look to their tribes or tribally based patron-client relationships to get things done. These mechanisms are generally quite effective, and subjects can often obtain what they need through these connections. (See Joseph Kostiner's and Christopher M. Davidson's contributions to this volume.)[58]

Reference to tribalistic patterns of politics recalls Sharabi's "neopatriarchy" and suggests the related terms "neopatrimonialism" and "patrimonialism." Max Weber introduced the term patrimonialism to describe the highly personalized ruling structure and bureaucracies in the Middle East, Asia, and parts of Africa. Like Sharabi's neopartriachy, neopatrimonialism is a modern incarnation of a traditional form of rule, augmented by the apparatus of the modern state.[59] In her study of the robustness of authoritarianism in the Middle East, Eva Bellin concludes that this robustness is due to the coercive apparatus. This apparatus's effectiveness results from several factors which obtain in the Gulf states, including patrimonialism. It enables elites to use favoritism and patronage to build a loyal base made up of people advanced through tribal and family connections. Patrimonialism, so strong in the GCC countries which have patrimonial monarchies, helps make regimes resistant to democratic reforms. The entire state, which constitutes one big coercive apparatus, sees little or no opening for reforms, since these might mean the end of family rule. In the GCC states, rule is family rule.[60] As shown in this book, patrimonial monarchical rule in the

---

58   Joseph Kostiner, "The Nation in Tribal Societies – Reflections on K.H. al-Naqib's Studies on the Gulf," in *Tel Aviver Jarbuch f ür deutsche Geschichte*, Vol. 30 (2002), pp. 212-22, and Madawi Al Rasheed, *A History of Saudi Arabia* (Cambridge University Press, 2002), particularly pp. 188-217.

59   On Weber's patrimonialism, see Max Weber, *Economy and Society* (New York: Bedminister Press, 1978). Shmuel Eisenstadt was apparently the first to use the term neopatrimonialism, in his *Traditional Patrimonialism and Modern Neopatrimonialism* (London: Sage Publications, 1973). See also Gero Erdmann and Ulf Engel, "Neopatrimonialism Reconsidered: Critical Review and Elaboration of an Elusive Concept," *Commonwealth and Comparative Politics*, Vol. 45, No. 1 (February 2007), pp. 95-119. Researchers have tended to conflate the two terms: I will use patrimonialism.

60   Others factors mentioned are fiscal health (in our case, oil wealth); maintenance of international support networks (this certainly obtains in the case of massive Western support for the GCC countries); and the lack of significant popular mobilization (popular mobilization has only occurred in Iran, during the Islamic Revolution). Eva Bellin, "The Robustness of Authoritarianism in the Middle East," *Comparative Politics*, Vol. 36, No.

GCC states goes a long way toward explaining not only the staying power of authoritarianism and the resistance to democracy, but also why limited liberalization has been chosen as a way for these regimes to cope.

There is one final obstacle to real democracy and liberalization in many of the Gulf countries. This is the presence of huge numbers of disenfranchised foreign workers. (See Onn Winckler's contribution to this volume.) In each of the countries in the Gulf Cooperation Council (GCC: Saudi Arabia, Bahrain, Qatar, Kuwait, Oman, and the UAE), the percentage of non-nationals in the population runs from a low of forty percent in Bahrain to a high of eighty percent in the UAE.[61] If one focuses in on the labor force, which might be said to be in an age range roughly equivalent to voting age, every GCC country has a labor force that is over fifty percent foreign (from a low of sixty percent in Bahrain to a high of ninety percent in the UAE).[62] Democratization can never take place without enfranchising this population, and certainly liberalization can never take place without opening up political space for it. Non-nationals have no role in any of the current liberalization policies in the GCC. They cannot vote, and their voices are nearly invisible in the liberalized political space created in the past few years. We therefore note this important feature of Gulf demographics, since if GCC countries do not address this issue, which they are unlikely to do, any talk by Gulf leaders of liberalization may be, as they say in the Middle East, *kalam fadi*—empty words.

༜

This book puts political liberalization in the Gulf on the map. It helps explain why democracy is unlikely to occur in the near future, and why political liberalization has taken root instead. Of course, it is an interim assessment only, as it must be. Through it the reader of this book will discover

---

2 (January 2004), pp. 139-57. Jason Brownlee stresses in a similar fashion that "patrimonial ties can help the regime endure...challenges and feat its domestic opponents." Jason Brownlee, "...And Yet They Persist: Explaining Survival and Transition in Neopatrimonial Regimes," *Studies in Comparative International Development*, Vol. 37, No. 3 (Fall 2002), pp. 35-63. As Brownlee points outs, for comparativists who debate the relative weight of structure vs. agency in democratic transitions, a focus on patrimonialism, which involves both, can contribute to a synthesis. On this debate and its Middle Eastern applications, see Marsha Posusney, "Enduring Authoritarianism: Middle East Lessons for Comparative Theory," *Comparative Politics*, Vol. 36, No. 2 (January 2004), pp. 127-38.

61   Statistics are from 2002, and are taken from Andrzej Kapiszewski, "Political Reforms in the GCC Countries: Are Monarchies of the Gulf Democratizing?", *Acta Asiatica Varsoviensia*, No. 15 (2002).

62   Statistics relate to 2002.

the varieties of political liberalization in the Gulf, through the expertise of the scholars assembled herein. The articles demonstrate that reforms have addressed economic and some social issues, but have not resulted in any fundamental redistribution of power.

This book is addressed both to the scholar and the practitioner. The articles included herein advance our understanding of the breadth and depth of political liberalization in this important regional arena.

The foregoing offered an analysis of the general issues associated with liberalization and democratization in the Middle East and the Gulf in particular. In the first part of this book, three authors examine Gulf region-specific aspects of liberalization. In the second part, the authors have carried out country studies. Kuwait receives extra treatment, with two chapters, since it has gone the furthest in its liberalization program. Unlike most studies of political development in the Gulf, which leave out Iran and Iraq, we have included chapters on these important countries in order to present a complete picture. Rather then trying to create a "handbook" of liberalization that would follow a shopping list of pre-determined items and force scholars from different disciplines into unfamiliar territory, it was decided that scholars and general readers would best be served by having each author discuss Gulf liberalization from within their own discipline and area of concentration. For instance, Onn Winckler, an economic historian, concentrates on labor issues, while Muhammad al-Atawneh, an authority on the history of Islamic law, examines clerics' views on liberalization in Saudi Arabia. Their contributions and others reflect these differences, enrich our understanding, and give added value to this collection.

The fast pace of developments in some of these countries has made the task of editing particularly challenging in keeping the chapters as timely as possible. The themes and trends outlined herein will be with us for years to come. That said, this is a dynamic region undergoing dynamic processes— witness the ever-changing situation in Iraq.

Joseph Kostiner, in his contribution to this volume, emphasizes that tribal or kin-based groups have traditionally provided Gulf societies with protection from the state. Kostiner's assertions bear out Tétrault's and Carapico's view (discussed above) that primordialism does not eliminate the chance for liberalization. In the process of state-formation, leaders did not destroy the kin-based structure of society, as they themselves were part of it. Instead, they incorporated it into the ruling system, and used it to extend and consolidate their rule, even as the kin-based structures afforded some degree of representation vis-à-vis the state. But demographic growth has made it harder to maintain the kinship basis of political ties, and the government has been forced to embark on some liberalization in order to relegitimize its rule. The bottom line remains, however, that in these "kin-ordered monarchies,"[63] the supremacy of the ruling family is maintained.

In her contribution, Jill Crystal reminds us that the semi-elected or partially-elected institutions in the Arab states of the GCC are created by the leaders in order to maintain power. The same goes for economic liberalization. These governments maintain repressive capacity and the willingness to use it. There are no political parties, and there is limited judicial independence. That said, writes Crystal, these moves have been dramatic and the fact that they are limited does not diminish their importance. The business community has mixed feelings about economic and political liberalization. While the former can increase profits, it threatens competition with those members of the community having particularly close ties to the ruling families. While individual merchants support political liberalization, as a whole the business community has no particular commitment to a parliament (but no animosity toward it either).

Onn Winckler examines the contribution of the GCC rentier state to the dual labor market (nationals in the public sector and non-nationals in the private sector) in the Gulf, and its implications for political liberalization. Until the mid-1990s, the employment of nationals was well taken care of: they were simply guaranteed employment in the public sector, and this served as the cornerstone of the rentier political economy. The regimes therefore did not have to resort to political liberalization for regime legitimization and survival. But beginning in the 1990s serious efforts were made to reduce the size of the foreign workforce, and this was helped by higher oil prices. Yet these regimes discovered that nationals could not compete in the private sector, and therefore unemployment of nationals increased, as did the employment of foreign nationals. Theoretically, argues Winckler, the increased oil prices since the mid-1990s might have increased the leverage of the state and maintained the rentier economy for future generations, yet in actuality high prices will not obviate the need for political liberalization, although they may slow its pace. This is because GCC populations continue to increase at rates that have led to a continued decrease in per capita GDP, despite higher oil prices. Unemployment of nationals is there-

---

63   A term well chosen by Nazih Ayubi, *Over-Stating the Arab State: Politics and Society in the Middle East* (London: I.B. Tauris, 1995), p. 224.

fore acute and will continue to function as a driver of political liberalization as the regimes seek to placate the opposition.

Our country studies begin with Saudi Arabia, the most populous and influential actor in the Gulf. Muhammad al-Atawneh asserts the centrality of religion and the influence of clerics in Saudi society, and therefore the necessity to address the approach of the establishment *'ulama* to ideas of liberalization and democracy. Nearly all laws in the kingdom are based on Islamic jurisprudence (*fiqh*), and this is a factor in providing legitimacy for the regime. In general, these clerics reject democracy as a Western innovation and as part of a Western intellectual invasion. According to al-Atawneh, the idea of democracy itself, where sovereignty rests with the people, is inimical to Wahhabi thought, since sovereignty rests ultimately with God. Given this view of democracy, al-Atawneh does not see it ever being achieved in Saudi Arabia. That said, certain liberalization measures can be and have been implemented, but not without the consent of the *'ulama.*

On the other end of the liberalizing spectrum from Saudi Arabia is Kuwait. This country's role as the harbinger of liberalization—and in its own case, even democracy—in the region merits a double-barreled examination. Mary Ann Tétreault concentrates on gender as a prism for assessing Kuwaiti political development. The lack of universal suffrage until May 2005 galvanized women's groups. Opposition to women's rights comes from both liberals and traditionalists who fear that women will demand equal personal status. Thus getting the vote does not assure equal status. It could lead to an unhelpful increase in tension between different sectors of the population, not helped by a newly freed broadcast media which emphasize sensationalism over dispassionate analysis. That said, demonstrates Tétreault, liberalizing Kuwait economically and politically is unambiguously democratizing.

As Michael Herb notes, Kuwait sets the standard for political development in the Gulf. Its legislature is elected, yet the executive branch (the amir and ministers) is not. Herb argues that Kuwaiti political development is likely to follow the trajectory of European absolute monarchies that developed into constitutional ones. Kuwaitis support the institution of the monarchy, and while there are those who want to limit its power, they like having the royals around. The constitution, remarks Herb, does allow the parliament to bring about full democracy, although it has shown reticence to do so. The reasons do not have to do with the rentier argument that oil makes for strong rulers, since the parliament can restrain the ruler. Nor does it have to do with intimidation of the parliament, rigging of elections, or a ban on political parties. Rather, he concludes, the single factor preventing democracy in Kuwait is the failure of the opposition to unite around an agenda of political reform. Like Tétreault, he is bullish on the prospects for democracy in Kuwait.

John Peterson's chapter is on Bahrain, a country with a majority Shiʻa population ruled by the Sunni Al Khalifa. Despite this situation, stresses Peterson, the history of opposition to the monarch has led to unity amongst opposition forces of all stripes. Taking his cue from the rentier thesis, Peterson maintains that as it is the first post-oil Gulf economy, strains are being felt in Bahrain first. King Hamad's initial reforms upon assuming the throne elicited some excitement, but appear to have been little more than cosmetic, a tool for staying in power. Peterson argues that Islamist forces in Bahrain, both Sunni and Shiʻi, constitute positive pressure toward liberalization, and increasing the stake of Islamists in the participatory process will have a salutary effect on their commitment to political reform, since they will benefit from it. Limitations on liberalization are the result of pressure from conservatives within the ruling Al Khalifa, as well as from their patrons, the Al Saud and the Al Nuhayan of Abu Dhabi, who head the UAE. The influence of King Hamad's conservative uncle, Prime Minister Khalifa bin Salman, who was responsible for much of the oppression of the 1990s, continues to be felt. Within Bahrain, the jury is still out with respect to King Hamad's reform, with some disappointed and demanding much more, and others having faith that liberalization will continue.

On the face of it, in Qatar, as Elisheva Rosman-Stollman makes clear, there is little reason for reform. The country is wealthy, it is relatively homogenous, and there is no opposition to the royal family. Ironically, it is the lack of internal opposition that allows the Amir, Hamad bin Khalifa Al Thani, more freedom in implementing change. Low voter turnout for elections to the Central Municipal Council in 1999 indicated either a lack of enthusiasm for reform or a sober assessment of the possibility of any real change coming about. Reforms are merely cosmetic, designed mostly to appeal to Western eyes and irritate more conservative Gulf neighbors. Amir Hamad desires to turn Qatar into a regional power (witness the recent expansion of al-Jazeera to English-language broadcasting in November 2006), and amongst numerous steps he has taken, one has been liberalization. Projecting a democratic profile raises Qatar's image in the West, and its slower-to-develop GCC allies can hardly protest, given the current pro-liberalization atmosphere amongst most of the GCC populations.

In Oman, the least developed of the GCC states, elections to the fully-elected Consultative Council were held in 2003, with the participation of both men and women as candidates and voters. This body exists alongside an appointed upper chamber and possesses some limited power to propose legislation, and really has little more than advisory powers. Voter registration and turnout were quite low, and fewer candidates ran than in earlier elections. According to Uzi Rabi, this was due to the limited mandate given the Council, and the fact that political rallies were banned and canvassing in public areas was discouraged. In essence, maintains Rabi, the entire exercise is designed to co-opt important tribal and business elites, and is a continuation of earlier methods of rule. While younger and Western-educated Omanis view the Council with skepticism, members of the Council have been seen questioning ministers during televised sessions. Ministers are becoming more responsive to members' concerns, but any important liberalization will be a slow and complex process, Rabi concludes.

In the United Arab Emirates, writes Christopher M. Davidson, politics remain based on direct lines of communication between citizens and rulers, and recent efforts to expand formal participation through semi-elected councils have yet to amount to much more than window dressing. Patrimonial politics, the rentier state, and economic liberalization have all but obviated the need for significant political liberalization. While economic liberalization has forced some social and political liberalization for the moneyed foreign residents of the UAE, it remains to be seen if rights extended to the increasingly demanding expatriate population might not have a spillover effect and force the government to extend similar rights to citizens. But they would have to demand them, and the current rentier system treats them so well that doing without these rights might be a small price to pay for a life of luxury.

Iraq and Iran are not usually included in books on the Gulf, since the member countries of the GCC have more in common in terms of regime type (they are all monarchies) and social composition. The fact that they have chosen to organize themselves as the GCC, pointedly leaving out Iraq and Iran, proves this point. Along with Afghanistan, Iraq is the poster child for the Bush administration's policy of democracy promotion, and America's heavy military involvement necessitates a look at Iraq in any study of political liberalization in the region. Going way beyond liberalization, the

US goal in Iraq is full democratization. Yet in Iraq, unlike in other Gulf countries, heterogeneous "primordial" loyalties block attempts at a power-sharing, democratic model. According to Ofra Bengio, universal suffrage, granted under the watchful eye of the US, did not guarantee democracy. The major ethnic groups, and factions within these groups, view "democracy" as a tool for furthering their own needs. The Shiʿis crave "democracy for the majority," which will enshrine their status as the largest ethnic group in Iraq. The Kurds follow a federative vision, which would insure their autonomy. The Sunnis, on the other hand, opposed democratization as it threatened to undermine the hegemony they had enjoyed since the founding of modern Iraq, and viewed the American presence as the main threat to that hegemony. Bengio concludes that Iraq's fate is an unfortunate one: it really needs an autocratic government to rule it, but that is incompatible with democracy. Under these circumstances, the best that can be hoped for is that previously disenfranchised ethnic groups will finally be represented in any government.

Like Saudi Arabia, Iran defines itself as an Islamic state. But unlike in Saudi Arabia, in Iran there is an intense public debate amongst the clerics on the meaning of democracy in an Islamic state. In his chapter, Meir Litvak draws the fault lines and challenges presented by this debate. Litvak examines the approach of four trends—hard-line, dominant, reformist and liberal—to three issues: popular sovereignty vs. the rule of the jurisconsult, civil liberties and concepts of freedom, and the contrasting of Western democracy with Islamic democracy. Litvak remains hopeful, concluding that the constitutional mechanisms which resemble democracy, even while deprived of their democratic essence, will eventually combine with pressure from below, pluralism within the clergy, and real efforts to reconcile Islam and democracy to produce an effective and democratic system in Iran.

ఴ

In late 2004, the Moshe Dayan Center for Middle Eastern and African Studies of Tel Aviv University assembled some of the best minds on Gulf issues to discuss liberalization in the region. The workshop was convened by Joshua Teitelbaum. This book is the culmination of the research done for, and in the three years after, that workshop. During that period, what has happened in the Gulf has only become more salient. I would like to thank the former director of the Dayan Center, Prof. Asher Susser, for his support and encouragement of this project, and his assistant, Ilana Greenberg, who is both efficient and kindhearted. The current director, Prof. Eyal Zisser, has extended all help requested. As always, office help from Roslyn Lon and Elena Kuznetzov proved to be the best. The Dayan Center Librarian, Marion Gliksberg, and the director of the Press Archive, Haim Gal, were ever ready to provide needed research materials. I thank them all.

This book is dedicated to my three amazing girls, Dena Avigail, Rivital, and Ayalah. They are a tremendous source of joy and pride to me and to my wife and closest friend, Jacqueline.

1

LIBERALIZATION AND ITS LIMITS IN THE GULF STATES

Joseph Kostiner

Despite intensive economic modernization, wealth, education, and social mobility since independence, the oil-rich Arab Gulf states remain autocratic. Theorists point to these factors, particularly wealth, as correlating with liberalization and democratization.[1] It is proposed herein that the age-old presence and social salience of tribal and/or kin-based, clan-like groups typical of Gulf state societies[2] are a unique contributing factor to what theorists might see as an anomalous situation. These groups have functioned to cushion the effects of government autocracy and remove some of its sting, thereby limiting the intensity of demands for democratization and allowing autocracy to continue its reign.

These types of groups have traditionally provided the citizens of these states—be they from the elite or the lower classes—with protection from their leaders and governments. During World War I and the inter-war period, as these states emerged through a process of state-building and the strengthening of state leaders, an unwritten code seemed to prevail that maintained this

---

1   On the association between democracy and indicators of national wealth, communication, industrialization, urbanization and education, see Seymour Lipset, *Political Man: On the Social Bases of Politics*, new and updated edition (Baltimore: The Johns Hopkins University Press, 1981), and Marsha Pripstein Posusney, "Enduring Authoritarianism: Middle East Lessons for Comparative Theory," *Comparative Politics*, Vol. 36, No. 2 (January 2004), pp. 127-38. For a general discussion of why Middle East regimes remain autocratic, see Eva Belin, "The Robustness of Authoritarianism in the Middle East," *Comparative Politics*, Vol. 36, No. 2 (January 2004), pp. 138-57.

2   K.H. al-Naqib, *Al-Dawla wa al-Mujtlama' fil-Khalij wal-Jazira al-'Arabiyya* (Beirut: Markaz Dirasat al-Wahda al-'Arabiyya, 1976).

common social framework intact. It is true that the states' rulers reinforced their military, administrative and economic capabilities, but their governments, as they developed in the 1920s and 1930s, had an enveloping or encapsulating effect on society, rather than drastically changing it.

A new echelon of officials emerged to head these governments. Likewise, state law systems (drawing in various degrees on the holy law, *shari'a*) were imposed on societies. The military power of tribes and their raiding habits were contained (notably, in the subjugation during 1929-30 of the Saudi Arabian *Ikhwan*, a coalition of tribal leaders who had fought for the Saudi leadership during the expansion of the nascent state). Rulers' supremacy had to be maintained, at least passively, through citizens' compliance with the governing bodies.[3] However, the rulers did not cut deeper into social frameworks. They did not destroy the common kin-structures, neither did they try to remold them into other, class-based or sectoral solidarities (*'asabiyyat*). They rather coalesced with or against existing clans, forming alliances with most of them or isolating others.

Several reasons can account for the rulers' motives in maintaining this system. The kin-based groups constituted the common nuclei of Gulf societies. The rulers themselves belonged to clans, and each of them maintained his personal loyalty to his clan and cultivated its power. Hence, uprooting other clans and tribes could have led to tremendous opposition, possibly to bloody wars and to the destruction of the very fabric of their societies. Moreover, by forming coalitions with existing clans and tribes, including political alliances and intermarriage, rulers facilitated political stability and/or extended their social-territorial control over more tribes and clans.

Tribal and clan leaders naturally favored a system that kept their social framework intact. As Al-Azmeh has put it with respect to Saudi Arabia, "The absolute monopoly of power by one particular clan require[d] the maintenance of tribal particularism and of the social system of stratification prevalent in the desert."[4]

This system gave relative protection to Gulf societies from the potential unlimited autocracy of their leaders. An individual benefited from his clan's or tribe's physical defense, social services and economic cooperation as well as the legitimacy and reputation of his kin-group. In societies that did not tolerate (and made illegal) the formation of political parties and

---

3   See J. Kostiner, *The Making of Saudi Arabia* (London and New York: Oxford University Press, 1991).

4   A. Al-Azmeh, "Wahhabite Polity", in Ian Netton (ed.), *Arabia and the Gulf: From Traditional Society to Modern States* (Totowa, NJ: Barnes & Noble Books, 1986), pp. 75-90.

interest groups, the kin-based structures were the only time-honored and legitimate social framework. Researchers, therefore, regarded these structures as "corporate groups," that is, as segmentary organizations that maintain defense, employment, economic interests and a common identity for their members. The corporate groups also represented their members to the state.[5] They maintained a kind of protected autonomy from their governments, providing their members with the ability to exist under their own time-honored codes, economic conditions and family-personal values.

In addition, the kin-based structures formed a broad sociopolitical system. The governments legitimized such frameworks and preferred them to other sociopolitical bodies, thereby perpetuating their existence. Even when the bigger Bedouin tribes became sedentarized, clan-like and family-like structures were reproduced in both the settled and the remaining wandering populations, among modernized, educated people, as well as new business groups. By appearing as leaders of kin-based corporate groups, leaders retained the ability to protect their members and values as well as the legitimacy to represent themselves as entrepreneurs of business and construction, or as key figures in education and bureaucracy. As Naqib puts it, groups of kin-based structures were society's representatives vis-à-vis the governments, but were also trusted by the royal families. They represented tribal establishments, merchants, sectarian (mostly Shi'a) groupings, workers, and middle class professionals, as well as religious establishments and movements. The royal families recognized these structures and even regarded some of them as allies and partners in patron-client networks. Thus the system attested to their governments' readiness to permit a pluralist system composed of many kin-based units to prevail, and to enlist them through individual ties.

Another political practice pertaining to this system was the use of the *majlis*, an open meeting held periodically by a member of the royal family (sometimes holding a position in the government, or acting as regional governor) hosting lower ranking members of his community, or of lower-ranking families and tribal groups acquainted with him. Members of such groups usually came to ask for assistance to fend off demands of the state bureaucracy, to complain about the government's conduct or other matter relevant to citizens, or to ask for personal financial assistance. The *majlis* allows access to supreme leaders and makes it possible for them to extend their intervention (*wasta*) so as to ease a simple citizen's way in facing the

---

5   See the thesis of N. Ayubi, *Overstating the Arab State* (London: Tauris, 1994).

government.[6] Thus, the institution of the *majlis* combined with other advantages of the kin-based divisions in society to grant the citizens more protection, fulfillment of basic needs, identity, and representation vis-à-vis their governments.

Maintaining the kin-based system in Gulf societies, however, involved another angle as well. This concerned the governments' own role in the system: while rulers were not supposed to penetrate the family and tribal structures and were to respect their autonomy, the subjects were not expected to interfere with the governments of the royal families. This was the other side of the same coin: in return for the governments' concession to their societies, rulers retained an autonomous and uncontrolled legitimacy for governing. The royal families themselves decided who would be the representative families among the different social sectors, and with whom they would cooperate, by allotting them business opportunities and/or jobs in the state administration. The governments chose the targets for investment of oil wealth and what to develop in the public economy, as well as whom to advance and whom to suppress. They also kept full control of economic resources, notably oil and gas. These resources—at the sole disposal of the governments—enabled them to embark on massive construction and development operations without having to account for them to any political body, or to subject themselves to an effective audit. Moreover, the "ruling core" of the Gulf governments remained the members of the royal families, with their extensive privileges.

Political change in the Gulf states was therefore stymied by this political system: the autonomy of the kin-based groups on the one hand, and the uncontrolled power of the rulers on the other. Substantial reform—of the kind that would involve a considerable reshaping of the regime—could hardly evolve, since such changes could not be adopted both by the rulers and by the social groups without altering the balance of power between them. The only possible reforms were political adjustments, namely, changes that both rulers and social structures could easily adopt without substantially changing the privileges of each side or their mode of power-sharing.

---

6   "Al-Majalis al-Maftuha fil-Su'udiyya" [The open meetings in Saudi-Arabia], *al-Majalla*, July 2, 2000.

Modes of political adjustment

In Saudi Arabia, when some kind of political change was required, it was not introduced through popular vote or broad, people-based consensus. The people's councils in the Hijazi cities, which King 'Abd al-'Aziz "Ibn Saud" endorsed from the earlier Hashemite regime in 1925 and 1926, right after his forces had occupied the Hijaz, faded away under the new regime. Large political gatherings, consisting of free debates between Ibn Saud, the religious sages ('ulama) and representatives of the Ikhwan (religiously-zealous tribal forces who had attempted to enforce a warring and religious posture upon the Saudi state) ceased to exist as a vital forum of debate and decision-making after the Ikhwan's subjugation in 1929-30.[7] Thereafter, decisions involved the King and a small group of advisors and ministers. Some tribal leaders and supreme religious sages may have been called upon for consultation and advice, but the decisions if and how to readjust were confined to a small group of leaders and government officials.[8]

New problems of political readjustment became evident in the period between 1958 and 1964, when the rule of King Saud (r. 1953-1964) weakened and the rivalry between him and his brother Faysal (r. 1964-1975) intensified. Saud's rule was characterized by a lack of proper handling of the Kingdom's initial oil revenues, which led to a budgetary deficit. Likewise, Saud's policies concerning development and construction and the treatment of opposition groups, as well as the erratic turning from pro-Nasserist to pro-US and anti-Nasserist foreign policies, all called for reform. However, Faysal's policies in coping with these problems revealed several principles:

1. The ruler should recognize the requirement for certain changes.
2. These changes should neither subtract from the ruler's authority and privileges, nor subjugate him and the government to a constitution or a doctrine which is meant to control them and limit the scope of their decision-making. Faysal objected to any attempt of the "free princes," led by prince Talal, to introduce a constitution.
3. The required changes were engineered in order to avoid any impact on the relations between the ruler and the social structures—they were to impact only on the administrative sphere. Furthermore, they were to extend the ruler's administrative abilities, and strengthen the power

---

7   Kostiner, *The Making of Saudi Arabia*.

8   Mohammed Almana, *Arabia Unified* (London: Century Benham, 1982).

of the state. Faysal introduced new administrative functions, such as planning (notably "five-year plans"), a large state bureaucracy, and the recruitment of foreign experts in the relevant fields. Changes were introduced through a ruler's fiat without regard to input from society. Indeed, in the 1960s and 1970s, new ministries were established (for planning, petroleum, industry and commerce, justice and others), as well as new bureaucratic arms and new financial bodies to support the new ventures.[9]

4. Changes should improve the standard of living and social conditions. Education, health and employment infrastructural facilities were established.[10]

These principles demanded that no power-sharing processes should be considered. The ruler and the state bureaucracy were to run the process of reforms; the subjects were to have no part in it. Neither was the King put under any control. The changes improved socioeconomic conditions, rather than political rights and status. Reforms reflected the grace of a beneficent autocracy led by an ever-stronger ruler, generously granting his subjects an improved lifestyle.

Similarly, the Kuwaiti constitution of 1962, which laid the ground for election of a National Assembly, reflects the divisions between the ruler and the government on one hand and the leading social groups—the notables—as well as lower-ranking merchant families on the other. It is true that according to the constitution the ruler recognized the citizens' right to advise, even criticize the government and question its policies, and that this was a meaningful step towards citizens' participation in power politics, given the earlier history of Kuwait. In the past (the crises of 1921 and 1938) when the notable families initiated the formation of representative councils, the ruler, Shaykh Ahmad, rejected them, and in 1938 and 1939 he even tried to shut the councils down. However, Ahmad and later rulers acknowledged the ambitions of the notable families, and, for the sake of stability, were ready to accommodate these ambitions in the constitution.[11] The constitution, however, was presented to the Kuwaiti citizens as an instrument handed by the ruler, in his grace, to his people. The al-Sabah family was neither barred from nor limited in "exercising total monopoly of all instruments of politi-

---

9   S. Yizraeli, *The Remaking of Saudi Arabia* (Tel Aviv: Moshe Dayan Center, 1997).

10   H. Lackner, *A House Built on Sand* (London: Ithaca Press, 1976).

11   J.E. Peterson, *The Arab Gulf States, Steps Toward Political Participation* (Washington, DC: Praeger, 1988), The Washington Papers No. 131, pp. 35-41.

cal and economic power and its symbols."[12] Hence the Kuwaiti constitution allowed citizens only to criticize the ruler's methods of using the power he was holding, or the policies by which he did so. It was not intended to reshuffle the basic division of power by taking away power from the ruling family and the government and handing it to the citizens.

Moreover, in practice, Kuwait's rulers made it absolutely clear that there were limits to the criticizing and questioning of government policies. When the National Assembly became too troublesome in its criticism of the government and started acting as a core of anti-government opposition movements, the ruler used his prerogative (which had been included in the constitution) and prorogued the assembly in July 1986. Kuwait had to wait until October 1992 for its ruler, under the impact of his country's liberation from Iraqi occupation, to permit elections for a new National Assembly.

Managing crisis situations while maintaining autocracy

The resilience of the Saudi autocratic regime is best demonstrated in the rulers' handling of a crisis situation, such as those of the 1980s. The death of King Khalid and the accession to power of his successor, Fahd, on June 13, 1982 occurred during a period of sustained drop in oil prices, which reached a low of less than $20 a barrel in 1984-85 (after the record of over $41 per barrel that they had reached in 1981, under the shadow of the beginning of the Iran-Iraq war). Moreover, owing to Western states' policies of oil conservation and the use of non-oil means of energy, oil sales were also dropping. Saudi Arabian sales dropped from about 12m. barrels a day in 1981 to less than half of that in 1984-85. The financial shortage was evident in the budget and in an overwhelming need for cuts in public expenditure.

King Fahd's rise to power was accompanied by government statements about a need for scrutiny of public administration, and the firing of many public-sector employees.[13] There were reports of complaints from educated, "middle-class" elements, such as teachers, academics and journalists, about the government's policies and particularly about princes abusing their power.[14] Consequently, there were renewed promises from King Fahd to establish a Consultative Council (Majlis al-Shura); to sell government-owned

---

12 See the point by Abdulhadi Khalaf, "What the Gulf Ruling Families Do When They Rule", *Orient* 44 (2003), p. 548. The phrase draws on M.A. Tétrault, *Kuwait, Stories of Democracy* (New York: Columbia University Press, 2003).

13 *Financial Times*, June 6, 1983, August 18, 1983; *'Ukaz* (Mecca), May 30, 1983.

14 *Financial Times*, September 21, 1982, April 25, 1983; *al-Yamama* (Mecca), December 6, 1982.

businesses; and to recruit private-sector businessmen to invest in the state's industry and trade, in order to employ workers who had been or would be made redundant in the public sector.[15]

However, in 1985-86 it became clear that the government had neither taken any serious measures to encourage political participation nor balanced the lack of these with firings and closing down of government businesses. The government actually cut its investments in public construction, new contracts and imports. Moreover, the veteran oil minister, Ahmad Zaki al-Yamani, was sacked in 1986 to demonstrate that the government dealt with the person responsible for the declining oil income. Instead, Saudi leaders preferred socio-political stability: they avoided harsh cuts in expenditure, allowing subsidized food and government-employed jobs to continue. Thus, the distributional policies aimed at cultivating the living standard of society were maintained at all costs. Moreover, while the business sector was indeed encouraged to increase its activities in the economy, the Majlis al-Shura was not opened, nor was any institution established to allow more political participation.[16]

Saudi rulers simply used various administrative and economic means to deflect the impact of the acute economic crisis of the 1980s, and kept the spending on employment and food unchanged. For the Saudi rulers, the results were good: continuing the distributional policies served to maintain socio-political stability while keeping autocratic rule intact.

Kuwait, too, was beset by financial deficits and the need to restructure the economy, mainly through privatizing. Kuwait's case, however, developed along a different course. During the summer of 1982 the Suq al-Manakh, which had developed into an unofficial stock market drawing on the ready cash produced by the Gulf's oil boom, turned out to be no more than a bubble, and crashed. The government, which had not regulated the Suq, came under intense criticism from the members of the National Assembly.

The government's response was instructive. It let the heavy investors take the hit, so that no one could accuse it of responsibility for the crash. But it bailed out the small investors (whose share was only about 5 percent of the $94 billion worth of post-dated checks which had been used in the market). The government's rationale was to help the lower ranks of the business class

15   *Wall Street Journal*, January 3, 1984; *'Ukaz* (Mecca), May 22, 1984.
16   *Wall Street Journal*, December 18, 1983; *Time*, April 21, 1986; *New York Times*, October 1, 1986; *Economist*, November 8, 1986.

and prevent the downfall of these important elements.[17] The ruler acted as the financial savior of the people, and by so doing preserved both the socio-economic order and autocratic rule in Kuwait.

In the period that preceded the 1990s, far-reaching reforms that would permit real power-sharing between the ruler and the citizens in Saudi Arabia and Kuwait did not constitute a valid option for their rulers. However, one should also bear in mind that local societies, mainly organized according to tribal and family-like kin-groups, also favored a paternalistic, traditionally-based political system. They were no "revolutionary" elements. The middle classes' struggle for change suited the monarchical regime they were part of, and was not aimed to topple and replace it. A strategy of minor political adjustments, in a political system that hinged on distributional principles, was accepted by both rulers and their citizens in the period preceding the 1990s.

In the 1990s, notably as a result of the Kuwait-Iraq war of 1990-91, some of the fabric of Gulf regimes and societies changed. The dependence on Western forces to defend the Gulf states against Iraq tarnished the image of Gulf leaders as invincible, and made them appear hesitant and weak in the eyes of their societies. The old age and health difficulties of several Gulf leaders (in Saudi Arabia, Kuwait, and Bahrain for example) contributed to their declining aura. The demographic growth of local populations, notably in Saudi Arabia, whose population grew from about 8 million in the 1970s to around 23 million in the 1990s, made it difficult to retain the kinship-based political ties and the governments' preferences for certain families. Too many clan members who were not allied to government networks graduated from the developing educational system in the Gulf or Western universities, and competed for jobs or to join businesses. They were more ready than their predecessors to both criticize and defy government policies.

In addition, economic difficulties resulting from wartime spending and declining oil prices generated unemployment and a need for budgetary cuts and financial scrutiny. An atmosphere conducive to substantial reform developed among certain sectors of the populace, as well as leaders who were attentive to these social rumblings. Moreover, the delegitimizing propaganda of extremist Islamist groups, openly resisting the governments' efforts to cooperate with Western forces to destroy a Muslim state—Iraq—and to host them in the Gulf, made it necessary for the regimes to embark on reforms in an effort to relegitimize their rule.

---

17 *Wall Street Journal*, October 11, 1983; *Financial Times*, February 22, 1984.

2

ECONOMIC AND POLITICAL LIBERALIZATION: VIEWS FROM THE BUSINESS COMMUNITY

Jill Crystal

The last decade has seen the simultaneous expansion of political and economic liberalization in the Gulf. This chapter examines the relationship between these kinds of liberalization, and explores the various ways they combine in different Gulf states. It examines the interests that lead key groups to push for or against each kind of liberalization, the way these interests play out in different institutional settings, and the way indigenous ideologies are recast to embrace, or to critique, the market and representation.

Political liberalization

Political liberalization in the Gulf has generally meant the creation of partially-elected councils that advise an unelected monarch. These institutions have largely emerged in the last decade, although nearly all echo earlier aborted attempts at political liberalization. Kuwait, with the oldest continuous and most firmly established pro-democratic institutions, has gone the furthest in expanding contestation. There the decade since the Iraqi invasion has seen free elections for a genuinely legislative body, accompanied by lively and open political debate covering a range of issues, from economic liberalization to women's suffrage. Qatar, Bahrain, Oman, and the UAE have experienced more tentative political openings with elections for partially-appointed advisory bodies with more limited mandates, although in these states more modest contestation has been accompanied by greater participation by extending suffrage to women. Saudi Arabia remains at the other end of the political continuum, with promises of political openings accompanied by greater repression. A snapshot of each state follows.

Kuwait has had a fully-elected National Assembly since independence. Despite suspensions in 1976 and 1986, it has functioned over the years as a continuing forum for political debate. The Assembly is accompanied by a political environment largely protective of the civil and political rights that make political competition possible. Kuwait also has a relatively benign police apparatus. Suffrage was until recently limited to male nationals, but in May 2005 Kuwait's Assembly voted to extend suffrage to women, beginning with the next parliamentary election in 2007.

Qatar's experience has been far more tentative. Since the accession to power of the current ruler, Shaikh Hamad bin Khalifa Al Thani, who deposed his father in a bloodless coup in 1995, the country has seen significant political liberalization. Potentially the most important reform is Qatar's new constitution, adopted by referendum in April 2003. Other reforms include the holding of Municipal Council elections in 1999 and 2003 (and the granting of women's suffrage) and the removal of many press restraints. These reforms, however, are new and untested. While the constitution embodies many formal civil and political rights, these lack institutional guarantees. Whether these reforms are a temporary measure to secure popular and Western support during a difficult transition or steps towards a genuine expansion of political and civil rights is unclear.

Like Qatar, Bahrain has seen notable political liberalization, following the accession of Amir Hamad bin 'Isa Al Khalifa in 1999. In the fall of 2000 Hamad appointed additional members to the existing, appointed Consultative Council. He formed a Supreme National Committee which drafted a National Action Charter to replace the old constitution in December 2000. The Charter called for elections to a bicameral National Assembly with law-making authority to consist of an elected lower house and an appointed upper house. In February 2001, the new constitution was endorsed by popular referendum. In the fall of 2002, Bahrain held its first parliamentary elections since the short-lived Assembly of 1975. Other reforms followed: political prisoners were released and dissidents who had been fired from state employment were reinstated. These changes were particularly significant because they followed a harsh government crackdown from 1994 to 1998, in which the then Crown Prince and Defense

Minister Hamad himself played a pivotal role. The state security police, blamed for the harsh crackdowns of the 1990s, was now disbanded and replaced by a milder National Security Agency.[1] After that, however, reform stalled. In October 2002, Hamad (who in February had declared himself King and named his son, Salman, Crown Prince) issued a new Press and Publications Law. This law gave the Information Ministry expanded censorship powers and threatened severe penalties for criticism of the king or the political system. He also issued blanket immunity for any official suspected of human rights violations. A new amended constitution replaced the National Action Charter and deprived the National Assembly of any right to introduce legislation directly. As in Qatar, reform in Bahrain has not been institutionalized and its future rests very much with the personal decisions of the king (as J.E. Peterson argues in chapter 7).

In Oman, reform has been more gradual. In 1990, the Sultan established an appointed Consultative Council to replace an older appointed body created in 1981. In 1994, he increased its membership. In 1997 and again in 2000 and 2003, the government held elections to the body, expanding suffrage until by the 2003 elections virtually all adult nationals were eligible to vote. The Council was given a narrow mandate, primarily restricted to economic and some social matters, but it did enjoy the right to interpellate ministers. In 1996 the Sultan also established a Basic Law, the country's first constitution.

The United Arab Emirates has seen more modest political liberalization. It has an appointed National Council, albeit one with livelier debate than some of the other appointed councils. Although government officials have raised the possibility of holding elections, they have not yet done so.

Saudi Arabia has also seen political liberalization in the last decade, although by the standards of the region these reforms have been muted. In 1993, following liberal and Islamist pressure during the Gulf War, the government established an appointed Consultative Council. Following the attacks of September 11 and an increase in US pressure on the Saudi government to discredit those closest to al-Qa'ida, liberals saw an opportunity to push for more political liberalization. In January 2003, 100 intellectuals signed a petition, the "Strategic Vision for the Present and Future," to Crown Prince 'Abdallah, outlining a broad reform program calling for constitutional institutions, including an elected Consultative Council, and

---

1   Mohammed Almezel, "It's a Summer of Discontent in Bahrain," *Gulf News*, August 19, 2003.

protection of political and civil rights. On October 13, 2003, the government announced that elections would be held within the next twelve months for half of the members of the country's municipal councils. The following day the government allowed the Saudi Red Crescent Society to host a conference on human rights. At the same time, however, the government used riot police and live ammunition to break up a peaceful protest by Saudis objecting to the slow pace of reform.[2] Hundreds were detained. These moves continued a Saudi government crackdown in force on opposition that began with the 1996 Khobar bombings and accelerated with bombings in May and November 2003.

The Saudi experience highlights, albeit in sharp relief, the limits of political liberalization in the Gulf. For the most part, liberalization has occurred in the absence of violent opposition—in some cases, notably Qatar, in the absence of almost any visible opposition. But each state has retained a repressive capacity and a willingness to use it when opposition appears. In Saudi Arabia, the state has become more militant in pursuing opposition even as it has put forward promises to liberalize. In Qatar, political reforms have been accompanied by government moves to centralize the intelligence agencies, giving the ruler more direct control. Even without the use of force, in each state the government places clear limits on public opposition. The relationship between the executive and legislature is one-way. Nowhere does the permitted opposition voice the goal of electing (or overthrowing) the executive. Each state restricts representation as well as contestation: in Oman the electorate has expanded only gradually. In Kuwait, it was limited to men until May 2005. In Bahrain, the government drew the districts in such a way as to significantly limit the voice of the numerically dominant Shi'is.[3] When the government announced that the new legislature's appointed upper house would hold equal power with its elected lower house, the largely Shi'i opposition groups boycotted the elections. Civil society is regulated in each case. Public assembly is limited and political parties are banned. Judicial independence is limited. Still, for all these limitations, the movement in the last decade in the direction of democratization is dramatic. And it has been paralleled by a move toward economic liberalization.

2   Toby Jones, "Violence and the Illusion of Reform in Saudi Arabia," *Middle East Report Online*, November 13, 2003.

3   Nadeya Sayed Ai Mohammed, "Political Reform in Bahrain: the Price of Stability," *Middle East Intelligence Bulletin* Vol. 4, No. 9 (September 2002).

Economic liberalization

In the Gulf, economic liberalization refers to a fairly narrow package of policies. Economic liberalization has meant expanding the private sector in an effort to mobilize private capital with the goal of increasing employment opportunities for nationals (specific methods are detailed by Onn Winckler in chapter 3). This effort has been accompanied by legislative measures, of varying success, to require or encourage the substitution of national for expatriate labor. Perhaps the most dramatic form of liberalization, given the history and intensity of resource nationalism in the Gulf, is the move to attract foreign direct investment (FDI) in the energy sector in an effort to access foreign technology. Qatar has been among the more energetic and successful in this area, while Project Kuwait, an initiative to encourage foreign oil companies to develop the country's northern fields, has been hampered by parliamentary objections. Economic liberalization has also meant welcoming FDI more cautiously in other areas, such as tourism, civil aviation, health care and communications. Finally, economic liberalization has everywhere included the stated goal of cutting back the welfare state: limiting state subsidies and entitlements.

The success of the project has been limited. The Gulf states have made impressive moves in the direction of freer movement of goods and services, agreeing on a unified tariff in 2002, ahead of schedule, and moving ahead with an agreement in 2004 to move toward monetary union. Some restrictions on the freer movement of capital have been lifted. This has not, however, been accompanied by freer movement of labor. Economic liberalization has not generally been accompanied by increased transparency, with some exceptions in the energy sector. Corruption, often stratospheric, in the form of large commissions for large government contracts remains endemic throughout the Gulf, although some states have moved to limit such practices.[4] Finally, the Gulf economies remain overwhelmingly dependent on oil and natural gas and these resources are owned by the state.

One indicator of the limited success of economic liberalization is the level of FDI. According to figures compiled by the Kuwaiti Inter-Arab Investment Guarantee Corporation, the GCC states attracted about $162 million in FDI in 2001, out of the worldwide capital of around $735 billion. Outward investments surpassed inward in Kuwait (which had a

---

4   In the UAE, the government has recently mounted a campaign to limit corruption; see "UAE Risk: Risk Overview," *Economist Intelligence Unit*, October 22, 2003.

negative balance of $40 million), Saudi Arabia ($20 million) and the UAE ($156 million). Bahrain ($92 million) and Oman ($49 million) had a positive balance and Qatar did the best with $237 million in investment, largely in its gas sector.[5]

Of the Gulf states, Saudi Arabia moved most cautiously and was the last GCC state to join the World Trade Organization (WTO), in December 2005. Saudi Arabia began WTO entry talks in 1993 but these initially stalled over reforms that the Saudis argued contravened Islamic law. In 2001, a list it submitted of sectors closed to foreign investment (including oil, insurance, and telecommunications) was strongly criticized by the WTO. These problems were largely worked through and Saudi Arabia joined the WTO. Toward that end, and in the interest of attracting FDI, it abolished its sponsorship requirement, and now allows 100 percent foreign ownership in new projects (previously limited to 49.51 percent). The government has privatized some state enterprises and reduced tariffs to meet the new GCC guidelines. In June 2003, the Supreme Economic Council set up under Crown Prince 'Abdallah to promote economic liberalization approved a capital markets law which called for the creation of a body to regulate the stock market and license new financial institutions and a proposal to deregulate the transport system, including domestic aviation. The Consultative Council has monitored these changes with interest, but in the absence of a more open debating body, dissent has taken the form of clashes between the various bodies that oversee reform such as the Supreme Economic Council, Sagia (which must approve licenses for firms with foreign capital) and the various relevant ministries, such as the Commerce Ministry.[6]

Since taking power in 1995, the Amir of Qatar has taken several steps in the direction of economic liberalization in an effort to encourage foreign investment. Most significantly, he has moved to invite international oil companies to develop new oilfields and expand Qatar's production of natural gas, signing major new liquefied natural gas (LNG) deals with ExxonMobil, ConocoPhillips, and Shell to build the largest gas-to-liquids plant in the world. In December 2002, Qatar announced privatization of all electricity generation and water projects. Qatar has also opened up higher education to private, or at least American foreign investment. Where

5   Nadim Kawach, "GCC States Suffer amid Sharp Slowdown in Capital Inflow," *Gulf News*, November 20, 2003.

6   "Saudi Arabia's Political Outlook," *MEED*, Quarterly Report, Saudi Arabia, August 26, 2003.

foreign investors once required local partners, Qatar now allows 100 percent ownership in some areas.

Bahrain and the UAE have diversified in interesting ways as well. Bahrain has gone further than the other GCC states in granting the right to own property to foreigners.[7] In 2002, the government also enacted legislation allowing foreign workers to transfer sponsorships and allowing foreign investors to own up to 49 percent of companies listed on the Bahrain stock exchange. The UAE has introduced some of the most ambitious and certainly more curious economic plans outside the energy sector. Dubai intends to develop or expand an Internet City, Media City, yacht marina, indoor ski slope and tropical jungle, a palm-tree shaped artificial island, and upscale resorts.

Explaining liberalization

Economic and political liberalization share some similarities. Each is a top-down affair: a calculated, and limited, move by rulers to maintain power. That it occurs in the presence of pressure from below should not obscure this fact. Economic liberalization has been driven largely by the governments' fear that growing youth unemployment will metastasize into political dissent if jobs are not found, and by the hope that the private sector can postpone that day.

Political liberalization has been driven by a similar desire to maintain power and delay a day of reckoning. Elections can tame the opposition and marginalize the violent groups: Kuwait's Islamists and Shi'is participate politely, by comparison with their Saudi or (in the 1990s) Bahraini counterparts. Clearly, in Saudi Arabia, violence was a driving force in leading to the announcement of an opening in 2003. Announced measures of opening up were accompanied by increased state militancy against opposition groups. Should those measures fail to tame the opposition, they allow the ruler to gauge opposition strength and identify leaders to target for repression or cooptation. Elections everywhere in the Gulf also separate nationals (to whom suffrage is restricted) from the many expatriates (who today, as in the Arab nationalist 1950s, may bring dissident political ideas). That the elected bodies are clearly intended as a forum for the masses is evident in the fact that not only do members of the ruling family typically not run for office, but the rulers' key supporters, the police and military, can typically

---

7   Jasim Ali, "GCC Insights: Bahrain enacts liberal Foreign Ownership Law," *Gulf News*, August 17, 2003.

neither run nor vote; this reinforces the divorce between participatory and palace politics. Nonetheless, even when they are top-down affairs, the process of political liberalization and the process of economic liberalization have many supporters, and a few opponents. Both are driven, at least in part, by popular demands for reform.

The business community

While it is often taken as a given that the business community will support political and economic liberalization, reality is more complex. The business community's first interest is its economic well being. It assures that interest by lobbying the state (thus shaping policy formulation) and by colonizing the state bureaucracy (shaping policy implementation). While individual merchants support political liberalization, as a whole the business community has no particular commitment to a parliament (although it does not harbor any animosity toward it either). Where the strategy of working with and through the state bureaucracy has been largely successful in persuading rulers to protect core merchant interests, merchants continue to support the rulers. This support, however, is conditional and passive: merchants will temper or even end political support for rulers who ignore their economic needs. But as a group, the business community will support any regime that distributes wealth its way and guarantees the requisite investment stability. It will turn to political liberalization only when the regime fails it economically.

Economic liberalization is more enthusiastically embraced by business interests, but it too has its detractors. Those who embrace neoliberalism do so out of self-interest; there is no ideological commitment to the market in this community or anywhere else on the political spectrum. While some businesses gain from increased ties to the world economy, many of the older businesses, accustomed to government protection in the form of sponsorship requirements, lose their advantage as liberalization proceeds. Historically, the business community has benefited from close ties to the state. Moreover, members of the existing business community know that throughout the Gulf, but particularly in states with historically weaker business communities (such as Qatar or Saudi Arabia), those best placed to benefit from any expansion of the private sector are ruling family members. It is they, not the established businesses that will benefit most from moves to the market, even if their activities ultimately undermine such moves. For members of the ruling family, comparative advantage lies in rent seeking, not entrepreneurship; any move toward the market that privileges their access will undermine real movement towards economic liberalization by blurring rather than sharpening the distinction between the public and private sector.

Women

Women's suffrage has been hailed in the Western press as a key indicator of political liberalization. In the Gulf, however, it can be more accurately viewed as part of a legitimizing move on the part of the rulers that plays primarily to a Western audience. It has everywhere been a top-down affair: the one country with a women's suffrage movement, Kuwait, was among the last to extend suffrage to women. Where suffrage has been expanded, it has not been accompanied by any dramatic expansion of contestation.

A brief comparison of Kuwait and Qatar illustrates this point. In 1999, Kuwait's Amir announced a decree granting women suffrage. Popular opposition to women's suffrage among some leading (male) segments of the political elite, which expressed itself through Kuwait's much more open press, culminated in an Assembly vote rejecting the Amir's decision on suffrage on the constitutional grounds that it had occurred when the Assembly was out of session, a period during which the Constitution permits only emergency measures. Women's suffrage, they argued, was not an emergency situation. When women took the issue to court, hoping to challenge the election law that prevented them from voting, the issue worked its way up to Kuwait's Constitutional Court which upheld the Assembly's position. Women did not vote in Kuwait because a slim majority of those with suffrage (men) democratically opposed it. In Qatar, similar opposition also appeared in response to the Amir's similar 1998 announcement granting women suffrage for the 1999 municipal elections. An Islamist, 'Abd al-Rahman bin 'Umar al-Nu'aymi, in a rare show of public dissent, presented a petition to the Amir signed by eighteen others, objecting to women's suffrage (and to women's public participation in sports). He was arrested. This opposition, having no National Assembly to pressure, no clear constitutional right to pursue, and no court willing to entertain a constitutional issue, went nowhere. Women vote in Qatar not because it is an emerging democracy, but because the Amir said so.

This is not to say that women do not want suffrage; they do. Kuwait's suffrage movement is decades old. Suffrage was embraced enthusiastically by women in Bahrain, Qatar and Oman. Women in Saudi Arabia have voiced interest in having a role in whatever participatory institutions emerge. Nor is it suggested that women's rights are not a central issue in the Gulf. To the contrary, as elsewhere, the meaning of Islam and the role of Islam in politics—arguably the central issue of political discussion everywhere in the Muslim world—is often, if not typically, framed around women's issues. In those states where open public discussion is allowed, notably Kuwait, the status of women is one of the most important topics of debate between Islamists and liberals. Women themselves, however, are rarely central actors in this debate. Women in the Gulf welcome political liberalization, but the debate about the role of women in politics is not at its heart a debate about what women want.

If political liberalization, insofar as it extends to women's suffrage, is generally seen by women in the Gulf as a good thing, the record on economic liberalization is more ambiguous. Economic liberalization and cutbacks in state employment fall disproportionately on women who have benefited from professional employment and working conditions sensitive to the needs of working parents in ways that the private sector is not (for example, generous maternity leave, hours that match the schools'). The Saudis perhaps have grasped this and in 2004 lifted a ban that kept women from taking jobs in many fields and set aside land for an exclusively female industrial city, proposed by a group of Saudi businesswomen.[8] The most organized and vocal women in the Gulf have often supported economic liberalization; but they are also typically members of the merchant class, who would suffer least from the moves to the market.

Youth

Youth unemployment is a driving force behind economic liberalization throughout the Gulf. Saudi Arabia's case is not atypical. The unemployment rate among Saudis is officially around 15 percent but some estimates place it as high as 30 percent; among new graduates it is doubtless higher.[9] With more than half the population under the age of fifteen, policymakers see a crisis looming. Part of the answer lies in nationalizing the workforce and Saudi Arabia has announced a series of occupations that must be Saudized, for example jewelry stores and taxi companies. In 2002,

---

8   Syed Rashid Husain, "Industrial City for Saudi Women Soon," *Gulf News*, July 12, 2003; Thomas Lippman, "The crisis within," *Washington Post*, June 13, 2004, p. B01.

9   Najla Al Rostamani, "At the crossroads: Saudi Arabia in transition," *Gulf News*, November 25, 2003.

Saudi Arabia passed legislation requiring companies with 20 or more employees to have 30 percent Saudi nationals, with the ambitious and probably unrealistic goal of reducing the proportion of expatriate workers to 20 percent in a decade.[10] Similar moves have occurred in other Gulf states.

The problem, however, and the link to economic liberalization lie in the fact that most governments have already made significant progress in nationalizing the public workforce. If the process is to expand further, the private sector must nationalize its workforce as well. While the government can make its argument in nationalistic terms, resistance is cast in market terms: national labor is more expensive and less efficient than expatriate labor. In the UAE, for example, the Minister of Planning has conceded that the policy of nationalizing more of the workforce has not been successful despite ongoing government efforts: in 1995 nationals accounted for 9 percent of the workforce, but by 2000 the figure was 8.6 percent and declining.[11] Whether it is the government providing jobs or enacting rules that require the private sector to do so, short-term prospects for employment from the perspective of unemployed graduates lies with the state and not the private sector. There may (or may not) be long-term gain for the young in expanding the private sector, but by the time it happens, they will no longer be young.

Political liberalization also has mixed appeal to this population. Certainly age, like gender, is a universally important stratification politically. Schools create annual cohorts of graduates. People form different interests at different ages: young people are concerned with access to higher education and jobs, adults with their children's education, older adults with retirement. Economic crises (rising prices, falling prices) and political crises (1990, 2003) create watershed socializing events for a generation. Links established in youth, deepened by shared political experience, endure a lifetime, making age and generational change critical to politics. This is especially true in the Gulf where age is so great a culturally defining trait that seniority, even by a few months, confers authority, and where rapid improvements in public health and education have produced an unusually large and experientially different baby boom oil generation. It is less clear

---

10   Ibid.

11   Nadim Kawach, "National workforce to drop despite Emiritisation drive," *Gulf News*, October 28, 2003.

what this generational divide means.[12] Certainly the younger population is more educated but higher education does not confer similar beliefs, nor does it push people in a particular political direction, inclining them, for example, toward participatory politics or neoliberalism.

In the 1960s, Gulf citizens returned with Western education to become Arab socialists, in the 1980s to become Islamists. But the important difference may be a new style of politics: national in scope, inclusive in rhetoric. As Gregory Gause points out, college graduates have learned to develop personal networks that cut across family, tribal and other lines and can to a degree draw on those networks to mobilize people on political issues. This may increase as a generation receiving higher education largely at home rather than abroad emerges. The shared experience of this generation has created a national arena for politics and has forced all who wish to appeal to this generation to cast their issues "in general policy terms, as opposed to personal patronage terms."[13] This is not to suggest that members of a new generation do not identify along lines of class or sect, rather that they will have perhaps a greater ability to build bridges and alliances across lines, perhaps using the ideology and organization of generation as a fulcrum. Such skills would probably make for more effective participatory politics, although it is not clear how welcoming those institutions are to the young (the Gulf's most established participatory institution, Kuwait's National Assembly, is certainly dominated by an older generation).[14] But this outlook could also make them more effective underground organizers.

Expatriates

Expatriates are outside the political framework of the GCC states, but merit brief discussion nonetheless. Normally foreigners are easily contained through two mechanisms. First, the state has, in effect, privatized the policing of expatriates. The most important legal structure shaping expatriate

---

12   See Dale Eickleman, "Mass Higher Education and the Religious Imagination in Contemporary Arab Societies," *American Ethnologist*, Vol. 19, No. 4 (November 1992); Mamoun Fandy, *Saudi Arabia and the Politics of Dissent* (New York: St. Martin's Press, 1999), pp. 157-80; Mai Yamani, "The New Generation in the GCC: the Case of Saudi Arabia," in Rosemarie Hollis (ed.), *Oil and Regional Developments in the Gulf* (Washington: Brookings, 1998), pp. 136-48.

13   See Gregory Gause, "Political Opposition in the Gulf Monarchies," paper prepared for the conference on "The Changing Security Agenda in the Gulf," Doha, Qatar, October 24-26, 1997.

14   In the 1999 Assembly, 21 members were over 50, 21 were in their forties and only eight were in their thirties; see "Majority of Winners Educated," *Kuwait Times*, July 5, 1999.

labor is typically a residence law, whose application is left largely to the private sponsorship system and to the sponsor (who, for example, retains passports). Actively policing the large expatriate community is beyond the bureaucratic capacity of the government, and fortunately (for the state, not the expatriates) there is usually sufficient harmony of interest between the state and sponsors for daily control to rest with the private sector. Behind private control lies the public threat of deportation.

A second, less important mechanism for controlling expatriate labor is the labor law, which typically bans collective action outright and constrains expatriate labor in narrower ways. On the whole, these render the expatriate community relatively powerless. But this outcome is the result of effective state policy that evolved over decades. In the 1950s dissidents and expatriates engaged in serious political conversation. When expatriates and nationals have shared political interests, this system of state control, dependent as it is on private sponsors, can break down, as it did in the 1960s with Arab nationalists, in the 1980s in Bahrain and Kuwait with Iranians and the local Shi'i populations, and in the 1990s with expatriate Islamists and Saudi dissidents. Generally, the sense of national identity and of a national political community that governments have cultivated (in large part by invoking fear of the large expatriate community) has kept expatriates and locals apart. Where transnational movements like al-Qa'ida resonate with domestic opposition, these forms of control are less effective. This frightens rulers, as the existing barriers between expatriates and nationals are built on an assumption of national identity that transnational movements do not share. Expatriates (who are excluded) and the local opposition with whom they develop ties are in these circumstances unlikely to embrace polite participatory local politics.

Finally, sometimes, although less frequently, it is even the government rather than the opposition that brings expatriates back into the political equation, to strengthen its hand against domestic opponents. For example, in the weeks leading up the 2002 elections in Bahrain, thousands of expatriates, primarily Syrians, Yemenis and Baluchis in the armed forces, police and intelligence services were granted full citizenship, then ordered to vote. More than 10,000 Persian *bidun* were similarly naturalized. In July 2002 a new citizenship law allowed individuals from neighboring countries, who would be mostly Sunni, to obtain Bahrain citizenship.[15] This is not the norm, certainly; but it is not beyond possibility in some other countries,

---

15   Fred Lawson, "Bahrain" (Freedom House: forthcoming).

such as Qatar, where citizenship has been granted to some on the basis of political orientation, or the UAE, where the government, in part under US pressure, has granted citizenship to hundreds of Palestinians.[16] Such expatriates whose political participation rests solely on patronage and who are not socialized into local political norms are unlikely to embrace political liberalization as an ideal.

Liberals

As elsewhere in the Middle East, the major ideological divide in the Arab Gulf is between liberals and Islamists. Liberalism in the Gulf has generally shifted over the last few decades from an initial broad commitment to Arab nationalism and socialism to economic and political liberalization. Part of this shift is generational, but part of it is specific to the Gulf because of its wealth. There, even in the Nasserist era liberals lacked a natural constituency, and so always attracted a more polyglot following, including, from the beginning, members of the business community who used liberalism as a vehicle for expressing interest as well as ideological politics. In the 1970s, governments throughout the region also began looking to the liberals to balance the emerging Islamists.

In Kuwait, the liberal electoral defeat in 1981 was the turning point, causing the government to worry about growing Islamist strength. The 1990-91 Gulf War hastened this shift as liberals were forced to disconnect from their historical association with now discredited Arab nationalism. To reconstitute themselves, they moved toward political liberalization (advocating women's suffrage, legalization of political parties, and restraints on the ruling family, for example separation of the Prime Minister and Crown Prince) and toward economic liberalization, embracing the market. Unlike the Islamists, they now supported cuts in social spending to reduce budget deficits. In the 1999 elections, the liberals staged a comeback.

In Saudi Arabia, liberals in the Arab nationalist era were largely marginalized and did not become a significant force until they were able to recast their concerns in Islamic (although not Islamist) terms. There the first turning point was the Gulf War and the petitions that followed. The second was 9/11, although it took until 2003 and the wave of political violence inside Saudi Arabia for the Saudi government to become more receptive to the now more moderate liberal position, and to see its utility as a pos-

16   Fatma Al Sayege, "Post-9/11 Changes in the Gulf: the Case of the UAE," *Middle East Policy*, Vol. 11, No. 2 (Summer 2004), p. 122.

sible way to help balance Islamist radicals. They did this by encouraging a moderate center comprised primarily of moderate Islamists, but including some moderate liberals. The Saudi liberal position on political participation is similar to that of liberals elsewhere in the Gulf: an enthusiastic embrace of the concept and a call for more participatory institutions, elections, judicial reform, increased transparency and, in Saudi Arabia, limitations on the political control of the religious establishment. The liberal position on economic liberalization is more mixed. The Saudi liberal Strategic Vision of January 2003 had an economic reform package that included controls on public spending and measures against corruption, but also aimed at achieving social justice and equity among the provinces and improving public services and state employment. However, Saudi Arabia is different economically: compared with Kuwait, the UAE and Qatar, Saudi Arabia does have a population of dispossessed, one whose poverty has been publicly acknowledged in recent years.

In the smaller Gulf states, liberal voices have been present but muted. In Qatar, for example, from the 1950s on, whenever dissent has emerged, it has had a liberal component: a call for public participation and transparency. After the Gulf War, Qatar, like the other Gulf states, experienced a push for political liberalization: in 1991, some fifty Qataris signed a petition to the Amir calling for an elected council with some real legislative and investigatory powers and for a constitution that guaranteed democratic freedoms.

The liberals have shown resilience over the years, reinventing themselves ideologically and exhibiting organizational talent and tactical ability: developing allies while retaining their core support, accepting government support when it is offered, and seizing opportunities such as the aftermath of 9/11 to attack their opponents. Unfortunately for them, the Islamists have also shown similar adaptive abilities.

Islamists

The major competition liberals face comes from Islamists. In the parts of the Gulf where the constituency of dispossessed is smaller, Islamists initially articulated an ideological rather than an interest-based politics, taking over the moral void left by the decline of socialist ideologies and the rise of rampant materialism. They have appealed to a national and sometimes transnational audience using the indigenous and easily recognized symbols of Islam.

At the two extremes of political openness and political closure, Kuwait and Saudi Arabia, Islamists and liberals face-off most clearly. In Kuwait, the Islamists have shown political skill over the years, taking over associations and forming alliances along both lines of interest (reaching out to poorer Kuwaitis and less influential urban families, closed out of merchant politics) and lines of identity (forming alliances with Bedouin and even the Shi'a). In terms of political agenda, Islamists have focused on *shari'a* and education. The government allowed Islamic groups to grow during the 1950s and 1960s to balance the Arab nationalists, but shifted position when the Islamic groups gained strength. In the 1970s, the government built mosques and gave Islamic charitable organizations funding and media access. After the 1976 Assembly suspension, the government turned for support to the then apolitical Islamic groups, such as the Social Reform Society, which had not criticized the dissolution.[17] The growing strength of the Islamists was reflected in the 1981 electoral defeat of the liberals. Issues such as the *hijab* or men and women mixing in public (notably at Kuwait University) now rose to the top of the political agenda. This raised the government's concern, and after the reconstitution of the Assembly following the 1990 invasion, the Amir turned to the liberals to form a government and began supporting liberal positions (against segregation at Kuwait University and favoring limits on the fundraising activities of unlicensed Islamic charities—an issue to which the liberals were drawing attention even in the early 1990s). In Kuwait, then, the government has handled the Islamists in more or less the same way it has handled the liberals: approaching them when the liberals seemed threatening, distancing themselves when the Islamists became too strong. The result has been to incorporate the Islamists into the political system, making them advocates of that system. In 1976 and 1986, when the government closed the Assembly, it could turn to the Islamists for support; in the 1990s, when it again closed the Assembly, the Islamists joined the liberals in demanding elections.

In Saudi Arabia the regime established a different dynamic, with different results. Historically, the government has achieved a degree of hegemony by successfully insisting that every important question be cast in religious terms. Religion set the parameters of political discussion. Setting the parameters meant that the regime could decide what issues were debated. It did not just decide what the answers to political questions were, but what

---

17   Shafeeq Ghabra, "Balancing State and Society: the Islamic Movement in Kuwait," *Middle East Policy*, Vol. 5, No. 2 (May 1997), p. 2.

the questions were. Hegemony gave the regime a tactical advantage: liberal opponents were thrown off until they found a way to cast their own arguments in an Islamic framework. While the Saudi regime was hegemonic in controlling the parameters, it was not unchallenged within the parameters it set. Religious authority remained the only legitimate authority, but state religious authorities were not the only authorities. Opposition groups contested the government using the same frames of reference. While moderate Islamist voices remained, radical ones grew. They did not embrace the cautious political liberalization when it was finally proffered.

In Qatar, the distinction between the two camps is less clear. Islamism and liberalism were never separate, nor Islam really subordinate. Perhaps because Islamist discourse was neither marginalized nor hegemonic, Islamists have not made great strides in Qatar. The Islamic establishment has retained more influence, for example over the legal establishment, than elsewhere, and so inhabits some of the same ideological space contested by radicals. Occasionally, the Islamic establishment (as opposed to the Islamist opposition) has been a mild opposition force, but for the most part it has been supportive of the government. In return, the amirs publicly nod to this establishment at times (as in the creation of a new Ministry of Awqaf in 1992). Finally, there is probably simply less simmering discontent than in other, more closed states.

Islamists have mixed feelings about economic liberalization. Islamic teachings themselves are of course mixed: the Qur'an offers defense both of private property and of social justice. The poorer the state, the more Islamists are able to benefit from economic liberalization, moving into the vacuum created by the retreating state by providing social services. But Islamists were also among the earliest to see the benefits of globalization, beginning with the expansion of Islamic charities, initially under the Saudis. Many individual Islamists are wealthy and engaged in the private sector, and stand to benefit from moves to the market.

External forces

Rulers must also balance internal pressures for political and economic reform against external pressures. These pressures have been mixed. While outside dangers have often allowed rulers to postpone political reforms in the interest of national security, the Iraqi invasion of Kuwait produced the opposite effect. The Iraqi threat was a factor prompting Kuwait's Amir to summon the body initially, and to reconstitute it after the 1990 invasion.

53

As Herb argues, the Iraqi threat made both the ruling family and the opposition more inclined to compromise.[18] Outside support is equally problematic. The line between US support for democratization and US interference in domestic politics for its own ends is often blurry. Thus the Bush administration's announcement of a US Middle East Partnership Initiative in 2002, and continuing efforts to push a democratization initiative in the region, have met with some skepticism in the Gulf as elsewhere. Those who support political reform risk being branded as pro-American if US pressure to democratize is visible.

The Gulf states have influenced each other. Kuwait's example certainly made it easier for reformers in other states. Qatar and Bahrain have competed in political liberalization as they have in other arenas. Their extension of suffrage to women put pressure on Kuwait to do the same. The smaller states' experience in political liberalization has had a much more muted impact on Saudi Arabia which, having learned to live with pro-democratic experiments it initially found suspect, found little reason to emulate them. Only when political violence at home became untenable did the Saudis cautiously consider political liberalization.

The impact of external economic pressures are more ambiguous. Global economic pressures themselves are not new. The Gulf, built around long-distance trade, has been part of a global economy for centuries. The Gulf was also a central part of the post-World War II global economy that was, after all, very much driven by oil. Nonetheless, joining the WTO has been an incentive, most clearly for Saudi Arabia, to introduce many economic reforms. The rise in regional blocs has also encouraged the GCC to work toward a common tariff.[19] It is not lack of integration into a global economy but wealth that has buffered the Gulf from neoliberal pressures felt elsewhere. The region's wealth has meant that the GCC states are not subject to the same kinds of intense external pressure to liberalize. Oil-producing states, with, as Glasser argues, access to "nonconditional finance" and external capital, have milder economic crises and so have developed more popular electoral coalitions because they are able to ignore demands of the IMF pressed more effectively elsewhere. He points out that Kuwaiti

18 See Michael Herb, *All in the Family: Absolutism, Revolution, and Democracy in the Middle Eastern Monarchies* (Albany: State University of New York, 1999), ch. 6.

19 Under an accord to come into effect in 2005, the customs tariffs will gradually become a uniform 5.5 percent on basic commodities and 7.5 percent on other goods.

government expenditures on social-welfare projects actually increased during periods of declining revenues.[20]

Future prospects

Liberals and Islamists form the ideological divide for the near future. A real expansion of economic and political liberalization could divide or even unite them, depending on how affected groups react. Thoroughgoing economic reform, for example, might divide the business community between those firms that are less competitive, which might choose a rent-seeking strategy, and those that are internationally competitive or have interests spread across several sectors. These firms might focus on shaping broad policy related to the economy as a whole (casting it in terms of public interest). Governments actively interested in pursuing economic liberalization might even work deliberately to divide the business sector using these lines of cleavage. Those choosing a rent-seeking strategy might have little interest in pursuing political liberalization. Liberals and Islamists do not fall neatly into these two camps, and so moves toward the market might weaken their prominent positions.

The enfranchisement of women is likely to have little impact at first. Women bring in the women's vote and candidates' wives (and the rare female candidate) will hold women-only campaign events. The existing gender-based public segregation will continue. Women's voting might even lead to more of the internet campaigning pioneered in Kuwaiti elections. Women would likely champion the concerns men have, voting as members of families, sects and tribes, and as ideologues, liberals or Islamists. Even if empowering women as a corporate group was neither the intention nor the short-term outcome of suffrage, this might, however, be an unintended side-effect down the road. With time, women could develop their own agenda and pressure other blocs to include women's issues on their platforms. Liberals and Islamists would then develop a women's platform, articulated in terms of traditional women's concerns (family, children, education, social justice) and, depending on the economy and the price of oil, perhaps employment. Since economic liberalization and cutbacks in state employment fall disproportionately on women, liberals and Islamists might use this as a vote-raising issue. Liberals would probably support

---

20   Bradley Glasser, "External Capital and Political Liberalizations: a Typology of Middle
       Eastern Development," *Journal of International Affairs*, Vol. 49, No. 1 (Summer 1995),
       pp. 45-73 .

upper-class women as they have in the past, leaving Islamists to support the work-related concerns of women from poorer households (where their income is central). Or they could both abandon women: liberals, as has happened in Kuwait, by nominally supporting women's issues, but placing them low on their agenda; Islamists by espousing traditional family roles and the need to save jobs for men.

It is also possible that liberals and Islamists could learn to work together. Islamists in Bahrain have played a positive role in pushing the government toward more democratization and accountability. Islamists and liberals certainly behave in a civil manner toward each other in Kuwait. In Qatar, the divide between the two groups has never been sharp. In Saudi Arabia, where the political system requires an Islamic discourse, moderate liberals and Islamists have sometimes worked together.

One area where they have a shared commitment to reform is the legal realm. Judicial reform is at the heart of constitutional democracy and so of any serious effort to reform politically. Constitutional limitations, in states where they exist, exercise themselves through constitutional review, whether it is the judicial review of common law courts, the constitutional review bodies of civil law states, review by a council of religious scholars, or some other formal body. Constitutional limitations cannot exist in the absence of a set of institutionalized procedures that provide a review of the constitutionality of laws and enforce consistency between particular laws and basic principles that hold the government to the notion of rule of law, not men. Constitutional democracies cannot exist without independent judiciaries, and consequently judicial reform has been part of the political liberalization platform in each of the GCC states. Judicial reform is also central to economic liberalization. A market economy requires predictability. For a market to work efficiently, the business community needs to know what the rules are and know that the courts will systematically enforce them. An unintended consequence of economic restructuring may thus be to set in motion a more thoroughgoing legal reform that can benefit political liberalization as well, such as occurred in postwar Japan, where the impetus for overhauling the entire judicial system came originally from an effort to create a legal system more conductive to a market economy, yet led to reforms in criminal justice that expanded political and civil rights.

Legal reform is a potentially important issue because only a legal structure, a judiciary, has the power and patience to check tendencies towards state excesses. Parliaments and the press can draw attention to isolated acts of malfeasance but both lack the tenacity necessary for thoroughgoing reform that elicits continued responsible behavior. Only courts can provide this. Both Islamists and liberals understand this and so place legal reform, the call for the rule of law, on their agenda. The central demand of Islamists everywhere is implementation of the *shari'a*, which obviously puts judicial reform at the center of their agenda. Here they and the liberals share an important, though unacknowledged common ground: they both oppose government arbitrariness. Both would like to see arbitrary government replaced by the rule of law (God's or men's).

Each state has moved in the direction of a reformed judicial system. Kuwait has a constitutional court, albeit a somewhat timid one, and a quasi-independent legal structure. Qatar has perhaps the furthest to go, being one of only a handful of states in the region with no constitutional review (while the new constitution calls for an independent judicial agency, such an agency has not been established, nor has one ever existed in the past; Qatar has no constitutional court and no mechanism for constitutional review). Saudi Arabia is in many ways more liberalized in this regard. Not only does it have historically a more independent judiciary, independent both of the government and of schools of legal thought, but it has in place beside its *shari'a* courts a parallel system of administrative courts (called committees) administering administrative law (called regulations).

Any movement toward political and economic liberalization might thus set in motion a sustained movement for legal reform that both Islamists and liberals could embrace. Economic and political liberalization are distinct processes, driven by different forces and favored by different groups. Neither liberalization sets in motion an inexorable process of change. Governments can close markets just as they can open them, hold elections or jail the candidates. The expansion of either is most likely to occur when opponents across the political spectrum can find an issue they can all embrace.

3

LABOR AND LIBERALIZATION: THE DECLINE OF THE GCC RENTIER SYSTEM

Onn Winckler

The uniqueness of the GCC rentier system

The tremendous oil revenues which followed the October 1973 "oil boom" led to the development of a unique pattern of the "rentier state" in the Arabian Gulf oil-monarchies. The term "rentier state" refers to an economy in which the government's revenues consist largely of external "rent," such as oil and gas revenues and foreign aid.[1] For example, non-oil revenues averaged only 11.7 per cent of Kuwait's total governmental revenues during the 1990s.[2] The mark-up on oil is huge: it costs approximately $1 to produce a barrel of Gulf oil, but it fetched about $50 a barrel on average during the first four months of 2005 (over $100 for much of 2008).[3] While the vast majority of the rentier state's implications are economic, it is essentially a political system in which the ruler provides financial incentives (*inter alia*, no taxes, guaranteed public employment for nationals, free education and health care services, etc.) in exchange for the citizenry being content with

---

1   The term "rental revenues" refers to a situation by which increasing revenues are not derived from greater efficiency or from the introduction of new technologies and investments. Thus, the sharp increase in oil prices since October 1973 was not an outcome of increasing production costs, but rather resulted from changes in the oil market. See Alan Richards and John Waterbury, *A Political Economy of the Middle East*, second edition (Boulder, CO: Westview Press, 1996), p. 16.

2   Central Bank of Kuwait, *Economic Report-2000* (Kuwait, 2000), p. 198.

3   See, e.g., "OPEC Agrees to Raise Production, Seeking to End Oil-Price Rally," *Energy Bulletin*, March 16, 2005 (http://www.energybulletin.net).

little or no meaningful political participation. At its core, it is a system based on "no taxation, no representation."[4]

A major component of the GCC (Gulf Cooperation Council) rentier state is the creation of a unique employment pattern: the *dual labor market*. One market is for nationals who are employed almost exclusively by the public sector, with high salaries and good working conditions; the other market is the private sector, which employs almost exclusively foreign labor at low salaries.[5] Thus, while public sector employment was, and still is, considered to be the last resort in the non-oil Arab economies, it was the employment of choice for nationals in the Gulf oil economies.

The issue of migration to the GCC countries, which has been referred to as a "new [Arab] demographic order,"[6] has been covered extensively in the academic literature since the mid-1970s. Scholarly attention has been focused, mainly, on the scale of foreign labor in the GCC countries, the mechanism of the migration process, the motivations of the migrant workers, and the economic consequences, both on the national-macro level as well as on the individual-micro level, for the migrant workers and their families. The subject that has received the least attention is the migration and employment policies of the GCC countries, particularly during the past decade—a period in which the rentier system's linkage between the GCC states and their societies has substantially declined. It will be demonstrated that the change in the nature of the dual labor market through changing labor and immigration policies represents a cardinal ingredient in the overall decline of the rentier system in these

---

4   On the GCC rentier state, see Hazem Beblawi and Giacomo Luciani (eds), *The Rentier State*, Vol. II (London: Croom Helm, 1987); Hazem Beblawi, "The Rentier State in the Arab World," in Giacomo Luciani (ed.), *The Arab State* (London: Routledge, 1990), pp. 85-98; Nazih Ayubi, *Over-Stating the Arab States: Politics and Society in the Middle East* (London and New York: I.B. Tauris, 1995), pp. 224-40; F. Gregory Gause, III, *Oil Monarchies: Domestic and Security Challenges in the Arab Gulf States* (New York: Council on Foreign Relations Press, 1994), pp. 42-77; Uzi Rabi, "Majlis al-Shura and Majlis al-Dawla: Weaving Old Practices and New Realities in the Process of State Formation in Oman," *Middle Eastern Studies*, Vol. 38, No. 4 (October 2002), pp. 41-50.

5   According to official Saudi statistics, by January 2002, Saudi nationals represented only 15.6 percent of the total employees in the private sector (339,501 out of 2,181,047). Saudi Arabia Monetary Agency, *Thirty-Eighth Annual Report 1423* [2002], p. 48, table 2.5.

6   Georges Sabagh, "Migration and Social Mobility in Egypt," in Malcolm H. Kerr and El Sayed Yassin (eds), *Rich and Poor States in the Middle East: Egypt and the New Arab Order* (Boulder: Westview Press and Cairo: The American University in Cairo Press, 1982), p. 71.

countries, and is bound to have major implications for the future of political liberalization in the Gulf.

The uniqueness of the Gulf labor migration system

A common approach taken in recent academic literature regarding the GCC migration system is to suggest that it essentially resembles other global migration movements for employment purposes. Andrzej Kapiszeasky has argued:

Only from a legal point of view, is the situation of foreign workers in the GCC countries different from that in most other states in the world as expatriates nowadays have practically no possibility of obtaining permanent residency or being eligible for citizenship. Otherwise, labor migration to the GCC states shares many characteristics with other movements of this kind, and the de facto transformation of temporary immigrants into settlers cannot be ruled out.[7]

As Kapiszeasky explained further:

Thus, GCC states have become mother countries for an increasing number of non-nationals, despite the objectives set up by the authorities.... Thus, the development of modern societies in the GCC countries is already under way, although it is likely to take quite some time to develop all the bonds that a mature structure of this type requires.[8]

A similar view was expressed by Douglas Massey and associates, who claimed:

Despite these rather draconian labor market and immigration policies, migrant networks and social institutions have nonetheless arisen to promote the perpetuation of migration and the emergence of settled communities, especially among migrants from the Arab world.[9]

However, some superficial similarities notwithstanding, the migration system in the GCC countries differs quite radically from that of other international labor migration systems in five distinct ways:

1. *No citizenship available.* It is typical of Western-style migration that after some time, in most cases no longer than a few years, migrants are joined by their family members. Thus the migration process often ends with the migrant and his family becoming citizens of the host country. This was, and

---

7   Andrzej Kapiszeasky, *Nationals and Expatriates: Population and Labour Dilemmas of the Gulf Cooperation Council States* (Reading: Ithaca Press, 2001), p. 193.

8   Kapiszeasky, pp. 197-8.

9   Douglas S. Massey et al., *World in Motion: Understanding International Migration at the End of the Millennium* (Oxford: Clarendon Press, 1998), p. 159.

still is, the case in the US, Canada, Australia, France, and other European Union (EU) labor-importing countries. In contrast, since the early 1980s, the GCC authorities have imposed strict limits on the entry of family members. Moreover, it is nearly impossible for migrant workers to receive citizenship in one of the GCC countries, be they Arabs or non-Arabs.

2. *Lack of employment stability.* In contrast to Western countries, the position of foreign workers in the GCC countries is extremely unstable. According to the migration rules and regulations of the GCC countries, a foreign worker can be deported from the country without prior notice. This shaky position was evident in the 1990-91 Gulf crisis in the case of Palestinians and Jordanians in Kuwait and Saudi Arabia, and the Yemenis in Saudi Arabia, nearly all of whom were deported because of their leaders' support for Iraq. The United Nations Economic and Social Commission for Western Asia (ESCWA)[10] report on the returnees following the Iraqi invasion of Kuwait described the situation of the migrants who were forced to leave the host countries:

Millions of Arabs and other expatriate families that had settled long before in Kuwait, Iraq and Saudi Arabia had to evacuate their homes in a hurry, many of them leaving behind their properties and jobs... The belief of some emigrants that they would be able to settle forever in the host countries proved to be an illusion, revealing their unrealistic understanding of the conditions, principles and polices of emigration in these host countries.[11]

Moreover, whereas in the Western labor-importing countries religion is not a factor in granting citizenship—and prior to the events of September 11, 2001, it was even illegal in the US to inquire about a person's religion—in the GCC countries a non-Muslim cannot be naturalized under almost any circumstances. Two major factors account for the unstable position of the foreign workers in the GCC countries: first, in contrast to Western labor-importing countries, the GCC countries are not democratic. In Western labor-importing countries, the legal system itself provides protection for foreign workers through labor laws, civil rights, and the like. This

---

10   The ESCWA is a UN regional organization, based in Beirut, and its members include Egypt, Syria, Lebanon, Iraq, Yemen, the Palestinians, and the GCC countries. The organization is part of the Secretariat of the UN and is one of the five regional commissions which report to the UN Economic and Social Council. Funding of the organization is mainly from its member states. In many cases, the data provided by ESCWA are the only data available on GCC demographic trends and developments.

11   ESCWA, *Return Migration: Profiles, Impact and Absorption in Home Countries* (New York, December 1993), pp. 1, 10.

is not the case in the undemocratic GCC countries. Second, while assorted non-governmental organizations (NGOs) in the Western labor-importing democracies protect foreign workers from both the authorities and employers, such organizations do not exist in the GCC countries.

3. *Permanent settlement is not sought.* Whereas the aim of the vast majority of migrant workers to Western countries is to become citizens of the host country, the typical labor migration scenario in the GCC countries is that of a migrant worker who comes for several years only in order to earn as much money as possible before returning to his or her home country. "The vast majority of the migrants want to return home. Neither they nor the receiving countries view labor migration as permanent resettlement."[12] An Indian migrant worker, who was employed in the UAE together with his brother, described their employment motives in an interview for a field research project: "Together, we decided to save some money and establish a small business in Kerala...."[13] A research project conducted in the Syrian Euphrates Valley in the early 1980s by Annika Rabo reached a similar conclusion about the reason for migration from the Raqqa region to the GCC countries:

Young men may see migration to the Gulf as the only rapid means of gaining money to get married, to build a house, to buy a car or to invest in some business... those who have migrated...talk of the hardships in the Gulf... But they all say it is worthwhile since the pay is good.[14]

The initial aim of the GCC authorities was to prevent the settlement of foreign workers.[15] During the 1990s, the national diversification of foreign labor in the GCC countries advanced considerably. A major parameter in this area is the continuing increase in the share of non-Arabs within the total population of foreign workers. Beyond their economic advantage of being cheaper than Arabs, the Asian workers also have a clear socio-po-

---

12   Richards and Waterbury, *A Political Economy of the Middle East*, p. 384.

13   Sulayman Khalaf and Saad al-Kobaisi, "Migrants' Strategies of Coping and Patterns of Accommodation in the Oil-Rich Gulf Societies: Evidence from the UAE," *British Journal of Middle Eastern Studies*, Vol. 26, No. 2 (1999), p. 282.

14   Annika Rabo, *Change on the Euphrates: Villagers, Townsmen and Employees in Northern Syria* (Stockholm: Department of Social Anthropology, University of Stockholm, 1986), p. 101. Regarding the economic incentive of the Egyptian workers in the Arab oil states, see Delwin A. Roy, "Egyptian Emigrant Labor: Domestic Consequences," *Middle Eastern Studies*, Vol. 27, No. 3 (July 1991), p. 574.

15   See, e.g., in this regard: Peter N. Woodward, *Oil and Labor in the Middle East: Saudi Arabia and the Oil Boom* (New York: Praeger, 1988), p. 26.

litical advantage—the near-impossibility of marriage between a non-Arab non-Muslim and a GCC woman. This attitude toward the foreign workers is also mentioned by the young Saudis interviewed by Mai Yamani, who noted that: "Most of the young people interviewed prefer to maintain a social distance from the foreigners...."[16] The same perception was shared by other GCC countries as well. In retrospect, this part of the GCC migration policy was indeed successful.

4. *Foreign workers constitute the majority of the workforce.* In the Western labor-importing countries, foreign workers represent, in most cases, less than 10 percent of the total workforce,[17] and thus serve only as a supplement to the national workforce, in the vast majority of the cases employed in low-paying, low-status occupations. In the GCC countries, however, foreign workers have represented the vast majority of the workforce since the mid-1970s. In Qatar, the UAE and Kuwait, foreigners also represent the vast majority of the total population. This being the case, it is necessary to reject the notion of "integration" of foreign workers into the local society, where the indigenous population represents only a tiny fraction of the total workforce and population. Thus large-scale naturalization would turn the indigenous population into a minority. The situation in such countries as the US and Canada is, of course, totally different, as the number of naturalized migrants is very small in comparison to the indigenous national population. In addition, given that the vast majority of the foreign workers in the UAE, Qatar and Oman and, to a lesser extent, also in Kuwait and Saudi Arabia are not Arabs, the real meaning of mass naturalization of foreign workers is loss of the country's Arab-Islamic identity.

5. *An interest in cheap foreign labor.* In many developed labor-importing countries, the import of cheap foreign workers is only in the interest of the economic elite, but not in that of the whole population, because of the competition in the labor market, particularly in low wage occupations.[18]

---

16   Mai Yamani, *Changed Identities: The Challenge of the New Generation in Saudi Arabia* (London: The Royal Institute of International Affairs, 2000), p. 81.

17   Thus, for example, according to International Labor Organization (ILO) figures, by 1997 the foreign-born labor within the total labor force represented 9.9 percent in Austria, 9.1 percent in Germany, 6.1 percent in France, and 5.2 percent in Sweden. Among the OECD countries, only in Luxemburg, Switzerland, Australia, Canada, and the US did foreign workers' labor represent more than 10 percent of the total workforce. ILO, *World Employment Report-2001* (Geneva, 2001), p. 19, table 1.5.

18   In the case of Israel, for example, one of the most paramount factors in increased unemployment among nationals during the past decade was the availability of cheap foreign workers, either Palestinians until 1994, or from overseas since then.

In the GCC countries, however, the mass import of cheap foreign workers was until recently in the interest of both the authorities and the indigenous population. The availability of this type of worker enabled the GCC middle class, which constituted the vast majority of the indigenous populations, to employ cheap foreign workers in their small businesses and as domestic workers in their homes,[19] while the employment of the indigenous workforce was guaranteed in the public sector.

Moreover, since a foreigner was not allowed to work in the GCC countries without local sponsorship (*kafil*), many nationals used the system for easy profit by serving as a sponsor to foreign workers without even employing them.[20] For example, the economic weekly *MEED* reported in late 1996 that a UAE citizen could earn AED5,000 ($1,360) just by supplying a visa and sponsoring foreign workers.[21] The *kafala* system, labeled by Fred Halliday as "new slavery,"[22] produced a unique situation in which nationals could earn money strictly by virtue of their nationality. In effect, the liberal migration policies up to the 1990s represented one of the royal families' "gifts" to the indigenous populations, within the context of the rentier political system.

Thus the dual labor market system worked to ensure that no competition would emerge between the nationals and the foreign labor force. For example, the monthly salary of UAE university graduates was AED8,000 ($2,150) per year in the early 2000s, while high school graduates earned AED5,000 ($1,360) monthly—twice the salary of well-qualified and experienced Indian or East-Asian employees.[23] In the case of Saudi Arabia, one can find even larger wage gaps between national and foreign workers. According to a survey conducted in 1996-97 by the Saudi Central Department of Statistics, the average monthly salary of Saudi nationals was SR5,704 ($1,521), while it was only SR1,901 ($507) for foreign workers.[24]

---

19   According to the various estimates, by late 2004 some two million Asian maids were working in the GCC countries, representing more than 20 percent of the total foreign labor in these countries. *Middle East Online* (http://www.middle-east-online.com), updated October 18, 2004.

20   See, e.g., Roger Owen, *Migrant Workers in the Gulf* (London: Minority Rights Group, 1985), p. 8; "Gulf Population and Labour Force Structure," *The NCB* [National Commercial Bank] *Economist*, Vol. 5, No. 4 (June/July 1995), p. 10.

21   *Middle East Economic Digest (MEED)*, December 6, 1996, p. 34.

22   Quoted in Ayubi, *Over-Stating the Arab States*, p. 227.

23   Economist Intelligence Unit (EIU), *Country Profile-UAE, 2001*, p. 15.

24   Said Abdullah al-Shaikh, "Demographic Transitions in Saudi Arabia and Their Impact on Economic Growth and the Labor Market," *Saudi Economic Survey*, September 13, 2000, p. 19; p. 20, tables 3 and 4; EIU, *Country Profile-Saudi Arabia, 2003*, p. 33.

Therefore, even if the GCC authorities were to allow the foreign workers to bring their family members, for the vast majority it would simply be impossible to support them due to their low salaries relative to the high cost of living in the GCC countries.[25] Indeed, the sharp reduction in the foreign workers' salaries following the drop in oil prices in 1986[26] was the main factor contributing to the marked decline in the number of family members accompanying foreign workers. These financial considerations were only further exacerbated by the GCC authorities' change in preference from Arab to Asian workers and the increasingly tight regulations on accompanying family members.

The uniqueness of the GCC migration system is a function of the unique structure of GCC societies, which are based on a kinship or "tribal" system.[27] In effect, these "intimate societies" prevent others from becoming members of the unique kinship-rentier system, since those outside kinship networks would find themselves hard-pressed to integrate into what Hazem Beblawi has stressed is a "long tribal tradition of buying loyalty and allegiance ..., distributing favors and benefits to its population."[28] In many cases, foreign workers in the GCC countries are housed in work camps outside the cities. According to Qatar's 1997 population census, 116,774 foreign workers were living in such camps.[29]

The failure of GCC migration and employment policies prior to the mid-1990s

Following the October 1973 oil boom, all the GCC countries implemented liberal migration policies for three prominent reasons: small national workforces due to small indigenous populations; low rates of labor force participation; and lack of the professional skills needed for advancement.

25   See Baquer Salman al-Najjar, "Population Policies in the Countries of the Gulf Co-operation Council: Politics and Society," *Immigrants & Minorities*, Vol. 12, No. 2 (July 1993), p. 209.

26   By mid-1986, the price of a crude oil barrel was less than $10 as compared with $37 in 1981 (current prices). As a result, by 1986 the oil export revenues of the GCC countries amounted to only $38.3 billion as compared with $157.8 billion in 1981 (current prices). ESCWA, *Survey of Economic and Social Developments in the ESCWA Region, 1998-1999* (New York, 2000), pp. 45-6.

27   Philip Khoury and Joseph Kostiner, "Introduction," in Joseph Kostiner and Philip Khoury (eds), *Tribes and State Formation in the Middle East* (London and New York: I.B. Tauris, 1991), pp. 1-21. A wider discussion on this issue appears in Uzi Rabi's Introduction to his book, *New Oman* (Tel Aviv: Moshe Dayan Center, 2000), pp. 12-18 (Hebrew).

28   Beblawi, "The Rentier State in the Arab World," p. 89.

29   Qatar, *Annual Statistical Abstract*, 19th issue, p. 17, table 6.

Thus, during the "oil decade" (1973-82) the number of foreign workers in each of the GCC countries rapidly increased. Overall, by 1980, the number of foreign workers in the GCC countries was estimated at 2.9 million, as compared with 1.4 million only five years earlier, in 1975. During the first half of the 1980s this trend continued, and by 1985 the number of foreign workers in the GCC countries had climbed to 4.4 million, representing almost 70 percent of the total GCC workforces (see Table 1).

However, in 1982-83, following the end of the oil decade, the GCC authorities began to favor a policy of "nationalizing" their labor forces. This policy change was the outcome of several factors, the most prominent being the slowing down of economic development following the sharp decline in oil prices; the increase in unemployment among nationals, including open and especially hidden unemployment; the marked increase in the burden of providing services for foreign workers and their accompanying family members; and the increasing fear that the large number of foreigners would bring about social and political unrest. The changes in migration and employment policies resulted in the deportation of a large number of illegal foreign workers; limitations on the number of family members allowed to accompany foreign workers; reductions in government subsidies of public services for foreign workers and their accompanying family members, mainly in the areas of health care and education; the adoption of quota regulations for nationals in various economic fields; prohibition on the employment of foreign workers in certain job categories; and numerous measures to prevent foreigners from becoming permanent residents in the GCC countries, such as banning them from owning real estate.[30]

Notwithstanding the nationalization policy and the economic recession resulting from low oil prices and the Iraqi invasion of Kuwait, the number of foreign workers in each of the GCC countries continued to increase during the fist half of the 1990s, albeit at lower rates than in the previous decade (see Table 1). Overall, by the mid-1990s it was clear that four main obstacles had brought about the failure of GCC measures aimed at decreasing the dependence on foreign workforces. First was the unwillingness of nationals to accept jobs that they considered to be low paying or socially

---

30   On the GCC migration policy until the mid-1990s, see Onn Winckler, "The Immigration Policy of the Gulf Cooperation Council (GCC) States," *Middle Eastern Studies*, Vol. 33, No. 3 (July 1997), pp. 483-8; Onn Winckler, "Gulf Monarchies as Rentier States: The Nationalization Policies of the Labor Force," in Joseph Kostiner (ed.), *Middle East Monarchies: The Challenge of Modernity* (Boulder and London: Lynne Rienner, 2001), pp. 245-7.

Country	Nationals	Foreigners	Total	% Foreigners
1975				
Saudi Arabia	1,027	773	1,800	42.9
Kuwait	92	213	305	69.8
Bahrain	46	30	76	39.5
Oman	137	71	208	34.1
Qatar	13	54	67	80.6
UAE	45	252	297	84.8
Total	1,360	1,393	2,753	50.6
1980				
Saudi Arabia	1,220	1,734	2,954	58.7
Kuwait	108	384	492	78.0
Bahrain (a)	61	81	142	57.0
Oman	119	171	290	59.0
Qatar	15	106	121	87.6
UAE	54	471	525	89.7
Total	1,577	2,947	4,524	65.1
1985				
Saudi Arabia	1,440	2,662	4,102	64.9
Kuwait	126	544	670	81.2
Bahrain	73	101	174	58.0
Oman (b)	167	300	467	64.2
Qatar	18	156	174	89.7
UAE	72	612	684	89.5
Total	1,896	4,375	6,271	69.8
1990				
Saudi Arabia	1,934	2,878	4,812	59.8
Kuwait	118	731	849	86.1
Bahrain	127	132	259	51.0
Oman	189	442	631	70.0
Qatar	21	230	251	91.6
UAE	96	805	901	89.3
Total	2,485	5,218	7,703	67.7
1995				
Saudi Arabia (c)	2,545	3,945	6,490	60.8
Kuwait	148	614	762	80.6
Bahrain (d)	104	168	272	61.8
Oman	270	496	766	64.8
Qatar (e)	37	244	281	87.1
UAE (f)	95	855	950	90.0
Total	3,198	6,322	9,521	66.4
1999				
Saudi Arabia	3,173	4,003	7,176	55.9
Kuwait	221	1,005	1,226	82.0
Bahrain	113	194	307	63.2
Oman	312 (g)	503	815	61.7
Qatar (e)	37	244	281	71.7
UAE (e)	124	1,165	1,289	90.4
Total	3,988	7,114	11,102	64.1

2001-2002			
Saudi Arabia (i)	3,664	5,500	9,164	60.0
Kuwait (j)	276	1,104	1,380	80.0
Bahrain (i)	128	192	320	60.0
Oman (i)	316	604	920	65.7
Qatar (k)	43	367	410	89.5
UAE (i)	170	1,530	1,700	90.0
Total	4,597	9,297	13,894	66.9

Table 1: *Nationals and Expatriates in the GCC Labor Forces, 1975-2002* (figures in thousands)

— No data available.

(a) Data related to 1981.

(b) Data related to 1986.

(c) Data related to 1994.

(d) Data related to 1996.

(e) Data related to 1997.

(f) Since the UAE authorities published data for 1995 only for the total labor force, including both nationals and foreigners without distinguishing between them, these data were broken down by the author into 90 percent foreigners and 10 percent nationals, which was and still is the composition of the UAE workforce.

(g) Since the Omani authorities did not publish data on the size of the national workforce in 1999, only on the foreign workforce, the data on the national workforce in 1999 were calculated by the author on the base of the 1995 data (270,000 Omani national workforce) and an annual growth rate of 3.7 percent from then until 1999.

(h) Data related to 2001.

(i) Data related to 2002.

(j) Data related to 2003.

(k) There are no available data on the Qatari labor force since the 1997 census, either for nationals or for foreigners. However, adding an annual growth rate of 3 percent to the 1997 census data results reveals that by 2002 Qatar's indigenous labor force amounted to approximately 42,500. Regarding foreign labor, the calculation was as follows: by 2002, the foreign population in Qatar according to ESCWA figures numbered about 458,000. Taking into consideration an economically active rate of 80 percent, this reveals a foreign labor force of about 367,000.

Sources: Ministry of Planning, Central Statistical Office, *Annual Statistical Abstract*, various issues (Kuwait); Central Statistical Organization, Directorate of Statistics, *Statistical Abstract-1992* (Manama); Bahrain, Bahrain Monetary Agency, *Economic Indicators*, No. 5 (September 2004); Oman, *Statistical Yearbook*, various issues (Muscat); Oman, Ministry of Development, *The Fifth Five-Year Development Plan, 1996-2000* (Muscat, July 1997); Central Bank of Oman, *Annual Report-2001* (Muscat 2001); Central Bank of Oman, *Annual Report-2003* (Muscat, 2004); Saudi Arabia, Saudi Arabia Monetary Agency, *Thirty-Eight Annual Report 1423H* [2002G] (Riyadh, 2003); Qatar, The Planning Council, Secretariat General, *Annual Statistical Abstract*, various issues (Doha); J.S. Birks and C.A. Sinclair, *International Migration and Development in the Arab Region* (Geneva: ILO, 1980); J.S. Birks and C.A. Sinclair, *International Migration for Employment: Manpower and Population Evolution in the GCC and Libyan Arab Jamahiriya*, World Employment Programme Research, Working Paper (Geneva: October 1989); ESCWA, *Demographic and Related Socio-Economic Data Sheets for Countries of the Economic and Social Commission for Western Asia*, 1978-2001, various issues (Beirut, Baghdad, and Amman); ESCWA, *Population Situation in the ESCWA Region, 1990* (Amman: May 1992); ESCWA, League of Arab States, and UNFPA, "Arab Labour Migration,"

Meeting of Senior Official and Experts, Amman, April 4-6, 1993; The Kingdom of Saudi Arabia, Ministry of Planning, *Seventh Development Plan*, 1420/21-1424/25 AH. [2000-2004 AD] (Riyadh, 2001); Qatar National Bank, *Qatar Economic Review*, various issues (Doha); EIU, *Country Profile, Bahrain, Qatar, Oman, Saudi Arabia*, and the *United Arab Emirates*, various issues (London); Birks, Sinclair & Associates Ltd, *GCC Market Report, 1990 and 1992* (Durham, UK: Mountjoy Research Centre); Andrzej Kapiszewski, *Nationals and Expatriates: Population and Labour Dilemmas of the Gulf Cooperation Council States* (Reading, UK: Ithaca Press, 2001); Bahrain, al-Jihaz al-Markazi lil-Ihsa, *al-Ti'dad al-'Amm lil-Sukkan wal-Masakin wal-Mabani wal-Mansha'at-1991* (Manama, 1992); "al-Simat al-Asasiyya li-Sukkan al-Kuwayt wa-Quwwat al-'Amal fi Nihayat 1994," *al-Iqtisadi al-Kuwayti*, No. 324 (May 1995); Globaledge, "Country Insights-Statistics for Kuwait" (http://globaledge.msu.edu/ibrd/CountryStates, updated March 27, 2005; Human Right Watch, *Human Rights News*, "Population Statistics: Gulf Cooperation Council States" (http://www.hrw.org); MSN Encarta, "Bahrain" (http://www.encarta.msn.com/encyclopedia).

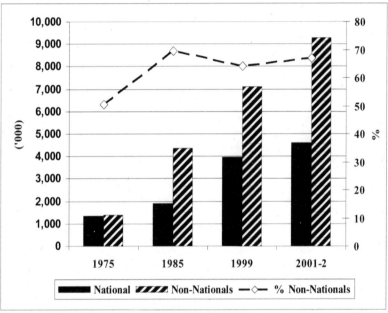

Figure 1: *Nationals and Expatriates in the GCC Labor Forces, 1975-2002* (figures in thousands)

undesirable, mainly in the private sector—even if the alternative was to be unemployed.[31] Second was the natural preference of private sector employers for cheap and disciplined foreign workers over nationals.

In this respect, GCC private sectors were no different from elsewhere in the world. According to one Saudi businessman, "If I have the choice

---

31   J.S. Birks, I.J. Seccombe and C.A. Sinclair, "Labour Migration in the Arab Gulf States: Patterns, Trends and Prospects," *International Migration*, Vol. 26, No. 3 (1988), pp. 267-86; Robert E. Looney, *Economic Development in Saudi Arabia: The Consequences of the Oil Price Decline* (Greenwich: JAI Press, 1990), p. 80.

between employing and paying a Saudi 4,000 riyals while I could pay a Filipino 1,000, of course I will employ the Filipino."[32] The third obstacle was the lack of skilled workers and high school and university graduates in technical occupations.

Fourth was the labor policy that allowed the import of foreign workers with almost no limitation as to scale, skill, or nationality.[33] Sa'id 'Abdallah al-Shaykh, the Chief Economist of the Saudi National Commercial Bank (NCB), correctly assessed Saudi labor policy:

... [It] created a wage structure that reflected the flexibility of importing different skills and not the extent of searching domestically. The relative scarcities of local labor skills did not affect the wage structure [for nationals] since demand for all needed skills could be met through imports.... Therefore, wages do not necessarily reflect the interaction of domestic labor supply and demand forces.... The implication of this is that both the level and the structure of wages that prevailed in Saudi Arabia have been determined independently from the supply of Saudi local labor.[34]

In the other GCC countries the labor market situation was quite similar. In the mid-1990s, the wage structure mechanism in the GCC labor markets was determined not by skill, but by nationality. Thus, while in all other labor markets the wage rate is a function of skill and supply/demand balance, in the GCC countries the wage rate was, and still is to a great extent, a function of nationality. The result was that labor force nationalization policy was efficient only in the public sector, in which the government, not the free market, determined the salaries and work conditions. In the private sector, however, the number of foreign workers continued to increase. Those nationals who worked in the private sector were likely to be either self-employed or close relatives working in the family business.

The dual labor market on the one hand, and the rapid increase in employment demand due to the high natural population increase rates on the other hand, led to a climb in the unemployment rates among nationals in each of the GCC countries.[35] According to a high-level Saudi Ara-

---

32   Mai Yamani, "Health, Education, Gender and the Security of the Gulf in the Twenty-First Century," in David E. Long and Christian Koch (eds), *Gulf Security in the Twenty-First Century* (Abu Dhabi: The Emirates Center for Strategic Studies and Research, 1997), p. 274.

33   On the various obstacles to the implementation of the GCC labor force nationalization policy until the mid-1990s, see, e.g., Winckler, "Gulf Monarchies as Rentier States," pp. 247-50.

34   Al-Shaikh, "Demographic Transitions in Saudi Arabia," pp. 15, 19, 21.

35   Onn Winckler, *Arab Political Demography* (Brighton and Portland: Sussex Academic Press, 2005), pp. 100-1.

bian official, unemployment among nationals in the kingdom had climbed to 20 percent by 2001.[36] The Saudi Prince Walid bin Talal estimated in November 2003 that the unemployment rate among Saudi nationals had reached as high as 30 percent, and that "we are creating an unlimited social problem."[37] Is the unemployment among nationals only "masked," as is argued by many,[38] or is it a "real" problem? In order to answer this crucial question, we have first to define the occupational characteristics of the foreign workers in the GCC countries during the 1990s. Broadly speaking, during the second half of the 1990s, one can identify five major groups of foreign workers in the GCC countries:

1. *Domestic service workers* employed in the homes of nationals as gardeners, nannies, and drivers, the latter mainly in Saudi Arabia where women are not allowed to drive. From a purely macroeconomic point of view, these workers are not necessary for running the GCC economies.[39] These workers, of course, are not subject to the GCC labor force nationalization policies and cannot be replaced by nationals under any circumstances on account of their extremely low salaries, sometimes even less than $100 per month.[40]

2. *Unskilled and semi-skilled factory laborers.* Their share in the total foreign workforce is substantial, for example, amounting to 20 percent in Saudi Arabia in 1996-97.[41] Their replacement by nationals would be quite problematic since their salaries are quite low and any legislated replacement would bring about an increase in production costs and a subsequent loss in profits. As the GCC economies become more integrated with the global economy, increased production costs due to the employment of nationals at the expense of foreigners could lead to the outsourcing of production itself.[42]

36 ESCWA, *Survey, 2001-2002*, p. 19.
37 *Middle East Economic Survey (MEES)*, 2 February 2004.
38 See e.g., Kapiszeasky, *Nationals and Expatriates*, p. 210.
39 The vast majority of these workers come from such countries as Sri Lanka, Pakistan, India, and the Philippines.
40 See in this regard Ugo Fasano and Rishi Goyal, "Emerging Strains in GCC Labor Markets," *IMF Working Paper*, No. 04/71, April 2004. (http://www.imf.org/external/pubs/ft/wp/2004/wp0471.pdf).
41 Al-Shaikh, "Demographic Transitions in Saudi Arabia," p. 20, table 5.
42 With regard to the Saudi Arabian dilemma in this issue, see Rodney Wilson, *Economic Development in Saudi Arabia* (London and New York: RoutledgeCurzon, 2004), pp. 105-6.

3. *Highly skilled foreign workers.* These includes managers of large companies, particularly the top managerial level of the oil and gas companies, almost all of whom are Westerners, mainly from the US and the EU countries. Although their importance to the GCC economies is as enormous as their salaries, their numbers are quite small and they do not have a significant impact on the overall GCC employment trends.

4. *Workers in the wholesale and retail trade.* These workers can be replaced relatively easily by nationals through legislations and regulations, as this area is not subject to international competition and does not suffer from a low social image.

5. *Construction workers.* From a purely economic point of view, it is possible to replace these foreign workers with nationals, as there is no international competition in this area. However, the construction industry suffers from a very low social image and thus would have to offer much higher salaries to nationals in order to attract them. While in Western industrialized countries the cost gap between the employment of local and foreign labor could be overcome through tax reduction in order to prevent huge cost increases, this is not a viable option in the GCC countries, since there is no taxation on housing. In fact the governments, not the citizens themselves, bear most of the housing cost through subsidized loans and generous grants. Thus the replacement of foreign by national labor in the construction sector would lead to a sharp increase in government expenditures on housing, not to mention the expected rise in spending on infrastructure.

From a purely economic point of view, nationals cannot replace a large percentage of GCC foreign workers under the current economic structure and employment policies. Therefore, it is clear that the high unemployment rate among the GCC nationals constitutes "real" unemployment rather than "masked" unemployment.

GCC migration and employment policies since the mid-1990s

In the mid-1990s, the GCC authorities realized that new and stricter measures would have to be taken in order to achieve their basic aims in the areas of employment and migration. The issues of employment, migration, and population growth began to receive more governmental and public attention than ever before. GCC rulers made numerous speeches on these matters, and the press issued a constant flow of articles on demographic and employment issues.

Most important, the issue of employment assumed a higher stated priority in GCC development plans, first and foremost in Saudi Arabia and Oman, the two most populous countries in the GCC.[43] For example, the Saudi Arabian Monetary Agency report for 2000 opened the Labor Force section by stating: "Attention given to the labor market in the Kingdom has greatly increased recently. Saudization of posts and creating employment opportunities for the Saudi labor force have become the most prominent challenges that face planners and policy makers."[44] The section discussing the employment policy in the Saudi Seventh Five-Year Development Plan for the years 2000-4 opened by stating: "Labor force development issues present some of the most important challenges for the Seventh Development Plan..."[45] As for Oman, within the framework of the "Oman 2020 Plan,"[46] the demographic issue was also given high priority.[47]

Overall, since the mid-1990s, the elimination of the dual labor market mechanism has become the most widely stated priority of the GCC governments' migration and employment policies. The specific rules and regulations of each country notwithstanding, it can be said that the migration and employment policies of the GCC states from the mid-1990s concentrated mainly on the following nine measures, some of them representing a new approach and others continuing previous plans and policies:

1. *Tightening the rules and regulations regarding the employment of foreigners in the private sector* in order to increase the jobs available to nationals, while obviating the need to compete with the much cheaper foreign workforce. All the GCC states took steps in this direction, without exception, from the late 1980s, but more extensively from the mid-1990s through the use of two mechanisms: first, there is the quota system, in which the government determines the minimum percentage of nationals to be employed in each economic area; second, the employment of expatriates in specific job categories has been prohibited so that only nationals can supply the demand in those areas. For example, in Saudi Arabia, Resolution no. 50 of 1995 required every establishment employing 20 or more workers to em-

43   See, e.g., *Saudi Economic Survey*, August 18, 1999, p. 5.

44   Saudi Arabian Monetary Agency, *Thirty-Sixth Annual Report 1421* [2000], pp. 257-9.

45   Saudi Arabia, Ministry of Planning, *Seventh Development Plan, 1420/21-1424/25 AH* [2000-2004 AD], p. 158. The current guidelines of the *Shura* dictate that by the year 2007, 70 percent of the workforce will have to be Saudi. Robert Looney, "Saudization and Sound Economic Reforms: Are the Two Compatible?" *Strategic Insights*, Vol. 3, No. 2 (February 2004) (http://www.ccc.nps.navy.mil/si/2005/Mar/looneyMar05.asp).

46   The Omani long-term development plan entitled, "The Vision for Oman's Economy: Oman 2020."

47   Oman, Ministry of Development, *The Fifth Five-Year Development Plan, 1996-2000* (Muscat, July 1997), p. 192.

ploy a minimum of 5 percent Saudi nationals.[48] This minimum percentage of Saudi nationals was increased to 25 percent in September 2000,[49] and again to 30 percent in 2002. The aim of the current Saudization policy is that the overall number of foreign workers in the Kingdom should not exceed 20 percent of the total indigenous Saudi population by the year 2012.[50] In order to enforce the Saudization regulations and decisions, the Saudi authorities established Saudization committees in the major regions of the kingdom under the chairmanship of the governors of the regions.[51]

In the case of Oman, the Central Bank issued a circular in July 1995 stipulating that by the year 2000, Omanis should hold at least 75 percent of senior and middle management positions in the commercial banks. Omanization calls for 95 percent of clerical positions and 100 percent of positions in all other areas to be held by Omanis. At the end of 1999, Omanis held 78.8 percent of all positions, with women making up 30 percent of the total. During 1999, the percentage of Omanis employed in senior and middle management levels in the commercial banks rose from 76.7 percent to 78.8 percent. There was a slight increase in the clerical percentage to 98.7 percent, while the non-clerical areas had already achieved 100 percent Omanization in 1998.[52] According to the plans, the Omani private sector was due to create more than 100,000 new work opportunities for young new entrants to the labor market during the period 2001-5.[53]

2. *Diminishing the gap between the costs of employing foreigners and nationals.* While the public sector can bear the gap between the costs of employing nationals and those of employing foreigners, the private sector must act in accordance with one rule, being profitable to the greatest extent possible. The only way to overcome the natural preference of the private sector to employ foreign workers is to diminish the current huge wage gaps between nationals and foreigners. Indeed, all of the GCC countries have been actively addressing this matter since the early 1990s by increasing the costs of employing foreigners through taxation, on the one hand, and by reducing the costs of employing nationals through governmental subsidies, on the other. In June

---

48   EIU, *Country Profile-Saudi Arabia, 2003*, p. 19.

49   ESCWA, *Survey, 2000-2001*, p. 35.

50   *The Middle East*, October 2003, pp. 54-55.

51   Saudi Arabia Monetary Agency, *Thirty-Eighth Annual Report 1423* [2002] (Riyadh, 2003), p. 324.

52   Sultanate of Oman, Ministry of Information, "Oman 2000" [http://www.omanet.com].

53   EIU, *Country Profile-Oman, 2003*, p. 23; *MEED*, May 4, 2001, p. 24.

2000, for example, the Saudi authorities established the Manpower Development Fund, whose aims were to subsidize the training of nationals for employment in the private sector and to assume a portion of their salaries for an interim period of two years.[54] In Oman, a significant measure taken to close the gap in employment costs between nationals and foreigners was the almost complete abolishment of the *kafala* system. Thus, for example, the new Omani labor law enacted in May 2003 prohibits nationals from taking payment from a foreigner in exchange for employment.[55]

3. *Directing new local entrants to the labor market toward the private sector.* The growing disguised unemployment in the public sector, combined with the rising percentage of salaries as a proportion of total governmental expenditures[56] and the increasing number of new nationals entering the labor force, has led the GCC authorities to the inescapable conclusion that the public sector can no longer absorb new entrants to the labor force. A *MEED* report on the Saudi economy from late 2000 noted in this regard: "The [Saudi] government has made clear through its words and actions that it sees private sector investment as the main driver of job creation."[57] In order to enhance the employment of nationals in the private sector, the Saudi Seventh Development Plan focuses on improving the productivity of nationals, increasing the private sector's capacity to employ a larger number of nationals, and establishing a comprehensive and reliable labor market database.[58]

The authorities of the other five GCC countries viewed the situation in a similar manner. For example, in mid-April 1998, the UAE Minister of Higher Education and Scientific Research asserted: "We call upon every private employer to play an active role in recruiting and employing national graduates."[59] By the end of December 1998, when oil prices were the lowest ever since the oil boom of 1973-74, the Bahraini Minister of Labor and Social Affairs declared that "the private sector has to play a major role

---

54   *Saudi Economic Survey*, August 30, 2000, p. 7.

55   Sultanate of Oman, Ministry of Information, "Oman Labour Law" (http://www.omanet. com).

56   In 1994, for example, salaries for public sector employees constituted about half of the Bahraini budget outlays. *MEED*, November 24, 1995, p. 26. By 2002, public sector salaries amounted to as high as 40 percent of total Kuwaiti government expenditures. *MEED*, October 10-16, 2003, p. 33.

57   *MEED*, December 1, 2000, p. 38.

58   Saudi Arabia, *Seventh Development Plan*, p. 157.

59   *MEED*, May 15, 1998, p. 25.

and share the responsibility of providing jobs."[60] These are only a few of many examples.

4. *Emphasizing technological education at the secondary and university level, in order to reduce dependence on foreign experts and skilled labor.* Taking Saudi Arabia as an example, only 6,000 of 31,000 physicians were nationals in the year 2000.[61] Indeed, according to recently published data, during the past few years there has been a steady increase in the number as well as the percentage of students in technical fields.[62] This issue received considerable attention in the Saudi Seventh Development Plan,[63] and the same trend can be found in the other GCC countries.

5. *Developing economic areas in which the share of nationals within the total workforce is already high or in which there is significant potential for work opportunities for nationals.* In this regard, it can be stated that since the 1980s, Bahrain has served as the economic "sensor" of the GCC countries, leading the region, together with Dubai, in economic diversification through such areas as oil-related industries, banking, and tourism. By 1999, the number of visitors to Bahrain was 3.2 million (the vast majority of whom were Saudis), as compared with 1.6 million in 1995. The percentage of the tourism industry in total GDP was 9.2 percent, and the percentage of employees in the tourism industry in the total number of employees was 16.7 percent.[64] Since the early 2000s, the Bahrainis have started to develop "health tourism" for affluent GCC nationals.[65]

Saudi Arabia has begun to promote the tourism industry as a new source of employment for the indigenous labor force, in addition to the purpose of encouraging the Saudi citizens to spend their holidays in the kingdom rather than abroad.[66] During the past few years, Qatar has also made efforts to develop its tourism sector through huge investments in top-of-the-range hotels in the West Bay area, such as Hyatt, Ritz-Carlton, and Interconti-

---

60   *MEED*, December 11, 1998, p. 22.

61   *Saudi Economic Survey*, 21 February 2001, p. 7.

62   See: ESCWA, *Statistical Abstract of the ESCWA Region-2000*, pp. 123-4, table II-2; Saudi Arabian Monetary Agency, Thirty-Sixth Annual Report 1421 [2000], pp. 45, 238-40.

63   Saudi Arabia, *Seventh Development Plan*, p. 116.

64   *MEED*, January 19, 2001, p. 33.

65   *Gulf States Newsletter*, October 31, 2001, p. 7.

66   On the Saudi Arabia tourism development during the past decade, see Gwenn Okruhlik, "Image, Imagination, and Place: The Political Economy of Tourism in Saudi Arabia," in Joseph A. Kechechian (ed.), *Iran, Iraq, and the Arab Gulf States* (New York: Palgrave, 2001), pp. 111-29.

nental.[67] But the most successful tourism development among the Gulf oil states is in Dubai. According to official UAE figures, in 2003 the tourism sector contributed 17 percent of Dubai's GDP directly and its indirect contribution was as high as 28 percent,[68] demonstrating the huge potential of the tourism sector both for economic diversification and as a major tool for creating new job opportunities for nationals.

6. *Preventing a rapid increase in female labor force participation rates.* Officially, all of the GCC countries, without exception, encourage women's employment. However, in practice, the social norms and, in the case of Saudi Arabia, the myriad rules and regulations limit the range of job opportunities actually available to Saudi women. Thus the labor force participation rates of women in the GCC countries are among the lowest, not only in comparison to other Arab countries but also worldwide, with the exception of Bahrain. The report of the Saudi Arabian Monetary Agency for 2000 noted the high cost of female education that is not returned because of the limitations on female employment, and reiterated the importance of expanding Saudi women's employment opportunities. Yet it claimed that such employment could only come about "in keeping with the conditions, characteristics and traditions of the society."[69]

While there is no doubt that increasing women's employment would contribute to the long-term growth of GCC economies and, in parallel, would bring about fertility decline, in the short run raising female labor force participation rates would substantially increase the number of new entrants to the labor market and would further escalate the already high employment pressures. Moreover, since the vast majority of the GCC female employees are currently employed in the public health and education systems,[70] increasing female labor force participation rates means absorbing them into the already bulging public sector.

7. *Deportation of illegal foreign workers.* A major barrier to implementing the labor force nationalization policies is the easy availability of illegal foreign workers. In addition, the large number of illegal foreign workers has shifted the balance of supply and demand in the labor market. Hence, since

---

67   *MEED*, June 16, 2000, p. 5.

68   "Dubai GDP Gets Tourism Boost," *Gulf News*, May 8, 2004.

69   Saudi Arabian Monetary Agency, *Thirty-Sixth Annual Report 1421H* [2000], p. 268.

70   For example, a report of the Bahrain Chamber of Commerce dated September 2002 indicates that Bahraini women represented less than 1 percent of the workforce in the private sector as compared with more than 40 percent in the public sector. *The Middle East*, January 2003, p. 23.

the mid-1990s, the enforcement of labor and immigration laws in all of the GCC countries has been enhanced through the implementation of three major measures. The first is the increased inspection of foreign workers and the immediate deportation of any illegal worker found. This measure was not new, and there was a period during the 1980s, particularly in the early years of the decade, when some relatively large-scale deportation of illegal foreign workers took place. However, the difference between the actions taken in the 1980s and the more recent measures lies in the extent of the governments' operations in this field.[71] The second measure is the increased inspection of foreigners at border crossings. In the case of Saudi Arabia in particular, this measure is crucial since the kingdom hosts the *Hajj* when nearly two million pilgrims enter the country. The third measure is the imposition of stricter penalties on private employers who employ foreign workers illegally.

8. *Religious justification of labor force nationalization.* Thus far, only Saudi Arabia has adopted such a measure. One of the Saudization measures in the Seventh Development Plan is that of "enlightening people through information media of the importance of work and its religious and social value."[72]

9. *Promoting fertility decline.* Since the mid-1990s, the authorities of the two most populous GCC countries, Saudi Arabia and Oman, have advocated fertility decline in order to alleviate future employment pressure.[73] It should be emphasized, however, that only Oman has adopted fertility decline as an official policy. In October 1994, the Birth Spacing Services Program was incorporated into the Omani governmental Maternal and Child Health clinics to promote the use of contraceptives, which are given free of charge in the clinics. Moreover, Sultan Qabus himself has promoted family planning in his public speeches. Indeed, by the year 2000, the percentage of married Omani women using family planning methods was 32 percent, as compared with 9 percent in the late 1980s. Likewise, the Saudi authorities have recently become more concerned about the wide-based age pyramid and its implications for future employment demand, even publicly acknowledging the seriousness of the demographic situation. A

---

71   On the development of the phenomenon of illegal foreign workers in the GCC and its scale, see, e.g., Kapiszeasky, *Nationals and Expatriates*, pp. 87-99.

72   Saudi Arabia Monetary Agency, *Thirty-Eighth Annual Report 1423* [2002], p. 319.

73   In the other four GCC countries, the indigenous populations are in any case very tiny. Thus, an anti-natalist policy in order to bring about a fertility decline is not relevant in their cases.

clear indicator of the changing Saudi fertility approach is the abolition in 1996 of the 1976 law forbidding the promotion, distribution, and use of contraceptives.[74]

Evaluating GCC immigration and employment policies

As the data reveal, there is no longer any doubt that from the mid-1990s, considerable progress was made in the implementation of employment and immigration policies in the GCC countries, particularly in Bahrain, the country with the lowest per capita oil revenues and proven reserves among the GCC countries. As early as 1995, 29.3 percent of the total employees in Bahrain's private sector were nationals. By 1999, according to ESCWA figures, 90 percent of Bahrain's public sector employees were nationals, and in the private sector as well, substantial progress was also achieved, with 66 percent nationals in the banking sector, 38 percent in the industrial sector, and 14 percent in the construction sector.[75] Overall, by 2003, Bahraini nationals comprised 29.2 percent of the total private sector employees.[76] However, despite the strict measures taken to favor indigenous workers and the steady increase in the number of national employees in the private sector, the total number of foreign workers in Bahrain continued to increase, reaching 192,000 in 2002 (see Table 1), while the total foreign population amounted to 261,463 in 2003, increasing from 239,391 in 2000—an increase of 9.2 percent within three years.[77]

In the case of Oman, although there was no significant decline in the number of foreign workers during the second half of the 1990s, a substantial decline in their number has been evident in the public sector. According to official Omani data, by 2001 the number of foreign employees in the private sector was 529,998, compared with 526,018 in 1994, while in the public sector their number declined from 35,812 to 27,161 in the corresponding years.[78] According to the latest available official data, by 2003 the number of foreign workers in the Omani public sector was 23,969, representing a further decline of 13.3 percent within two years.[79] On

---

74   On the anti-natalist measures taken by Oman and Saudi Arabia, see Winckler, *Arab Political Demography*, pp. 139-41.

75   ESCWA, *Survey, 1998-1999*, p. 53. See also EIU, *Country Profile-Bahrain, 2001-2002*, p. 19.

76   Bahrain, Bahrain Monetary Agency, *Economic Indicator*, No. 5 (September 2004), p. 4.

77   Ibid., p. 3.

78   Central Bank of Oman, *Annual Report 2001* (Muscat, 2002), p. 17.

79   Central Bank of Oman, *Annual Report 2003* (Muscat, 2004), p. 20, table 2.5.

the importance of Omanization for the Sultanate's future socioeconomic development, Sultan Qabus said that "work, whatever its nature, is a virtue."[80] On the success of the Omanization policy, the monthly *The Middle East* wrote as follows:

From the moment one enters the sultanate this [Omanization] influence is obvious. A large proportion of the airport staff at Muscat's Seeb International Airport are Omanis. The taxi driver who transports you to your hotel, the reception staff that greet you there, are all likely to be Omanis. And this is also true of manufacturing, industry, banking and most sectors of business.[81]

However, although Oman has indeed implemented some important measures in the area of labor force nationalization, it should be remembered that in 2002, approximately 90 percent of the private sector employees were still foreigners[82] and the overall number of foreign workers continued to increase, amounting to more than 600,000 in 2002, a net increase of approximately 100,000 from 1999 (see Table 1). According to the current Omani Five-Year Plan, the private sector was supposed to create more than 100,000 new work opportunities for young Omanis by the end of 2005. However, in the first year and a half of the plan, the number of Omani employees in the private sector increased by only 7,500—much below the plan's target.[83]

In the case of Saudi Arabia, a major positive indicator of the improvement in the implementation of Saudi employment policies in recent years is the steady reduction in the scale of workers' remittances. By 1999, the scale of Saudi workers' remittances was $14.06 billion, representing a decrease of $1 billion from 1998 and a decrease of approximately 25 percent (in real terms) as compared with 1994.[84] However, this success is relative and the progress in the Saudization of the labor force falls far below expectations. By January 2003, according to data provided by the Ministry of Labor, of the 7 million foreigners in the Kingdom, "at least 5.5 million of them are workers,"[85] representing a substantial increase from the 4.4 million in 1999 (see Table 1). Thus, despite the Saudization measures taken and the steady

---

80   Sultanate of Oman, Ministry of Information (http://www.omanet.om).

81   *The Middle East*, April 2003, p. 33.

82   *Gulf States Newsletter*, May 16, 2003, p. 9.

83   EIU, *Country Profile-Oman, 2003*, pp. 23-4. See also: ESCWA, *Survey, 2003-2004*, p. 55.

84   *MEED*, September 15, 2000, p. 29.

85   Human Rights Watch, "Population Statistics: Gulf Cooperation Council States" [http://www.hrw.org].

unemployment increase among nationals, the number of foreign workers continued to increase.

In Kuwait, the number of foreign workers continued to increase rapidly during the past decade, amounting to 1.1 million in 2003, as compared with 762,000 in 1995, representing an increase of 45 percent (see Table 1). Moreover, the changes in the immigration and labor policies during this period were quite minor. With oil production of almost 2.4 million b/d and 96.5 billion barrels of proven oil reserves,[86] and with a small national population of only 800,000, perhaps Kuwait can afford after all to stick to its current rentier policy. However, even in Kuwait, despite its comfortable economic situation, the authorities plan to change the current political-economic framework by launching a four-year plan aimed at cutting governmental subsidies and imposing public services fees and sales taxes.[87]

In Qatar and the UAE as well, the number of foreign workers continued to increase rapidly during the past decade with only marginal changes in their labor markets' structure and composition. Foreign labor in the UAE increased from 1,165,000 in 1997 to 1,530,000 in 2003, an increase of 31.3 percent. Qatar's foreign workers in 2002 were estimated to number 367,000, compared with 244,000 in 1997, representing an increase of as high as 50 percent (see Table 1). A major consequence of the rapid increase in numbers of Qatar's foreign workers was the equivalent increase in the workers' remittances that amounted to QR5.802 billion ($1.59 billion) in 2003 as compared with QR4.584 billion ($1.26 billion) in 1999, an increase of 26.6 percent in four years only.[88] This means that by 2003, almost 8 percent of Qatar's total GDP was outflow from the country through workers' remittances.[89]

Conclusions

Until the mid-1990s, the major factors that shaped the employment structure of the GCC countries, including the size of the foreign workforces, were not economic but political. During the second half of the 1980s and

86   U.S. Energy Information Administration (EIA), [http://www.eia.doe.gov/emeu/cabs/opecrev.html].

87   *Gulf States Newsletter*, February 21, p. 14; 16 May, p. 15; 25 July 2003, p. 15.

88   Qatar Central Bank, Department of Economic Policies, *Twenty-Seventh Annual Report* (Doha, 2004), p. 56.

89   By 2003, Qatar's total GDP was 74.351 billion QR ($20.426 billion). Qatar Central Bank, Department of Economic Policies, *Twenty-Seventh Annual Report* (Doha, 2004), p. 15.

the first half of the 1990s, the number of foreign workers in GCC countries continued to increase, even though oil prices were low and budgetary deficits high, sometimes more than 10 percent of GDP.[90] At the same time, the vast majority of the new nationals entering the workforce were absorbed into the public sector. This dual labor market mechanism, with its privilege of guaranteed public sector employment, serves as the major cornerstone of the GCC rentier political system—the "no taxation, no representation" formula. Political liberalization measures were therefore not necessary for regime legitimization and survival.

But during the second half of the 1990s, with the exception of Kuwait and to a lesser extent the UAE and Qatar, the GCC countries took substantial measures in order to reduce the number of their foreign workers. High oil prices since April 1999 have helped the GCC authorities to enhance their nationalization policies.[91] In this respect the Iraqi crisis, which has led to a sharp increase in oil prices, served GCC economic interests well.

However, even though the increase in the number of foreign workers was halted during the second half of the 1990s, this did not solve the unemployment problem among young GCC nationals. Their inability to compete with cheap foreign labor in the private sector remained, while the public sector is not a viable area for instituting the nationalization policy.

Yet paradoxically, increasing the available work opportunities for nationals in the private sector requires an equivalent increase in the number of foreign workers. This has been the case particularly in Oman, the UAE, and Qatar, as is clearly evident in the tourism industry. The most extreme example in this respect is Dubai. By 2002, despite the high oil prices, the oil sector contributed only 17 percent to Dubai's total GDP.[92] However, the "price" for this enhanced economic diversification and low unemployment rates among nationals was a rapid increase in the number of foreign workers,[93] which is at odds with the logic of the underlying policy of the GCC authorities to reduce dependence on foreign labor.

---

90   Thus, for example, the Saudi budget deficit in the fiscal year of 1992 was $10.5 billion, representing more than 10 percent of GDP. *The Middle East*, February 1994, p. 24.

91   By 2003, according to the EIA estimate, Saudi oil revenues amounted to $81 billion, compared with only $49 billion in 2001. Overall, by 2003 GCC oil revenues amounted to $141 billion, more than two and a half times the amount of 1998 revenues (EIA, "OPEC Revenues: Country Details," January 2004 [http://www.eia.dov.gov].

92   "Tourism to Outshine Oil in Dubai's GDP," *Gulf News*, August 12, 2003 (http://www.gulf-news.com).

93   Overall, during the period 1996-2002, Dubai's labor force, in which nationals constitute only 10 percent, increased from 390,380 to 663,372, representing an extraordinary

In order to promote labor force nationalization, Robert Looney suggests: "Reducing the relatively high wages in the public sector is likely to lower the reservation wage and increase the willingness of nationals to acquire skills...valuable to private sector employment."[94] Although decreasing the percentage of nationals employed by the public sector is a necessary step, it would constitute a socio-economic revolution that would significantly affect the political system as the current political formula of "no taxation, no representation" would diminish. Thus, transferring current national employees from the public to the private sector is not politically viable under the current rentier political system. However, as the privatization of government entities to enlarge the private sector in order to provide employment for nationals proceeds, this should have the effect of contributing to greater political openness, as businesses will demand it. In other words, private sector growth will be an engine of political liberalization.

It seems that only through political change that alters the fundamental rentier nature of the relationship between the ruling families and their citizenry can a solution be found to the two chronic problems of the dual labor market: high unemployment among nationals and the steady increase in the number of foreign workers. Primarily, these changes must take place by increasing "representation" in exchange for "taxation." There are some encouraging signs that such changes may be afoot—witness the establishment of the Consultative Council in Saudi Arabia in 1993, the 1996 Oman Basic Law and the 1999 elections in Qatar. Yet just how far GCC royal families will be willing to accept change still remains to be seen.

Thus far, political openness in the GCC countries has come about at the initiative of the rulers in their efforts to find a balance between the economic changes and the political systems. That is, greater political participation has not been brought about by public pressure through mass demonstrations or opposition actions against the royal families. In this respect, the GCC countries are no different from the other Arab states. This process of political openness is fundamentally different from the development of the "Western" democratic style, which was the result of increasing pressure for political participation by the new middle class that emerged from the Industrial Revolution. Thus, whereas democracy in Western European countries was the outcome, mainly, of regime weakness, the increased po-

---

increase of 70 percent within only eight years. Government of Dubai, Department of Economic Development, *Dubai Economic Statistics* (http://www.dubaided.gov.ae).

94   Looney, "Saudization and Sound Economic Reforms."

litical openness in the Arab countries, including the GCC countries, is more the result of a strengthening within the regimes that has allowed for increased political openness. Hence the most liberal political system among the GCC countries is in Qatar, with almost no visible opposition. On the other hand, in Saudi Arabia, where political opposition has been on the rise during the past decade, a degree of political openness has not been accompanied by any significant liberalization of the political system.

The economic problems of the past decade, particularly the increase in the unemployment of nationals, have forced the GCC royal families to adopt a modicum of participatory politics. The higher oil prices of the past few years, which theoretically might increase the leverage of the state and maintain the rentier system for future generations, will in practice not obviate the need for political liberalization, although they may slow its pace. This is because GCC populations continue to increase at rates that have led to a continued decrease in per capita GDP, despite higher oil prices.

However, in the meantime, the power of the royal families in these countries has not been significantly narrowed in practice. The small amounts of political change that have occurred in the GCC countries during the past decade were primarily due to the state's inability to significantly reduce the unemployment of nationals. This had led to a diminishing of the scale of the rentier system, particularly in the employment and subsidies areas. But these regimes are solid and stronger than ever, and can be expected to enjoy nearly absolute power, at least for the foreseeable future.

4

SAUDI ARABIA: WHY THE '*ULAMA* ARE STALLING LIBERALIZATION

Muhammad al-Atawneh

Introduction

In a recent study, the scholar Jean-François Seznec wrote that there was hope for democracy in Saudi Arabia. According to Seznec, stirrings of proto-democratic trends are observable today in Saudi Arabia among certain social groups—including even some circles of the royal family—who would like to see more liberalization and participation. Moreover, democratic dynamics are not totally alien to Saudi culture: "There is a preexisting culture of consultation and discussion inherited from the Bedouin and Arab traditions of *majlis*. It has a leadership that is used to negotiating on most issues within its own group (and to a certain extent with other groups)."[1] Seznec stressed, however, that further evolution of democratization "can only be with the encouragement, or at least approval, of the king." In other words, democratization of the Saudi state should take place from the top down.[2]

One cannot doubt Seznec's observation that quite a bit of pressure for political and social reforms, including in democratic directions, has taken place recently in Saudi Arabia.[3] The completion of elections for half the

---

1   Jean-François Seznec, "Stirrings in Saudi Arabia," in Larry Diamond, Marc F. Plattner and Daniel Brumberg (eds), *Islam and Democracy in the Middle East* (Baltimore and London: Johns Hopkins University Press, 2003), p. 82.

2   Seznec, "Stirrings in Saudi Arabia," p. 82.

3   For example, a new Memorandum of Advice [*mudhakkirat nasiha*] was submitted by 104 intellectuals and '*ulama* to the then Crown Prince 'Abdallah, calling for comprehensive reforms in Saudi Arabia. See *al-Quds al-'Arabi*, January 30, 2003.

members of municipal councils in 2005 appears to be the government's response to such pressure, as well as to the increasing criticism of the Saudi regime.[4] It is clear that as far as Saudi Arabia is concerned, reforms in general, and democratization and liberalization of the Saudi political system in particular, cannot take place without the support, or at least the consent, of the royal family as a major power center in the authoritarian Saudi state.

Yet, efforts at political liberalization in Saudi Arabia are made more complex because of the strong fusion of religion and state in the kingdom.[5] It is prominent even among Middle Eastern countries in this respect, with its judicial and constitutional system that operates on traditional Islamic legal principles: the Qur'an and Sunna form its constitution, Islamic *fiqh* is the basis of the laws of the state, and there is no comprehensive system of "man-made" legislation. The religious establishment plays a vital role in the state judicial system, and religious scholars, or *'ulama*, are responsible for legislation and judicial procedures, perhaps more than in any other Middle Eastern country. Moreover, the *'ulama* maintain a strong influence over politics. They provide legitimacy for political measures, thereby contributing to the political stability of the Saudi dynasty for over two centuries.[6]

---

4   *Al-Sharq al-Awsat*, October 15, 2003; Joshua Teitelbaum, "Between the International Hammer and the Local Anvil: Municipal Elections in Saudi Arabia," *Tel Aviv Notes*, March 15, 2005 (http://www.tau.ac.il/jcss/tanotes/TAUnotes129.doc).

5   The question of whether Islam is compatible or incompatible with democracy has been the subject of heated debate among Western scholars over recent decades. Most scholars have endeavored to explore the extent to which religion is compatible with the basic tenets of democracy: pluralistic competition, free debate, and regular electoral accountability. Answers have never been an absolute yes or no, and scholars have usually preferred to delineate the *line* between the in/compatibility of Islam and democracy. See William Zartman, "Islam, the State, and Democracy: The Contradictions," in Charles E. Butterworth and William Zartman (eds), *Between the State and Islam* (Cambridge, UK and Washington, DC: Woodrow Wilson Center and Cambridge University Press, 2001), pp. 231-44; Shukri B. Abed, "Islam and Democracy," in David Garnham and Mark Tessler (eds), *Democracy, War, and Peace in the Middle East* (Bloomington, IN: Indiana University Press, 1995); Ali Reza Abootalebi, *Islam and Democracy: State-Society Relations in Developing Countries, 1980-1994* (New York and London: Garland Publishing, 2000), pp. 60-76; John L. Esposito and John O. Voll, *Islam and Democracy* (New York, Oxford: Oxford University Press, 1996), pp. 11-33; Forough Jahanbakash, *Islam, Democracy, and Religious Modernism in Iran (1953-2000): From Bazargan to Soroush* (Leiden, Boston, Cologne: E.J. Brill, 2001), pp. 20-50.

6   The role of the *'ulama* in Saudi Arabia was worked out by the historical alliance of 1745 between Shaykh Muhammad Ibn 'Abd al-Wahhab (d. 1792), the founder of the Wahhabi movement, and Muhammad Ibn Sa'ud (d. 1765), the ancestor of the Sa'udi dynasty. On the basis of this alliance, Ibn Sa'ud became the political leader, while Ibn 'Abd al-Wahhab became the supreme religious authority and spiritual leader of the first Sa'udi-Wahhabi state (1745-1818). For more on the *'ulama*'s functions in modern Saudi Arabia, see Frank Vogel, *Islamic Law and Legal System: Studies of Saudi Arabia* (Leiden: E.J. Brill, 2000), pp. 169-221.

Thus Saudi Arabian reforms in general, and in fundamental spheres such as the relationship between religion and state in particular, should not only garner the support of the political elite, as noted by Seznec; they need also to enjoy the support and full cooperation of the *'ulama*. In other words, in Saudi Arabia, where changes must be carried out via the *shari'a*, the *'ulama* represent the best means for attaining them. How then, does that critical social group, the *'ulama*, relate to democracy? Is there any room for democracy in their world outlook? Finally, to what extent do such positions either advance or block reforms in democratic directions? Answering these and related questions necessitates an examination of the *'ulama*'s writings and legal opinions (*fatawa*) on politics and democracy. An emphasis will be placed on the official *'ulama*, or those who are the members of the Board of Senior *'Ulama* (*Hay'at Kibar al-'Ulama*, hereafter BSU), and the Permanent Committee for Scientific Research and Legal Opinions (*al-Lajna al-Da'ima lil-Buhuth al-'Ilmiyya wal-Ifta* hereafter: CRLO).[7] The goal of this article is to deepen our understanding of the contemporary Saudi-Wahhabi *'ulama*'s position on democracy, for without the approbation of the *'ulama*, it is very unlikely that political liberalization, let alone democracy, will make significant strides in the kingdom. As will be seen, the official *'ulama* are likely to make this very difficult.

Debating democracy in the contemporary Islamic world

Democracy in its Western form has evoked many controversies among contemporary Muslim scholars and jurists. Raghid El-Solh divided the scholars' attitudes toward democracy into three major groups:[8]

1. Those that reject democracy as a foreign concept that has been imposed by Westernizers and secular reformers upon Muslim societies. For the extremists among this group, democracy is nothing but apostasy, on account of its denial of the fundamental Islamic affirmation of the sovereignty of God. According to El-Solh, those holding these views are less likely to be the ones participating in elections. Many limit themselves to participating

---

7   These two institutions, led by the Grand Mufti, constitute the "religious pyramid" in current Saudi Arabia, providing the ultimate statements on *shari'a*; they complement each other. While the BSU issues formal *fatwa*s on major public issues, the CRLO is responsible for conducting research, administering private *ifta*, and providing administrative support for the BSU.

8   Raghid El-Solh, "Islamist Attitudes Toward Democracy: A Review of the Ideas of Al-Ghazali, Al-Turabi, and 'Amara," *British Journal of Middle Eastern Studies*, Vol. 20, No. 1 (1993), p. 58.

in intellectual debates in the media, and others remain aloof from the political dynamics of their societies.

2. Those who believe that true Islam and democracy are compatible. This group argues that Islam is inherently democratic, and all of the principles and practices of democracy are integral to it. Hence the democratization and the Islamization of Muslim societies are more or less the same process. Among the Islamists who belong to this group is Hasan al-Turabi, the leader of the Islamic National Front in the Sudan.

3. Those that place an emphasis on democracy in its representative forms. These seem to be less skeptical than members of the first two groups about the possibility of implementing democracy in Islamic society. Moreover, some extend the argument to affirm that under the conditions of today's world, democracy can even be considered a requirement of Islam. Scholars have been known to bring historically important concepts from within the Islamic tradition together with the basic concepts of democracy as understood in today's world. El-Solh names two prominent Egyptian proponents of this idea: Muhammad 'Amara, a well-known writer on Islamic affairs, and Shaykh Muhammad al-Ghazali, a leading Egyptian Muslim Brotherhood thinker.

Wahhabis, democracy, and the West

Wahhabis, who are more suspicious of foreign cultures than any other Islamic group, belong to the first category. Historically, the Wahhabis opposed admixtures of Islamic thought with foreign cultures, thereby condemning the rational school of Mu'tazila and accusing it of corrupting true Islam by adopting Greek philosophy. The Wahhabis rejected *kalam*, or Islamic dogmatic theology, including Ash'arism, and insisted that innovations such as mysticism and asceticism, philosophy and polemic theology, cult and ritual are foreign to the Qur'an.[9]

In contemporary Wahhabi discourse, Western influence on Islamic societies has been described as an intellectual invasion (*ghazw fikri*) by which the West endeavors to turn the Islamic nation away from its beliefs in favor of Western cultural perceptions. Shaykh 'Abd al-'Aziz Bin Baz, who is considered to be the most authoritative contemporary Wahhabi

9   Ahmad Bin 'Abd al-Raziq al-Dawish, *Fatawa al-lajna al da'ima lil-buhuth al-'ilmiyya wal-ifta wal-da'wa wal-irshad*, 13 vols (Riyadh: Maktabat al-'Ibikan, 2000), 2:181-211; 3:152-3, 162-3, 177-8.

scholar,[10] expressed his concern regarding intellectual invasion on more than one occasion. According to Bin Baz, this is nothing but a war undertaken by the West in order to influence Islamic societies via various methods such as school curricula, print publications, and television. For Bin Baz, this war is far more serious than military war, since it aims for secrecy, seeking to achieve subtle objectives initially, so that the invaded nation neither perceives it, nor attempts to halt it, nor stands in its way—thereby falling victim to it.[11]

Bin Baz therefore urged Muslims to beware when encountering Western culture, such as when traveling or studying in the West. For example, he called upon the Saudi government to institute a selection process for students seeking to travel to the West to complete their studies in various fields.[12] Indeed, a royal decree promulgated in 1984 limited students' travel to studying disciplines that could not be studied in Saudi Arabia.[13] This prohibition was mainly aimed at recent high school graduates. The reason given was to prevent these young adults from being exposed to permissive societies and cultures that differ widely from conservative cultures such as that of Saudi Arabia.

The Saudi Wahhabis' negative attitude toward the West is articulated in the conceiving of democracy as an integral part of Western culture. The 'ulama as well as the Saudi government reject democracy as incompatible with Saudi society and culture. According to former King Fahd, Islam provides a systematic and fully integrated system of governance that is not necessarily compatible with Western democracy. In the King's words:

The democratic system that is predominant in the world is not a suitable system for the peoples of our region. Our people's makeup and unique qualities are different from those of the rest of the world. We cannot import the methods used by people in other countries and apply them to our people. We have our Islamic beliefs that constitute a

---

10   Bin Baz filled a long series of important international and local religious functions. Among the most outstanding in Saudi Arabia were his roles as the head of the Dar al-Ifta (1975-99) and Grand Mufti of the Kingdom from 1993 until his death in May 1999, at the age of 89.

11   See Bin Baz's legal opinion regarding this in Muhammad bin Sa'd al-Shuway'ir (ed.), Majmu' fatawa wa-maqalat mutanawwi'a, 13 vols. (Riyadh: Maktabat al-Ma'arif, 1997), 3:438-346.

12   See Bin Baz's legal opinions in Majallat al-Buhuth al-Islamiyya, the quarterly publication of the General Presidency of the Administration of Scientific Studies, Fatwa, (Religious) Instructions and Preaching, Kingdom of Saudi Arabia, 6:466-7 [hereafter MBI]; see also al-Shuway'ir, Majmu' fatawa wa-maqalat mutanawwi'a, 4:195.

13   Royal Decree No. 19851 of July 1, 1981, revised by Decree No. 438/8, of December 11, 1984.

complete and fully-integrated system. Free elections are not within this Islamic system, which is based on consultation [*shura*] and the openness between the ruler and his subjects before whom he is fully responsible... In my view, Western democracies may be suitable in their own countries, but they do not suit our countries.[14]

As one might guess, the main argument for rejecting democracy by King Fahd was the incompatibility of democracy with Islamic values. Islam provides a "complete and fully-integrated system" that is consistent with Islamic society, while democracy in its Western form remains alien to this Islamic system, at least as conceived by the Wahhabis.

An investigation of contemporary Wahhabi theological and political thought sheds more light on the extent to which the Wahhabi ideology of the official *'ulama* is compatible or incompatible with democracy. This examination will focus on three of democracy's most basic tenets: sovereignty (*siyada, hakimiyya*), pluralism (*ta'addudiyya*), and freedom of expression (*hurriyyat al-ta'bir*).

Sovereignty

Sovereignty lies at the core of much contemporary Islamic debate on democracy. For the Wahhabis, similarly to most contemporary Muslim scholars, sovereignty ultimately rests with God, who is the source of all authority and has made the law, defining good and evil, the licit and the illicit (*al-halal wal-haram*). Members of the Muslim community (*umma*) are God's subjects; the community's laws are divine; its property is God's property; its army is God's army; and its enemies are God's enemies.[15]

Also, God's sovereignty assumes that the divine legislative will seeks to regulate all human interactions, that *shari'a* is a complete moral code that prescribes for every eventuality. Bin Baz argues, for example, that the term worship (*'ibada*) includes all human actions, whether explicit or latent. Accordingly, one must completely submit to God's will as it manifests itself particularly in the Qur'an and the Sunna. For this reason, the Qur'an is much more than the highest source of the Islamic *corpus juris*; it is a con-

14   *Al-Siyasa*, March 28, 1992.

15   'Abd al-'Aziz Bin Baz, "*Wujub tahkim shar' Allah wa-nabdh ma khalafahu*," in Muhammad Ibn Sa'd al-Shuway'ir, *Majmu' fatawa wa-maqalat mutanawwi'a*, 1:72; see also idem, "*al-Radd 'ala man ya'tabiru al-ahkam al-shar'iyya ghayr mutanasiba ma' al-'asr al-hadir*," in ibid., 1:415; idem, "*Hukm al-Islam fi man za'ama anna al-Qur'an mutanaqid aw mushtamil 'ala ba'd al-khurafat aw wasafa al-rasul bi-ma yatadammanu tanaqqusahu aw al-ta'n fi risalatihi*," in ibid., 1: 82-8. See for example Bernard Lewis, "Politics and War," in Joseph Schacht and C.E. Bosworth (eds), *The Legacy of Islam* (Oxford: Clarendon Press, 1974), p. 159.

stant source of inspiration. It constitutes an eternal constitution appropriate for any time and place, and thus it contains the basic principles of Islamic law and provides the platform for developing political, legal, and moral norms. [16]

Hence, it is incumbent upon Muslims to obey only the Qur'an and the Sunna's instructions. To substantiate his arguments, Bin Baz provided nine verses, all of which command obedience to God and His Prophet's instructions. One of these verses is: "But no, by thy lord, they can have no (real) faith, until they make thee judge in all disputes between them, and find in their souls no resistance against thy decisions, but accept them with the fullest conviction [4: 65]." Another verse is:

"O ye who believe! Obey Allah, and obey the Messenger, and those charged with authority among you. If ye differ in anything among yourselves, refer it to Allah and His Messenger, if ye do believe in Allah and the Last Day: that is best, and most suitable for final determination [4: 59]."[17]

A quick glimpse at all the verses indicates that they all relate to the doctrine of allegiance and enmity in Islam (*al-wala wal-bara*), under which Muslim allegiance must be pledged only to God and His Prophet.[18] Accordingly, Bin Baz rejected other political ideologies that spread in the Arab world, such as communism and nationalism.[19] He stressed, "He who thinks that human rules [are] better than those of God, or even resemble them [God's rules], thereby endorsing replacing them by positive rules or human orders, is an unbeliever."[20]

However, God does not seek to regulate all human affairs, actually leaving human beings considerable latitude in regulating their own affairs as long as they observe certain standards of moral conduct, including the preservation and promotion of human dignity and well-being. In other words, while sovereignty belongs to God, it has already been delegated in the form

16   'Abd al-'Aziz Bin Baz, "*Wujub tahkim shar' Allah wa-nabdh ma khalafahu*," in Muhammad b. Sa'd al-Shuway'ir, *Majmu' fatawa wa-maqalat mutanawwi'a*, 1:72.

17   Ibid., pp. 268-9; other Qur'anic verses cited by Bin Baz were: 42:10; 5:44, 45, 47, 50, 51; 9:23.

18   On the doctrine of *wala wa-bara* in contemporary Wahhabi legal and theological thought, see Ahmad b. 'Abd al-Raziq al-Dawish, *Fatawa al-lajna al da'ima lil-buhuth al-'ilmiyya wal-ifta wal-da'wa wal- irshad*, 2:41-89.

19   Bin Baz, "*Hukm man yutalib bi-tahkim al-mabadi al-ishtirakiyya wal-shuyu'iyya*," in Muhammad bin Sa'd al-Shuway'ir (ed.), *Majmu' fatawa wa-maqalat mutanawwi'a*, 1:268-71.

20   Idem, "*Wujub tahkim shar' Allah wa-nabdh ma-khalafahu*," in ibid., 1:79.

of human agency.[21] This precept explains God's commands of honoring human beings and the miracle of the human intellect—an expression of the abilities of the divine. For Bin Baz, the fact that God honored the miracle of the human intellect and the human being as a symbol of divinity is sufficient for justifying a moral commitment to protect and preserve the integrity and dignity of that symbol of divinity.[22] The questions remain, however: who are God's representatives on earth, and what are the limits of their authority?

Wahhabi political theory is based on the premise that the purpose of government in Islam is to preserve the *shari'a* and to enforce its dictates. To maintain and enforce the *shari'a*, a temporal ruler is needed, and obedience to him is a religious obligation. However the ruler must consult the *'ulama*, who are designated as those most authorized to clarify the instructions of the *shari'a*. Relying on the teachings of his predecessors—principally Ibn Taymiyya and Ibn Qayyim al-Jawziyya—the founder of Wahhabism, Shaykh Muhammad Bin 'Abd al-Wahhab (d. 1792), divided the ruling hegemony of the state between the *'ulama*, who were the authority with regard to jurisprudential matters, and the *umara* or rulers, who ruled and presumably consulted the *'ulama*.[23]

---

21   The issue of God's sovereignty [*hakimiyyat Allah*] was raised early in Islamic history by a group known as the Khawarij, when they rebelled against 'Ali Ibn Abi Talib, the fourth Rightly Guided Caliph. The Khawarij were initially part of 'Ali's camp until he agreed to arbitrate his political dispute with a competing political faction led by Mu'awiya (the founder of the Umayyad Dynasty, 661-750). For the Khawarij, this represented an arbitrary acceptance of the dominion of human beings instead of that of God. 'Ali responded by calling upon the people to gather around him, and brought a copy of the Qur'an, instructing it to speak to the people and inform them regarding God's law. The people were shocked and exclaimed, "What are you doing? The Qur'an cannot speak, for it is not a human being!" 'Ali then explained that this was exactly his point: the Qur'an is but ink and paper, and does not speak for itself. Instead, it is human beings who give effect to it according to their limited judgments and opinion. See Muhammad Ibn 'Ali Ibn Muhammad al-Shawkani, *Nayl al-Awtar Sharh Muntaqa al-Akhbar* (Cairo: Dar al-Hadith, n.d.), 7:166; Shihab al-Din Ibn Hajar al-'Asqalani, *Fath al-Bari bi Sharh Sahih al-Bukhari* (Beirut: Dar al-Fikr, 1993), 14:303.

22   Bin Baz, "*Wujub tahkim shar' Allah wa-nabdh ma-khalafahu*," in Muhammad b. Sa'd al-Shuway'ir (ed.), *Majmu' fatawa wa-maqalat mutanawwi'a*, 1:79; A Qur'anic verse states: "Behold, thy Lord said to the angels: I will create a vicegerent on earth." They said: "Wilt Thou place therein one who will make mischief therein and shed blood? Whilst we do celebrate Thy praise and glorify Thy holy (name)?" He said: "I know what ye know not," Qur'an [2:30].

23   The link between religion and the state was stressed in the teachings of other classical scholars such as al-Ghazali and Ibn Taymiyya, who linked the Islamic state with religion; see A. Layish, "'Ulama and Politics in Saudi Arabia," in M. Heper and R. Israeli (eds), *Islam and Politics in the Modern Middle East* (London and Sydney: Croom Helm Press, 1984), pp. 56-7.

This formula manifested itself in the alliance of 1745 between Ibn 'Abd al-Wahhab and Muhammad Ibn Sa'ud (d.1765), the founder of the Saudi dynasty, which in turn created the *'ulama-umara* alliance of mutual support which obtains until this day.[24] Under this arrangement, Muhammad Ibn Sa'ud became the political leader, while Ibn'Abd al-Wahhab became the supreme religious authority and spiritual leader of the first Sa'udi-Wahhabi state (1745-1818).[25] Nonetheless, no specific, precise model regulating the cooperation between the *'ulama* and the rulers was provided, nor were their respective spheres of authority delineated. Most important, however, according to this alliance, the Wahhabis can recognize no separation between religion and state.

For the most part, contemporary Wahhabi *'ulama* embraced the classical stance of their predecessors, determining that God's representatives should be the *'ulama* and *umara.*[26] Bin Baz argues, for example, that the function

---

24   The treaty between Ibn 'Abd al-Wahhab and Ibn Sa'ud is well known and treated by many works. See for example 'Abdallah al-Salih al-'Uthaymin, *Ibn 'Abd al-Wahhab: Hayatuhu wa-fikruhu* (Riyadh: Dar al-'Ulum, 1987), pp. 53-8; M.J. Crawford, "Civil War, Foreign Intervention, and the Question of Political Legitimacy: A Nineteenth-Century Saudi Qadi's Dilemma," *International Journal of Middle East Studies* Vol. 14 (1982), pp. 227-48; Muhammad Kamil Dahir, *al-Da'wa al-Wahhabiyya wa-atharuha fi al-fikr al-Islami al-hadith* (Beirut: Dar al-Salam lil-Tiba'a wal-Nashr, 1993), pp. 50-2.

25   In practice, Ibn 'Abd al-Wahhab filled a wide range of positions in the first Saudi-Wahhabi state, such as Grand Mufti, Supreme Judge, and Official Administrator of Religious Affairs, thereby nominating judges (*qadis*), preachers (*murshids*), and *'ulama* throughout the peninsula. His authority even extended beyond religious affairs, to include such areas as politics, economics, and military affairs. The Najdi historian Ibn Bishr noted that the authority of the Shaykh was as influential as that of the ruler (*amir*): "Neither 'Abd al-'Aziz nor anyone else received anything without his permission. He made the moves for war. The opinions and statements made by Muhammad Ibn Sa'ud and his son, 'Abd al-'Aziz, were based on the Shaykh's statements and thinking." Ibn 'Abd al-Wahhab's *fatwas* and instructions were enforced in most cases by the Committee for Commanding Right and Forbidding Evil (*hay'at al-amr bil ma'ruf wal-nahi 'an al-munkar*) or, as it is called by the Wahhabis, *mutawwi'a*, which was appointed by the Shaykh himself. Any community member who did not fulfill his religious obligations or violated the principles of the *shari'a* as interpreted by the Wahhabis was harshly punished. See Dahir, *al-Da'wa al-Wahhabiyya*, p. 165; 'Abd Allah al-Salih al-'Uthaymin, *Ibn 'Abd al-Wahhab*, p. 71; George Rentz, "Wahhabism and Saudi Arabia," in Derek Hopwood, ed., *The Arabian Peninsula: Society and Politics* (London: Allen & Unwin, 1972), p. 57; Joseph Kechichian, "The Role of the 'Ulama in the Politics of an Islamic State: The Case of Saudi Arabia," *International Journal of Middle East Studies*, Vol. 18, No. 1 (1986), p. 53; 'Uthman Ibn Bishr, *'Unwan al-majd fi tarikh Najd* (Riyadh: Maktabat al-Riyadh al-Haditha, n.d.), p. 15; M. Cook, *Commanding Right and Forbidding Wrong in Islamic Thought* (New York: Cambridge University Press, 2000), p. 167; David G. Edens, "The Anatomy of the Saudi Revolution," *International Journal of Middle Eastern Studies*, Vol. 5, No. 1 (1974), pp. 7, 50-64.

26   One should note that changes have been introduced into the traditional relationship between religion and state as a result of the recent incorporation of the *'ulama* into the state's administration. According to some scholars, these changes have resulted in the loss of independent power. See Ayman al-Yassini, *Religion and State in the Kingdom of Saudi Arabia*

of the *'ulama* in a Muslim state is to interpret God's will through analysis and exegesis of His words, while the function of the *umara* is to apply such interpretations.[27] Hence, *'ulama* and *umara* should be obeyed as long as their instructions are consistent with the *shari'a*. This stance was expressed in Bin Baz's legal opinions and writings. The following legal opinion was particularly important in this respect:

Query:
To whom does obedience to authority-holders (*wulat al-umur*) belong, *'ulama* or *umara*?

Response:
God, exalted may He be: "O ye who believe! Obey Allah, and obey the Messenger, and those charged with authority among you. If ye differ in anything among your-selves, refer it to Allah and His Messenger, if ye do believe in Allah and the Last Day: that is best and most suitable for final determination." [4:59]. The authority-holders are the *'ulama* and the *umara* of the Muslims, who must be obeyed on condition that their decrees match the will of God, and do not contradict it. Thus the *'ulama* and *umara* must be obeyed in doing good, for only in this way will peace and safety reign and will the usurped be saved from the usurper, while disobedience will cause anarchy so that the strong will usurp the weak. If, however, the decree is issued counter to the will of God, neither the *'ulama* nor the rulers should be

---

(Boulder, CO and London: Westview Press, 1985), p. 59; A. Layish, "'Ulama and Politics in Saudi Arabia," p. 53; A. Layish, "Saudi Arabian Legal Reform as Mechanism to Mod-erate Wahhabi Doctrine," *Journal of the American Oriental Society*, 107 (1987), p. 292; Mordechai Abir, *Saudi Arabia in the Oil Era: Regime and Elites; Conflict and Collaboration* (London and Sydney: Croom Helm Press, 1988), p. 29; Summer Scott Huyette, *Political Adaptation in Saudi Arabia: A Study of the Council of Ministers* (Boulder, CO: Westview Press, 1985), p. 117; O.Y. Al-Rawaf, "The Concept of Five Crises in Political Develop-ment: Relevance to the Kingdom of Saudi Arabia," PhD dissertation, Duke University, 1981, p. 527. However, attributing the decline of the *'ulama* to their incorporation into the state administration requires further consideration. It is more likely that via this in-corporation, the *'ulama* increased their influence over official policies and governmental circles. In other words, by holding official positions, they became players from within the power structure. Had they remained external to the government, their influence would have diminished. In any event, the *'ulama* continued to exercise influence over several areas, including nearly all legal and religious affairs. They even managed to increase their power over time by expanding their control over other ministries and religious agencies such as the Ministry of Justice, the Ministry of Islamic Affairs and Endowments, Call and Guidance, the Ministry of Pilgrimage, and the Committee of Commanding Good and Forbidding Wrong, Preaching and Guidance of Islam at Home and Abroad, as well as supervision of girls' education, notaries public, mosques and *awqaf*, and finally the World Muslim League and the World Assembly of Muslim Youth. Thus, the *'ulama* continue to play a significant role, at least in influencing the social and internal policy of the govern-ment.

27   'Abd al-'Aziz Bin Baz, "*al-umara wal-'ulama yuta'un fi al-ma'ruf li-anna bi-hadha tas-taqim al-ahwal*," in Muhammad Ibn Sa'd al-Shuway'ir, *Majmu' fatawa wa-maqalat mutanawwi'a*, 7:115-22. See also al-*Sharq al-Awsat*, May 5, 1993.

obeyed. An example would be a decree to drink wine or to deal with usury. However, no opposition must be raised against the rulers, even when not fulfilling the *shari'a*, but rather they must be advised through ways of tranquility.[28]

By opening his reply with Qur'anic interpretation, Bin Baz postulates a broad basis to the ruler's activity. For him, this command clearly establishes the obligatory and unqualified duty of obedience on the part of the ruled. Moreover, he interprets "the ruler" to include political leaders as well as *'ulama*. To substantiate this Qur'anic evidence, Bin Baz next draws on the Sunna, along with an extension of the principle of protecting the public well-being (*maslaha*). Bin Baz states that obeying the ruler is connected to obeying God and His Prophet, thereby emphasizing the importance of obeying rulers.[29]

According to Bin Baz, the only reservation regarding the obligation to obey is in the case of a ruler or person of authority whose orders violate the *shari'a*. One must not, however, oppose a ruler who does not act in accordance with the *shari'a*, but rather enlighten him to the fact of his having acted in opposition to the *shari'a*. Bin Baz thus based his arguments mainly on the principle of *maslaha*—a principle that appears as a basic concept in Muslim legal and political thought, by means of which the ruler's actions are legitimized within the doctrinal framework of *siyasa shar'iyya*.[30] Basing himself on this principle, Bin Baz established obligatory obedience even to those royal decrees and rules that are not mentioned by the *shari'a*, such as regulations regarding traffic, road accidents, employer-employee relations,

---

28   Due to the length of the response, only a section is quoted. The full response may be found in al-Shuway'ir, *Majmu' fatawa wa-maqalat mutanawwi'a*, 7:115.

29   Ibid., pp. 115-22.

30   *Siyasa shar'iyya* means "administrative practice [*siyasa*] within the limits assigned to it by Islamic law [*shari'a*]". In Saudi Arabia today, *siyasa shar'iyya* is arguably the most important tool in the hands of the Monarch when conducting the affairs of state under the aegis of Islamic law. *Siyasa shar'iyya* provides the theoretical and practical base that enables the cooperation between government and *'ulama*. Moreover, the King's authority, based on *siyasa shar'iyya*, is supported by the Basic Regulations of the Kingdom of Saudi Arabia [*al-nizam al-asasi*]. For example, Article 55 of these regulations states: "The King shall undertake the governing (*siyasa*) of the nation based on *siyasa shar'iyya*, in accordance with [*tibqan*] the rules [*ahkam*] of Islam…" Similarly, Article 67 states: "The regulatory authority shall have jurisdiction to enact regulations [*nizams*] and bylaws [*lawa'ih*] in order to attain welfare and avoid harm in the affairs of the state, in accordance with the general rules [*qawa'id*] of the Islamic *shari'a*…"; see Kingdom of Saudi Arabia, "*al-Nizam al-asasi lil-hukm*," May 1992, p. 15; Vogel, *Islamic Law and Legal System*, pp. 169-70, 341-3. For more on *siyasa shar'iyya*, see 'Abd al-Fattah 'Amru, *Al-siyasa al-shar'iyya fi al-ahwal al-shakhsiyya* (Amman: Dar al-Nafa'is, 1998); 'Abdallah Muhammad al-Qadi, *Al-siyasa al-shar'iyya: Masdar lil-taqnin bayna al-nazariyya wal-tatbiq* (Tanta: Matba'at dar al-kutub al-jam'iyya al-haditha. 1989); Yusuf al-Qaradawi, *Al-Siyasa al-shar'iyya fi daw' nusus al-shari'a wa-maqsiduha* (Cairo: Maktabat Wahbah, 1998).

and social welfare, the claim being that rules of this sort deal with the well-being of the public.

As mentioned above, neither classical Wahhabis nor their predecessors divided authority between *'ulama* and *umara*. Thus, little was written by contemporary Wahhabis about the scope of the king's authority. Apparently, the only treatment of this subject is related to the penalty for brigandage (*hiraba* or *muharaba*), defined as a *hadd* criminal act.[31] In 1975, while reforming the *shari'a* courts and the criminal law procedure, the CRLO issued a legal opinion determining that the courts' jurisdiction consists of identifying the type of crime and proposing the punishment according to its severity. The final decision regarding the punishment was within the king's purview, so that he may accept or reject the courts' recommendation by his judgment. It was furthermore established that the king should approve penalties for severe crimes, such as execution and dismemberment, and in general any physical punishment, and that he is entitled to approve the punishment as set by a court of law, or to instruct the relevant authority to revise or reconsider it.[32]

Pluralism[33]

For the Wahhabis, genuine Islam was demonstrated in the life of the early Muslims in the first three centuries after the Hijra, which set the foundations of Islam. The Wahhabis sought a return to the religious thought and practice of the forebears (*al-salaf al-salih*), as well as devotion to their opinions. [34] In other words, being *salafi* is the only way by which a Muslim assures membership in the sole "saved sect" (*al-firqa al-najiya*) which is mentioned in the *hadith*: "And this community [*umma*] will split into

---

31   Class of crimes defined according to content and penalty in Qur'an and Sunna, plur. *hudud*.

32   Sa'd Ibn Zafir, *al-Ijra'at al-jina'iyya fi jara'im al-hudud fi al-mamlaka al-'arabiyya al-sa'udiyya wa-atharaha fi istitbab al-amn* (Riyadh: Maktabat Fahd al-Wataniyya, 1999), 2:393; see also Royal Decree No. 8/1849 from June 5, 1982 based on the BSU's *fatwa* No. 85, September 10, 1981.

33   On Islam and pluralism, see Abdulaziz Sachedina, *The Islamic Roots of Democratic Pluralism* (Oxford, New York: Oxford University Press, 2001), pp. 3-22.

34   Al-Dawish, *Fatawa al-lajna al-da'ima*, 2:165-6; 'Abd al-Rahman Bin Qasim, *al-durar al-saniyya fi al-ajwiba al-najdiyya* (Riyadh: Dar al-Ifta, 1385/1965), 7:48; Hrair Dekmejian, "The Rise of Political Islamism in Saudi Arabia," *Middle East Journal*, Vol. 48, No. 4 (1994), pp. 635-8; on the *salafi* trend in the contemporary Islamic world, see H.A.R. Gibb, *Modern Trends in Islam* (University of Chicago Press, 1947), pp. 17-38; M.H. Kerr, *Islamic Reform: The Political and Legal Theories of Muhammad 'Abduh and Rashid Rida* (Berkeley, CA: University of California Press, 1966), pp. 103-53.

seventy-three sects, all of them in the Hellfire except of one."[35] On the basis of this *hadith* and other traditions, Muslims must unequivocally follow the Prophet and his companions' steps in all their thoughts and deeds.

Muhammad Ibn 'Abd al-Wahhab stressed that God commanded people to obey Him alone and to follow the teachings of the Prophet: "As for *ijtihad*, we are imitators of the Book, the Tradition, the Virtuous Ancestors, and the Four Imams".[36] The *salafiyya* trend, then, is an embodiment of what the Prophet left for his community (*umma*). Hence, anyone who departs from it will cause splitting, and fall into the sects that have been threatened with the Fire.[37] Contemporary Wahhabis remain to a great extent faithful to the tenets of their forefathers in this respect as well. They maintain Salafism as the spirit of their legal and theological philosophy. This adherence comes across clearly in their *fatwa*s and writings. For instance, the CRLO described the *salafi* concept as follows:

Salafiyya is derived from *salaf*, who were the companions of the Prophet, and the *imams* from the first three centuries who were announced in the hadith: 'The best of the people are those who belong to my century, then those who follow them [the second century], then those who follow them [third century]...*salafi*s are those who follow the footsteps of the *salaf* who, in turn, followed the Book [the Qur'an] and the Sunna and called for following them and acting according to their directions...[38]

Most importantly, however, contemporary Wahhabis often stressed the superiority of the Wahhabiyya as a *salafi* movement, comparing it with other Islamic groups. A BSU member, Shaykh Salih al-Fawzan, made this clear when he stated:

To say that the *salafi* movement resembles any other Islamic movements is wrong. The *salafi* movement is the only one that must be followed by adopting its ap-

---

35   Tirmidhi, *Sahih*, 2643. The *hadith* identified the members of the "saved sect" as those who follow the Prophet and his companions' (*sahaba*) traditions.

36   Muhammad Ibn 'Abd al-Wahhab, *Mu'allafat al-shaykh al-imam Muhammad Bin 'Abd al-Wahhab*, 12 vols. (Riyadh: Imam Muhammad Bin Sa'ud Islamic University, n.d.), 1:225-7.

37   Ibid.; further CRLO *fatwa*s in this respect can be found in al-Dawish, *Fatawa al-lajna al-da'ima*, 12: 241-242; 2:143-181. Notably, the Wahhabi perception of Salafism was rejected by many modern movements and scholars, who claimed that this trend of Salafism is nothing but an independent legal school of thought. The prominent Syrian Shaykh Sa'id Ramadan al-Buti argues, for example, that Salafism is no more than a blessed historical period (*marhala zamaniyya mubaraka*) that resembles others in Islamic history. See Muhammad Sa'id Ramadan al-Buti, *al-Salafiyya: marhala zamaniyya mubaraka li madhhab Islami* (Damascus: Dar al-Fikr, 1988), pp. 132-44.

38   *Fatwa* No. 1361 in al-Dawish, *Fatawa al-lajna al-da'ima*, 2:165.

proach, joining it, and doing *jihad* with it. Therefore, Muslims are not permitted to follow any other movement, since they all are straying movements…[39]

Basing themselves on this perception of Salafism, contemporary Wahhabis maintain intolerance toward others, whether Muslims or non-Muslims, and even toward other Wahhabis who do not engage in the "canonical" perceptions of the official religious establishment, which considers itself the Wahhabi mainstream. This intolerance is clearly demonstrated in the BSU's response to the demands of the Committee for the Defense of Legitimate Rights (CDLR) and the Movement for Islamic Reform in Arabia (MIRA), two Saudi opposition movements.[40] The BSU cast doubt on these movements' purposes, thereby declaring them illegitimate movements. For example, on May 12, 1993, the BSU issued a communiqué denouncing the CDLR as incompatible with *shari'a*:

The Council [BSU] finds the behavior of those who signed the document [of the CDLR] strange. The Council unanimously denounces this organization as illegitimate, because Saudi Arabia is a country that rules according to Islam. Islamic courts are all over the country, and no one has been prevented from complaining about any injustice to the specified agencies or to the Ombudsman.[41]

The Wahhabis are intolerant toward other Islamic movements such as Sufis and Shi'is. This intolerance is clearly expressed in the CRLO's response to a questioner who asked whether he can pray in a Sufi mosque or gathering place (*zawiya*):

You should not pray with *Sufis* in their praying room, and you must beware of their companionship and mixing with them in case you are afflicted with what they have been afflicted with. So perform your prayers in another mosque where they uphold the Sunna and are steadfast upon it.[42]

According to the CRLO, not only is praying with Sufis prohibited, but so is even contacting and mixing with them. Although Wahhabis did not declare Sufis to be infidels (*kuffar*), they treat them as such. Therefore the

39 *Fatwa* No. 209 in 'Adil Ibn 'Ali bin Ahmad al-Fridan (ed.), *al-Muntaqa min fatawa fadilat al-Shaykh Salih bin Fawzan bin 'Abdallah al-Fawzan* (Beirut: Mu'assasat al-Risala, 1999), 1:361; see also the interview with Shaykh Bin Baz regarding this, in *al-Muslimun*, July 28, 1996.

40 For a further account of these movements, see Joshua Teitelbaum, *Holier Than Thou: Saudi Arabia Islamic Opposition* (Washington, DC: Washington Institute for Near East Policy, 2000), pp. 28–42.

41 Quoted in Mamoun Fandy, *Saudi Arabia and the Politics of Dissent* (New York: St. Martin's Press, 1999), p. 120.

42 *Fatwa* No. 6250 in al-Dawish, *Fatawa al-lajna al-da'ima*, 2:207.

CRLO proposed alternative mosques run by "those who abide by the Sunna," another title that Wahhabis-*salafis* attribute to themselves.[43]

The official Wahhabi *'ulama* express anti-Shi'i sentiments in their *fatawa* and publications. The CRLO determined, for example, that eating Shi'i food or intermarrying with Shi'is, or even shaking their hands, is forbidden.[44] Shaykh 'Abdallah Bin Jibrin, a former member of the BSU, went even further when he declared that killing the Shi'a, whom he called *rafida* (rejecters of the first three Caliphs), was not a sin.[45] The *'ulama's* critique referred to all versions of Shi'ism. For instance, the *'ulama* denounced the mainstream Twelver Shi'is for their arguments about the distortion of the Qur'an by the third Caliph, 'Uthman, and the negation of the authentic Sunni *hadith* corpus, such as al-Bukhari and Muslim, which they replaced with new sources based on the twelve *imams*.[46]

The Wahhabis are also intolerant of other monotheists (Jews and Christians). This intolerance is demonstrated in the writings and *fatwa*s of the BSU and the CRLO. For instance, a legal opinion on religious unity was issued by the CRLO, which rejected the call "for the unification of religions"—that is, Islam, Judaism, and Christianity—in the mass media.[47] The call referred to accelerating tolerance among the people of these religions through sharing religious activities with them, such as building mosques, churches, and synagogues in one area, especially in universities, airports, and public squares; printing the Qur'an, the Torah, and the New Testament in one book; and conducting joint conferences, in both the East and the West. The CRLO rejected this suggestion, arguing that it blatantly contradicted the principle that Islam superseded all religions that preceded it. That is, calling for unity of religions would imply a serious admission that religions are equal and that people on earth may adopt whatever they wish of them equally. This would involve a denial of Islam as the purest of all the religions, a denial that the Qur'an is the only true book and the Prophet Muhammad is the seal of all the prophets and messengers—all articulated in the Qur'an, the Prophetic traditions, and the opinions of the

---

43   Ibid.

44   Fandy, *Saudi Arabia and the Politics of Dissent*, p. 200; al-Dawish, *Fatawa al-lajna al da'ima*, 2: 263-9.

45   *Al-Jazira al-'Arabiyya*, No. 11, December 1991.

46   *Fatwa* No. 11461, in al-Dawish, *Fatawa al-lajna al da'ima*, 2:269.

47   *Fatwa No. 19402, dated 25 Muharram 1418 A.H [June 1, 1997]*, signed by 'Abd al-'Aziz Bin Baz, President, 'Abd al-'Aziz bin 'Abdallah Al al-Shaykh, Vice President, Salih bin Fawzan al-Fawzan, member, and Bakr bin 'Abdallah Abu Zayd, member.

prominent classical scholars. For example, a Qur'anic verse states: "If any one desires a religion other than Islam (submission to Allah), never will it be accepted of him; and in the hereafter he will be in the ranks of those who have lost (all spiritual good)" [3:85]. Also:

"Say: 'O People of the book! Come to common terms as between us and you: that we worship none but Allah; that we associate no partners with Him; that we erect not, from among ourselves, lords and patrons other than Allah. If then they turn back, say ye: 'bear witness that we (at least) are Muslims (bowing to Allah's will)'" [3:64].

Building mosques, churches, and synagogues in one area was rejected as well, in accordance with Ibn Taymiyya, who denounced churches and synagogues as worship places:

Churches and synagogues are not God's houses, but rather Allah's houses are the mosques. Rather, they [churches and synagogues] are houses of apostasy [*kufr*] even though God's name is mentioned in them. Houses are judged according to the creed of the people. These people rejected God's last Prophet and as such they are *kuffar* [disbelievers], and hence their houses are but houses designated for the worship practiced by the *kuffar*.[48]

Therefore, sharing religious activities with Jews and Christians, such as attending their conferences or symposia, and affiliating with assemblies in such places, is forbidden. Also, printing the Torah and the Bible even independently, let alone printing them together with the Qur'an in the same book, is totally forbidden. According to the CRLO, the Qur'an is the only Book that should be abided by, in accordance with the verse:

"To thee we sent the Scripture in turn, confirming the Scriptures that came before it, and guarding it in safety: so judge between them by what Allah hath revealed, and follow not their vain desires, diverging from the truth that hath come to thee..."[5:48].

Nonetheless, the CRLO noted that calling non-Muslims, in general, and the people of the Book, in particular, to Islam is not only permitted, but is incumbent on all Muslims, in accordance with the explicit texts of the Qur'an and the Sunna. It should be carried out, however, within the context of the laws of Islam. Therefore debates, meetings, and dialogue with non-Muslims which are likely to "enable them in achieving their desires, fulfilling their aims, breaking the bonds of Islam, and bending the fundamentals of Islamic faith are all considered invalid, rejected by Allah,

---

48   Ibid.

His Messenger, and all believers."[49] The *'ulama* found support in another Qur'anic verse: "…And follow not their vain desires, but beware of them lest they beguile thee from any of that (teachings) which Allah hath sent down to thee…" [5:49].[50]

Freedom of expression

The Wahhabis pay much attention to the principle of "Commanding Good and Forbidding Wrong" (*al-amr bil-ma'ruf wal-nahi 'an al-munkar*) as a fundamental duty of every Muslim. This principle was made clear by the *hadith* which reads:

"… try to stop it [the evil] with his hand [using force], if he is not in a position to stop it with his hand, then he should try to stop it by means of his tongue [meaning he should speak against it]. If he is not even able to use his tongue, then he should at least condemn it in his heart. This is the weakest degree of faith [Muslim]."

Contemporary Wahhabis interpret this *hadith* as meaning that it is incumbent on Muslims to warn and reprimand the evildoer, and to try to stop him or her from doing evil.[51] Beyond this, Muslims should openly and publicly condemn evil and show the course of righteousness that the evildoer should adopt. That is, there is not only a right to express an opinion in public, but an obligation on Muslims, whether individuals or groups, to urge changes.[52] Therefore, they implored Muslims to speak out when they encounter any transgression of the *shari'a*, or in calling others to Islam (*da'wa*). For example, in an interview with the Kuwaiti magazine *al-Mujtama'*, Shaykh Bin Baz instructed Saudi young people not to leave electronic means of communication in the hands of those who are not Muslims: "There is no doubt that the use of communication to expose the truth disseminated by *shari'a* laws, exposing heresy, and warning against it [are] our loftiest aims, if not duties and prescriptions of the highest order."[53]

---

49 Ibid.

50 Ibid.

51 Al-Fridan, *Al-Muntaqa*, 1:196-205; Bin Baz, "*al-Amr bil-ma'ruf wal-nahi 'an al-munkar huwa sabab salah al-mujtama' kama annahu huwa safinat al-najah*," in al-Shuway'ir, *Majmu' fatawa wa-maqalat mutanawwi'a*, 3:264-7.

52 One must note that while Commanding Good and Forbidding Wrong is interpreted by some scholars as an early guarantee of the freedom of speech, others regarded it as the exact opposite. See Cook, *Commanding Right and Forbidding Wrong*, pp. 32-46.

53 See interview with Bin Baz in al-Shuway'ir, *Majmu' fatawa wa-maqalat mutanawwi'a*, 5:271.

Freedom of expression in politics, however, is heavily restricted and must be exercised in a secret manner. This principle is clearly expressed in the BSU response to the advice (*nasiha*) proffered to the King by the two Saudi opposition groups mentioned above, the CDLR and MIRA. The official *'ulama* denounced the advice offered by these groups, arguing that advice should be given in private. According to the BSU, if advice became public, then the aim behind it would be politicized and used to bolster the advising group's stature.[54] The BSU's critique was rejected by the opposition groups, who were intolerant of the *'ulama*'s approach to solving problems behind the scenes and providing advice in secret.[55] Accordingly, they called on people to view official *fatwas* with much more suspicion, especially those that were issued to legitimize the regime's actions.[56]

Another example of opposition to advice being given publicly is the *'ulama*'s response to the demonstrations in Riyadh preceding the first Gulf War in the early 1990s. Shaykh Bin Baz stated, for example, that demonstrations are not part of solutions and reforms, but rather a major cause of internal conflict (*fitna*) and evil among people. According to him, demonstrations in which people "marching in streets and shrieking are not the right way to bring about change and *da'wa*. Reforms and changes should be through correspondence in a polite manner."[57]

Shaykh 'Abd al-'Aziz Al al-Shaykh, the current Grand Mufti, noted, "Such behavior [demonstrating] is forbidden by Islamic law, since it is an anarchic act that never serves any objectives of the nation [*umma*]." He added, "These [demonstrations] are forbidden innovations [*muhditha munkara*] that one must avoid."[58] Shaykh al-Fawzan stated that demonstrations are foreign to Islam, since Muslims throughout history never engaged in such activities. According to Shaykh 'Abd al-'Aziz Al al-Shaykh, Islam supports order and mercy among its members, not anarchy [*fawda*], disorganization [*tashwish*], and the arousing of riots. Achieving rights should be

54 Fandy, *Saudi Arabia and the Politics of Dissent*, p. 120.

55 The Saudi official *'ulama* believe in presenting advice (*nasiha*) to the ruler in private concerning how better to govern according to Islamic law; Mordechai Abir, *Saudi Arabia, Government, Society, and the Gulf Crisis* (London: Routledge, 1993), p. 192.

56 Ibid.

57 www.sahab.ws/4036/news/1553.html, quoted from Muhammad Bin Fahd al-Hasin, *al-Fatawa al-shar'iyya fi al-qadaya al-'asriyya* (Riyadh: Dar al-Akhyar, 2003).

58 *Al-Sharq al-Awsat*, October 27, 2003.

carried out in a peaceful manner and via legitimate ways, not by demonstrations that lead to bloodshed and destruction of property.[59]

Conclusions

It should be clear from the foregoing that it is impossible to reconcile the ideas of democracy as commonly understood with official Wahhabi thought. This is manifest in the attitude of the official *'ulama* toward the basic tenets of democracy: sovereignty ultimately rests with God, and the *'ulama* and *umara* constitute the agents on earth for interpreting and implementing His sovereignty. Salafism is the only spiritual source for legal and theological philosophy, and freedom of speech in politics is limited to the offering of advice (*nasiha*) in a secret manner. These interpretations are inimical to the normative understanding of democracy.

Democracy in its Western forms is far from being achievable in contemporary Saudi Arabia. The problem is further complicated because democratization of the Saudi state would jeopardize the traditional Saudi-Wahhabi political system based on the *'ulama-umara* alliance. Reforming the system means that both these traditional elites would lose power in favor of other segments of society. Therefore, the *'ulama,* as well as the royal family, are quite content with the current situation, which allows them to preserve their power.

While "democratization" of the Saudi state in a Western style seems to be impossible, nevertheless some measures of political liberalization are possible. They can occur via much more political participation of other segments of the society, freedom of speech, and tolerance of cultural pluralism within the Saudi state. Such political liberalization should be from the top downward and must garner the support or at least the consent of the *'ulama,* as a critical group in advancing or blocking reforms in democratic directions.

---

59   www.sahab.ws/4036/news/1553.html, quoted from Muhammad Bin Fahd al-Hasin, *al-Fatawa al-shar'iyya fi al-qadaya al-'asriyya* (Riyadh: Dar al-Akhyar, 2003).

5

KUWAIT: SLOUCHING
TOWARDS DEMOCRACY?

Mary Ann Tétreault

Introduction

The fall of the Berlin Wall inaugurated pressure for democratization across the world, including Kuwait, where invasion and occupation had strengthened popular demand for greater political participation and governmental accountability. Yet following liberation, the Kuwaiti regime managed to reinstate itself virtually intact. It spurned overtures from the secular opposition to cooperate on liberalizing the economy, worked to defeat liberal candidates for parliament, and maintained alliances with Islamist and tribalist forces. Politics as usual seemed to be the order of the day, but beneath the façade of normality, long-term forces continued to press toward further political, economic, and social opening.

Gender politics, economics, and the media are three areas worthy of attention as harbingers of political liberalization in Kuwait. Gender politics is a frequent locus of analysis and contention in non-egalitarian societies. Gender inequality exists in multiple nested tyrannies, making it an excellent metaphor for other forms of social and political oppression.[1] In Kuwait, parallel contestations over impediments to agency and equality occur with respect to gender and other lines of division. Examining gender politics highlights ambivalence and instrumentality in conflicts over

---

1   For example, see David G. Marr, *Vietnamese Tradition on Trial, 1920-1945* (Berkeley: University of California Press, 1981), pp. 58-9.

greater egalitarianism in the political system as a whole, along with the attitudes and institutions that support or impede democratization.

Another locus of opening is economic. Kuwait is a signatory to treaties and conventions underpinning the global trade and investment regime, but economic liberalization is still very much in process. The conventional view holds that state ownership is the highest bar to liberalization and that simple divestiture would open the economy automatically. Yet even greater impediments to liberalization in Kuwait are systems that discriminate against and among Kuwaiti investors to control potential political and economic competitors. The domestic debate over bringing Kuwait into conformity with WTO-mediated norms is one attempt to use international institutions to democratize the economy and, through it, the regime.[2]

Kuwait also has been affected by a media revolution exemplified by the availability of regionally-produced satellite news broadcasts which broke the Western monopoly on electronic sources of information by offering news and commentary from an Arab point of view.[3] The Qatar-based Al-Jazeera covers Usama bin Ladin's activities. It has broadcast footage of US bombings in Afghanistan, Israeli military attacks on Palestinians, and civilian casualties, property destruction, and terrorist attacks generated by the invasion and occupation of Iraq. The shift in values represented by the displacement of US-based to regionally-based mass media outlets accompanies a shift in media consumption. The new TV networks challenge the primacy of Kuwait's lively print press as the primary source of regional and international news. As in the West, the move from print to television as the medium of choice for news and information changes the content and quality of political discourse. Television gives images a higher priority than analysis, reducing the quantity of information and range of viewpoints represented in the public square. The Kuwaiti public square remains large and active but generational shifts in media preferences may foreshadow shifts in political preferences. This change is likely to accelerate to accommodate the entry of female candidates in national and local elections.

---

2   Mary Ann Tétreault, "Pleasant Dreams: The WTO as Kuwait's Holy Grail," *Critique: Critical Middle Eastern Studies*, Vol. 12, No. 1 (Spring 2003), pp. 75-93.

3   Naomi Sakr, *Satellite Realms: Transnational Television, Globalization and the Middle East* (London: I.B. Tauris, 2001).

Gender and liberalization

For forty-two years, Kuwait's electoral law permitted any male first-category citizen[4] twenty-one years of age or older to vote and run for office, but it denied political rights to Kuwaiti women. This changed in May 2005 when women attained full political rights. The campaign for woman suffrage in Kuwait was long and contentious, and its achievement took appreciable effort by the Prime Minister to overcome objections from Sunni Islamist and tribal members of the National Assembly. The old electoral law had coexisted with Kuwait's constitution, which guarantees female and male citizens equal rights. Yet legal discrimination between men and women extended beyond political rights, inscribed in laws limiting women's rights to travel, to qualify for some state benefits, such as housing, and to pass their nationality to their children. This lack of political rights stimulated the development of women's organizations, leaving as an important legacy of the long struggle for political rights years of experience of organizing and building coalitions across disparate groups and interests. Middle- and upper-class women were the first to organize voluntary associations to lobby for political rights and for fundamental changes in Kuwait's family law. As Islamist groups and movements gained ground domestically in the late 1970s, religious organizations also became venues for women's political participation.

Kuwaiti feminist activism grew out of the individual freedom Kuwaiti women have enjoyed for more than half a century. Debate about women's emancipation first emerged in the local press in the 1950s, initiated by young Kuwaiti men who were part of the Arab nationalist movement then agitating for modernization throughout the region as a whole.[5] Women's rights constituted one of several justifications for their assault on existing traditions and customs, and was part of a larger struggle against ignorance, backwardness, and retrograde customs and traditions.[6] The young reform-

---

4   Citizenship categories are becoming less relevant since the National Assembly gave political rights to the sons of second-category (naturalized) Kuwaitis, who are eligible for all state benefits but are not permitted to vote or run for office. Naturalization is comparatively rare and the number of second-category Kuwaitis is small.

5   See, for example, Adeed Dawisha, *Arab Nationalism in the Twentieth Century: From Triumph to Despair* (Princeton University Press, 2003). The contribution of Arab nationalism to the Kuwaiti opposition in its early years is touched on in John Daniels, *Kuwait Journey* (Luton, UK: White Crescent Press, 1971).

6   The same strategy had been followed by young modernizers in Vietnam a generation earlier—see Marr, *Vietnamese Tradition on Trial*—and, during the same period, by young Egyptians: see Leila Ahmed, *Women and Gender in Islam* (New Haven: Yale University Press, 1992).

ers published newspapers and magazines and invited Kuwaiti women to express their views in sections of these publications—called *Rukn al-Mar'a* or the Women's Corner—reserved for discussions of "women's issues."[7] Women also gained public exposure as members of the workforce, a result of universal education, health care, and job opportunities offered to citizens regardless of their sex. But when feminist activists demanded legislation that would give them equal social and political rights, the government and parliament were outraged and women were deserted by some of their erstwhile allies. Meanwhile, Islamist women's groups grew in response to the tacit alliance between the regime and religious leaders during the first of two periods of extra-constitutional parliamentary suspension.[8] The broadening of the women's movement had no effect on equal rights legislation, however. It was regularly rejected by the parliament beginning in 1971, and the likelihood of its achievement receded in most Kuwaitis' minds with every defeat. Following the liberation of Kuwait from Iraqi occupation in 1991, many citizens anticipated that women's resistance activities would be rewarded by enfranchisement, but the Amir failed to act on these expectations, while Sunni Islamists continued their intense opposition to women's rights.

Several proposals to restrict women's access to education and employment were considered by the first post-liberation parliament of 1992, and suffragists responded by coordinating their activism more closely. In 1995, they established the Women's Issues Committee (WIC), a network to harmonize the activities of liberal voluntary associations campaigning for women's political rights. The Graduates Society established a Women's Development Committee, and the Women's Cultural and Social Society (WCSS), the only survivor of Kuwait's earliest feminist organizing, intensified its campaign for woman suffrage. Islamist women also joined the suffrage movement, among them a prominent Shi'i activist, Khadija al-Mahamid. In 1997, several WCSS board members joined their male colleagues to found and lead a new democratic political grouping, the Nation-

7   Haya al-Mughni, *Women in Kuwait: The Politics of Gender*, 2nd ed. (London: Saqi Books, 2003); Haya al-Mughni and Mary Ann Tétreault, "Engagement in the Public Sphere: Women and the Press in Kuwait," in Naomi Sakr (ed.), *Women and the Media in the Middle East* (London: I.B. Tauris, 2004), pp. 120-37.

8   Jill Crystal, *Oil and Politics in the Gulf: Rulers and Merchants in Kuwait and Qatar* (New York: Cambridge University Press, 1990); Jill Crystal, *Kuwait: The Transformation of an Oil State* (Boulder, CO: Westview Press, 1992); Mary Ann Tétreault, *Stories of Democracy: Politics and Society in Contemporary Kuwait* (New York: Columbia University Press, 2000).

al Democratic Movement, NDM, demonstrating both women's political maturity and acceptance of their authority by male activists.

The Amir declared himself a champion of woman suffrage in May 1999, when he issued a decree granting full political rights during the first constitutional dismissal of parliament in Kuwaiti history. Suffrage forces were elated but, much to their disappointment, that November the Amiri decree was voted down; two weeks later, an identical measure introduced by members of parliament to remove the taint of Amiri pressure also was defeated. The loss might have been expected given the absence of effort by the government to mobilize pro-suffrage forces during and after the July 1999 election. Even so, many observers were surprised by evidence of either second thoughts or a political deal between suffrage opponents and two prominent pro-suffrage members, the opposition merchant Ahmad al-Sa'dun and the Shi'i Islamist Husayn 'Ali al-Qallaf, whose abstentions on the second vote ensured that the politics rights bill would fail.

Kuwaiti women began to rethink their suffrage campaign strategy following the 2003 election. The 2003 parliament was disappointing, a lackluster body dominated by "independents," mostly tribal members less interested in legislating than in raking in the perquisites of membership in the National Assembly. Kuwaiti feminists soon concluded that their efforts would be better devoted to lobbying the government. They also quietly dropped the old suffragist rationale that Kuwaiti women had "earned" their political rights in recognition of their contributions to family, society, and economy and, after 1991, because of their exemplary efforts on their country's behalf during the Iraqi occupation. After the 2003 election, Kuwaiti women increasingly spoke of political rights in terms of citizenship and entitlement. As the T-shirts worn by pro-women's rights demonstrators proclaimed, "Women are Kuwaitis Too."[9]

Still, in late 2004 and early 2005, parliamentary debates on women's rights seemed to be shaping up as just another episode in what had become a familiar story. This phase culminated in April 2005, when a mean-spirited measure that would have allowed women to vote and run only for municipal offices passed at its first reading and, when it came up for the second and final reading, was defeated on the floor. Due to a technicality, however

---

9   Mary Ann Tétreault, "Kuwait's Parliament Considers Women's Rights, Again," *Middle East Report Online*, September 2, 2004, at http://www.merip.org/mero/mero090204. html; and Mary Ann Tétreault, "Women's Rights and the Meaning of Citizenship in Kuwait," *Middle East Reports Online*, February 10, 2005, at http://www.merip.org/mero/ mero021005.html.

(twenty-nine members had abstained), the session was declared as lacking a quorum, putting the bill back on the table. Two weeks later, when it came up again, cabinet members suddenly introduced a substitute proposal granting women full political rights in elections at all levels. The biggest surprise in the new measure was an "order for urgency" that would allow it, if passed, to become law in a single session. This audacious maneuver kept the antis from mobilizing public protests to keep weakly committed members of the anti-suffrage coalition in line. Indeed, the antis' coalition eroded as a handful of tribalist members joined Liberals, Shi'a, and the cabinet to pass the bill. The first appointment of a woman to the cabinet came four weeks later when a political scientist, Masuma al-Mubarak, was named Planning Minister, despite loud complaints on the floor from Sunni Islamists and unreconstructed tribalists.

In April 2006, a by-election for the municipality of Salmiyya became Kuwaiti women's first opportunity to compete and to vote. Two women ran in the eight-person field and one of them, Jinan Bushahri, an engineer who works for the Kuwait municipality and the first woman to become an official candidate in Kuwaiti elections, came in second. It was a more than respectable result, especially given the make-up of the district:

[O]verriding tribal and sectarian factors do not allow either of the female candidates any chance of victory. The most likely candidate to win is the nominee from the 'Awazem' tribe who would succeed his [fellow tribesman] who used to occupy the seat previously. The Shiite candidates strongly protested the authorities' overlooking of the secret sub-elections, prohibited by law, held by the Awazem tribe which gave their candidate a strong push in the elections. According to unofficial estimates, the inhabitants of the province include 28,000 voters divided between 16,000 Sunnis, 8,000 of which belong to the Awazem tribe, and 11,000 Shiites, the largest Shiite voting pool in Kuwait.[10]

It may be too early to assess the impact of women's entry into the political sphere, but it is not too early to speculate about the government's motivations in opening the door. A glimpse into these motives is suggested by the assessment of the *al-Hayat* reporter quoted above.

The Kuwaiti regime had sought stability since the late 1970s by nurturing an alliance with retrograde political forces whose primary attraction was their appeal to "traditional" popular constituencies. This alliance reflected the regime's distrust and fear of Arab nationalist modernizers and resentment at their demands for greater political and economic openness. Islamists and

---

10   *Al-Hayat* (London), April 5, 2005, reported in *Mideast Wire*, April 5, 2005.

tribalists were viewed as ideologically more compatible with the regime, as well as easier to assemble into pro-government voting blocs. Recently, these once-welcome allies have come to be seen differently, as sources of potential danger to a ruling family that is reorganizing internally.

Tribes are cohesive political factions and the larger ones, like the ruling family itself,[11] are relatively autonomous corporations with formidable negotiating power. A law passed by the 1996 parliament sought to abolish "tribal primaries"—pre-declaration elections in which the number of tribal candidates is winnowed to one or two—because, in heavily tribal constituencies, they virtually guaranteed the election of at least one clan member and thereby the power of the tribe itself. But as we saw above, in spite of this law an 'Awazim tribal primary chose the ultimate victor in the 2006 Salmiyya by-election. Similarly, tribal primaries were not challenged in the 2003 parliamentary elections, although they had been in 1999.

Flouting the law on tribal primaries with impunity is one way in which the tribes show their power. The other is to apply that power to demanding material rewards in exchange for political support. The hold-up of the women's rights bill offers one example. Tribal MPs were reported to have demanded increases in government support payments to their constituents, and possibly even cash on the line for themselves, in return for their votes.[12] High oil prices have emboldened them to increase their demands in this regard, going so far as to insist that the government pay off bank loans—"with compensation for families that have not taken out loans."[13] The never-ending list of tribalist demands has heightened concern at top levels of the regime that structural impediments (such as salary and retirement payment commitments) will constrain its ability to rationalize the domestic economy (see below).

The other pillar of the regime has been Sunni Islamists, courted from 1977 by the late Amir Jabir al-Ahmad (r. 1977-2006) and also by the Crown Prince he appointed, Sa'd al-'Abdallah. Shaykh Jabir aimed to counter the

---

11   The corporate organization and power of the Al Sabah and other "dynastic monarchies" are traced in Michael Herb, *All in the Family: Absolutism, Revolution, and Democracy in the Middle Eastern Monarchies* (Albany, NY: SUNY Press, 1999).

12   During the fall of 2005, struggles over who would succeed the dying Jabir al-Ahmad spilled over into the newspapers, where a member of the al-Salim branch accused the dominant al-Ahmads of corruption and gave as an example millions of dinars in payoffs made to unnamed tribal MPs to ensure that they would vote for the women's rights bill. See also Melanie Britto, "Legislative Blitz Amends Election Law: Women Win Political Rights," *Arab Times*, May 16, 2005.

13   Omar Hassan, "Kuwaitis Eye Huge Cash Handouts," *Middle East Online*, August 11, 2005, at http:www.middle-east-online.com/english/kuwait/?id=14951.

liberal opposition whose Arab nationalist components had provoked the 1976 closure of the parliament, in part by forcing the nationalization of Kuwait's hydrocarbon industry. Over time, Islamists came to dominate the bureaucracy of the Education Ministry—education is a particular focus of Islamist movements generally, for several reasons.[14] In Kuwait, the ministry offered protected spaces for recruitment, a means to influence the ideas and habits of the next generations of students, and a reservoir of jobs for activists. By the 1980s, it became obvious that the occupants of this Islamist citadel had generated a pool of graduates whose specialization in majors concentrating on religion and culture left them unable to compete in a national job market.[15] Today, despite a shortage of competent Kuwaiti nationals, youth unemployment remains an economic and social problem.

Among the dangers presented by the growing population of unemployed young men is their attraction to *jihad* abroad and to Islamist gangs at home. Kuwaiti "Afghans," jihadists who have returned to Kuwait from fighting in Afghanistan, Bosnia, and Chechnya, were involved in several attacks on foreigners mobilizing for the 2003 invasion of Iraq. They also "drove to Falluja" to fight with Iraqi insurgents against the Americans in November 2004. A gang calling itself the "Desert Flogging Group" beat a Kuwait University student and broke her arm for appearing in public without a veil. A few years later, erstwhile desert floggers were among the "Peninsula Lions," former followers of Sulayman Bughayth, an individual who appeared among the top leadership of al-Qa'ida. Members of this group were charged with a rash of violent acts including attacks on police in early 2005.[16]

In response, Kuwaiti officials have tightened rules for transferring funds abroad, to limit economic support for jihadist campaigns. These include restricting the activities of religious charities, thought to be an important source of funding for Islamist activities. One of the strategies for addressing the education problem has been to charter private universities. In addition to introducing direct competition that already has stimulated curricular and other reforms at Kuwait University, these new institutions helped to compensate

---

14   See Olivier Roy, *The Failure of Political Islam*, trans. Carol Volk (London: I.B. Tauris, 1994), esp. chap. 3.

15   Interview with Sulayman Mutawwi' in Kuwait, May 1990.

16   See, for example, Daniel Pearl, "Kuwait is Divided over Support of U.S." *Wall Street Journal*, October 24, 2001; Mary Ann Tétreault, "Advice and Dissent in Kuwait," *Middle East Report* 226, Spring 2003, pp. 36-9; Mary Ann Tétreault, "Terrorist Violence in Kuwait," *Foreign Policy in Focus—Commentary*, February 23, 2005, at http://www.fpif.org/commentary/2005/0502kuwait.html.

for the difficulty Kuwaiti students faced in studying abroad in the United States, and are expected to graduate students whose skills are more closely matched to the needs of the local economy.[17] An indication that winds of change could reach the ministry itself is that the first government assembled following the multi-amir leadership transition in early 2006 features a new Education Minister aiming to shake up the bureaucracy.[18]

Some observers have speculated that the enfranchisement of women became a state project because women are envisioned, however (un)realistically, as a suitably "conservative" substitute for overly demanding tribalists and Islamists as mainstays of the regime. Inasmuch as women are conservative, I surmise that they are less so in terms of issues and programs than as forces for reform rather than revolution.[19] Citizens also hope that women will be a moderating force, but less against revolution than against rampant and still-rising government corruption. While either of these might be too much to hope for, women are quite likely to ask policy makers to provide for the needs of children and families beyond the mere payment of child allowances and provision of schools and health clinics. Here, women are envisioned as spokespersons for now neglected issues whose thoughtful resolution stands to benefit the nation as a whole.

What Kuwaiti men fear, however, liberals as well as traditionalists, is that women will want equal personal status. The first mass mobilization of Kuwaiti women took place in the 1970s under a charismatic and organizationally gifted middle-class woman, Nuriyya al-Sadani. Sadani founded one of the first women's organizations in Kuwait, the Arab Women's Development Society (AWDS). The AWDS was militantly activist, unlike its merchant-class sister organization, the WCSS (also established in 1963). In 1971 it organized the first Kuwaiti women's conference, which closed by preparing and submitting a petition to the parliament that demanded, in addition to full political rights, equal opportunity in employment, female inclusion among special attorneys empanelled to draft a new family

---

17   Interviews in Kuwait June 2003; December 2004, March 2006.

18   Mary Ann Tétreault, "Three Emirs and a tale of two transitions," *Middle East Reports Online*, February 10, 2006, at http://www.merip.org/mero/mero021006.html; Ibrahim al-Khalidi, "Tabtabaei plans to 'reshuffle' all assistant undersecretaries: Minister discusses ways to improve MoE," *Arab Times*, April 17, 2006.

19   Haya al-Mughni, "Women's Movements and the Autonomy of Civil Society in Kuwait," in Robin L. Teske and Mary Ann Tétreault (eds), *Conscious Acts and the Politics of Social Change* (Columbia: University of South Carolina Press, 2000), pp. 170-87; Mary Ann Tétreault, "A State of Two Minds: State Cultures, Women, and Politics in Kuwait," *International Journal of Middle East Studies*, Vol. 33, No. 2 (May 2001), pp. 203-20.

law, child allowances for working mothers (then provided only to male heads-of-household), and restrictions on polygyny. Whatever their strategies turn out to be, the addition of women to the political scene could give new energy to citizen activism across an unprecedented broad spectrum of interests.

Economic liberalization

Economic liberalization has ceased to constitute a neat line dividing liberals from Islamists in Kuwait. Both groups are quite variegated. Liberals encompass political liberals who want to open the regime and may or may not support economic liberalization, and neo-liberals who want to liberalize the economy and may or may not be Islamists. During the 1999 parliament, the economic positions of liberals and neo-liberals coincided so frequently that the US political scientist Pete Moore called the resultant coalition a "liberal-business alliance."

Political labels in Kuwait are often deceptive. "Liberal," with its multiple meanings, is a problematic concept by itself; so is "business," which includes members of the ruling family whose domestic private investments run on an inside track to which they and their close allies have sole access. Ruling-family businessmen compete with traditional merchants and with newer, middle-class businessmen who formerly were a dependent constituency of the regime. Merchant and middle-class Islamists also have business interests and sometimes take neo-liberal positions. Examples include Khalid Sultan, a merchant-class Salafi member of the 1981 parliament who ran unsuccessfully in 1985 and 1992; and 'Abd al-Wahhab al-Wazzan, a Shi'i merchant and former minister who held the portfolios of both Trade and Industry and Labor and Social Affairs in the first government formed after the 1999 parliamentary election, and is a member of the Board of the Kuwait Chamber of Commerce and Industry.

The neo-liberal/Islamist business consensus supported changes in the labor law in 2001 to give Kuwaiti private-sector employees the same government allowances for dependents that had been available only to state employees. Both neo-liberal and Islamist businessmen had pressed for this change to level the playing field between private and public employment and stimulate private-sector employment of Kuwaiti nationals; liberal influence is visible in the law's limitation on the number of children covered to five per family. Support for privatization also cuts across Islamist and secularist parliamentarians, and class interests shape ideas about how au-

tonomous the private sector should be and whether large domestic investors should be allowed to take strategic positions in the national economy.

Merchants are the most likely to embark on strategic investments, but
their histories as large investors offer mixed messages to the regime. Some
merchants accumulated enough capital in the late 1950s to bail out the
ruler after corrupt family members had looted the treasury,[20] but economic
relations between the ruler and the merchants were far from one-sided. Assisted by a large, interest-free deposit by the then Amir 'Abdallah al-Salim,
five merchant families established the National Bank of Kuwait, an institution that broke the monopoly of the British Bank of the Middle East and
remains the strongest private-sector financial institution in the country.
Other merchants displayed what Khalid Buhamra called "a short breath"
when, in the wake of the oil revolution, adjustment resulted in losses for
the joint-venture, public-private tanker and petrochemicals companies in
which they owned substantial shares.[21] Private-sector owners were eager
to sell out to the state in what were then unprofitable companies. Now,
strategic positions in segments of the state-owned oil company, the Kuwait
Petroleum Corporation (KPC), are coveted by the former eager sellers as
well as by large international oil companies (IOCs).

As a first step in the privatization of state oil interests, a 1993 World
Bank report recommended selling domestic gasoline stations, preferably to
different proprietors to encourage competition in the retail gasoline market, and phase out price supports for motor fuels. This suggestion was resisted by large investors because ownership of a single retail gasoline outlet
offers little prospect of owner autonomy or market power. They compare
it with the first post-nationalization government-initiated oil privatization scheme, the Equate subsidiary of the Petroleum Industries Company
(PIC), another affiliate of KPC. Equate is owned 45 percent by PIC (that
is, by the Kuwaiti government), and 45 percent by Dow Chemical, formerly Union Carbide. The last 10 percent went into a holding company,
Bubiyan, whose shares are traded on the Kuwait Stock Exchange. "It was
sold to the public, to 300,000 people. . . . [But] after five years, there are
many fewer shareholders."[22]

This more-than-arm's-length relationship between the citizen shareholders and their investment in Bubiyan evokes a Veblenian critique from

---

20   Crystal, *Oil and Politics in the Gulf,* p. 75.

21   Interview in Kuwait, 1990.

22   Interview with businessman Salah al-Turkayt, 2002.

Kuwaiti industrialists and large investors. Rather than looking at portfolio investment as what Veblen called "absentee ownership," access to profits without responsibility,[23] they see it as a ploy to shut them out of decision-making authority. One businessman, Salah al-Turkayt, noted:

> It's true the private sector has part [of Equate] but only 10 percent. The real problem is how this was given. The initiative was from the government. . . .We'll give 10 percent to the private sector but the private sector was totally bypassed. We'll create Bubiyan after PIC and Union Carbide has filled everything. We'll have members from the PIC board and then public shares. Everyone was a subscriber. [But the Bubiyan] board knew nothing about the project. It had no decision power whatsoever. They had to nominate one person, one [to represent the Bubiyan owners] on the whole board of Equate. . . . From day one they were told, bring your money, but with no information, no transparency. . . . This company was created with no decision from its [board] members and no history of petrochemicals, no strategy. To do this again would be very bad.[24]

Al-Turkayt speaks of skills and experience that were "wasted" when Equate was set up, but the subtext of this message is control. Portfolio investment leaves control with boards of directors and managers. Small shareholders can "bring their money," but they do not sit at the table where strategic decisions are made.

Wealthy Kuwaiti investors outside the ruling family are more ambivalent than negative about foreign participation. Some see themselves as engaged in a tacit alliance with outside investors and professionals inside the company, defending its interests against the ruling family's merchant cronies and the bureaucrats overseeing tendering. Just such an image was projected as responsible for differences in performance between two KPC affiliates, the relatively efficient joint-venture production operation in the Divided Zone and operations in the fully nationalized Kuwait Oil Company (KOC), the domestic producing arm of KPC.[25] Similarly, Bubiyan investors tend to support Dow/Union Carbide against the government. They "hated bureaucracy and delays and always were with Union Carbide in terms of pressure."[26]

Not surprisingly, labor interests are strongly opposed to privatization because it threatens the jobs of Kuwaiti nationals. Parliamentary opposi-

---

23 Thorstein Veblin, *Absentee Ownership: Business Enterprise in Recent Times: The Case of America* (New Brunswick, NJ: Transaction Books, 1923/1997).

24 Interview with Salah al-Turkayt, 2002.

25 Mary Ann Tétreault, *The Kuwait Petroleum Corporation and the Economics of the New World Order* (Westport, CT: Quorum Books, 1995), pp. 92-8.

26 Interview with Salah al-Turkayt, 2002.

tion comes from members representing the outlying areas, whose residents are more likely to depend on public-sector jobs. Before the recent war-fueled economic boom, the pro-labor position was framed as a justice issue. In addition to support from Islamists from outlying areas like Mubarak al-Duwayla, urban liberals with Arab nationalist backgrounds such as Ahmad al-Khatib and 'Abdallah Nibari also took the side of workers against the wealthy. Complex cross-cutting views are embodied in these parliamentary coalitions. Isma'il Shati (1992), Nasir al-Sani' (1992, 1996, 1999), and Ahmad al-Du'ayj (1999), Sunni movement Islamists,[27] are supporters of privatization, but Islamist neo-liberals do not speak for all Islamists. Secularist neo-liberals and liberals also are split over this issue. Class seems to trump religion but increasingly, alliances with factions of the ruling family trump class.

A defining moment in the privatization debate occurred on December 4, 2001, when 'Abdallah Nibari spoke in support. Nibari had led the forces for nationalizing Kuwait's oil industry in the 1970s, and was the most prominent liberal in the National Assembly after Ahmad al-Khatib retired in 1996. He was attacked by the former National Assembly Speaker Ahmad al-Sa'dun, a liberal who has become a single-minded opponent of virtually every initiative coming from the government. Ahmad was joined by the Islamists Walid Tabtaba'i, a Salafi, and Walid al-Jari, a Muslim Brotherhood member endorsed by his tribe. Nibari had help from the Islamist Ahmad al-Du'ayj and the secularist liberals 'Abd al-Wahhab al-Harun and Ahmad al-Rubi'. Completing the tangle of cross alliances were the most vociferous opponents of the measure, Musallim al-Barrak and Khamis Talaq 'Uqab, both representing tribal districts and both affiliated with the broadly based—liberal—New Democratic Movement.[28]

The conflict on the floor focused on the employment effects of privatization. Most of the speakers agreed that privatization would end "disguised unemployment" through economic rationalization which would eliminate workers and positions. Many expressed fears that rationalization also

---

27   "Movement Islamists" belong to organized groups and control substantial resources that may or may not be available to their unorganized political and social allies. The dates in this paragraph refer to the parliaments in which each man served.

28   The New Democratic Movement was organized following the 1996 election. Its remnants are part of a new strategic umbrella called the Alliance, structurally reminiscent of the Women's Issues Committee, which also incorporated several groups united around the issue of suffrage. The Alliance takes a limited number of positions and offers to assist any candidate or officeholder who supports them. (Interviews in Kuwait, December 2004 and March 2006.)

would replace Kuwaitis with lower-cost foreign workers. Part of the debate dealt directly with oil privatization, a measure many in parliament opposed strongly:

[Khamis Talaq] Oqab said KOC recently subcontracted a KD 130,000 deal which [if the work had been undertaken by KOC directly] could have employed 15,000 Kuwaitis. Instead, only seven percent of the 4,500 employees are Kuwaitis, while the chairman of KOC says he wishes he has (*sic*) the authority to replace the foreigners with Kuwaitis.

"We are not justifying a non-Kuwaiti workforce, while some get filthy rich," he said. He said the new rich, who embezzled after the stock market collapse and Kuwait Oil Tankers Company crash, want to take over the country.

"[Nibari] tried to expel foreign contractors in the '70s but now wants foreign investors," he said.[29]

The protean meaning of privatization to political liberals like Nibari had changed. It reflected a hope that economic forces could check the power of the regime and its Islamist and tribalist allies whom they see not only as threatening their civil liberties but also as cannibalizing the state. In the face of repeated failures to extend political democratization, rationalization and privatization became solutions preferred by many Kuwaiti liberals for ending incompetence and corruption in state agencies. The government and recent parliaments cooperated on measures to attract foreign investment, even eliminating the restrictions on foreign ownership and portfolio investment adopted during the reign of Amir 'Abdallah al-Salim to protect the nascent private sector. In the fall of 2003 the government agreed to allow full foreign ownership of Kuwait-based enterprises, subject to its approval of individual projects. But tangled webs of regulation remain. Few are directed toward health and safety or quality assurance, and they all make it difficult for a non-Kuwaiti to contemplate doing business in Kuwait without a local agent, a costly (and graft-ridden) requirement under the old law which has been formally abolished.

The government advocates reform but focuses on foreign investment, not liberalizing investment opportunities for Kuwaitis. Exceptions include support for private-sector joint ventures such as the new private universities in which ruling family members are heavily invested, and questionably legal real estate schemes operated by their cronies. Opening the domestic economy to foreign investors could rip the "disguise" from much of the crypto-un-

---

29   *Arab Times*, December 5, 2001.

employment now hidden behind state ownership and private-sector protections, but it could also constitute another mechanism for diverting state resources into the bank accounts of the rulers. The main case in point is Project Kuwait, a scheme to open the northern oil fields to private investment by international oil companies. The government and parliament have been at loggerheads over this issue since it was invented in the 1990s as a strategy to plant corporate "hostages" along Kuwait's border with Iraq, thereby ensuring external intervention to reverse any future Iraqi invasion.

Now that Saddam is gone and post-Saddam Iraq continues to implode politically, the danger Iraq presents to Kuwait is not invasion but spillover from sectarian and civil war. Here, those nominated as external saviors have already shown themselves incompetent to prevent or reverse. The Iraq war, in addition, has boosted oil prices, offering an indigenous alternative source of capital for developing Kuwait's oil production capacity. This undermines a second argument for Project Kuwait, which is that it will bring in necessary external financing, although the argument for expertise and technology transfer remains intact, strengthened by deteriorating yields from Kuwait's oldest oilfields and the need to replace obsolescent infrastructure throughout the hydrocarbon sector. The last, underlying issue is the same as it was during the nationalization crisis of the 1970s: who will determine the future of Kuwait's hydrocarbon industry and who will profit from its expansion?

The outcome of the vote on Project Kuwait rests on the relative strength of younger members of the ruling family, now openly seeking parliamentary allies and exploring avenues that appear to offer advantages they can deploy to move up in the line of succession. The present Oil Minister, Ahmad al-Fahd, is said to control the votes of a dozen or more parliamentary "independents" from the tribal areas, people who might have been expected to vote against Project Kuwait because the rationalization it would inaugurate works against the economic interests of their voting constituencies. Yet the women's rights vote showed how susceptible these members are to rewards of other kinds. Thus, the coming debate and vote on Project Kuwait, coupled with the impending showdown over a parliament-initiated legislative redistricting project that Ahmad al-Fahd hopes to hijack or quash, could be another defining moment. As this reveals the relative positions of aspirants to the position of amir and the shape of the coalition with which the ruler expects to govern, it will determine whether Kuwaitis or their rulers will take the leading role in shaping the private sector as a whole.

MARY ANN TÉTREAULT

The new media and populist modernization

Some of the most important characteristics of modernity are psychological. Modernity generates desires for private rights, individual autonomy, and political liberty.[30] This is why what I have called "the politics of private desires"—that is, a self-referential orientation whose spread from elites to mass publics threatens the doyens of "traditional" cultures, social organizations, and regimes—remains prominent in Kuwait. Psychological modernity characterizes Kuwaitis who identify themselves as modern and cosmopolitan. It also characterizes movement Islamists who project a parochial traditionalism. Although they attract followers who define themselves as "traditional," Islamist movements are modern—arguably postmodern.[31] They appeal to "junior" men from respectable and even wealthy families who, in imperial Europe, would have been sent to make their fortunes in the colonies. They appeal equally to young men from the popular classes whose future prospects are threatened by modernization and economic liberalization. Women also flock to Islamist banners, some drawn by fear of social change and others by the prospect of wielding public influence from the protected spaces of their homes. Among prominent Sunni Islamist leaders are Kuwaiti neo-liberals, strong social conservatives who welcome economic liberalization because they believe it will help them to move up—another hallmark of modernity. In parliament, they continue to advocate making the *shari'a* the sole source of Kuwaiti law despite the setback represented by the outcome of the campaign for women's rights. They are as much examples of interest-based—modern—politics as they are of "traditional" outlooks.

The appeal of Islamism enabled Islamists to regain their popularity in Kuwait rapidly following the September 11, 2001 attacks on the United States. Kuwait's Islamists were tarnished by revelations of Kuwaiti participation as organizers, financiers, and fighters in Usama bin Ladin's operations. Liberals criticized them openly and made successful demands on the government to supervise Islamist-run "charities." This first popular disenchantment with Islamism did not last very long, however. It was reversed by reports of civilian casualties from US bombing in the Afghan war and the openly pro-Israel stance of US President George W. Bush in response

---

30   Yaron Ezrahi, *Rubber Bullets: Power and Conscience in Modern Israel* (Berkeley: University of California Press, 1997); Peter J. Taylor, *Modernities: A Geohistorical Interpretation* (Minneapolis: University of Minnesota Press, 1999).

31   See Aziz al-Azmeh, *Islams and Modernities*, 2nd ed. (London: Verso, 1996).

to the acceleration of violence in Israel and the Palestinian Authority territories in the spring of 2002. Public opinion polls in the early summer of 2002 reported that nearly 80 percent of Kuwaitis believed that US military action in Afghanistan was unjustified.[32]

The "you are either with us or against us" stance of the US government makes such attitudes risky for a country that is acutely dependent on the United States for strategic security. Kuwait relinquished more than a third of its land area to US military control during the preparatory phases of the Iraq war and supported the United States in public statements by government representatives, provoking negative responses from some other Arab governments. But despite Kuwaiti hopes that the US-UK invasion of Iraq would ultimately improve security region-wide, it also provoked the anti-American responses I noted earlier, which included attacks on US personnel stationed in Kuwait and Kuwaiti participation in clashes between Iraqi insurgents and US forces.

Modernity and post-modernity in the form of rising diversity in public opinion underlie Kuwaiti citizens' divergence from the official, pro-US position of their government. Those who cheered the prospect that al-Jazeera would replace CNN and the BBC as the most widely viewed television news sources in the Gulf saw it as a forum for political opposition and thus a channel for democratization. Now al-Jazeera has been joined by other Arab-owned and -operated stations, and local programming in Kuwait that features critical perspectives on current issues. Although they have been criticized as overly ideological and just as likely to skew the truth as the Western-based networks they have replaced in most Kuwaiti homes, these news outlets are widely perceived and valued as representing a local, formerly excluded point of view.[33]

Arab television news networks have changed the mechanisms generating and propagating Kuwaiti popular culture. Before the Iraqi invasion, broadcasts from state-owned and -operated stations carried little international news and virtually no coverage of domestic politics.[34] Kuwaitis relied on locally produced newspapers and magazines for information. These outlets

---

32   *Sixty Minutes,* "Kuwait: Ten Years Later; Most Kuwaitis Not in Support of the United States' Stand on Terrorism," CBS News, broadcast June 9, 2002.

33   Mamoun Fandy, "Information Technology, Trust, and Social Change in the Arab World," *Middle East Journal,* Vol. 54, No. 2 (Summer 2000), p. 394; N. Janardhan, "New Media—In Search of Equlibrium," in *After Saddam,* ed. Mary Ann Tétreault and Andrzej Kapiszewski (Boulder, CO: Lynne Rienner, forthcoming).

34   Tétreault, *Stories of Democracy.*

provided a wide spectrum of news and opinion in normal times but were operating under censorship in 1990, during the second extra-constitutional closure of parliament, which was accompanied by a harsh curtailment of civil liberties.[35] The invasion highlighted the inadequacy of state-controlled media. Although the government had access to US satellite photographs of Iraqi troop movements on the border, censorship left most Kuwaitis ignorant of the looming danger.

The regime wanted to control the press because of its history as a stronghold of the opposition. Kuwaiti merchants had originally launched newspapers and weekly magazines to mobilize a constituency for political reform. During the 1930s, before Kuwait had its own print press, the opposition National Bloc, which had substantial support among Kuwait's leading merchants, used the Iraqi press to publish its reform program. Magazines blossomed after World War II, promoting modernism, offering articles on current national issues, and publicizing the new reforming trends elsewhere in the Arab world.[36]

The print press became the premier institution of Kuwait's "political space" following the adoption of the constitution in 1962. To candidates in Kuwait's first parliamentary election (1963), newspapers offered a national forum for discussing the issues of the day in their myriad analyses and opinion pieces. These publications still tend to reflect the interests of their owners, mostly businessmen, but because virtually every political grouping and major institution has its own magazine, taken as a whole the print press represents a broad range of perspectives. Prominent Kuwaitis contribute regular opinion pieces to newspapers and magazines, most of them written by regular columnists. In some university departments, writers receive credit toward promotion for their columns and articles.

Most Kuwaitis read several newspapers and magazines. They discuss what they read with family, friends, and neighbors, at work and at *diwaniyya*s, regular meetings that take place in private homes. Most *diwaniyya*s are restricted to men but a few, notably the *diwaniyya* of Rasha al-Sabah, a cousin of the Kuwaiti ruler, are open to both sexes. Kuwaiti women have begun to host *diwaniyya*s. Rula Dashti, a businesswoman and long-time feminist activist, inaugurated her weekly *diwaniyya* in 2002.

---

35   Ghanim Al-Najjar, "Human Rights in a Crisis Situation: The Case of Kuwait After Occupation," *Human Rights Quarterly*, Vol. 23 (2001), pp. 188-209.

36   Muhammad Rumaihi, *Beyond Oil: Unity and Development in the Gulf*, trans. James Dickins (London: Macmillan, 1986), p. 99.

Regular attendance at *diwaniyya*s institutionalizes channels for direct communication among people with similar tastes and interests. Most have a core of regular participants who are close friends, relations, and/or clients of the host. Other guests may come frequently or seldom; some Kuwaitis routinely visit several gatherings in the same evening. Attendance at *diwaniyya*s honors the host, and they attract crowds when the host invites important visitors or schedules a debate on a topic of general interest. Political candidates host their own *diwaniyya*s and flock to others to debate issues and meet voters, often advertising speakers and debates in advance in the newspapers to boost attendance. What people say at *diwaniyya*s often appears in the press, both in news reports and in opinion columns.

Newspapers and *diwaniyya*s are interdependent modes of political communication spreading information and opinion and creating precisely the kind of "imagined" national community that Benedict Anderson argues is the product of a literate population and a commercial print press. Even more important for democratization, these uniquely Kuwaiti venues together form a "space of appearance" in which activists mobilize support, issues and personalities are nationalized and normalized, and coherent— though far from unitary—perspectives on social and political life are formed, criticized, adjusted, and propagated.[37]

Young men begin attending *diwaniyya*s with their fathers as little boys where they are introduced to the mores and interests of their social group, as well as to the personalities and issues that define the domestic political scene. They learn to be respectful to their elders, to listen and argue, and also to tolerate if they do not entirely share the opinions of the father and his peers. Important sites of cultural reproduction and discipline, *diwaniyya*s are not uniformly idyllic experiences for everyone, especially young men who are moving away from markers of "traditional" identity and likely to be objects of their elders' sarcastic humor.

The attachment of Kuwaiti youth to socializing at *diwaniyya*s appears to have dropped off since liberation in favor of watching girls in shopping malls and hanging out in internet cafes.[38] Internet use in Kuwait is concentrated between 4 pm and midnight, the hours when tea at home and family visiting normally take place.[39] Kuwaiti youth spend many leisure hours

---

37   Benedict Anderson, *Imagined Communities*, rev. ed. (London: Verso, 1991); Hannah Arendt, *The Human Condition* (Garden City, NY: Doubleday Anchor, 1959).

38   *Christian Science Monitor*, April 26, 2000.

39   Deborah Wheeler, "New Media, Globalization and Kuwaiti National Identity," *Middle East Journal*, Vol. 54, No. 3 (Summer 2000), p. 433.

with peers, shrinking the time available for inter-generational socializing. A Kuwait University dean, 'Ali Tarrah, links rising drug addiction to Kuwaiti fathers' absence from the home—a result of their obsessive attendance at *diwaniyya*s to which their sons no longer accompany them.[40]

Many Kuwaitis are becoming regular television watchers. Like other media television also creates imagined communities among regular viewers, but without the direct participation and avenues for activism offered by *diwaniyya*s and the print press. Jürgen Habermas argues that the social environment of television consumption and its qualities as a medium eliminate both reasons and opportunities for discussion and analysis. Television viewers become passive consumers of media products rather than informed and active citizens.[41] Electronic media shield speakers and opinion makers from direct exposure to consumers, despite the popularity of call-in shows which, in reality, offer little more than the appearance of participation. These qualities of electronic media were less influential in the Middle East when television stations dispensing news and public affairs programming were either Western networks or government-owned. Viewers had fewer ways to evaluate the reliability of what they were watching as compared to what they read in the newspapers or heard at *diwaniyya*s, but together these multiple sources of world and regional news and opinion offered different perspectives and spaces within which to analyze and criticize reports from all sources.

This changed during the 1990-91 war, in part because the obvious partisanship of Western television coverage repelled Middle Eastern viewers.[42] They welcomed the new Arab networks as more reliable and accurate, but it is likely that they merely trade Western biases for Arab biases.[43] In addition, the social environment of electronic media consumption does not change whether programs originate in Washington or Doha. Even in Kuwait, should television news and public affairs viewing shrink the time devoted to traditional media for news and analysis, politics could descend toward Habermasian norms of passivity.

---

40   *Los Angeles Times*, February 12, 2003.

41   Jürgen Habermas, *The Structural Transformation of the Public Sphere: An Inquiry into a Category of Bourgeois Society*, trans. Thomas Burger and Frederick Lawrence (Cambridge, Mass.: MIT Press, 1991).

42   Edmund Ghareeb, "New Media and the Information Revolution in the Arab World: An Assessment," *Middle East Journal*, Vol. 54, No. 3 (Summer 2000), p. 401.

43   Janardhan, "New Media."

Television-generated passivity contributes to public ignorance and creates an environment where mass support can be mobilized through deliberate misinformation and partisan manipulation of public opinion. How this works is shown in the results of polls probing Americans' attitudes toward the conflict in Iraq which were conducted from January through September 2003. A "substantial portion of the [US] public had a number of misperceptions that were demonstrably false" with regard to three key issues pertaining to the Iraq war: whether or not US forces had discovered evidence that Saddam Husayn was working closely with al-Qaʻida; whether or not they had found weapons of mass destruction in Iraq; and whether or not world public opinion supported the US position on the war.[44] The quality of media outlets, more than any other factor including the partisanship of the respondent, explained the bulk of divergence between facts and beliefs. Significantly, 80 percent of those relying on the populist Fox News "misperceived" or were mistaken about one or more of the three issues, whereas only 23 percent of those who relied primarily on public broadcasting stations, PBS (TV) and NPR (radio), were mistaken about one or more issues. Reinforcing the importance of the content and quality of the media outlet for opinion formation is the apparently perverse finding that watching more often and paying better attention do not necessarily lead to a more accurate understanding of events. "[O]verall, those who pay greater attention to the news are no less likely to have misperceptions. Among those who primarily watch Fox, those who pay more attention are more likely to have misperceptions. Only those who mostly get their news from print media, and to some extent those who primarily watch CNN, have fewer misperceptions as they pay more attention" to the news.[45]

The relevance of these findings to Kuwaiti politics cannot be overstated. One of the strongest democratizing institutions in Kuwait is the space created by widespread consumption of news and opinion in the print press and at *diwaniyya*s. This unique combination of media gets the news out while it encourages participants to compare and contrast what they have heard and read and make the sources accountable for what they report. *Diwaniyya*s also allow individuals to test their understanding of events and have their misperceptions corrected. In consequence, most adult male Kuwaitis are

44   Steven Kull, "Misperceptions, the Media and the Iraq War," Program on International
       Policy Attitudes/Knowledge Networks poll, 2 October 2003, quote on 1.
45   Kull, "Misperceptions," p. 16.

well informed about national and international issues and have a noteworthy capacity for making inferences and developing independent opinions.

Shifts in media consumption patterns threaten both pillars of the Kuwaiti information regime. First, the turn toward television as a source of news, especially if the viewer watches only one network and that network offers limited—and biased—coverage, increases the tendency toward unquestioned acceptance of information due to the modality of television consumption and the danger of misperception arising from the quality of the broadcast source. Second, should the trend away from *diwaniyya*s by young men continue into adulthood, the loss of this participatory venue for opinion formation could diminish the capacity of average Kuwaitis to develop reasoned judgments about national and international politics. Internet use among young people is growing rapidly, but despite its potential as a source of multiple political viewpoints and information, the internet is not an adequate substitute for the unique space of appearance created by wide newspaper readership and mass participation in *diwaniyya*s.

Conclusions

Politics in every nation consists of more than what can be read in the news or seen on TV. It also exists within social forces whose barely perceptible shifts, individually and together, change the nature of the political environment, including who is represented, what kinds of resources each can bring, and how much of what kind of space is available for conducting democratic politics. All of these have the potential to affect the conduct of politics and also to shape its outcomes.

Enlarging citizenship to include women ends male monopoly of political authority and opens a route for successful challenges to the rules underpinning male domination. Kuwaiti women launch themselves as equal participants in politics with public-sphere experience gained from their jobs, voluntary activities, and access to the print press. Yet an important lesson of history is that enfranchisement by itself is no guarantee that women or their interests will be represented in government, especially since, in light of the sleight-of-hand maneuver necessary to change the electoral law in Kuwait, we cannot assume without empirical verification that women's rights have majority support among the Kuwaiti population or even among Kuwaiti women. At another level, although Kuwaiti women long have been highly visible actors in society and the economy, and their political activity on behalf of themselves and others was widely accepted well before May 2005, we also must ask whether this acceptance is likely to be furthered or retarded as they enter mainstream politics. Indeed, women in the United States actually lost status after they achieved political rights,[46] while women in Eastern Europe lost many protections as well as reproductive rights in the transition to market democracy.[47]

Whether the subject is political power or material benefits, we are speaking of winners and losers, not simply female winners and male losers but persons whose life chances are limited or enhanced by either the status quo or political change. Similar concerns about winning and losing shape the debate on economic opening, but to view the lineup on this issue as merely labor-versus-capital elides other conflicts responsible for the long stand-off between social forces arrayed on both sides of this issue. Looking only at "economic" issues, we can see contests between proponents of foreign as opposed to domestic investment, between portfolio and directly managed investment, and the nature of the balance between social protection and reliance on market forces to regulate the economy. Here the struggle between the children of the old merchant clans and ambitious sons of the new middle class intersects with the struggle over women's political rights as women join the competition for access to resources that are in the power of the state to allocate. They also intersect with maneuvers by members of the Al Sabah who see in them opportunities to build support for their political aspirations. Economic opening also could bring the presently submerged conflict between Kuwaitis and the 62 percent of the population made up of non-Kuwaitis into sharper focus.[48] Whoever thinks that economic liberalization is the "easy" first step toward political democratization should look a little more closely at how this process actually works in an economical situation.

Indeed, it is the power of economic opening to force changes in political regimes that shifts the positions of actors engaged in these various contests. It also invites a reconsideration of interests broadly conceived. Persons on

---

46   See, for example, William McNeill, *Everyone Was Brave: The Rise and Fall of Feminism in America* (New York: Quadrangle, 1969); Anne Phillips, *The Politics of Presence* (Oxford: Clarendon Press, 1995).

47   Mary E. Hawkesworth, "Democratization: Reflections on Gendered Dislocations in the Public Sphere," in Rita Mae Kelly, Jane H. Baynes, Mary E. Hawkesworth and Brigitte Young (eds), *Gender, Globalization and Democratization* (Boulder, CO: Roman and Littlefield, 2001), pp. 223-36.

48   See, for example, al-Najjar, "Human Rights"; Anh Nga Lonva, *Walls Built on Sand: Migration, Exclusion, and Society in Kuwait* (Boulder, CO: Westview, 1997).

any side, including ruling family members, cannot be entirely confident that their interests will be maximized by the positions they take. WTO-conforming regulations slice through the interests I have sketched here in ways that generate winners and losers within groups as well as among them. Rational choice models and neo-conservative ideologies submerge interests that cannot be defined in economistic terms, and are not good sources for useful predictions as to whether shifts in the balance of social and political forces are more likely to lead to democratization, populism, or even fascism.

The proliferation of electronic mass media in Kuwait, like the enfranchisement of women, is a clearly democratic trend, but even here what the ultimate impact on democratization will be is unpredictable. If television were to displace newspapers and *diwaniyya*s as the primary medium of news and analysis, the results are likely to be retrogressive. Regardless of the content and bias of any individual news outlet, most television viewing takes place outside the spaces of appearance that are the *sine qua non* of democratic political life. Even if Kuwaitis do not slide into the same television-induced passivity that characterizes US media consumers, momentous legal changes could alter its public spaces in negative ways. A new press law, passed in March 2006, could flood the print-press market with special-interest publications that would dilute the unique national forum formerly sustained by a limited number of newspapers (five Arabic-language and two English-language dailies). Kuwait is noteworthy for the national forum created by its local media which ensures the quality of its spaces of appearance and their production and consumption by many persons across the social and political spectrum. Indeed, in recent years print-press outlets and *diwaniyya*s have expanded the number, kinds of persons, and range of views represented there. Columns written by mostly middle-class university faculty members appear among news and opinion articles reflecting the merchant-class positions of owners of Kuwaiti dailies. The purchase of *Al-Watan* by a member of the ruling family who regards the old merchant clans as his personal and political enemies, and welcomes contributions from Islamists and tribalists who share his anti-merchant views, also contributes to the diversity represented in the same news outlet, as well as among the several that the average Kuwaiti reads every day.

The *diwaniyya* as an institution supports merchant-class status and power and thus the social group from which the most effective societal checks on the regime have come. Middle-class Kuwaitis also host *diwaniyya*s but, like *diwaniyya*s in the homes of members of the ruling family, they rarely achieve the political authority exercised from the *diwaniyya* "castles" erected by merchants to defend their interests against the regime. Female candidates challenge the status of the *diwaniyya* as the premier political venue during political campaigns. Women will be expected to conform to persistent social norms limiting socialization among unrelated men and women, and to the amendment tacked on to the woman suffrage law by Islamists, requiring women to conduct themselves according to the precepts of Islamic law during campaigns and elections. Female candidates are likely to favor campaign venues such as televised debates and public meetings where their behavior can be seen to be proper by the audiences they hope to reach. This could diminish the authority of the merchant class, not only because people would be drawn to other venues to vet candidates and discuss platforms, but also because *diwaniyya* groups would become less effective as sites for concentrating votes to elect particular candidates.[49] Usually this power is exercised negatively, against a particular candidate, but *diwaniyya* strategies also concentrate the vote for particular individuals through pledges of support and decisions to cast "one-eyed" ballots, that is, votes for only one rather than the two persons each voter is entitled to choose.

Pressures to open up Kuwait, politically and economically, come from domestic and outside forces. None is unambiguously democratizing while all carry the real possibility of increasing political polarization and domestic conflict. Opening could intensify the already nasty competition between young men and professional women, and between middle- and merchant-class forces. It is likely to increase competition between citizens and the foreign workforce they depend upon, and bring that mostly sublimated conflict into uncomfortable prominence. A commercial press covers conflict because that is what sells newspapers, and by according prominence to controversy, this coverage changes the shape and flavor of politics. Television coverage penetrates further than the print press, yet offers fewer nuances and less information than traditional Kuwaiti media. Television too is drawn to conflict, but the way it reports tends to polarize consumers, in part because television viewing impoverishes their information base. Whether and how well Kuwait's traditional participatory institutions can channel the results of expanding the national political universe in positive ways will determine whether the massive changes in gender relations, the economy, and the parameters of public space it is undergoing will prove to be democratizing or not.

---

49   Such "*diwaniyya* voting" is described and analyzed in Tétreault, *Stories of Democracy.*

6

KUWAIT: THE OBSTACLE OF
PARLIAMENTARY POLITICS

Michael Herb

Kuwait sets the standard for political development in the Gulf. The first dynastic monarchy in the Gulf emerged there in 1939, when members of the ruling family, as a group, seized control of the Kuwaiti state, initiating the system of government-by-clan that we see today throughout the Gulf.[1] Kuwait has the most liberal constitution of the Gulf monarchies, and it has the longest experience with elections and parliamentary politics. An examination of Kuwait's progress toward greater political participation, and the obstacles in the way of that progress, not only helps us to understand Kuwaiti politics, but also, in all likelihood, any future movement toward democracy in the other Gulf monarchies.

Kuwait's 1962 constitution gives the Kuwait parliament (the Majlis al-Umma, or National Assembly) a substantial degree of power. The parliament, however, has not used its powers to the fullest in pursuit of greater democracy. In this chapter I examine this relative failure, and how the events of 2006 promise to change this situation. I argue that Kuwait tends to make progress toward democracy only when the parliamentary opposition overcomes its internal differences and demands concessions from the ruling family. I begin with a discussion of the Kuwaiti political system, emphasizing the way that monarchism shapes any future path toward de-

---

1   Jill Crystal, *Oil and Politics in the Gulf: Rulers and Merchants in Kuwait and Qatar* (Cambridge University Press, 1990); Michael Herb, *All in the Family: Absolutism, Revolution, and Democracy in the Middle Eastern Monarchies* (Albany, NY: State University of New York Press, 1999).

mocracy. I then examine the factors that shape the use of parliamentary powers under the rules of the constitutional system.

Democratization in monarchies

Students of democratic transitions typically look for free and fair elections as the marker of a transition to democracy. Kuwait, however, has seen five relatively free and fair parliamentary elections since 1992, and yet is not democratic. This is because the ruling family selects the ministers who form the government: put differently, while the legislative branch of government is elected, the executive branch is not. Deputies in the parliament have the power to remove ministers that they do not like, and occasionally they have used this power. But the initiative in appointing ministers remains with the amir. In this, Kuwait's political system resembles European constitutional monarchies before they made transitions to full democracy. This is not surprising, since Kuwait's constitutional structure comes straight from the European monarchical tradition, with particular care taken to make the elected parliament compatible with the continued political dominance of the ruling family.

Kuwait's institutional similarity with European monarchies extends to its likely path to democracy. A half-dozen European monarchies made transitions from absolutism, to constitutional monarchy, then to democracy.[2] In the phase of constitutional monarchy, monarchs appointed governments, but parliaments had some powers to approve or disapprove of the monarchs' choices. These systems democratized when "parliamentarism" was achieved—that is to say, when parties in the parliament won the right to appoint the prime minister and the other ministers, and the monarch lost the right to veto these choices.[3]

There were many constitutional monarchies in the nineteenth and twentieth centuries, but only a few achieved democracy in an unbroken evolution from absolutism through constitutional monarchy and to parliamentarism. Yet the odds are good that Kuwait will accomplish exactly this. In

---

2   I use the term "constitutional monarchy" here in its original nineteenth century sense: a monarchy bound by a constitution, but not stripped of power.

3   Nathan J. Brown, *Constitutions in a Nonconstitutional World: Arab Basic Laws and the Prospects for Accountable Government* (Albany, NY: State University of New York Press, 2002); Michael Herb, "Princes and Parliaments in the Arab World," *Middle East Journal* 58 (Summer 2004). On the term parliamentarism see Heinz H. F. Eulau, "Early Theories of Parliamentarism," *Canadian Journal of Economics and Political Science*, Vol. 8 (February 1942). In the European monarchies, a full transition to democracy typically required both an expansion of the suffrage and parliamentarism.

no small part, this is simply because the alternatives are even less likely. Kuwait's ruling family is going nowhere: most Kuwaitis like having the ruling family around, and its detractors limit their ambitions to making the amir a figurehead. No organized group of Kuwaitis, inside or outside Kuwait, wants to get rid of the monarchy altogether. Nor is it likely that the monarchy could be rendered a figurehead by the military, or by some other authoritarian group, as were the Thai or Japanese monarchs. The ruling family controls the military. The parliament today is clearly the main contender to replace the ruling family as the central power in the Kuwaiti political system. The status quo may prove durable, but the clear alternative to the status quo in Kuwait is parliamentarism. This is also true of the other five Gulf monarchies, albeit to a lesser degree in some cases, and thus Kuwait's path toward parliamentarism may show the way toward democracy in the other Gulf monarchies as well.

Constitutional monarchy in Kuwait

Kuwait's constitution defines the ground rules for the sharing of power between the parliament and the ruling family.[4] These rules are important in Kuwait: they are generally followed quite closely, as the succession crisis of early 2006 vividly demonstrated. The essence of the distribution of power between the parliament and the monarchy is thus: the amir appoints a prime minister, who then appoints a cabinet. The parliament can remove ministers and it can block legislation. Each side, in effect, can check the other: parliament does not have to accept a government it does not like, but it lacks the constitutional power to appoint one of its own choosing. A constitution such as Kuwait's can permit democracy, but only if the parliament makes it clear that the monarch has no choice but to appoint a cabinet selected by parliamentary parties, and if the monarch accedes to this demand.

Kuwait has a unicameral parliament of up to 65 members. Fifty are elected, while up to fifteen additional members hold seats by virtue of appointment to the cabinet.[5] The parliament can interpellate individual ministers and follow the interpellation with a motion of confidence. The inter-

---

4   An English translation of the constitution can be found at http://www.oefre.unibe.ch/law/icl/ku__indx.html (accessed November 10, 2004).

5   The total number thus depends on the size of the cabinet, but in any case the cabinet cannot exceed sixteen members, at least one of whom must always be an elected member of the parliament.

pellation is a device borrowed from the European constitutional tradition.[6] The term is translated in Arabic as *istijwab*. It has been translated back to English—infelicitously—as "grilling" in the English-language press of the Gulf. Ministers cannot vote on motions of confidence, and as a consequence elected members alone decide questions of confidence, via a simple majority of the elected members who do not hold cabinet seats.[7]

The parliament cannot formally vote to remove confidence in the prime minister, but it can accomplish much the same thing by declaring that it cannot work with him.[8] This is accomplished via a majority vote of elected deputies, excepting ministers. In the end, a vote of no confidence in the prime minister amounts to a vote of no confidence in the government as a whole. If the prime minister loses this vote of confidence the constitution then calls on the amir to dismiss either the prime minister or the parliament. The prime minister loses his job if the parliament returned in the subsequent elections again declares its inability to work with him.

The parliament can also block legislation, though the constitution dilutes the powers of elected deputies by giving all members of the cabinet (including those who did not win election) the right to vote on legislation. The government votes as a bloc. As a result, the government can pass legislation opposed by a majority of the elected members of parliament. Nonetheless, a super-majority (at most, 33 members of parliament) can block legislation favored by the government, and has done so, most notably in 1999 when the parliament denied women the vote by a vote of 30 to 32.[9] Overall, the parliament enjoys substantial powers, particularly when compared to other Gulf countries whose constitutions much more seriously hedge the ability of their parliaments to remove ministers and block legislation.[10]

Under Kuwait's constitution, the amir appoints the prime minister, who in turn appoints the ministers. Appointees to cabinet posts are of two sorts: those from the ruling family, and those outside the family. Prime ministers

---

6   Interpellations of individual ministers were important, for example, in French parliamentary life in the later part of the nineteenth century. James W. Garner, "Cabinet Government in France," *The American Political Science Review*, Vol. 8 (August 1914).

7   Abstaining, or failing to show up for the vote, amounts to a vote in favor of the minister.

8   In May of 2006, Kuwaiti newspapers and politicians used the term *istijwab* to describe a proposed vote of inability to work with the Prime Minister.

9   Parliament is able not only to block legislation, but also to pass legislation over the objections of the government. If the amir does not like a law passed by the Assembly, he can send it back for reconsideration. If it passes again with a two-thirds majority or in a later session by a majority, the measure becomes law (Articles 65 & 66).

10   See Herb, "Princes and Parliaments in the Arab World."

have retained tight control of the process of appointment of ministers from outside the ruling family. Shaykh Sa'd, who formed eleven governments between 1978 and 1999, typically appointed cabinets by first asking prospective members if they would, as a matter of principle, be willing to serve. He did not tell them who their colleagues would be, or what post they would hold. This conserved his power, and gave non-*shaykhs* little ability to impose their wishes on Sa'd. By March 2007, however, parliamentary blocs came to have an organized role in the appointment of the government, at least in the sense that the prime minister met with each bloc individually, soliciting the opinions of its members on the formation of the new government. Some blocs nominated prospective ministers, while others demurred. The overall effect, however, was to recognize the degree to which the opinions of the parliamentary blocs influenced the chances for success of any new government.[11]

The ruling family monopolizes the post of prime minister and the other core portfolios (the "ministries of sovereignty"). The constitution does not explicitly demand this, though it very carefully allows it. The family makes appointments to these posts by consensus and the prime minister lacks the power to make unilateral decisions. The number of *shaykhs* in the cabinet has typically ranged between five and seven (in Kuwaiti usage, a "*shaykh*" is almost always a member of the ruling family).[12] Until 2003, the prime minister was also always the crown prince, which made direct challenging of the prime minister by the parliament difficult.

The amir has wide powers of dissolution: he can dissolve and call new elections if the prime minister declares that he cannot work with the parliament. In this case, new elections must be held within two months. This is a substantial stick to wield against the parliament, as the electoral advantages of incumbency in Kuwaiti elections are modest. In 2003, 42 sitting deputies ran for reelection, of whom 17 did not return.[13] This is typical of recent elections.

Of course, the most serious threat the ruling family can deploy against the parliament is to suspend the parliament altogether. Such suspensions violate the constitution, but have formed a crucial part of the balance of power between the parliament and the ruling family.

---

11 *Al-Qabas*, March 15, 2007.

12 For a detailed examination of how these families work, see Herb, *All in the Family*.

13 This includes two deputies who lost tribal primaries.

Obstacles to democracy

This constitutional framework sets out the ground rules for politics in Kuwait. It does not determine, however, the distribution of power between the parliament and the ruling family. Indeed, the constitutional structure can accommodate a distribution of power ranging from near absolutism to full democracy. The actual balance between parliamentary and monarchical power depends on the degree to which the parliament effectively exercises its constitutional powers.

The puzzle of Kuwaiti politics, especially in recent years, is just why the parliament has expressed only a limited desire to use its constitutional powers to demand a transfer of real authority from the ruling family to the parliament, at least up to the spring of 2006. I will explore several possible explanations:

1. Oil prevents democracy.
2. The ruling family intimidates deputies by threatening to suspend the parliament.
3. The government steals the elections and distorts voter preferences through the design of the electoral system.
4. The government corrupts the parliament by buying the votes of deputies.
5. The ban on political parties blocks further progress toward democracy.
6. The Kuwaiti electorate hesitates to support a transition to full democracy.
7. Lack of opposition unity prevents progress toward democracy.

Of these, I will argue that the most convincing explanation for the failure of the parliament to use its powers to the fullest lies primarily in the inability of the opposition to unite around a reform agenda, which itself owes much to hesitation among Kuwaiti voters concerning the wisdom of making a full transition to democracy.

Oil

When measured in per capita terms Kuwait is one of the world's richest oil exporting countries. Scholars often attribute the authoritarianism of oil-rich states to the malign influence of petroleum on politics. While I cannot evaluate the overall argument here, I will make some comments concerning how oil detracts from, and contributes to, the prospects for democracy in Kuwait.

Oil wealth has lifted Kuwait from relative poverty to real affluence, and along the way has led to a sharp increase in educational levels and in the size of the Kuwaiti middle class. It has contributed to the construction of a reasonably effective Kuwaiti state, one that receives better scores on measures of governance than would be expected were Kuwait to lack oil.[14] All of these factors have a positive impact on the prospects for democracy in Kuwait, and make it more likely that Kuwait, if it ever democratizes, will stay that way.

Oil, however, likely also has negative effects. Oil plausibly makes Kuwaiti voters more satisfied with their government than they would be were Kuwait to lack oil altogether. It is an accepted finding of the literature on regimes that they tend to be more secure in economic good times. Oil, of course, does not guarantee good times: sometimes oil revenues contract and budgets shrink. Yet many Kuwaitis are well aware that they have it good by the standards of their parents, their grandparents, and their region. While they do not necessarily give the ruling family much credit for this (after all, the al-Sabah did not put the oil in the ground) oil wealth does contribute to a sense of relative contentment. We can contrast this, for instance, with the bubbling discontent often seen in Yemeni politics, or in the monarchy of Nepal, both of which have a standard of living close to that which we might expect to find in Kuwait were it to lack oil (which Yemen has, but less abundantly). Moreover, the past few years have seen steady increases in the price of oil, and this no doubt helps the regime—as would economic growth resulting from something other than natural resource exports. Of course, were Kuwait to make a transition to democracy, oil revenues would also have a stabilizing effect on its democracy.

Oil revenues, it is often thought, strengthen rulers. If we accept the adage that power follows money, the rulers of Kuwait ought to have an unassailably strong position. The state owns the oil, and the state receives the proceeds. Wealth flows from the state to society. Yet Kuwaiti society hardly lies prostrate before its rulers. Instead, Kuwait's ruling family faces a variety of real constraints on its power, constraints imposed by the constitution, by the parliament, by the bureaucracy, and by the prevailing norms of political life in Kuwait. Over 90 percent of Kuwaitis who are employees work for the state, and many who own businesses receive contracts from the state. Yet state employees evince remarkably little fear of retaliation for

---

14   Daniel Kaufmann, Aart Kraay and Massimo Mastruzzi, "Governance Matters IV: Governance Indicators for 1996-2004," *World Bank Policy Research Working Papers Series*, No. 3630 (2005).

participating in opposition groups or campaigning for opposition candidates. Deputies receive a guaranteed pension after they leave office, and the merchant families, despite their partial reliance on government contracts, have long formed a locus of opposition to the ruling family. It appears that constraints limit the power of the government, despite oil: laws protect government employees, as do Kuwait's political norms. Given the existence of this multitude of constraints even in the presence of vast oil wealth there is no reason to think that oil, in itself, explains the absence of democracy in Kuwait. If oil is compatible, in Kuwait, with the emergence of a powerful parliament, with widespread freedom of expression, and with a deeply entrenched norm of respect for the spirit and letter of the constitution, why is oil not compatible with democracy?

Fairness of the elections

While the al-Sabah have occasionally suspended the parliament, the ruling family has generally held reasonably free and fair elections. Of the eleven elections held under the 1962 constitution, the government has interfered in the process of counting ballots only once, in 1967. Election contests receive extensive coverage in Kuwait's largely free press. Voters have ample opportunities to determine the ideological viewpoints and positions of candidates. The government imposes no unusual barriers to candidacies: essentially any Kuwaiti citizen who meets the basic eligibility requirements (which no longer include being male) can put his or her name on the ballot.

Vote buying is the main procedural problem in Kuwaiti elections. Kuwait, which is hardly a large country to start with, was until recently divided into no fewer than 25 electoral districts. Each district elects two members to the parliament, and each voter casts ballots for two candidates. Each of the 25 districts has a modest number of voters, ranging from just over 2,200 to 10,700 registered voters in 2003. This helps aspiring candidates to buy votes, since relatively few votes must be purchased. Partly as a consequence, votes are dear: in a recent by-election, a price of $150 per vote was described in the Kuwaiti press as a "trifle."[15] Votes in the 2006 election were reported to be going for as much as the equivalent of $3,000. The government, of course, is not the only purchaser of votes, since a seat in Kuwait's parliament is a highly valued commodity. Yet the government has the money to spend, and is widely accused of spending it in at least some races.

---

15   Al-Qabas, April 10, 2006.

Many Kuwaitis harshly criticize vote buying. Indeed, the 2006 elections were fought largely over the issue of political corruption, with the opposition pitted against what it saw as anti-reform elements in the ruling family and the National Assembly. The Kuwaiti papers featured frequent articles about vote buying, and the opposition exhorted voters to avoid it. Islamist groups, as they had in the 2003 elections, pointed out that it violated Islamic teachings. Billboards appeared inveighing against the practice: a particularly vivid billboard showed a Kuwaiti purchaser of votes walking with a chain attached to the necks of three other Kuwaitis, who were crawling behind him—these were those who had sold their votes and, by implication, themselves.[16]

The focus of the Kuwaiti opposition on political corruption can only be salutary, but should not lead observers (and perhaps Kuwaitis too) to exaggerate the size of the problem: for all the noise surrounding the issue of vote-buying, it does not ensure that pro-government candidates usually win. In fact, the opposition wins most seats. Moreover, pro-government candidates tend to do best in districts in which voters are more likely to favor the government, so that we cannot attribute the presence of all pro-government deputies in the parliament to vote buying. That said, anything that makes vote buying more difficult will likely increase, at least somewhat, the size of the opposition in parliament.[17]

Many Kuwaitis fervently believe that the division of Kuwait into 25 districts in 1980 biased election results against political reform, and there can be little doubt that the ruling family intended to reduce the size of the opposition in the parliament when it unilaterally redrew voting districts in 1980.[18] This redistricting is blamed for a multitude of sins. First, it made vote-buying easier, since a small margin of votes often separates winner from losers in these districts. Second, the redistricting made it more difficult for ideological groups to win seats.[19] Third, the redistricting sharply reduced the Shi'i presence in parliament, and the Shi'a moved into the opposition after 1979.[20] Fourth, the redistricting increased the number of tribal deputies in the par-

---

16   *Al-Qabas*, June 6, 2006.

17   Thus one of the benefits of enfranchising women was that it increased the number of voters, and the number of votes that must be purchased to influence an election.

18   Dabbi al-Haylim al-Harbi, *Al-Nizam Al-Intikhabi Fi al-Kuwayt* [*The Electoral System in Kuwait*] (Kuwait: al-Siyasi lil-Nashr wa al-Tawzi', 2003).

19   The report of the committee of the council of ministers tasked with coming up with a new system noted some of these problems. See *al-Qabas*, May 5, 2006.

20   The plan to reduce the number of districts to five alleviated the under-representation of the tribes and the Shi'a, but did not end it.

liament, and the tribes then voted more often with the ruling family than did non-tribal Kuwaitis (the *hadar*); to a lesser degree that still continues.[21] This was exacerbated by the ruling family's naturalization, in the 1960s and 1970s, of thousands of members of the tribes in an effort to counterbalance the influence of urban Kuwaitis in the parliament.[22]

None of this, however, prevented the opposition from winning a decisive victory in the elections of 2006, held under the 25 district system. While the new five district system is unlikely to live up to the hopes of its more fervid supporters, neither is it likely to help the government regain control of the parliament.

Parliamentary corruption

In recent years the government has bought not only the votes of Kuwaitis at the polls, but also the votes of deputies voting on issues on the floor of the parliament. A disgruntled *shaykh* charged that it cost the family over $20 million in payoffs to deputies to secure the right of women to vote in the parliamentary ballot of 2005.[23] While the exact figure may or may not be accurate, the ruling family is credibly suspected of spending substantial sums, in this period, to influence parliamentary votes. Somewhat similar charges were made in 2001 when the government faced a serious threat of losing a vote of confidence in its Minister of Finance, which would have led to the collapse of the government as a whole. The press reported that the government handed out a substantial number of jobs to the constituents of wavering members of parliament to secure their votes. Since the appointment of the current Prime Minister in 2006, however, this practice has declined: there is still a bloc of parliamentary deputies controlled by the government, but the faction of the ruling family that advocates the unbridled use of patronage and political money to manipulate parliamentary votes has not been given the green light to use the resources available to swing parliamentary votes. This policy has helped the Prime Minister maintain the support of the main parliamentary blocs, but has resulted in a decline in the government's ability to win parliamentary votes.

---

21   See the article in *Al-Qabas* summarizing research by Muhammad 'Abd al-Jabir and Jasir Karm, April 9, 2006.

22   Anh Nga Longva, "Nationalism in Pre-Modern Guise: The Discourse on Hadhar and Bedu in Kuwait," *International Journal of Middle East Studies*, Vol. 38, No. 2 (May 2006).

23   *Nibras*, October 11, 2005; *al-Tali'a*, November 14, 2005.

The threat of an unconstitutional suspension of the parliament

Almost all authoritarian regimes have an elected parliament: when parliaments challenge rulers, the leaders of most authoritarian regimes steal the elections. The al-Sabah, by contrast, have more often simply shut down the parliament and locked the doors. The al-Sabah have done this twice. In 1976 the al-Sabah suspended the parliament, as a result of both modest pressure from the parliament for reforms and a regional environment hostile to political participation: the ruling family reopened the parliament in 1981. Again in 1986 the Amir suspended the parliament, and went so far as to replace it with an unconstitutional, and largely impotent, Majlis al-Watani (or National Assembly) in 1990. Only after liberation from Iraqi rule were elections held again under the 1962 constitution, in 1992.

This habit provides a potential explanation for the failure of the parliament to seriously press the ruling family for democracy. If deputies think that their demands will result only in the closing of the parliament, they might well make a strategic decision to avoid direct challenges of the ruling family. In the year following the opposition victory in the 2006 elections, there was much talk in Kuwait of an unconstitutional suspension of the parliament. Yet it was also increasingly clear that the time when such an option could seriously be considered had passed, and that the ruling family had neither the political resources nor the will to unilaterally reduce the constitutional powers of the parliament.[24]

One indication of the ruling family's acquiescence to the constraints of constitutional life can be found in the succession crisis of early 2006. When Amir Jabir died his cousin Sa'd came to power, but Sa'd suffered from dementia and could not rule. In the Gulf, ruling families, not parliaments, decide who rules. Yet the Kuwaiti constitution and Kuwaiti law specify that only parliament can depose an existing amir. Faced with a choice, the ruling family decided to follow the letter of the constitution, going to the parliament to depose the Amir. This was done at a considerable cost to the prestige and power of the family. It is not likely to be a coincidence that the redistricting issue came to a head within six months of the disputed succession, and the crisis resulted in a resounding defeat for the authoritarian branch of the ruling family.

---

24   This observation is based on interviews in Kuwait in the spring of 2007, including interviews with politically influential opponents of political reform.

The ban on political parties

In the end, parliamentarism requires political parties: only via parties, and parties with discipline, can the parliament establish durable preferences for a slate of ministers to form the government. In the absence of parties the parliament cannot have durable preferences and the monarch will have the dominant voice in appointing the prime minister.

By law, political parties are prohibited in Kuwait. This, however, is not an insuperable barrier to parliamentarism, especially because electoral and parliamentary blocs act as *de facto* parties. Blocs of like-minded candidates have long cooperated in Kuwaiti elections, dating back to the 1960s when Arab nationalists won numerous seats in the parliament. Today, a number of formal political organizations run candidates in elections, and a number of deputies in the parliament belong to these groups. Other candidates may accept the endorsement of one (or more) of these groups without formally joining. The electoral system, however, makes no provision for parties: each voter, under the new electoral system, will vote for four candidates from among a large number of candidates in his or her district. While candidates will likely form lists, only their individual names will appear on the ballot. This is by design: the dismal experiences of other Arab states with political parties have long made parties an object of suspicion among Kuwaitis.

In the parliament, blocs have emerged in recent years and now have a central role in parliamentary politics. The parliamentary blocs are not always coterminous with organizations that field candidates in elections: the Islamist Bloc in parliament, for example, includes representatives of the two *salafi* groups, the Muslim Brothers, and a variety of independents. The populist Popular Bloc, by contrast, is mostly a parliamentary bloc with little presence in elections. The Independent Bloc exists solely as a parliamentary group, its members running—as the bloc's name suggests—as independents in elections, although in practice the Independent Bloc amounts to a pro-government party, one often affiliated with the anti-reform elements in the government and the ruling family.

An examination of important votes in recent assemblies does not reveal consistent discipline among the members of the important parliamentary blocs, though there is variation among the blocs. The Muslim Brothers demonstrate more discipline than any other parliamentary group and this increases the political power of the organization. The Popular Bloc also enjoys some discipline, while the Islamist Bloc as a whole is not very disciplined at all.

As noted above, the parliamentary blocs have come to have a more formal role in the formation of new governments via meetings with the prime minister and through the announcement of candidates for ministerial positions. The prime minister takes these consultations seriously because the support of parliamentary blocs for prospective ministers helps to ensure that they will not be subjected to an early interpellation, with the subsequent difficulties that any interpellation causes.

In the absence of reforms to make parties part of the electoral process, legalizing parties in Kuwait, alone, would not make parliamentarism much more likely. That said, voting by party lists in elections, for example, would likely give a substantial boost to bloc discipline in the parliament. In the end, however, sustained party discipline in the parliament itself may follow, rather than long precede, parliamentarism. One can well imagine that the nascent parliamentary parties that currently exist in the form of parliamentary blocs could well turn into disciplined parties if there were an active need to support a specific government, rather than merely an occasional opportunity to kick a specific minister out of office.

Ambivalence about democracy

Kuwaitis have ambivalent feelings about democracy and about the role of their ruling family in political life. The opposition has recently won clear majorities in parliamentary elections, but the central opposition demands are not for a transition to democracy but instead for limitation on the power of the ruling family. The two are related, but they are not the same thing. The opposition—and a clear majority of Kuwaitis—have a strong attachment to the 1962 constitution and react strongly to any suggestion that the powers of the parliament should be circumscribed. And the opposition also wants to keep the ruling family in its place: Kuwaitis across the political spectrum tend to be proud of the fact that their ruling family does not put on the airs of the ruling families of the rest of the Gulf. At the same time, there is virtually no support in Kuwait for a republic and there is a good deal of trepidation about the consequences of a transition to parliamentarism in which parliamentary blocs would determine the composition of the government. Thus opposition demands tend to focus on weakening the ruling family's control of politics while not explicitly seeking to end it. As a consequence the parliament, which enjoys substantial powers under the constitution, does not fully use the full measure of its powers to press the ruling family to democratize.

Political divisions among deputies

While there is widespread support in Kuwait for limiting the power of the ruling family, there are a variety of other issues which tend to divide Kuwaitis, and divide the parliamentary opposition. Frequently, opposition deputies make up a majority of the deputies in parliament, as they did in the 1999, 2003 and 2006 parliaments, and in some of the previous parliaments going back to the 1980s. Yet, except during the spring and summer of 2006, the issues that have dominated the attention of the Kuwaiti parliament are not, in the end, about political reforms that would increase the power of the elected parliament at the expense of the ruling family. Instead, parliamentary politics frequently revolve around issues that divide the deputies who support reform. Three major types of cleavages run through the Kuwaiti opposition: these are based on identity and sect, culture and religion, and economics.

Kuwaitis divide themselves into three main identity groups: the Shi'a, the Sunni *hadar* and the Sunni tribes. The Shi'a have held around five seats in recent assemblies. Before the Iranian revolution (and before the re-districting that reduced their parliamentary representation) the Shi'a reliably voted for the government. The Iranian revolution pushed the Kuwaiti Shi'a into the opposition, though in recent years the Shi'a have elected a number of pro-government deputies.

Just over half of the deputies in recent parliaments have had a clear tribal affiliation. In the past, tribal (or *badu*) deputies tended to support the ruling family, though from the 1980s onwards the Islamist opposition has made serious inroads in tribal districts. The populist Popular Bloc formed in 1999 competes with Islamist groups for opposition votes in tribal districts.

Those Sunnis who do not identify politically with a tribe are generally counted among the Sunni *hadar*, and make up perhaps 35 percent of the electorate. In the 1960s and 1970s, the Sunni *hadar* formed the locus of opposition to the ruling family in the parliament, electing a number of Arab nationalist candidates. As the left has declined, Islamists have won some seats in *hadar* districts, as have liberals. Pro-government candidates have always won at least some *hadar* seats, though pro-government candidates have always had less success in *hadar* districts than in tribal districts.

Economic issues divide Kuwaitis into roughly two groups. Most Kuwaitis who are employees work for the Kuwaiti state, and these Kuwaitis receive relatively generous paychecks for what is often a modest effort. Their salaries might best be thought of as a cross between a payment for services rendered to the state and a payment from the national trust fund. These Kuwaitis tend to press for increases in government wages and other forms of direct income support from the state. On the other side of the class divide we find Kuwaiti business owners and those with Western education and marketable skills: these Kuwaitis tend to view less well off Kuwaitis as parasitic dependents on state largesse. These Kuwaitis support the growth of the private sector and restraint in raising wages in the public sector. Economic cleavages intersect with identity in Kuwait: tribal Kuwaitis tend to be less well off and more dependent on state employment, while the Sunni *hadar* are better off and more likely to be business owners. The Shi'a fall into both groups.

Religion and culture form the final great divide in Kuwaiti politics. Sunni Islamists support a larger role for Islam in public life and generally represent culturally conservative Kuwaitis. For many years, their signature issue was the amendment of the constitution to make Islamic law *the* (rather than *a*) source of law in Kuwait, and the Sunni Islamists voted against giving women the right to vote in 1999 and 2005. Islamists are found among both tribal and *hadar* Sunnis. There are Islamists too among the Shi'a, though their Islamism is tempered by their community's minority status in Kuwait: the Islamization of public life in Kuwait means, in effect, the dominance of a Sunni form of Islam.

In parliament we find three opposition blocs (a fourth bloc consists of "independents" close to the government). The Sunni Islamists formed the largest bloc in the most recent assemblies, with around 14 members in 1999 and from 16 to 18 in the 2003 and 2006 parliaments. The bloc is split among three groups: the Muslim Brothers and two *salafi* political groups. Some members are independents. The bloc is wholly Sunni and has members from both tribal and *hadar* districts. Economic issues split the Sunni Islamists down the middle.

On the other side of the culture wars we find two groups: the liberals and the Popular Bloc. An informal bloc of liberal and nationalist deputies numbered eight members in the 1999 Majlis, and somewhat fewer in the 2003 Majlis. After the 2006 elections, the bloc announced its existence formally, in keeping with the increasing role for blocs in Kuwaiti politics: it again had eight members. All members of the bloc in the 2006 parliament are Sunni and *hadar* and none are tribal. The bloc's members tend to agree on the three main issues of Kuwaiti politics: they support limits to the power of the ruling family, they are economically in favor of reform (and thus not very receptive to demands of Kuwaitis for more hand-outs from the state), and they oppose the Islamization of public life.

Finally, the Popular Bloc had ten members in the 1999 parliament, six in the 2003 parliament, and seven in the 2006 parliament. Its politics are best described as populist, and it represents the interests of those Kuwaitis who are relatively less well off. The Popular Bloc opposes the political program of the Sunni Islamists, and in tribal districts there is electoral competition between Sunni Islamists and candidates of the Popular Bloc. Thus the non-Islamist vote tends to split, going to the liberals in the Sunni *hadar* areas and the Popular Bloc (and other independents) in the tribal areas. Ironically enough, however, the Popular Bloc is a parliamentary coalition that also includes the Shi'i Islamists. There is a logic to this based on common economic interests and a common opposition to the Sunni Islamists, though the coalition is made more difficult by anti-Shi'i bias among many Sunni tribal Kuwaitis.

The Independent Bloc is a loose grouping of Kuwaitis who typically—though not always—vote for the government. The most reliable are the "service deputies," noted above for the government services that they provide to their constituents. These deputies also receive direct financial support from the government and the ruling family, though the degree of this support has apparently declined recently.[25] Despite the relatively large size of the Independent Bloc, the number of deputies who always vote with the government is small: of the 50 elected deputies in the 2003 Majlis, only nine voted with the government on three crucial issues: the 2004 vote of confidence in the Minister of Finance, women's political rights, and the 2006 referral of the redistricting plan to the constitutional court.[26] The nine reliably pro-government deputies hail mostly from tribal districts, and are not Shi'i.[27] The actual pro-government bloc, however, is somewhat larger than this, as the government collects its chips with some of the pro-government deputies only when it really needs to, leaving them free to vote against the government on issues of particular resonance in their electoral districts.

---

25   Interviews in Kuwait in spring 2007.

26   The government mustered all of its supporters to help pass the legislation giving women the right to vote.

27   Three are of one tribe (the 'Awazim), and four come from just two districts (the 18th and 24th).

Patterns in parliamentary politics

Table 1 shows a number of key votes in the parliament since 1995, with a summary of the issue and the voting breakdown.[28] We can roughly divide government-parliament relations in Kuwait in the period since liberation into three periods. Up to the spring of 2006, the government typically prevailed in disputes with the parliament even though the opposition frequently had a majority. In the spring and summer of 2006, the opposition united and forced the ruling family to agree to redistricting. Since then the opposition has not typically displayed much unity but the government nonetheless has suffered several stinging defeats in parliament. The result is a weakened government and ruling family, but a parliament that is unable to play a dominant role in guiding the government. Kuwait thus suffers from a lack of coherent direction that is much remarked in the press in Kuwait and the Gulf.

The first interpellation after independence set the tone for post-liberation parliamentary politics until recently. The experience of occupation weakened the position of the ruling family, and the opposition was widely said to have won a majority in the 1992 elections. Yet the one interpellation of the 1992 parliament, in 1995, set liberals against Islamists. The Minister of Education was the target of the interpellation, and liberals allied with the government to defend him. This split, pitting liberals against Islamists, reappeared in later assemblies. Islamist and *badu* votes defeated the expansion of the suffrage to women in 1990: the government forced the legislation through in 2005 only by calling in its chips with a handful of pro-government tribal deputies, prevailing on them to vote for women's political rights. A 2003 vote of confidence in Dayfallah Sharar, the Minister of State for Affairs of the Council of Ministers, illustrated the weakness of the liberals in parliament: the vote to remove confidence gained only 15 supporters (including most Shi'a), against the combined opposition of Islamists, the *badu*, and pro-government deputies. We also see the failure of a liberal/Shi'i coalition in 2005, when Islamist and tribal deputies forced the resignation of the Shi'i Minister of Information, under threat of a vote of confidence which he appeared poised to lose.[29] While the government lost

---

28   Data are drawn from the Kuwaiti dailies, including *al-Ra'i al-'Amm*, *al-Qabas*, and *al-Watan*, along with the London-based *al-Hayat* and the weekly paper of the Majlis al-Umma, *al-Dustur*. All of these data are also available at http://www2.gsu.edu/~polmfh/database/database.htm.

29   It did not help his case that liberals offered only lukewarm support, as a result of his failed efforts to appease the Islamists while in office.

Year	Issue	Results	Votes (opposition listed first)	Voting blocs
1995	Vote of confidence in Ahmad al-Rabi', the Minister of Education.	Government won.	21 to remove confidence.[1]	Islamists, many tribal deputies.
			17 to retain confidence. 4 abstentions.	Liberals, most pro-government deputies.
1999	Women's right to vote.	Government lost.	Exact results unavailable.	Liberals, Shi'a.
				Islamists, tribal deputies (including those close to the government).
2000	Vote of confidence in 'Adil al-Sab'i.	Government won.	19 to remove confidence.	Popular Bloc. Shi'a and non-Islamist tribal deputies.
			26 to retain confidence. 3 abstentions.	*Hadar* and Islamists.
2002	Vote of confidence in Yusuf al-Ibrahim, the Minister of Finance.	Government won.	21 to remove confidence.	Tribal deputies (except pro-government), most Shi'a, Popular Bloc, Islamists.
			22 to retain confidence. 3 abstentions.	Liberals, non-Islamist *hadar*, pro-government deputies, some Shi'a.
2003	Voice of confidence in Dayfallah Sharar, Minister of State for the Council of Ministers.	Government won.	15 to remove confidence.	Liberals and Shi'a.
			30 to retain confidence.	Islamists, tribal deputies, and government deputies (Popular Bloc split).
2003	Vote of confidence in Mahmud Nuri, Minister of Finance.	Government won.	21 to remove confidence.	Many Islamists, liberals, Popular Bloc, Shi'a.
			25 to retain confidence. 3 abstentions.	Pro-government deputies, independents, some Islamists.
2004	Redistricting vote.	Government won.	19 for 6 abstained (for).	Liberals, Popular Bloc, most Islamists.
			21 against redistricting.	Pro-government deputies, two tribal *salafis*.

---

[1] Votes of confidence succeed only with "a majority of the deputies who constitute the assembly, less the ministers." (Article 101)

2004	Petition to investigate the deal made by a company associated with he anti-reform Minister of Energy.	n/a	22 signed.	Islamists, liberals, Popular Bloc.
			28 did not sign.	Pro-government deputies, some moderates.
2005	Threatened vote of confidence in Minister of Information.	Government lost (minister resigned before vote).	n/a	Islamists, tribal deputies.
				Liberals, Shi'a.
2005	Women's right to vote.	Government won.	23 elected deputies against.[1]	Islamists, most tribal deputies.
			21 for women's rights.	Liberals, all Shi'a, tribal deputies closest to the government.
2006	Reducing the number of electoral districts from 25 to 5.	Opposition won after new elections called.	29 deputies in pre-dissolution parliament supported plan for 5 districts.	Popular Bloc, almost all Islamists, liberals and all *hadar* except service deputies.
			17 opposed.	Pro-government deputies, mostly from tribal districts.
2006	Government assumption of consumer loans.	Government won.	20 elected deputies voted for.	Tribal deputies (except some Islamists).
			24 elected deputies voted against.	Sunni *hadar,* Muslim brothers.
2007	Interpellation of Ahmad al-Abdallah.	Government lost.	Minister resigned before vote of confidence	Islamists, Popular Bloc.
				Independents, Liberals (weak support for minister).
2007	Interpellation of Ali Jarrah.	Governement lost.	Minister resigned before vote of confidence.	Popular Bloc; National Bloc (liberals); many Islamists.
				Independent bloc, Muslim brothers.

Table 1: Voting patterns in selected parliamentary votes, and issues, in parliaments since liberation

---

[1]   The government can vote on regular legislation: the vote totals given for the 2005 vote on women's political rights are for elected deputies only.

some of these battles, these losses hardly advanced the issue of political reform in Kuwait: instead, they advanced the cultural agenda of the Islamists while demonstrating the power of the Islamists in alliance with the tribes.

Other issues revealed a second major cleavage in Kuwaiti politics, one between the tribes and the *hadar*. In 2000, a coalition of *badu* deputies forced a vote of confidence in the Minister of Housing: he survived in part because he had Islamist support, and some tribal Islamists voted for him, along with almost all Sunni *hadar*. The government had a substantially more difficult time defending the liberal Minister of Finance in 2002. The minister attracted support from the *hadar*, but because he was a liberal, some *hadar* Islamists voted against him. He survived on the basis of *hadar* votes and the votes of pro-government tribal deputies.

On most of these issues, the government prevailed. It did so because, in the end, these issues split the opposition. In many ways, this is not surprising: as in any society, a multitude of political issues concern the average Kuwaiti, and political reform is but one of these. The role of Islam in politics, along with economic issues, matters a great deal to Kuwaitis, at times more than issues of political reform.

In the spring of 2006, however, the opposition united around the issue of reducing the number of electoral districts. Successive governments announced their support for some form of redistricting, but found one reason or another to delay and postpone any actual decision on the subject. In April 2006, a committee of the council of ministers proposed a five district system, with each district having ten members. The opposition embraced this, and the government as a whole voted to present the plan to parliament at a meeting in the middle of May. Twenty-nine elected deputies—that is, a sizeable majority of the elected deputies—signed a statement supporting the five district plan. The supporters included all of the opposition: liberals, Popular Bloc and Islamists alike. It included deputies from the main identity groups in Kuwaiti society, the *hadar*, Shi'a and tribes. Moreover, the redistricting plan received this support despite the fact that it underrepresented the tribes and the Shi'a, like all other districting plans in the electoral history of Kuwait.[30]

A few days prior to the parliamentary session the government changed course and proposed a ten district arrangement. Then, in the parliamentary session itself, the government supported calls to refer the plan first to the constitutional court. The opposition saw this as yet another delaying tactic,

30   See *al-Qabas*, May 5, 2006 for an overview of the plan.

and the 29 deputies who signed the statement walked out of the parliamentary chamber. Three opposition deputies then submitted a formal request to interpellate the Prime Minister, for the first time in Kuwaiti history. At the same time, a popular movement sprang up, holding public demonstrations demanding that the government implement the five district plan: the protesters adopted the color orange, after the Ukrainian pro-democracy activists. Protests extended even to the parliamentary hall itself, where protesters loudly voiced their support when reform deputies withdrew from the floor of the parliament; and they earlier chanted slogans hostile to the Minister of Energy, a *shaykh* seen as the leader of the anti-reform elements in the ruling family.

The Amir responded to all of this by dissolving the parliament and calling elections, held on June 29, 2006. The election campaign focused on the issue of political reform, to a greater degree than any campaign since that of 1992, and it became clear that the election results would serve as a referendum on the issue of redistricting.

The opposition convincingly won the 2006 elections. Of the 29 deputies in the previous parliament who supported electoral reform, 21 held their seats, one retired, and seven lost. By contrast, of the 18 former deputies who opposed reform, nine were reelected and nine lost their seats (of the three who took no position, one returned and two lost their seats). The opposition majority grew to well over 30 members, about half of them Islamists and the rest divided between liberal/nationalists and the populist Popular Bloc.

The government chose compromise over confrontation in response to the opposition's victory at the polls. The *shaykh* who led the anti-reform faction of the ruling family did not return to the government (this was Ahmad al-Fahd) and his ally, Dayfallah Sharar, also lost his cabinet seat. The government then agreed to the redistricting plan that it had so long resisted, and Kuwait is to be divided into five ten-member districts for its next parliamentary elections. In the fall of 2006, the three main opposition blocs formed an umbrella bloc (*kutla al-kutal*) and set out a common agenda. The umbrella bloc achieved some successes, notably the dismissal of the unpopular Minister of Information, who had during the election campaign threatened to poke his finger in the eye of his critics.[31]

---

31   *Al-Qabas,* July 8, 2006.

Opposition unity, however, did not endure.[32] The government successfully defeated a proposal (of the sort that only makes sense in Kuwait)
for the government to assume consumer debts. But in the spring of 2007
parliamentary interpellations led to the resignation of two members of the
ruling family from the government, one of them from the central ruling
lineage of the family. This was not a result of coordinated action across the
opposition blocs. The liberal/national bloc offered some tepid support to
the first minister, and the Muslim Brothers did the same for the second.
Yet in both cases the split in the opposition was not enough to save the
ministers, both of whom resigned rather than face likely defeat in a vote
of confidence. The two interpellations also showed the power of a political calculus whereby the various opposition blocs hesitate to aggressively
support ministers from the al-Sabah out of fear that the bloc would be
perceived by the electorate as a defender of the ruling family. Yet when the
possibility of an unconstitutional suspension of the parliament bubbled
again to the surface in the fall, the blocs held a series of meetings to coor-
dinate their response, illustrating again the degree to which defending the
1962 constitution unites the political opposition in Kuwait.

Conclusion

Kuwait's constitution gives its parliament substantial powers, and the fair-
ness of the elections enables the opposition to win parliamentary majorities. Recent events in Kuwaiti politics, especially in the summer and fall
of 2006, show just how much power the constitution affords a political
opposition that is united in its demands against the ruling family: a united
opposition pushed through a redistricting plan and ousted the leading anti-
reform *shaykh* from his position as Minister of Energy. Yet the three opposition blocs that compose the opposition have other priorities in addition
to political reform, and on these issues they are seriously split. Moreover,
the Kuwaiti electorate, while it supports limits to the power of the ruling
family, has an ambivalent attitude, at best, toward the notion that parliamentary blocs should appoint the government. Before 2006, the government had some success in splitting the opposition and winning important
battles with the parliament. Since the elections in the summer of 2006,
the government has lost much of its capacity to protect its members from
votes of confidence in the parliament. The result of this is a difficult political situation: a government that cannot protect its members or formulate

32   *Al-Qabas,* March 30, 2007.

a coherent vision, a parliament that is split over many issues and lacks the authority to govern, and a Kuwaiti public that fears the consequences of parliamentary supremacy but does not want a dominant ruling family either. To resolve this conundrum—and a resolution may be a long time in coming—Kuwait needs to move either toward the authoritarian model of the rest of the Gulf or toward parliamentary formation of governments. Recent trends, and the balance of power in Kuwaiti politics, suggest that absolutism is less likely than democratization.

7

BAHRAIN: REFORM—PROMISE AND REALITY

J.E. Peterson

The six member states of the Gulf Cooperation Council (GCC) are among the world's last true monarchies. The ruler of each state enjoys unparalleled power and other members of his ruling family hold most key positions in the government, as well as enjoying many other privileges. Despite significant steps toward institutionalization and the creation of governments that are frequently responsive, the structure and authority of these monarchical systems remain virtually unchallenged. The debate over democratization—a process that has touched the Middle East the least of all regions of the world—has acquired impetus in the Gulf only recently, quickened by the events of September 11, 2001 and the war in Iraq. The question of the future of liberalization in the GCC states is complicated by the continued legitimacy of the traditional pattern of leadership, as well as by uncertainty over the role that Islamists might play in the process.

Developments in Bahrain are particularly illustrative of the promise and the pitfalls of nascent democratization or liberalization in the region. Islamist forces in the country, among both the minority Sunni and majority Shi'i, constitute positive pressure toward liberalization, and increasing the stake of Islamists in the participatory process will have a salutary effect on their commitment to political reform, since they will benefit from it. Limitations on liberalization are the result of pressure from conservatives within the ruling family and its patrons, the rulers of the UAE and Saudi Arabia.

છ૦

Among all the GCC states, the pressures for change are particularly strong in Bahrain. As it is the Gulf's first post-oil economy, many of the stresses in

Bahrain will soon be felt elsewhere in the Gulf. Among these are the privileged status of the ruling family, the Al Khalifa, the need to deal with declining oil revenues, control over increasingly unpalatable corruption, and the
generation of employment for dramatically growing numbers of youth.

Bahrain's modern history has been frequently turbulent because of fric-
tions between its ruling family and the majority of its population. From
1961 until 1999 Bahraini politics consisted of a condominium between the
ruler, Shaykh 'Isa bin Salman, and the Prime Minister, his brother Shaykh
Khalifa bin Salman. While Shaykh 'Isa seemed content to reign, Shaykh
Khalifa took the more active role in deciding policy and running the government. The result was something of a "good guy, bad guy" partnership.
Shaykh 'Isa made himself accessible to the people and retained considerable
respect and loyalty. Meanwhile, Shaykh Khalifa appointed government officials including the cabinet, supervised the build-up of the security forces,
and allegedly became the richest person in Bahrain with extensive holdings
in land, hotels, commercial property (including office buildings leased by
government ministries), and profits on government contracts. Family and
tribal allies grew rich with him.

The last of many periods of unrest, an especially prolonged and violent
episode throughout much of the 1990s,[1] ended with the accession of Shaykh Hamad bin 'Isa Al Khalifa in March 1999 (he proclaimed himself King
in 2002). His initial moves seemed to defuse a highly volatile situation and
produced expectations of a truly new era in Bahraini politics. But perhaps
expectations soared unrealistically high. The pace of reform seemed to slow
noticeably after calm had settled over the country. The government remained largely unchanged (Shaykh Hamad's hard-line uncle was retained

1   The 1994-99 uprising has been covered in Louay Bahry, "The Opposition in Bahrain:
A Bellwether for the Gulf?" *Middle East Policy*, Vol. 5, No. 2 (May 1997), pp. 42-57;
Munira Fakhro, "The Uprising in Bahrain," Human Rights Watch/Middle East, *Routine
Abuse, Routine Denial: Civil Rights and the Political Crisis in Bahrain* (Washington, DC,
June 1997); Joe Stork, "Bahrain's Crisis Worsens," *Middle East Report*, No. 204 (July-
September 1997), pp. 33-5; Louay Bahry, "The Socioeconomic Foundations of the Shiite
Opposition in Bahrain," *Mediterranean Quarterly*, Vol. 11, No. 3 (Summer 2000), pp.
129-43; Abdul Hadi Khalaf, "The New Amir of Bahrain: Marching Side-Ways," *Civil
Society*, Vol. 9, No. 100 (April 2000), pp. 6-13; David M. Ransom, "Bahrain: New Emir,
New Vision," *Middle East Insight*, Vol. 16, No. 3 (June-July 2001), pp. 35-36, 71; Naomi
Sakr, "Reflections on the Manama Spring: Research Questions Arising from the Promise
of Political Liberalization in Bahrain," *British Journal of Middle East Studies*, Vol. 28, No.
2 (November 2001), pp. 229-31; Falah al-Mdaires, "Shi'ism and Political Protest in Bahrain," *DOMES: Digest of Middle East Studies*, Vol. 11, No. 1 (Spring 2002), pp. 20-44;
and J.E. Peterson, "Bahrain's First Reforms Under Amir Hamad," *Asian Affairs* (London),
Vol. 33, Part 2 (June 2002). Additional material and insights were gathered during visits
to Bahrain in 1985-86, 1990, 1999, and 2001.

as Prime Minister), the atmosphere of discrimination against the majority Shi'i population continued, and the restricted character of the new parliament caused widespread disappointment. Bahrain appeared to be stuck at a crossroads. Would the spirit of dialogue and conciliation continue, or would re-emerging differences mark a return to confrontation—perhaps not as overt and violent as that of the 1990s but just as damaging?

In large part, the key to future developments lies in the personality and intentions of the King. Considerable confusion surrounded the motivation of King Hamad. Were his initial reforms instituted simply to calm the unrest and arrest international criticism, or was he committed to continuing essential reforms and simply in need of time to carry them out safely? The question is not simply academic. In all the Gulf monarchies, the ruler holds disproportionate authority in decision-making and policy formulation and his decisions are the single most important factor in setting the direction of state action. King Hamad's namesake in Qatar, Amir Hamad bin Khalifa, has been committed to a path of gradual reform since his accession in 1995, even though there is little burning pressure for such reform in Qatar. Bahrain's pattern of cyclical unrest, underlying economic motivations, and unresponsive ruling family require a leader dedicated to long-term political reform.

Bahrain also provides a case study for the predominant role that Islamists are likely to play in any liberalization of political participation in the Gulf. The great majority of the political groupings in Bahrain are Islamist. The strongest of these are also from the majority Shi'i population and opposed to the government. Because of the sectarian political divide, the government supports the Sunni Islamist parties which did well in the 2002 and 2006 parliamentary elections.

Bahrain's Islamists, at present at least, are committed to legal participation within the system. None of the recognized groups advocates the overthrow of the government and, like most Bahrainis, all profess a wish to see the retention of an Al Khalifa ruler, albeit with significant changes and reforms to the present system. While the largest of the Shi'i Islamist parties chose to boycott the 2002 elections, they were joined in this action by the largest of the secular parties. They boycotted not because the elections were democratic but because they were not seen as democratic enough.

In short, Bahrain's experience demonstrates that Islamist opposition can be positive in pressuring governments toward more responsive accountability and increased participation. Indeed, it can be reasonably argued that any process that increases the Gulf's Islamists' stake in participatory politics will strengthen their commitment to a reformed and energized system. And this is most likely to be true for Shi'i Islamists.

The accession of Hamad bin 'Isa and the promise of change

Not a lot was expected of the new Amir when he acceded in 1999. Shaykh Hamad bin 'Isa had been thought to be under Saudi influence and had a close personal connection with Shaykh Zayid bin Sultan Al Nuhayan, the Amir of Abu Dhabi and President of the United Arab Emirates. Most importantly, his uncle, Shaykh Khalifa bin Salman, had served as Prime Minister since Bahrain's independence in 1971 and virtually ran the state during the reign of his easy-going brother Shaykh 'Isa while he promoted his own financial interests.

Within months of his accession, Shaykh Hamad instituted a number of reform measures that had immediate and strong impact. He opened dialogue with opposition leaders in his palace and in the homes of Shi'a religious figures. The most prominent opposition leader, Shaykh 'Abd al-Amir al-Jamri, who had been held under arrest for most of the period of unrest, was convicted in July of espionage and inciting unrest.[2] Shaykh Hamad ordered his release the following day. Eventually all of the detainees from the unrest were released and Bahrainis in exile were welcomed back. On National Day (December 16), he announced elections for municipal councils and the right of women to vote in them. A further step was the abolition of the State Security Law and Court, one of the protesters' key demands.

Other measures followed in 2000. A key demand of the opposition for decades had been the removal of the Briton Ian Henderson, the long-serving head of security. Henderson had been named an advisor in December 1996 and his post as head of the State Security Investigations Directorate abolished. In July 2000, he abruptly resigned as advisor and left the country permanently. On September 27, the Amir appointed 19 new members of the Consultative Council (*Majlis al-Shura*) and promised that it would be converted to an elected body after about five years.[3] Nineteen members of

2   Jamri was born in 1936 and studied Islamic law at Najaf in Iraq. Following his return to Bahrain, he was elected to the National Assembly of 1973-75 and then served as a judge in the Shi'i *shari'a* court until 1988. He has been active in the opposition since 1992. Bahry, "Opposition in Bahrain," p. 56.

3   The *Majlis al-Shura* had been created in 1992, apparently in response to the presentation to the Amir of a petition calling for restoration of the National Assembly. Human Rights Watch/Middle East, *Routine Abuse, Routine Denial*.

the Council were Shi'i. Shaykh Hamad had begun already to draw a group of intellectuals around him to discuss changes, and around October he promised that there would soon be a national dialogue over the constitution. This period was also marked by a significant expansion of the freedom of speech and of the press. For the first time in decades, Bahrainis felt free to discuss political matters in public and the air was full of high spirits and talk of "democracy." The immediate consequence was to bring a quick end to confrontational and sometimes violent opposition activities.

The trust engendered amongst the general population by the new Amir was increased when he promised a return to the constitution of 1973 and created two committees to this end: one to draft amendments to the constitution to ready it for implementation and the other to prepare a national charter. An Amiri decree of November 23 appointed 46 members of a Supreme National Committee to prepare a draft charter that would spell out "the general framework of the future course of the state in the fields of national action and formulate the role of state institutions and their constitutional authority."[4] The deliberations of the committee to prepare the charter, headed by the Heir Apparent, Shaykh Salman bin Hamad, were transparent to the public. Initially, the government planned to have the charter approved by a popular forum of some two thousand carefully selected Bahrainis convened for this purpose. However, some members of the committee, believing this to be an attempt to give the appearance of a democratic regime without the substance, resigned from the committee. The government was thereupon forced to rethink the idea and devised the idea of a referendum.[5]

But as it turned out, the activities of the constitutional committee, headed by the Minister of Justice, Shaykh 'Abdallah bin Khalid Al Khalifa, and composed of seven ministers, were not transparent. The committee did not meet publicly and did not take into account any of the recommendations of the other committee or of the popular petitions.

The recommendations of the committees were made public on December 14 with announcement of a National Charter to reaffirm the constitutional premise of the government and to formulate certain amendments to the constitution (the charter is discussed more fully below). The charter proposed that Bahrain should become a constitutional kingdom and that a bicameral legislature should be established with one elected house and a

---

4   Reuters, November 23, 2000.

5   Interviews in Bahrain, January 2003.

second appointed one. Shaykh Hamad reaffirmed these provisions in his second National Day speech on December 16.

The public, however, wavered in its support of the charter and the Amir. The charter was uncomfortably vague about how the new parliament would be constituted, stating only that "the first council shall be formed through direct and free elections and shall have legislative attributes. The second council shall be appointed and shall comprise people of experience and competence who will offer their advice and knowledge when needed."[6]

A worried Amir agreed to meet with four leading Shi'i religious figures a week before the referendum. The meeting was held at the home of Sayyid 'Abdallah al-Ghurayfi, who had been exiled during the unrest, with Shaykh 'Abd al-Amir al-Jamri also present. The Amir looked over their list of demands, which included a demand that legislative power would belong to the elected body alone and that the function of the Consultative Council would be only consultation, and then signed the document. Copies of the document with the Amir's signature and photographs of him signing it circulated widely throughout the country. The Amir also promised to make his agreement public and the following day, the Minister of Justice made an announcement of reforms to be introduced. The Amir's son, Shaykh Salman, also affirmed the reforms in a press conference.[7]

Shaykh Hamad went to the homes of other religious leaders to discuss the proposed changes. Meetings were held nearly every day at his palace with groups of journalists, opposition figures, representatives of civil society, and former exiles. He even met with the leaders of the secular liberal movement, most of whom had been in extended exile, who went away convinced that they had been invited not to exchange views but were expected simply to listen to a summary of what he intended to do.[8]

The government took other measures as well to secure a positive vote. All of the political prisoners, numbering about a thousand, were released between December 2000 and the referendum and, in late January, all restrictions on the movement of Shaykh al-Jamri were lifted.

The organized opposition prevaricated on whether to oppose or support the charter but eventually advocated that the electorate, consisting of all male and female Bahrainis over the age of twenty, should vote yes. As a result, government fears of a less-than-convincing result were not realized

6   Text of the National Charter, as published in the *Bahrain Tribune*, December 21, 2001.
7   Interviews in Bahrain, January 2003.
8   Interviews in Bahrain, January 2003.

and the charter received a resounding 98.4 percent of the vote in favor of the proposed changes.

The victory of the referendum seemed to signal a significant change in the conduct of Bahrain's politics. The Prime Minister, Shaykh Khalifa bin Salman, announced during a cabinet meeting on February 18 that the government would abandon the State Security Law, enacted just before the National Assembly was suspended in 1975, and abolish the State Security Court. This had been one of the opposition's key demands and both the draconian law, which permitted long periods of detention without formal charges, and the court, which existed outside the judiciary system, had prompted widespread criticism from abroad.

A general amnesty announced on February 5 brought immediate results and nearly all exiles had returned, at least for a visit and to assess the situation personally, by the end of April. Among them was Shaykh ʻAli Salman, a young Shiʻi religious leader whose arrest in November 1994, while protesting the detention of Shiʻi villagers after runners in a marathon were stoned, had been a principal spark of the unrest. In addition, citizenship was granted to more than a thousand *bidun*, those people born in Bahrain but denied citizenship. For the following year, the situation seemed stabilized and the outlook positive. On February 14, 2002, Shaykh Hamad declared himself King of Bahrain and announced that municipal elections would be held on May 9 and parliamentary elections on October 24—an acceleration of the original timetable.

But the details of the new parliament revealed by the government at this time raised fresh misgivings and marked an end to the period of optimism. The enthusiasm for King Hamad shown in the first two years of his rule soon waned. In the end, the amended constitution (popularly derided as a "new constitution") was presented to the people as a given, rather than as an instrument to be discussed and negotiated. The vagueness of the bicameral representative body, as described in the National Charter and approved in the referendum, was translated into a bicameral legislature with an elected lower house and an appointed upper house.

The municipal elections were held as scheduled on May 9, 2002, with run-offs for closely contested seats on May 17. Initially, the two largest political organizations—al-Wifaq and the National Democratic Action Society—were undecided on whether to participate, although five other major groups agreed to field candidates despite their concern over the manner in which electoral districts had been created. The first elections in thirty-two years created great interest and a total of 306 people competed for the fifty seats, thirty of the candidates being women. About 51 percent of Bahrain's eligible voters elected an all-Islamist council with twenty-three Sunnis and twenty-seven Shi'is. No female candidates made it past the first round of voting. Despite the Islamist label, successful candidates appeared to be elected on individual merits without much organized party planning. [9]

The next step was parliamentary elections. Although political parties have never been legal in Bahrain, a number of *de facto* parties emerged at this time, calling themselves societies rather than parties. Most, but not all, were Islamist in character and there were both Sunni and Shi'i Islamist organizations. It should also be remembered that the lines were mixed even within the Islamist parties: as one political activist pointed out, his family is Sunni, his wife is Shi'i, and his sister participates in the Shi'i Islamist party al-Wifaq.[10] The principal political groupings in Bahrain included the following:

1. *Al-Wifaq (jam'iyyat al-wifaq al-watani al-islamiyya)*:[11] a Shi'i Islamist party that enjoys the largest support and dominates the Bahraini political scene. Its leader is Shaykh 'Ali Salman who had been forced into five years of exile in London.[12] Before the 1990s, elements of al-Wifaq operated clandestinely and were known as the Islamic Enlightenment. It has no known ties, past or present, to the Iranian government. Its decision to boycott the parliamentary elections was apparently necessary in order to avoid a split within the party.[13]

2. The *National Democratic Action Society* (NDAS; *jam'iyyat al-'amal al-watani al-dimuqrati*): the most prominent secular party with a mixed Sunni and Shi'i membership, headed initially by 'Abd al-Rahman al-Nu'aymi, a long-time leftist activist who spent thirty-three years in exile. Formed in April 2001, the NDAS sought to group all the leftist groups, including liberals, Ba'this, the Arab Nationalists' Movement (ANM), and Communists, under its umbrella, but the Communists and some other groups left after two months. It also boycotted the parliamentary elections.

9   On the elections, see Reuters, May 10, 11, 18, 2002; Associated Press (AP), May 12, 2002.

10   Interview in Bahrain, January 2003.

11   Its full name translates as the Islamic Society for National Unity.

12   Shaykh 'Ali Salman Ahmad Salman came from a poor Shi'i family and had received a fellowship to study at King Sa'ud University in Riyadh, Saudi Arabia, before pursuing theological studies in Qom, Iran. Interviews in Bahrain, January 2003.

13   Interviews in Bahrain, January 2003.

3. The *Nationalist Group* (*al-tajammu' al-qawmi al-dimuqrati*): a secular Ba'thist party made up of both Sunnis and Shi'is, with Dr Hasan al-'Ali as its vice-president.

4. *Islamic Action* (*jam'iyyat al-'amal al-islami*): the more outspoken of the Islamic Shi'i groups, headed by Shaykh Muhammad 'Ali Mahfuz. Shaykh Muhammad had headed the Islamic Front for the Liberation of Bahrain, which was active during the 1990s unrest from its base in Tehran and openly advocated the overthrow of the Al Khalifa.

5. *Al-Wasat* (*al-wasat al-'arabi al-islami al-dimuqrati*): an Islamic nationalist party, mostly Sunni, and including some Nasserists. It is headed by 'Abdallah al-Huwayri.[14]

6. *Islamic Platform* (*al-minbar al-watani al-islami*): a Sunni Islamist party regarded as being associated with the Kuwait al-Islah/Muslim Brotherhood party. Although Dr Salah al-'Ali is the declared president, its real head is said to be Shaykh 'Isa bin Muhammad Al Khalifa, a former Minister of Labor and Social Affairs and uncle of the King.

7. *Asalah*: a Sunni Islamist party linked to the *salafi* movement and headed by 'Adil al-Ma'awida. The party won six seats in the Council of Deputies (*Majlis al-Nuwwab*) and is regarded as pro-government.

8. The *Islamic League* (*al-rabita al-islamiyya*): a Shi'i Islamist group regarded as pro-government and headed by Muhammad 'Ali Sitri, the Minister of Municipalities and a member of the original National Assembly. It won three seats in the Council of Deputies, although it is believed that none of its members would have been elected if al-Wifaq had not boycotted the elections.

9. *Islamic Education* (*jam'iyyat al-tarbiya al-islamiyya*): a Sunni Islamist group seen as pro-government and headed by Khalid al-Mu'ayyad, a brother of the former Minister of Information, Tariq al-Mu'ayyad.

There exists, in addition, another Shi'i Islamist group headed by the journalist 'Abd al-Wahhab Jawad, but it follows a different Shi'i school from that of the Islamic League.

While these nascent parties appear to represent the full range of Bahraini political opinion, they remain more fluid than ideologically driven. The emphasis in Islamist parties, particularly the Shi'i groups, is not on replacement of the existing system but on ensuring that the system adheres to Islamic values. These are generally defined in such a way that cooperation is

---

14   Its full name translates as the Arab Islamic Democratic Middle Path.

readily maintained with liberals who espouse a relatively more "secularist" approach to politics. Because the concrete goals of both camps are broadly similar, they are able to sustain a loose coalition. The Sunni Islamist parties stand apart, generally speaking, in that they seem more accommodationist and are more predisposed to work with the government, which is dominated by Sunnis; indeed, their opponents claim that they are supported by the regime because they are more malleable and stand as a bulwark against the Shi'i majority.[15] What nearly all groups share is a conviction that so far Bahrain has seen only the beginning of acceptable change.

Throughout the year 2002, political debate in and among the parties centered on whether to boycott the elections on the principle that the new parliamentary system did not conform to the 1973 constitution as King Hamad had promised. On the one hand, there was considerable support for eschewing participation on the grounds of principle: if "the people" caved in on the question of the constitution at the beginning, the government would have "won" and would be free to change the rules of the game whenever it liked. On the other hand, by boycotting and thus remaining outside the parliament, the parties risked forfeiting their right to speak for "the people" and could find it impossible to enter the arena in the future. In the end, a coalition of the first four parties listed above, including the two biggest (al-Wifaq and the NDAS), chose to boycott.

The Consultative Council was dissolved on February 16, 2002, two days after King Hamad announced that parliamentary elections would be held in October. At the same time, he produced an amended constitution and minor changes to the country's flag. Then, on July 3, details of the new parliament's composition were released: the new parliament (al-Majlis al-Watani) would be composed of a 40-seat elected lower house (Majlis al-Nuwwab or Council of Deputies) and an upper house (Majlis al-Shura or Consultative Council) with 40 appointed members who could be drawn from the ruling family, former cabinet ministers and retired military officers. Candidates for office were required to be literate Bahrainis, male or female, and at least thirty years old. All Bahrainis over the age of twenty were eligible to vote, although the question of voting privileges for military personnel was deferred.[16] Another decree barred the societies from taking part in the elections, although this was later rescinded.

15   For similar reasons, the regime in Kuwait followed a strategy of supporting Sunni Islamists to counter the influence of the liberals.

16   Details were reported by Reuters, July 3, 2002.

As a consequence, al-Wifaq and three other parties jointly announced in September their intention to boycott the election. Thus the 190 individuals, including eight women, who registered as candidates were independents or drawn from other parties. Shaykh 'Ali Salman, the president of al-Wifaq, justified the action by claiming that "[d]ue to the nature of the new constitution, the parliament will be crippled and weak.... People would be more politically active if they were electing a parliament with full legislating and monitoring powers, but I believe participation will be low as can be seen from the number of candidates."[17] (More than 300 had registered as candidates for the municipal elections earlier the same year.) The King's concern was evident in a televised address a few days before the election when he urged voters to consider, "What shall fathers and mothers say to their sons tomorrow if we boycott the future?"[18]

In the end, some 53 percent of eligible voters participated, slightly more than the 51 percent recorded in the municipal elections. Nineteen members, including three running unopposed, won seats on October 24, while the other twenty-one seats were decided in run-off elections held a week later. Not surprisingly, because of the boycott, Sunni Islamists won about one-half of the total seats. Two women made it into run-off elections but did not gain seats. The King quickly appointed a new *Majlis al-Shura*, as well as a new cabinet with his uncle remaining as Prime Minister, and inaugurated the parliament on December 14. A Sunni Islamist, Khalifa al-Dhahrani, was elected speaker of the Council of Deputies.

There was an encouraging sign in 2006 when the largest of the opposition groups, al-Wifaq, and the next largest, the National Democratic Action Society (also known as al-Wa'd), announced their intention of participating in the November 2006 parliamentary elections, thereby reversing their boycott of the initial elections four years previously. It was a controversial decision, however, and some of al-Wifaq's hardliners split off to form al-Haq, a new rejectionist party. The atmosphere was further disturbed by the "Bandargate" affair. In September 2006, an employee of the Bahrain government, of British citizenship but of Sudanese origin, made public a collection of documents that detailed corruption within the government and pointed to government efforts to fix the parliamentary elections. Although the government denied the veracity of the documents and deported

---

17   Interview with Reuters, October 6, 2002. Al-Wifaq claimed to have received 50.28 percent of the votes in the municipal elections.

18   AP, October 21, 2002.

the employee, the affair confirmed opposition suspicions that the Al Khalifa and the regime would never allow free elections. The government took strong action to prevent discussion of the matter, including blocking the NDAS website.[19]

The Shi'i Islamist opposition did relatively well in the elections. Al-Wifaq captured eighteen of the total of forty seats in an election that saw an encouraging 72 percent of the electorate voting. On the other hand, no NDAS candidate was elected and the Sunni Islamist groups al-Asalah and Islamic Platform captured seven and five seats respectively. Sunnis outnumbered Shi'a in the final analysis by twenty-two to eighteen. One woman won a seat in the parliament when she faced no opposition in her constituency, but a prominent female activist running under the NDAS banner accused the government of rigging the results in her constituency and then quashing a legal challenge to the results. Al-Dhahrani was re-elected speaker of the Council of Deputies and the king appointed twenty Sunnis, eighteen Shi'a, one Christian, and one Jew to the upper house.[20]

The inauguration of the new parliament in 2002-3 had contributed to the emergence of an atmosphere in Bahrain that was undeniably calmer and more positive than it had been four years earlier. The unrest of the 1990s had shuddered to an uneasy halt. People were freer to express their opinions and to organize within limits. The government under the new king had responded to some of the grievances and addressed them with certain changes. But many underlying factors remained unresolved.

The political atmosphere was disturbed in October 2002 by the return of Col. 'Adil Fulayfil. Regarded by many in Bahrain as the most notorious official in the security forces and accused of being the forces' main torturer, Fulayfil had fled the country illegally on May 3, 2002, soon after allegations of extortion and embezzlement prompted an official investigation into his activities. Although he seemed to be comfortably esconced in Australia, where he made numerous property purchases, he made an equally abrupt return to Bahrain in late November. Once there, he was said to be quietly residing in his home and not under arrest.[21]

19   *Khalij Times* (Dubai), September 27, 2006; Reuters, October 15, 2006; AFP, November 3, 2006.

20   AP, October 17, December 4, 2006; AFP, October 17, November 29, 2006; Reuters, November 26, December 5, 2006; *Financial Times*, November 26, 2006; *Gulf News* (Bahrain), November 27, 2006.

21   Reuters May 5, 2002; *Gulf Daily News* (Bahrain), May 9, 2002 and August 9, 2002; Reuters, August 28, 2002; Human Rights Watch email of December 17, 2002; interviews in Bahrain, January 2003.

It is not clear whether Fulayfil's return was forced by the prospect of facing legal action in Australian courts or simply facilitated by the promulgation of Royal Decree 56/2002 on October 23. This decree granted amnesty to members of the security and intelligence services for acts taking place prior to the general amnesty decree of February 2001. To many, this appeared to be an attempt to prevent any action being taken against the security forces, regardless of the legality of their actions, including torture.[22]

No action was taken against Fulayfil in the following years and Ian Henderson even returned to Bahrain. Meanwhile, political activists continued to run afoul of the government both before and after the 2006 parliamentary elections. Several activists calling for a boycott of the election were arrested and other activists were detained in early 2007 on charges of publicizing the Bandargate affair. At the same time, demonstrations continued to take place from time to time, principally over economic problems and unemployment.

Given the lack of movement through the mid-2000s, it seemed to many that the fundamental problems of Bahraini politics had not really changed and that the dialogue for change had reached an impasse. It was uncertain how much the King was committed to true reform. Furthermore, his uncle, Shaykh Khalifa bin Salman, remained Prime Minister and in daily charge of many of the most important aspects of the government, the Al Khalifa retained their dominance of senior government positions, and the key complaint of corruption remained largely untouched. During the 1990s, nearly all walls in the Shi'i villages had been covered with graffiti, only to be quickly whitewashed or made illegible by the security forces. In the following decade, the graffiti were back with its terse exhortations of "No National Charter," "Death to Khalifa," and "Death to America."

Reformer or pragmatist: initial reforms and unresolved grievances

While democratic reforms in Bahrain have been significant since the accession of King Hamad, they have been limited and serious questions can be and are being raised about whether the process of reform will continue

---

22   Amnesty International press release, November 29 2002, online at http://web.amnesty.o rg/802568F7005C4453/0/80256AB9000584F680256C800054851C?Open&Highligh t=2,bahrain; Human Rights Watch letter to King Hamad of December 17, 2002, online at www.hrw.org/press/2002/12/bahrain1217ltr.htm; REDRESS letter to the Bahraini ambassador in Geneva, December 17, 2002, online at www.vob.org/english/e-main.htm; interviews in Bahrain, January 2003. At the same time, Ian Henderson's deputy, Shaykh 'Abd al-'Aziz bin 'Atiyatallah Al Khalifa, was promoted to the post of Governor of Manama. Interviews in Bahrain, January 2003.

in the future. Much of this speculation revolves around the personality and intentions of King Hamad himself. Is he a true reformer or simply a pragmatist? Is he committed to taking the risks to truly transform and democratize the Bahraini political system or has he taken just the minimum steps necessary to stabilize his state and ensure continued Al Khalifa rule in the same manner as before?

Those who regard him as a true reformer point to the real gains made to correct injustices and to seek the trust of the people. They point to his termination of the antiquated and uniquely Bahraini policy of exiling dissidents. He ordered the release of all political detainees, whose detention had been another unsavory feature of Bahraini politics for a century. Furthermore, he rescinded the draconian State Security Law and abolished the State Security Court, both organs of essentially political control. Under his reign, the long-time British head of security resigned and left the country, his deputy was moved to a post as governor, and the chief torturer, in the eyes of dissidents, abandoned his post after the initiation of an investigation into his financial affairs. One elected deputy remarked that ten or fifteen years ago, he was among those who felt that the system must be completely overthrown; now, however, he believed that change could be achieved within the system and that the process of change was only beginning.[23]

It can be argued that the wheels of change have slowed because King Hamad can only proceed slowly. Too much change too quickly risks spinning the process out of control. The legislative process in Bahrain is untested and the opportunities for mistakes and the degeneration of debate into personal antagonisms are numerous.

Furthermore, the King faces considerable opposition from the conservative majority of the Al Khalifa, who argue that King Hamad is in danger of repeating the mistakes of the 1970s when the government concluded that it was necessary to suspend the first parliament. Some family members—as well as other Al Khalifa allies—fear the loss of their privileged status and government jobs, not to mention the possible airing of murky financial dealings.

King Hamad must take into account the advice and concern of the leaders in Riyadh and Abu Dhabi with whom he is close. Bahrain is highly dependent on Saudi Arabia for the gift of much of its oil production, for the contribution to its economy made by the thousands of Saudis who cross the causeway to spend weekends in the island state, for the close military ties between the two countries, and simply because Saudi Arabia is a far

---

23   Interview in Bahrain, January 2003.

bigger and more powerful country with an intense and justifiable anxiety over what happens in its close neighbor. In addition, King Hamad was undoubtedly guided by his close personal relationship with Shaykh Zayid bin Sultan Al Nuhayan, the President of the United Arab Emirates and Amir of Abu Dhabi, who died in November 2004. King Hamad was a frequent beneficiary of Shaykh Zayid's largesse, and as Shaykh Zayid made no moves toward democratic representation in either Abu Dhabi or the UAE over the course of his long years of rule, it can be reasonably assumed that his counsel was conservative in this regard. Matters do not seem to have changed under his successor, Shaykh Khalifa bin Zayid.

Most importantly, the key constraint on the King's authority and freedom of action must be the continued presence of his uncle, Shaykh Khalifa bin Salman, as Prime Minister. Shaykh Khalifa has spent more than thirty years in this office strengthening his position, effectively running the country during the reign of his late brother Shaykh 'Isa, surrounding himself with loyal supporters, and shaping the personnel and structure of the government to suit his purposes. While, as heir apparent, King Hamad served as commander-in-chief of the armed forces, Shaykh Khalifa exercised control of the security forces through his control of the Ministry of the Interior. Much of the ire of the dissidents during the 1990s unrest, and before and after, focused personally on Shaykh Khalifa.

Others argue that King Hamad's motivations were, at best, mixed. King Hamad was fully aware that it was necessary to bring the unrest to an end and he sought to avoid inheriting the bad reputation of the past. He recognized the pressing need to make some changes, such as curbing corruption and granting limited freedom of speech. At the same time, however, he holds the same view as the Prime Minister on the need to control the country through the appointment of senior members of the Al Khalifa to key positions. This has prevented the reform program from seeing further light. True reform, as one opposition leader argues, requires sacrifices. The King must reach a firm decision on how to deal with the Prime Minister but he has done nothing, probably because of opposition from the family.[24]

There are some who would argue that King Hamad should be given the benefit of doubt; perhaps he genuinely did wish to institute reforms but did not have a clear idea of how far he wished to go; and he may have run up against stiffer opposition from his uncle Shaykh Khalifa than he had anticipated. They do not believe that King Hamad sees the present

---

24   Interview in Bahrain, January 2003.

developments as the final step; instead, he may have a more evolutionary process in mind.[25]

The impact of September 11, 2001 is also cited as a reason why further reforms may have been placed on hold. One Islamist leader argued that the genuine momentum for change might have led to further reform but September 11 had a negative impact, making the regime more cautious. The government contended that the world had changed and therefore there was no place for Islamists, and that "concessions" made to Islamists must be revoked. Taking the positive view that the international situation will not remain the same forever, this leader argued that the Islamist opposition believes it must work closely and cooperatively with the government for more reforms in the future.[26]

These positive views, however, are not universally shared and appear to constitute a minority opinion. Certainly, many Bahrainis have concluded that King Hamad is simply a pragmatist. They argue that he had no choice but to offer political concessions because Bahrain faced continuing unrest domestically and was isolated internationally. The demonstrations and violence had an undeniably serious and negative impact on tourism and the financial sector. Human rights supporters in Britain and other countries were successfully arguing their case in the media and threatening legal action against Bahraini officials and Ian Henderson, the head of security.

They further argue that the proof of a pragmatic strategy lies in the abrupt change of attitude between King Hamad's first eighteen months—when he took the initial steps to release prisoners and welcome back the exiles—and the subsequent period after the referendum was approved. During the first period, Shaykh Hamad was easily accessible and engaged in dialogue both at his palace and in the homes of opposition leaders. After the referendum, gaining an audience became nearly impossible and the constitutional changes and details of the new parliament were simply announced and not open to debate.

As one opposition leader put it, in the beginning the government needed to deal with the opposition and it was easy to meet with King Hamad. After the referendum, the government no longer needed to deal with the opposition and it became very difficult to see him. During the pre-referendum process, Shaykh Salman bin Hamad said in a meeting that perhaps only 51 percent of people would agree to the National Charter, demonstrating

---

25   Interview in Bahrain, January 2003.

26   Interview in Bahrain, January 2003.

the low expectations held by the government. But because the opposition threw their support behind the charter, it received a 98.4 percent approval. Afterwards, the opposition tried to get an audience with King Hamad and wrote letters to him in an attempt to discuss the constitution. "We did our best to cooperate with the government, to push for new changes," one opposition leader declared. "We wish to tell the government to listen and that the government still needs the opposition. We are the people who are needed to keep people under control." Instead of listening, he averred that the government takes no steps to keep crises from occurring. He drew a comparison with Morocco where changes have been much more significant: for decades there was no dialogue with the opposition, but then the government opened up and the head of the opposition was now Prime Minister; the government listened and did as people demanded. But the government of Bahrain still does not listen, he complained.[27]

Even Shaykh 'Ali Salman conceded that the government had made some corrections of mistakes of the past: (1) it eliminated the State Security Law; (2) it freed political prisoners; (3) it eliminated exile for opposition figures. He also saw other positive developments: (1) the right to organize as political or civil societies; (2) all those opposed to the regime over the past three decades have been allowed to return to Bahrain and to work overtly in Bahrain; (3) freedom of speech exists, as well as freedom of the press; (4) trade unions have been established; and (5) although the outcome of the October 24, 2002 election may be contestable, just the opportunity for people to go to the polls has created a new atmosphere. Even so, he maintained that this was only part of the story.[28] Another human rights activist remarked that people had paid the price for these positive developments over the years in opposing and applying pressure on the government. In his view, changes were the result of a purely pragmatic decision by King Hamad; he concluded that, after all, "that's politics and King Hamad played it well. We can credit him for the liberties but we still have to safeguard our constitutional rights."[29]

As a consequence, the atmosphere in Bahrain in 2003 and into 2004 was tinged with considerable disappointment. Violent confrontation appeared to have been consigned to the past but many of the essential reforms urged upon the government over the last thirty years were still no closer to be-

---

27   Interview in Bahrain, January 2003.

28   Interview in Bahrain, January 2003.

29   Interview in Bahrain, January 2003.

ing addressed. Bahraini youth may become more radicalized, particularly if unemployment continues unabated and little is done to redress discrimination against Shi'is, and this may entail a return to sporadic violence.

In the meantime, Bahrain's opposition remains uncertain and divided. While distinctions in some cases reflect the Sunni-Shi'i divide, as well as a divergence between Islamic and liberal ideologies, the fundamental differences largely flow from disparate assessments of King Hamad and his policies. Individual and party thinking tends to vacillate between the two poles of rejecting King Hamad's changes as inadequate and accepting them on faith that liberalization is and will continue to be an evolving process. In particular, heated discussion continues to swirl around a long list of specific grievances, the most important of which are summarized here.

1. *The National Charter.* Much of the opposition argues that the National Charter was ambiguous and conflicting but the people had no choice but to accept it: either they voted in favor in order to get rid of the State Security Law and Court and bring back the exiles, or they would be turning their back on change. Their choice boiled down to either remaining in a situation of oppression or trying their chances with a badly drafted document. The charter, they contend, put forward a promise to expand democratic participation and not simply to return to the 1973 constitution, a promise that King Hamad affirmed in writing.

Some members appointed to the Supreme Committee for the National Charter suffered disappointment from the beginning. They believed their function was to discuss and then write the charter. Instead, a completed charter was handed to them at the first meeting and they were expected to look it over and approve it. They wanted to examine similar charters in Morocco, Egypt, and elsewhere, and to incorporate relevant points into the Bahraini charter, but the government contended there was not enough time, since deliberations began on December 3 and the government intended to finish the work of the committee by December 16. In addition, the members were told that King Hamad and the National Charter should be empowered above the constitution. This prompted five members of the committee to resign.[30]

---

30 The other thirty-five were said to have remained on the committee because they feared the loss of business with the government or the loss of their jobs. The five who resigned were then victims of a government campaign to discredit them. When a Kuwaiti newspaper reported allegations against them, the five sued the paper in Kuwaiti courts and won. They were, however, unable to take any action in Bahrain. Interview in Bahrain, January 2003.

The opposition contended that the approval given the government by the referendum was for a return to the 1973 constitution at a minimum. Instead of making only two changes (renaming the country a kingdom and establishing a bicameral parliament), they charged that King Hamad had altered the 1973 constitution completely and done so without seeking the agreement or even the input of the people. Objections to the new system embodied in the National Charter arose because, first, it was enacted in an unconstitutional way and, second, it completely changed the constitution against the rights of the people.[31] Some of those who stood for election and won seats in the *Majlis al-Nuwwab* argued that their presence would enable them to work for changes to the new constitution. However, the chances of amendments being made successfully are slim, since any change requires the vote of a two-thirds majority of both houses combined.

2. *The amended or "new" constitution.* In the words of one activist, "the ruling family gave Bahrain the 1973 constitution but then they took it away. The people wanted a return to the 1973 constitution but they returned us to 1873."[32] The same activist remarked that he had been told by one of the King's advisors that King Hamad never believed in the 1973 constitution and that outsiders had forced it on Bahrain. But as heir apparent and Minister of Defense, King Hamad pledged in the opening session of the 1973 National Assembly to respect the constitution. Thus, the activist argues, he has accepted it and is bound by it. The King has used the charter as a way around the constitution in order to propose very limited amendments to his new "amended constitution" as it is officially termed.[33]

---

31   Interview in Bahrain, January 2003. The "Opinion on the Constitutional Issue" (draft, January 2003) prepared by a number of Bahraini lawyers concludes that "the referendum on the National Action Charter is a sort of political referendum that was intended to reflect the views of the people on these general thoughts and principles, and pave the way for reconciliation. But it certainly does not contain any legal rule of any legislative nature, particularly what might be interpreted as a mandate that empowers the Amir alone, to amend the constitution."

32   Interview in Bahrain, January 2003.

33   Interview in Bahrain, January 2003. The "Opinion on the Constitutional Issue" cited above quotes the 1973 constitution, article 104, clause (a) as stating: "Notwithstanding the provisions of Article (35) of this Constitution, for an amendment to be made to any provision of this Constitution, it is stipulated that it shall be passed by a majority vote of two-thirds of the members constituting the Assembly and ratified by the Amir." In addition, the opinion rejects the claim that "the document issued in February 2002 is an amended constitution in response to the public will expressed in the National Action Charter" because the Explanatory Memorandum to the 2002 Constitution states "that the National Action Charter resulted in repealing all the provisions contained in the 1973 Constitution."

3. *Constitutional monarchy.* The National Charter declared that "the time has now come for Bahrain to be among the constitutional monarchies with a democratic system that achieves the aspirations of its people for a better future," by implication like the United Kingdom and other European parliamentary states. Instead, Bahrainis point out that their king rules as well as reigns, the newly constituted parliament has little power, and the powers of the elected membership are equally balanced by the powers of the appointed upper house.[34]

As another opposition leader pointed out, Bahrain has not become a constitutional monarchy "like the great constitutional monarchies elsewhere in the world." Instead, the new constitution makes the legislature subordinate to the executive. It leaves all power in the hands of the king and the prime minister. No one can make a new law or stop a law being made unless the king and/or the prime minister agrees. This, it is contended, shows that there has been no real change.[35]

4. *The new parliament.* The powers of the new parliament have been circumscribed by comparison with the older National Assembly. Under the 1973 constitution, the National Assembly was to consist initially of 30 elected members and a maximum of 14 government ministers serving as *ex officio* members (similarly to Kuwait); the number of elected members was to rise to 40 during its second legislative term. Under the 2002 constitution, the National Assembly consists of the same number of 40 elected members but 40 members appointed by the government have replaced the 14 government ministers. Not only are the numbers of elected and appointed made equal but the president of the Consultative Council (the upper house) is given voting rights in case of a tie, thus providing a 51 percent majority for appointed representatives.

Originally, King Hamad promised that the appointed upper house would be purely consultative and legislative functions would be reserved for the elected lower house. Instead the two bodies together are considered

---

34   One opposition figure argued during a discussion with Shaykh Hamad on February 9, 2002 that Shaykh Hamad had no power to change the constitution. At first, Shaykh Hamad agreed. But then his Egyptian constitutional advisor intervened to say that while the right did not exist in the constitution, it derived from the assertion of the Supreme Committee for the National Charter that the charter empowered the ruler above the constitution. This assertion had been contained in a draft of the covering letter for transmission of the charter to Shaykh Hamad but, after some committee members objected, the letter was redrafted and another letter placing the National Charter under the constitution was sent in its place. Interview in Bahrain, January 2003.

35   Interview in Bahrain, January 2003.

to be the legislative body. In addition, any amendments to the constitution require a two-thirds majority of the combined houses. As one Bahraini lawyer puts it, "the 2002 Constitution's Parliament is no more than a modified version of the previous Consultative Council. The difference is only that one half is elected and the other half is appointed."[36]

Under the 1973 constitution, the government could suspend the parliament for two months but then was required to hold new elections. Under the amended constitution, the government can suspend the parliament for four months without elections but the King also has full discretion to postpone elections without any time limit if the government advises him that new elections should not be held. In addition, the 1973 constitution mandated that an audit bureau be created and made subordinate to the National Assembly. The 2002 constitution removed the bureau's function of reporting to the National Assembly, and a royal decree in July 2002 ordered the audit bureau to report directly to the King, thus removing the legislature's ability to monitor the state's financial affairs.[37]

It should be noted that not all Bahrainis are so critical of the parliament; in particular, not surprisingly, those elected to it are not. One of the Sunni Islamist deputies points out that the government is not part of the new parliament and it cannot vote even in the Consultative Council. In fact, all participants in the National Assembly are new, apart from the Speaker.[38] The new parliament was a positive development because small things could be changed from inside the Council of Deputies, even though the Consultative Council represented the old system and government.[39]

Another Sunni Islamist deputy remarked that reforms and democracy must be introduced gradually since the country was not able to absorb it fully all at once. This, he added, was the cause of the trouble in the 1970s with the confrontation in the National Assembly and the numerous strikes. The regime needed to become used to changes and to learn to trust the people. In his view, the essential and urgent problem is corruption, particularly because the government is a one-man show. Everyone likes freedom but it has its boundaries in order to assure that all can be free. "Freedom is like salt in the food: too little and it is tasteless, too much and it is inedible."[40]

36   Jalila Sayed Ahmed, draft commentary on "Constitutional Issues: Bahraini Women's Political Rights," January 5, 2003.
37   "Opinion on the Constitutional Issue."
38   Interview in Bahrain, January 2003.
39   Interview in Bahrain, January 2003.
40   Interview in Bahrain, January 2003.

Another Shi'i observer who disagreed with the opposition's decision to boycott the election argues that it is better to have an elected body that annoys, questions, and attacks the government as an opening step in a continuing process. Because of the boycott, he notes, the parliament is composed of very low quality people who, for example, demanded that the government change the parliament's laws without realizing that they had the power to do so themselves.[41]

5. *The uncertain legality of political parties.* Although restrictions on civil societies and the activities of sporting or social clubs have been relaxed, political parties are still forbidden. This is why political groupings employ the term "society" (*jam'iyya*) in their titles. Everyone knows the parties and what they stand for and the government generally tolerates their unofficial existence. However, this did not prevent the government from harassing the parties. Al-Wifaq held its first annual conference in January 2003 in defiance of the government's demand that it should not be called a conference because that denoted it was a political party. After al-Wifaq booked the Exhibition Hall for its conference, the government forced the hall's management to cancel the booking. The organization then arranged for and booked the hall of a sporting club, but again the government forced cancellation of the booking. The opening of the conference finally took place in the hall of the Medical Society, which was far too small to accommodate all the attendees, and most people listened to the speeches outside under a tent in light rain.

6. *The security services.* Bitterness remained deep over the continued unimpeded role of the Bahraini security forces. No action has been taken against any security official with regard to allegations of abuses during the uprising. As one activist noted, "Many [activists] were imprisoned simply for speaking up for their rights. Alright, they have been released. But those of us who were imprisoned for five years have been punished while those who committed the crimes of torture have not been punished."[42] Allegations of widespread use of torture continued to reverberate around the country.

Meanwhile, senior officers of the security forces have been rewarded. Ian Henderson retired to Britain with a medal from the government but has since returned. His deputy, Shaykh 'Abd al-'Aziz b. 'Atiyatallah Al Khalifa, has been promoted to minister of state. 'Adil Fulayfil returned without prosecution. Furthermore, as mentioned previously, Decree 56/2002 pro-

---

41   Interview in Bahrain, January 2003.

42   Interview in Bahrain, January 2003.

vided amnesty for members of the security services on an equal basis with opposition figures.

The composition of the security forces remains unchanged, with the Al Khalifa and their Sunni allies monopolizing command positions and a high proportion of the ranks consisting of non-Bahrainis. The United Nations High Commissioner for Human Rights, Mary Robinson, chided the King on this matter when she visited Bahrain in March 2002.[43]

The security services continue to operate in the same manner as before, although they are slightly less obtrusive. It could, however, be argued that this suited the purposes of the government by showing that public safety was endangered in the absence of tough measures, as for example in the 2002 New Year's Eve riots (discussed below).

7. *Corruption and the role of the ruling family.* There has been no change in the status of the ruling family, which largely remains above the law and continues to reap unfair economic benefit from the system. Tales abound of the top members of the family taking over nearby islands as their personal estates, owning hotels, shopping malls, and office buildings. Poorer members of the family earn a comfortable income through so-called "free visas": expatriate workers pay a fee of about $1,300 to an Al Khalifa to get a work visa, and then they must find their own jobs and continue to pay their sponsors $25 or $50 a month out of a salary that may not be more than $160. This contributes to a continuing climate of corruption at all levels of government.[44] Indeed, one opposition figure charges that the principal reason why the Al Khalifa and other government officials oppose democracy is that it threatens to expose their record of corruption.[45]

In addition, there seems to be increased prevalence of family members in government positions: in 2007, fourteen of the twenty-six ministers were from the Al Khalifa and they predominate in other recent government appointments.

8. *Continued discrimination against the Shi'is.* Many Shi'is argue that nothing has been done to alter their inferior social and economic situation. One activist pointed out that the village of Sitra is the poorest part of Bahrain and endured the most arrests during the unrest. After the release of

---

43   Reuters, March 3, 2002.

44   In this connection, the opposition hailed the arrest of a former general manager of a Bahrain bank on charges of corruption but reiterated its demand that 'Adil Fulayfil should also stand trial. *Gulf Daily News* (Bahrain), March 6, 2003.

45   Interview in London, January 2003.

the detainees in 1999, the people of Sitra carried King Hamad on their shoulders. Now the same people, he said, are angry: they are still poor and unemployed, and those that do have jobs receive a salary of only about BD 150 ($390) on which to maintain a family of five or more.[46]

Others cite figures to the effect that only 10 percent of the top 500 government positions are held by Shi'a (who form approximately 70 percent of the total Bahraini population), or that there is only one Shi'i among the approximately 40 under-secretaries, or that none of the 600 officers in the *Diwan al-Maliki* (King's Office) are Shi'i.[47] Indeed, it is held that the government actively encourages sectarian conflict for its own purposes by persuading Sunnis that the Shi'is threaten them and the system. While many Sunnis supported the demands and objectives of the mainly Shi'i-led unrest of the 1990s, they are said to have kept quiet in order to save their jobs or business prospects.[48]

9. *Naturalization policy.* It is alleged that the government is embarked on a substantial policy of naturalization of Arab Sunnis from Jordan, Syria, and Yemen—especially employees of the security forces and their families—in order to alter the sectarian balance.[49] Opposition figures have claimed more than 100,000 naturalizations, although the government contends that the total is 60,000, consisting mostly of Iranians long settled in Bahrain, the majority of whom are Shi'i.[50]

Bahrain's tentative liberalization: an assessment

There is no doubt that considerable progress was made in the first years of King Hamad's reign. But there remains widespread disappointment at the limited number and nature of changes he has instituted, and there is considerable doubt that further progress will occur in the foreseeable future. At best, Bahrain's political liberalization may be regarded as a work in progress. If another referendum were held today, undoubtedly the National Charter would not get anywhere near the 98.4 percent acceptance it once received. The opposition is determined to keep up both internal and external pressure on the government to carry through promises that it feels

---

46   Interview in Bahrain, January 2003.

47   Interview in Bahrain, January 2003.

48   One person pointed out that permission was required from the security forces for employment even in the private sector. Interview in Bahrain, January 2003.

49   Interview in Bahrain, January 2003.

50   Interview with senior Bahraini government official, Washington, DC, July 2007.

have been made but not kept. This resolve lay behind the announcement on March 3, 2003 that six parties (al-Wifaq, al-Wasat, Islamic Action, NDAS, Democratic Platform, and Nationalist Forum) had joined forces under a new "charter of unity" that underscored their opposition to the amended constitution.[51] Similarly, the parties talked of organizing a popular petition with 100,000 signatures to present to the government.[52] But efforts to publicize this effort and to collect signatures were stoutly resisted by the government, which arrested nineteen activists for conducting illegal activities and undermining the state and put fifteen of them on trial in May 2004. The societies were forced to abandon their campaign as a *quid pro quo* for the release of the activists.[53]

Three preliminary conclusions give concern for the future. First, parliament has not been particularly effective. An attempt to legalize the recognition of societies as political parties seems to have been inconclusive. Complaints continue to be voiced about the low quality of MPs. Islamist MPs have raised confrontational issues a number of times and succeeded on one occasion in obtaining the lifting of a ban on women driving while veiled. One of the few major tests of parliament's legitimacy and will to act independently vis-à-vis the government occurred in the first part of 2004 over the investigation into the handling of two government-managed pension funds. The Council of Deputies established a commission to investigate the problem, over the government's objections, and produced a lengthy report in January that detailed extensive mismanagement and corruption. Again over the government's objections, the ministers responsible for the funds were called before the house and questioned. The government succeeded in limiting the scope and duration of the questioning, and prevented the Prime Minister from appearing. The matter was effectively shelved, no one was punished, and the funds have remained in a precarious state, facing insolvency by 2007.[54]

Second, the passage of time without significant further change seems to confirm that King Hamad is simply a pragmatist. In other words, since he has control and he has peace, why should he go any further down the path to reform and change?

51   *Gulf Daily News* (Bahrain), March 3, 2003.

52   Interview in Bahrain, January 2003.

53   *Gulf News* (Dubai), May 3, 10, 13, 2004; Reuters, May 3, 2004; *Gulf Daily News* (Bahrain), May 4, 10, 15, 2004; BBC Online News, World Edition, May 6, 2004.

54   *Gulf News* (Dubai), January 4, 23; April 29; May 31, 2004; Abdulhadi Khalaf, "Bahrain's Parliament: The Quest for a Role," *Arab Reform Bulletin,* Vol. 2, Issue 5 (May 2004).

Third, developments in 2003-7 exhibited a growing division between the leadership of the opposition—relatively moderate and committed to working within the system—and younger, more radical elements, who pushed the envelope, demand more change immediately, and were less likely to listen to their leaders. Hardliners captured eight of eleven seats on the executive of al-Wifaq in the January 2004 elections.[55] Al-Wifaq's decision to participate in the 2006 elections provoked a formal split. Even more important, this period saw a growing number of incidents—some of them violent—including protests at the US embassy, attacks on policemen, Shi'i demonstrations against entertainment and the drinking of alcohol, the arrest of website organizers who were viewed as critical of the government, and actions against women's and human rights activists.[56]

These incidents suggest the possibility of a split between leadership and radical followers, particularly if widespread unemployment and discrimination against Shi'is continues, with a possible return to chronic violence and diminished control over the opposition. The incidents also indicate a return to hardline responses by the security services. The fear of a downward spiral back into violence may have prompted the King to replace the long-serving Minister of the Interior, Shaykh Muhammad bin Khalifa, with the chief of staff of the Bahrain Defense Forces in 2004. However, Shaykh Muhammad's departure from the scene was nearly inevitable in any case, given his age and poor health.

Bahrain's experience since 1999 has demonstrated that a sustained opposition movement with moderate goals and a willingness to enter into dialogue can achieve positive results. It has also confirmed the fundamental role that Islamists can and do play in guiding and orchestrating this opposition. Furthermore, Bahrain's Islamists have been quick to organize their efforts, to recruit support for their cause in the West, and to utilize the web, e-mail lists, and press contacts to present their case. They have also been very receptive to alliances with secular liberals and across sectarian lines. This, however, may be a phenomenon unique to Bahrain because of the long history of strife and anti-government agitation by most Bahraini communities.

At the same time, though, Bahrain's recent experience also illustrates the pivotal role played by traditional rulers and the continued strength

---

55   *Gulf News* (Dubai), January 9, 18, 2004.

56   AP, March 24, 2003; *Gulf Daily News* (Bahrain), October 5, 2003. Reuters, October 22, 28, 2003; *Gulf News* (Dubai), October 26, 2003; Reuters, 17, 18 December, 2003; *Gulf News* (Dubai), March 15, 2004; AP, March 24, 2004; *Gulf News* (Dubai), March 28, 2004. Reuters, March 18, 2004; *Gulf News* (Dubai), April 23, 2004.

of their positions. While Bahrain's opposition undoubtedly can rightfully claim success for obtaining the recent reforms enacted by the regime, they were presented more as concessions by the ruler and less as the restoration of rights of the people. In Bahrain, as elsewhere in the Gulf, the ruler's authority remains unhampered and the ruling family is still a privileged caste. Shortly after independence in 1971, Bahrain adopted its first formal constitution, formally declaring that sovereignty rested in the people, and established a freely elected parliament. Even after the recent reforms, Bahrain still has far to go to return to the promises of liberalization made some thirty years ago, let alone being transformed into a truly constitutional monarchy.

Bahrain in the context of change in the Gulf

The answer to the question posed at the beginning—whether King Hamad is a true reformer or simply a pragmatist—may lie in between. The real crux of the system of politics in the Gulf is whether ruling families will gradually loosen their control and acquiesce in the eventual emergence of constitutional monarchies. In recent years, the Gulf states have instituted practical moves to answer domestic demands and international pressure— for example, the restoration of the National Assembly in Kuwait and the establishment of the appointed Consultative Council in Saudi Arabia.

However, moves toward liberalization and greater participation essentially are presented as "gifts" of the ruler. In no cases have rulers given up total authority over finances, defense, the media, and the interior. The closest to such change is Kuwait where the National Assembly has exercised its ability to contest government decisions, including arms purchases and financial questions.

Pressures for change are growing throughout the Gulf. Demographic pressures and rising unemployment threaten to alienate youth in most GCC countries. Corruption and abuses by members of ruling families are causes of complaint in every country. Liberals criticize regimes for not permitting participation in decision-making and more personal freedoms. Islamists attack corruption and deviance from Islamic values. Economic stagnation has been the norm—mitigated only by the bounty provided by high oil prices—and true economic development is stymied by top-heavy governments run by aging rulers and self-absorbed families.

In the short run at least, it is likely that Islamists will be the major beneficiaries of political liberalization throughout the Gulf. In Saudi Arabia, the decade-plus since the 1991 Gulf War has produced a number of highly vocal Islamist opposition figures and most observers believe that Islamists would dominate any elected Consultative Council.[57] A close observer of the UAE political scene estimates that if full elections were held for the Federal National Council, Islamists would comprise some two-thirds of the body. Together with tribalists who would probably win half of the remaining seats, they would form an anti-American alliance of perhaps 90 percent.[58]

Most prominent Islamists have focused on demands for reform and not revolution. There is a wide variety of groups and beliefs in the Gulf states. Extremists, where they exist, are in a tiny minority, and widely condemned even by other Islamists.[59] Most Islamist groups—whether Salafi, al-Islah/ Muslim Brotherhood, or Shi'i—are committed to working within the system. A prominent Islamist in Qatar, jailed for three years for submitting a reform petition to the Qatari *Majlis al-Shura* and refusing to apologize for it, declares that he will petition again when the time is right and risk another imprisonment. He has no objections to joining cause with other, non-Islamist, groups in future petitions.[60]

The growth of Islamist groups in Bahraini politics has been driven in part by sectarian divisions, which lead political organization to take the form of Islamist parties. Shi'i Islamist groups spearheaded the opposition during the 1990s and form some of the most important political groupings today, while Sunni Islamist groups have emerged partly in response to the challenge they see from the Shi'i groups. Kuwait's ruling family also supported Islamists to counter the liberals. But in recent years, the government has become alarmed by Islamist strength, although it is too weak to confront them.[61] It should be noted that Islamist groups in Kuwait and Bahrain diverge on many issues. Bahraini Islamists believe that women should

---

57   This belief has been prevalent at least since the 1980s. Interviews in Saudi Arabia, December 1985.

58   Interview in the UAE, January 2003.

59   In a press conference after his election to the new parliament, Shaykh 'Adil al-Ma'awida, the head of al-Asala in Bahrain, denied that Bahraini Islamist groups had any ties to extremists, noting that he had visited Afghanistan during the period of the Taliban and al-Qa'ida but did not agree with their philosophy because they held "apostate ideas to which we are opposed." In his words, "We look like them, but do not belong to them," adding, "When the United States supported them, we in Bahrain set up youth camps and spoke against the apostates and their apostasy. ... Some people were happy for what happened on 11 September, but we were sad." *al-Hayat* (London), November 1, 2002.

60   Interview in Qatar, January 2003.

61   Interviews in Kuwait, January 2003. As a consequence of growing Sunni Islamist power, the government has courted Shi'i Islamists as a counter.

participate fully in politics and society, in contradistinction to Kuwaiti Islamists. Bahrainis are not so doctrinaire in their insistence on application of
the *shari'a* and Kuwaiti Islamists would not ally themselves with socialists
and leftists as the Bahraini groups have.[62]

In the end, the path to democracy in the Gulf is far more tortuous and
uncertain than is often considered. Liberalization has been evident nearly
everywhere, but often with such slow progress that it seems impercepti-
ble. For the GCC states, the unanswerable question is whether this slow
advance will suffice to mollify increasingly impatient citizens. The answer
lies more in the resilience of and modifications to the relationship between
ruler and ruled than in strategies imposed from the outside.

---

62 Interview in Bahrain, January 2003. The Bahraini political commentator Ibrahim Bashmi
    explained the domination of the political arena by Islamists by saying they "have been
    closer to the people; they have the mosques, the charities and the ability to influence
    people with all their talk of the Holy Quran." On the other hand, he explained that the
    liberals have been "absent" since the National Assembly was dissolved in 1975. "They
    isolated themselves. They were alienated and people could no longer understand what
    they were talking about because younger generations have been influenced by the rise of
    Islamism with the Iranian revolution and other religious movements." *Gulf Daily News*
    (Bahrain), October 27, 2002.

8

QATAR: LIBERALIZATION AS
FOREIGN POLICY

Elisheva Rosman-Stollman

Since assuming power in a bloodless coup in 1995, Amir Hamad bin Khalifa Al Thani has taken a number of steps toward democracy in Qatar, the most publicized being the municipal elections in March 1999. Many observers have seen these steps as the Amir's attempt to embark on a program of democratization, but is this indeed the case?

As will be demonstrated, upon close examination, each of the major changes that Shaykh Hamad has initiated fits into a pattern of cosmetic reforms. These gestures look promising when seen through the eyes of Western media and governments, and are not too disturbing to the Qatari people, but result in little long-term effect. On the other hand, these steps usually generate a stir in the Gulf itself and sometimes in the Arab world at large—possibly the only effects the Amir hopes to achieve.

This chapter will present Shaykh Hamad's reforms and examine the reasons for them and their effects. It will also try to assess whether these are substantive changes, designed to begin a new era of more open and democratic rule in Qatar, or merely a way of "making waves" and attention-getting in a region composed of monarchies.

When studying the period since the 1995 coup in Qatar, one can detect two main types of change: the introduction of popular participation in government; and legislation affirming human rights and political freedoms. Assuming that Shaykh Hamad's policies indicate democratization, or at least the appearance of democratization, it seems that he has accepted a wide definition of democracy, measured by the existence of free and equal political participation and representation; fair, honest and periodic elections; and freedom of expression and association.[1] Accordingly, as will be illustrated below, regarding the participation aspect, the Amir began the democratization process by introducing a certain measure of participation in government through the establishment of an elected municipal council and a permanent constitution. Changes in the area of human rights and freedoms included promotion of women's rights, freedom of expression and cultivating dialogue with human rights organizations.

Before analyzing the situation in Qatar, it is important to point out that in many ways this amirate is a unique entity in the Gulf. Doha does not need to worry about its economic future and the country is, relatively, ethnically and religiously homogenous, with no opposition to the ruling family.[2] This places Qatar in a situation where internal pressures are not as great as those in other countries in the vicinity. Not having to deal with internal pressure and problems most probably allows the Amir more freedom in the initiating and implementing of reforms.

The Amir has also taken steps toward privatization and minor economic reform.[3] When discussing democratization in the Gulf states at large, most scholars note that economic liberalization in the Gulf is an important factor. Since the Gulf monarchies seem to follow the "no taxation without representation" rule, the drop in oil reserves tends to upset the informal social contract in these countries.[4] However, compared to its neighbors,

---

1   Following the classification suggested by Gabriel Ben-Dor at the conference in honor of Bernard Lewis, "Democracy, Liberalization and Civil Society: Israel, the Middle East and Islam," Jerusalem, February 18, 2003. This is a very condensed definition; a more detailed one can be found in Samuel P. Huntington, *The Third Wave: Democratization in the Late Twentieth Century* (Norman: University of Oklahoma Press, 1991), pp. 5-10. Indeed, the characteristics stated may be seen as the indicators of "Western" democracy, which many see as incompatible with Muslim societies such as that of Qatar. However, as this chapter claims that part of the motivation for democratization in Qatar is that country's wish to be perceived as a democracy in the eyes of the West, such indicators are relevant and may be used. This does not mean to imply that only one model of democracy exists, but rather that certain characteristics must exist in order for a given regime to be considered a democracy. It is also worth noting that in order to escape problems of imprecision and misinterpretation, the definition this paper adopts is a procedural one, following Huntington's lead (*Third Wave*, p. 6).

2   See chapter on Qatar in Anthony Cordesman, *Bahrain, Oman, Qatar and the UAE: Challenges of Security* (Boulder, CO: Westview, 1997), pp. 213-89.

3   See Andrew Rathmell and Kirsten Schultze, "Political Reform in the Gulf: The Case of Qatar," *Middle East Studies*, Vol. 36, No. 4 (October 2000), pp. 53-5.

4   For a detailed explanation of this idea see: Joshua Teitelbaum, "Bahrain, Qatar and the UAE: Tradition in the Service of the Present and the Future," in Joseph Kostiner (ed.), *The Gulf States: Politics, Society, Economics* (Tel Aviv: Moshe Dayan Center for Middle Eastern and African Studies, 2000), pp. 37-9, in Hebrew.

Qatar has not suffered economically.[5] Its oil reserves remain relatively high[6] and its natural gas reserve (the North Field) provides it with another source of income. Although these natural resources are finite, they allow Qatar more economic security than many of its neighbors and promise that Qatar will remain wealthy, at the very least in the near future.[7]

On the other hand, due to a certain amount of privatization that has also begun to take place,[8] the Qatari market took a significant plunge in 2004.[9] This result was to be expected and analysts predict that the market will revive substantially in the next few years. For example, in its recent synopsis of the Qatari economy, the Second Al Iktissad Wal Aamal Group concluded that "Qatar is on track to become the largest exporter of LNG [liquid natural gas] by 2010 and oil production is planned to rise."[10] In other words, Qatar should not encounter financial trouble in the near future. For all these reasons, when searching for motivation to democratize, in the case of Qatar the changing economic atmosphere cannot be regarded as a deciding factor.

GCC countries' leaders understand that making themselves more attractive to the West holds economic benefits, and that liberalization may be their only hope for retaining power; however, economic reform in these countries[11] has not been accompanied by sweeping political reform.[12] Addi-

5   Although Qatar has begun to cut subsidies and taken certain steps to cut costs in government, it still has not felt the true bite of economic troubles. See Joshua Teitelbaum, "Qatar," in Bruce Maddy-Weitzman (ed.), *Middle East Contemporary Survey (MECS), Vol. 22:1998* (Boulder: Westview Press, 2001), pp. 518-19.

6   See, for example, a report on the surge in oil reserves in the Gulf which emphasizes Qatar's salutary position: *Gulf News* (Dubai), July 9, 2003.

7   Cordesman, pp. 236-56.

8   See for example *Gulf News* (Dubai), May 25, 2003. For further details on the process in the petroleum industry, see also Abdullah Bin Hamad Al-Attiyah, "Speech of H.E. Abdullah Bin Hamad Al-Attiyah, Minister of Energy and Industry, Chairman of Industries Qatar, on the Introductory Meeting for Industries Qatar Company" (May 4, 2003) (http://www.qp.com.qa/qp.nsf/0/2929691cac19cd4a43256d1c0061384c?OpenDocument).

9   SHUAA Capital, *Insight: Gulf Capital Markets* (May 2005), pp. 3-4. (http://www.shuaacapital.com/shuaacapital/uploads/publications/SHUAA(SHUAA%20Capital%20INSIGHT)(1646).pdf).

10 Al Iktissad Wal Aamal Group, *Second Qatar Economic Forum: Synopsis* (May 2007) (http://www.iktissad.com/events/QEF/2/synopsis). For a similar predication: SHUAA Capital, *Insight: Gulf Capital Markets* (May 2005), p. 7. (http://www.shuaacapital.com/shuaacapital/uploads/publications/SHUAA(SHUAA%20Capital%20INSIGHT)(1646).pdf).

11 For example, on January 1, 2003 the GCC launched the pan-GCC Common External Tariff (5 percent) and Customs Union. John Duke Anthony, "Qatar's Heightened Profile," *GulfWire Perspectives*, October 27, 2002 (http://www.arabialink.com/GulfWire/GWP_2002_10_27.htm).

12 For a listing of economic reforms in the Gulf see Rathmell and Schultze, pp. 47-62.

tionally, as Rathmell and Schulze point out, there is little evidence linking economic and political reforms in the Gulf and in Qatar in particular.[13] For these reasons, this study will concentrate on the political aspect of the Qatari reforms and will not examine the economic liberalization aspect.

Popular participation

The Central Municipal Council. In his first step toward popular participation, in November 1997, the Amir announced the creation of the Central Municipal Council (CMC). The Council was to have twenty-nine members who would hold office for four years. Its mandate was to oversee application of the decisions and laws of the Ministry of Municipal Affairs and Agriculture, and to advise the ministry regarding issues of food and public hygiene.[14] Voter registration began in October 1998, but response was far from overwhelming. Only 22,000 citizens, out of 46,000 eligible voters, registered.[15] The lack of enthusiasm might have been caused by the fact the council was not granted real authority and its decisions were to be considered "recommendations," with no binding power.[16] Another reason could be that the older generation of citizens did not want to participate in the decision-making process, preferring the current political arrangement between citizens and government.[17]

Free municipal elections were held in Qatar for the first time on March 8, 1999. Women were allowed to vote and stand for election.[18] Of the 227 candidates, six were women, although none of the women were elected to office.[19] Voter turnout was almost 80 percent; however, it should be stressed that, as noted, less than 50 percent of those eligible to vote actually registered and members of the armed forces and police were not allowed to vote.[20]

---

13   Rathnell and Schultze, pp. 47-62.

14   *Middle East Times* (Egypt), March 7, 1999.

15   Teitelbaum, "Qatar," *MECS 1998*, p. 514. The population of Qatar is estimated at about 800,000 people. See CIA Factbook, "Qatar," (http://www.cia.gov/cia/publications/factbook/geos/qa.html#People).

16   *Middle East Times*, March 7, 1999.

17   Teitelbaum, "Qatar," *MECS 1998*, p. 514.

18   Qatar Ministry of Foreign Affairs website, November 2002 (http://english.mofa.gov.qa).

19   *ArabicNews.com*, March 9, 1999. A woman became a member of the CMC in March 2003 after her opponent, her cousin, withdrew his nomination. See *The Peninsula* (Doha), March 5, 2003.

20   Teitelbaum, "Qatar," in Bruce Maddy-Weitzman (ed.), *MECS 1999* (Boulder: Westview Press, 2001), p. 499. Perhaps as a result of the lack of participation, the Amir announced that all government schools would elect their own student councils and almost all students participated in these elections in October and November 1999.

Nevertheless, neighboring countries felt threatened by this step, especially Saudi Arabia.[21] The elections seem to have caused discomfort in the Arab world. In contrast to enthusiastic Western reporting, Arab media coverage attempted to minimize the meaning and impact of the elections. For example, the Egyptian daily *Al-Ahram* was careful to note that the "council itself has no real power."[22] The *Middle Eastern Times* noted that the elections were not "so much a result of public pressure, of which there is none or very little, but because the Emir...feels that the introduction of a limited form of democracy could be more beneficial to the long-term development of his country."[23] It was also noted that twenty-two Islamic scholars had petitioned the Amir not to enfranchise women and that he rejected the petition, saying that Islam did not discriminate against women.[24]

In practice, when the fanfare of the elections dissipated, it seems that the members of the CMC took their positions quite seriously. Thinking they would have the ability to bring about change, they began fighting for executive power almost immediately and succeeded partially in June 2002.[25] Frustrated by a lack of power, members of the CMC voiced their complaints to the press and were not content to sit at their desks and do what was obviously expected of them: to look like a democratically elected committee and keep their collective mouth shut. As their term came to a close, most CMC members did not seek reelection, because of their feeling that "the body is practically without any executive powers."[26] This implies that contrary to expectations, Qataris, at least those who bothered to participate either as candidates or voters, believed their ruler intended to adopt some form of democracy and were therefore disillusioned when the CMC did not live up to hopes for it.

The second elections for the CMC were held in April 2003. Only ninety-three candidates registered, far less than the number of candidates in the first elections.[27] Electoral participation was estimated at 25-40 percent.[28] Although these elections were barely mentioned in the foreign media, they

21   *Alexander's Gas and Oil Connection*, Vol. 4, No. 12 (June 20, 1999).
22   *Al-Ahram* (Egypt), March 11, 1999.
23   *Middle East Times* (Egypt), September 27, 1998.
24   *Middle East Times* (Egypt), September 27, 1998.
25   *The Peninsula* (Qatar), June 3, 2002.
26   *The Peninsula* (Qatar), October 5, 2002.
27   *The Peninsula* (Qatar), June 1, 2003.
28   The percentage depends on the source of the estimate see: *ArabicNews.com*, April 8, 2003; *Gulf Times* (Qatar), April 8, 2003.

were indeed held at a regular interval (four years) and in accordance with the law. In other words, despite obvious problems, the CMC entered its second term of office in what seem to be fair, honest and periodic elections. This had no precedent in Qatar.

While it may seem that the CMC and the elections are a significant step toward democracy, it appears that this reform was engineered from above with little input or response from below. Had the CMC indeed been a concrete step in building democracy, one would have expected to see higher voter participation and not such a drastic drop in the number of candidates. It seems that Qataris did not see any real point in participating in the democratic "game," whether because they had little or no wish for democracy, or out of disillusionment with the actual democratic product they observed. The Amir did not grant the council tangible power, indicating that he himself did not intend to share power with the people. The fact that the second elections received little foreign coverage highlights that the Amir had no incentive to publicize the fact that Qatar could boast free and periodic elections. Once the West was aware of elections taking place and the Amir reaped the publicity dividend, there was no need to remind the world that Qataris were not truly participating in government and those who were, were not satisfied with the results.

The permanent constitution. The second aspect of popular participation was the drafting of a permanent constitution. Qatar's first constitution was issued in 1970, before independence, and amended after independence in 1972.[29] In July 1999, the Amir appointed a thirty-two-member committee to set up an elected council under a permanent constitution.[30] The committee was chaired by 'Abdallah bin Salih al-Khulayfi, the dean of Qatar University, a US-educated economist. The committee was instructed to submit its conclusions to the Amir within three years.[31] When establishing the committee, the Amir announced that the constitution "must be based on Gulf, Arab and Islamic reality, as well as on original Arab traditions and the principles of the Islamic religion."[32] It seems such a statement was directed more toward a Gulf audience, trying to soften a step perceived as threatening, but also highlighting the fact it was taking place. Shaykh Hamad was effectively telling his neighbors that he realized they would be

---

29   Qatar Ministry of Foreign Affairs website, November 2002 (http://english.mofa.gov.qa).

30   Ibid.

31   *ArabicNews.com*, July 14, 1999.

32   *ArabicNews.com*, November 10, 1999.

unhappy with this action but it would take place nevertheless, portraying it as a truly traditional step and placing them in a negative light.

As promised, in July 2002, a written draft of a permanent constitution was submitted to the Amir for approval.[33] The constitution finalized succession laws in the amirate (articles 8-13, 16) and also stated that a "Ruling Family Council," composed of members of the royal family, would be appointed by the Amir, composed of members of the royal family (articles 14-15). It did not elaborate on the role of this council. In practice, such a council already exists: the Amir established the "Council of the Reigning Family" in July 2000. He heads the council while the heir apparent serves as vice chair. The council includes thirteen more, mostly younger, members of the ruling family, who approve of the Amir's reforms.[34]

The Amir's powers are described in detail in Articles 67-75. In dealing with separation of powers, the constitution states that the executive wing is to be headed by the Amir, the legislative authority will be given to an Advisory Council and the judiciary is to be independent, although "all verdicts shall be issued in the name of the Amir." (Article 63) The draft also upheld freedom of speech (including the press) (article 47-8), freedom of economic activity (article 28), freedom of worship (article 50) and freedom of assembly and association (articles 44-45), although political parties are still prohibited.[35]

The constitution announced the establishment of a parliament (*Shura*, Advisory Council—AC), comprising forty-five members, two-thirds of whom would be elected by popular vote, and prescribed the criteria for eligibility for membership, the manner of election, the rights and duties of the AC, and its general conduct (articles 76-116). The Amir may dissolve the AC at will, although he must state a reason for his decision and "it is not permissible for the council to be dissolved for the same reason twice" (article 104). Elections for a new council must be held within six months of the dissolution.

The constitution also included articles on human rights, banning torture and unlawful imprisonment (article 36), and adopting the principle of innocent until proven guilty in a fair trial (article 39).

---

33   The draft also appeared in the local press when it was voted upon by the general public. For the English translation see: http://www.thepeninsulaqatar.com.

34   Teitelbaum, "Qatar," in Bruce Maddy-Weitzman (ed.), *MECS 2000* (Boulder: Westview Press, 2002), p. 485.

35   *Arab News* (Saudi Arabia), April 30, 2003.

The Amir approved the draft, but only in April 2003 did Qataris themselves have the opportunity to endorse the constitution in a referendum. In order to encourage Qataris to vote on the subject, probably in consideration of their record in both previous CMC elections, seminars were organized and local papers publicized remarks by various ministers and public figures calling on citizens to participate.[36]

The campaign culminated the night before the vote, when in a televised address the Amir urged Qataris to participate in the referendum. Shaykh Hamad emphasized that the idea of "consultation" (*shura*) is an original Arab and Islamic idea.[37] The Amir also declared that

there is a critical and urgent need in our Arab and Muslim *umma* to practice these principles [of dialogue, consultation and deliberation between leaders]. Had popular participation, consultation institutions, democracy and the principles of social justice been prevalent, the condition of the *umma* [Islamic Nation] would not have arrived at where they are now. Our states and societies would have been able to practice their influence in the international community with credibility and effectiveness, emanating from the citizen's pride in belonging to his homeland and his aspiration for a better future in [the] planning and forming of which he participates.[38]

Appealing to common feelings in the Arab world regarding the "unjust decline of the *umma*," this speech was probably directed toward the older generation of Qataris who had so far been unwilling to take part in the democratic process. At the same time, such phrases were doubtlessly aimed at a greater audience than the Amir's subjects. The idea that democracy is the key to returning the *umma* to its original greatness places the democratically-inclined Amir within the Islamic fold and his opponents outside it. Qatar is not rebelling against the norms of the Arab world, but is rather the voice of reason calling to return the *umma* to its rightful greatness.

On April 29, 2003, the day of the referendum, the Foreign Minister was interviewed after casting his vote. He praised the Amir for taking this step, saying that "political stability and democracy in any country, especially when institutions are placed into an appropriate legal framework" would enhance Doha's international position.[39] The Foreign Minister was asked whether the step would have ramifications for the rest of the region

---

36   See, for example, the article on a seminar held by the Ministry of Justice and remarks on the subject by the Minister himself: *The Peninsula* (Qatar), April 23, 2003; remarks by the Minister of Civil Service Affairs and Housing, *The Peninsula* (Qatar), April 28, 2003.

37   *Arab News* (Saudi Arabia), April 30, 2003.

38   Text of the Amir's speech as translated in *The Peninsula* (Qatar), April 29, 2003.

39   *The Peninsula* (Qatar), April 30, 2003.

and noted that "any country has the right to take the decision it deems appropriate for it, provided that such a decision would not harm other countries."[40] Being quoted in an English-language paper ensured that this statement, as well as the Amir's speech given the previous night, would attract Western attention.

According to an enthusiastic local press, approximately 96 percent of the voters endorsed the constitution,[41] and the Western world voiced its approval. Western media covered the vote on the constitution in Qatar,[42] and various prominent Western officials praised Doha.[43] The Amir finally promulgated the constitution in June 2004,[44] and it came into effect in June 2005.[45]

In another important move, the Amir issued a new labor law allowing the creation of workers' associations (*tanzimat*).[46] Although these associations are prohibited from "any activity related to religion or politics" (article 119.1), workers' unions may be able to utilize their power in matters that are not only work-related. Perhaps as the "societies" in Bahrain did (see Peterson's chapter in this volume), the associations could one day evolve into political parties. However, only Qataris are allowed to join such associations and only a workplace with at least 100 Qatari workers is allowed to create an association (article 116). Since most of the workforce is composed of expatriates, it will be interesting to see if associations will indeed be created and in what occupations. In any case, the majority of workers will still be unprotected by the associations, although the law does allow for the creation of joint committees of all workers and employers to negotiate work terms (articles 124-127). The new law was scheduled to take effect in November 2004,[47] and was finally promulgated in May 2005.[48] By the end of 2007, a number of associations were formed, despite

---

40   *The Peninsula* (Qatar), April 30, 2003.

41   Qatar News Agency (QNA - Arabic), April 30, 2003 (http://www.qnaol.com).

42   See for example CNN coverage: *CNN.com*, April 27, 2003.

43   See for example *The Peninsula* (Qatar), 21 April, 2003; *Washington Post*, April 30, 2003.

44   *Al-Watan* (Qatar), June 9, 2004.

45   Carnegie Endowment for International Peace, *Arab Political Systems: Baseline information and Reforms – Qatar* (July 2005), p. 2. (http://www.carnegieendowment.org/files/Qatar_APS.doc#_Toc106983994).

46   For an English translation of the new law, see: *The Peninsula* (Qatar), May 20, 2004.

47   *Al-Watan* (Qatar), May 20, 2004.

48   Carnegie Endowment for International Peace, *Arab Political Systems: Baseline Information and Reforms – Qatar* (July 2005), p. 8. (http://www.carnegieendowment.org/files/Qatar_APS.doc#_Toc106983994).

bureaucratic difficulties. These include the fishermen's association, the musicians' association and the journalists' association.[49]

Although elections were scheduled for the end of 2004, and later for 2005, no steps toward constructing the AC have been taken and the Amir continues to rule as before. As will be demonstrated below, many freedoms endorsed by the constitution do not exist in practice and there is still no independent judiciary. These points indicate that the constitution is also primarily a "photo-opportunity" reform, although it has potential to evolve into something more concrete.

Human rights and freedoms

In the sphere of human rights and freedoms, it seems the Amir has decided to focus on three main points: freedom of expression, women's rights, and establishing ties with human rights organizations. These three areas of change are highly visible and results were evident almost immediately.

Al-Jazeera satellite channel and freedom of expression. Shortly after taking power, Shaykh Hamad disbanded the Ministry of Information, in effect abolishing censorship in the amirate. The founding of the al-Jazeera satellite channel also marked a boost in freedom of expression as it is portrayed as an independent channel and frequently causes international and inter-regional tension by its critical coverage of various countries, particularly the US and Israel. Despite its alleged autonomy,[50] the royal family is the major shareholder of the channel. Al-Jazeera does not normally criticize the Qatari government, accepting that such a step would most probably have an adverse affect on the channel.[51] It does, however, criticize other Arab regimes, causing much resentment in the Gulf and the Arab world.[52]

The Qatari regime seems to have benefited from its claim that al-Jazeera is merely practicing its right of freedom of expression. The Qatari Foreign

49   US Government, Country Reports on Human Rights Practices: Qatar, 7 March 2007 (http://www.state.gov/g/drl/rls/hrrpt/2006/78861.htm). See also Al Jabar, website of the journalists' association (under construction): http://www.aljaber.net.

50   In an interview, the Qatari Foreign Minister reiterated that al-Jazeera "does not reflect public policy in Qatar." See Louay Bahry, "Interview with Foreign Minister of Qatar, HE Sheikh Hamad bin Jassem bin Jabr Al-Thani," *Middle East Insight*, Vol. 5, No. 5 (2000).

51   Bahry, pp. 118-27.

52   John Duke Anthony, "Qatar's Heightened Profile," *GulfWire Perspectives* (October 27, 2002) (http://www.arabialink.com/GulfWire/GWP_2002_10_27.htm). For a description of various hurt parties in Jordan, Kuwait, Iraq, Libya and the Palestinian Authority see Joshua Teitelbaum, "Qatar," *MECS 1998*, p. 516; Joshua Teitelbaum, "Qatar," *MECS 1999*, p. 503; Joshua Teitelbaum, "Qatar," *MECS 2000*, p. 486.

Minister, Shaykh Hamad bin Jasim, publicly noted several times that al-Jazeera caused problems for the Qatari regime.[53] But it seems that the assertion of how much trouble the channel is for the Amir does not express a heartfelt sentiment. In practically the same breath, the Foreign Minister noted that the people of the region "deserve not just one al-Jazeera, but 10 al-Jazeera"[54] in order to give them a better idea of what goes on in their vicinity. Such claims are calculated to proclaim publicly, "It isn't only you who suffer from tongue-lashings in al-Jazeera, we suffer too, but it is for a greater good." But since this "greater good" is contested by the rest of the region, these statements are only relevant beyond the Gulf, where they make a favorable impression in Washington and Europe. The Qatari regime's official refusal to curb al-Jazeera despite complaints only enhances its claim of protecting democratic values.

On the other hand, it has become evident that the Arab leaders are aware of the channel's popularity. Both Usama bin Ladin and Saddam Husayn chose al-Jazeera as the venue for pronouncements while in hiding.[55] It seems that whatever the Qatari leadership had in mind when it chose to allow al-Jazeera a large degree of freedom, it is quickly taking on a life of its own. During 2004, the channel antagonized the United States with its coverage to the point where Secretary of State Colin Powell told the amirate that the channel was harming bilateral relations. Qatar then agreed to tell the station to "review its coverage."[56] It is true that at present al-Jazeera can still be controlled, but it is quite possible that this will not always be the case.

An additional development concerning freedom of expression came with the drafting of a new press law in March 2002 that was denounced by many Qatari journalists, since it allowed journalists to be imprisoned for their writing.[57] In practice, it seems that freedom of expression is still restricted, both officially and unofficially.[58] In June 2001, Ahmad 'Ali, the editor of

---

53   For example, "Al-Jazeera is a headache for me": Jonathan S. Kessler, Marshall Berger, Edmund Ghareeb and Laura DeKrock, "It is Important to Build Democracy in All Arab Countries: Interview with Qatar's Minister of Foreign Affairs Sheikh Hamad Bin Jassem Bin Jabr Al-Thani," *Middle East Insight*, Vol. 16, No. 4 (September-October 2001).

54   Kessler, et al.

55   Conversely, this has caused much speculation regarding the channel's true connection to terror. See for example Michael Isikoff and Eric Pape, "Al-Jazeera: Too Close to Terrorists?" *Newsweek*, September 22, 2003.

56   *BBC News*, April 30, 2004 (http://news.bbc.co.uk).

57   *The Peninsula* (Qatar), March 10, 2002.

58   See report on Qatar by The Committee to Protect Journalists (CPJ), (http://www.cpj.org/attacks02/mideast02/qatar.html).

al-Watan newspaper in Qatar, was physically attacked by three men related to the ruling family after his newspaper published articles criticizing government policies.[59] In its 2007 report, ranking countries according to freedom of the media, Reporters without Borders (RSF) ranked Qatar as number 79 out of 169. This is an improvement from past rankings. However RSF still categorizes Qatar as having "noticeable problems."[60] Although al-Jazeera is showcased as an independent channel, and thus as an indicator of free speech, inside the amirate much remains to be desired concerning freedom of expression. On the other hand, this process is by no means over and it is conceivable that one day other forms of local media might try to emulate al-Jazeera.

Women's rights. Qatar has advanced the status of women in the last decade. In 1999-2000, female students accounted for 72 percent of the total student population of the University of Qatar, and in 1998 only 24 percent of women aged 20-24 were married. But, in contrast, Qatar has not ratified the UN 1979 Convention on the Elimination of All Forms of Discrimination against Women. In general, Qatar is considered a male-dominated society, where women's conduct is sanctioned by social norms.[61]

Nevertheless, the steps to empower women are perhaps the most striking element in Qatar's reforms. One of the indications of this trend is the creation of a *de facto* Qatari "First Lady", a position that does not exist even theoretically elsewhere in the Gulf. The second of the Amir's three wives, Shaykha Muza bint Nasir al-Misnad, is highly visible, traveling abroad unaccompanied by her husband,[62] entertaining high profile guests,[63] sponsoring events and heading public institutions (mostly health and edu-

---

59 *Amnesty International Annual Report 2002: Qatar* (http://web.amnesty.org/web/ar2002. nsf/mde/qatar!Open). The attack was also described in the report of Reporters without Borders (RSF) in 2002 (http://www.rsf.org/article.php3?id_article=1451&var_ recherche=qatar).

60 RSF, *Third Annual Worldwide Press Freedom Index 2007* (http://www.rsf.org/article. php3?id_article=24025). Additionally, see map: RSF, *Middle East and North Africa*, November, 2007 (http://www.rsf.org/rubrique.php3?id_rubrique=43).

61 UNESCWA (Economic and Social Commission for Western Asia) Report on the situation of women in Qatar: (http://www.escwa.org.lb/divisions/sdd/women.html). See also Carnegie Endowment for International Peace, *Arab Political Systems: Baseline information and Reforms – Qatar*, (July 2005), pp. 7-9. (http://www.carnegieendowment.org/files/ Qatar_APS.doc#_Toc106893994).

62 As she did during 1997. See Joshua Teitelbaum, "Qatar," *MECS 1998*, p. 513.

63 Such as a highly visible visit from Shaykha Fatma bint Mubarak, wife of the then UAE leader, Shaykh Zayed Al Nuhayan. See *ArabicNews.Com,* January 30, 1999.

cation related).[64] More important, Shaykha Muza's activities are covered by the local as well as the regional press. This indicates that the media, at least, regard her as the First Lady. Other royal consorts in the Gulf monarchies are normally neither seen nor heard.[65]

It is possible that Shaykha Muza is the driving force behind the changes in the amirate's policy toward women. However, without her husband's blessing, none of the changes in Qatari women's rights would have come about. Conversely, the Amir benefits from having a "visible" wife who can serve as a persuasive advocate of his reforms. This is especially true when Shaykha Muza speaks to an international audience. For example, during a visit to Paris in 2003, Shaykha Muza stated: "In Qatar we have begun a series of radical educational changes at all levels.... As we redesign the educational system in Qatar, we are simultaneously introducing democratic reform into our political structure."[66] Hearing such statements from the First Lady is convincing, attracts much attention in the foreign press and generates favorable publicity for the amirate.

As discussed above, women were allowed the right to stand for election and vote in the March 1999 and April 2003 elections. Women's right to vote was opposed in Qatar by a group of clerics who submitted a petition to the Amir in June 1998. The petitioners, including three members of the ruling family, argued that placing women in positions of power was contrary to Islamic law.[67] Consequently, one of the leaders of this group, Shaykh 'Abd al-Rahman al-Nu'aymi, was jailed.[68] Although none of the women running was elected to the CMC in 1999, one woman was elected

---

64   See, for example, the website of the Qatar Diabetes Society (http://www.diabetes.com), where Shaykha Muza is portrayed as a driving force; and the site of the American Women's Association of Qatar, which lists events sponsored by the First Lady (http://www.qatar-info.com). For the full official description of Shaykha Muza's activities as First Lady see: "The Role of H.H. the Wife of H.H. the Emir," *Qatari Women, 2001* (http://english.mofa.gov.qa).

65   For a more detailed description of Shaykha Muza's actions, see Louay Bahry, "Elections in Qatar: A Window of Democracy Opens in the Gulf," *Middle East Policy*, Vol. 6, No. 4 (June 1999), pp. 118-27.

66   *The Peninsula* (Qatar), June 24, 2003.

67   Teitelbaum, "Qatar," *MECS 1998*, p. 513.

68   Mervat Diab, "Unveiling Democracy," *Al-Ahram* (Egypt), November 5, 1998. Amnesty International has attempted to follow the treatment of al-Nu'aymi, unsuccessfully. See *Amnesty International Annual Report 2000: Qatar* (http://www.web.amnesty.org/web/ar2000web.nsf/f5ea2b18926bc708802568f500619c95/3dc4ef458b982ac8802568f200552960!OpenDocument).

to the council in April 2003 and during May 2003, a first woman minister was appointed by the Amir to head the Ministry of Education.[69]

Several women were also granted individual privileges. A woman was given permission to practice law in Qatar for the first time in February 2000. She had applied for a license in 1989 but had not received any response. On her second attempt she was backed by the Amir and succeeded.[70] Women were also accepted into the Qatari police force in June 2003 when 107 female cadets graduated from Qatar's police academy.[71] The fact that such steps were publicized underlines how unusual they are and how they are actually an exception to the rule regarding women's conduct in Qatar. However, contrary to most of the reforms orchestrated by Shaykh Hamad, these steps are significant in that they apparently generate public discomfort. In general, the Amir does not seem to launch initiatives he feels Qataris will not endorse; but on the issue of women's rights he has apparently taken a bolder approach.

The improvements in the status of women, mirrored in their growing percentage in higher education and the increasing numbers of relatively older unmarried women, are probably the most impressive of these developments. Most of these accomplishments are not publicized in Qatar and receive much less media time than the other issues discussed here. They also may cause grumbling within traditional Qatari society: unmarried and educated daughters are tangible results that Qatari families can experience more acutely than a woman on the CMC.

Qatar has also become involved in various UN-affiliated projects dealing with human rights and women's rights. Delegates to such functions were usually women, or delegations headed by a woman, often from the ruling family. For example, Qatar's representative to UNICEF is Shaykha Ghalya bint Mohammad bin Hamad Al Thani of the royal family.

A memorandum of understanding (MoU) signed at UNESCO headquarters in June 2003, under which Qatar made an initial grant of $15 million to an international fund promoting higher education in Iraq, was signed by Shaykha Muza, who is the special envoy of UNESCO in Qatar.[72] The fund established was to be jointly administered by UNESCO and the

---

69   *Gulf News* (Dubai), May 7, 2003.

70   *ArabicNews.com*, February 17, 2000.

71   *Gulf News* (Dubai), June 9, 2003.

72   *The Peninsula* (Qatar), June 24, 2003.

Qatar Foundation for Education, Science and Community Development, also headed by the First Lady.[73]

In June 2000, Qatar sent a delegation, headed by the Amir's sister, Shaykha Hasa bint Khalifa, to the UN General Assembly session entitled "Women 2000: Gender Equality, Development and Peace for the Twenty-First Century".[74] In her statement, Shaykha Hasa outlined steps taken by the Qatari leadership toward advancing the status of women. The fact that the event was deemed important enough to send a delegation, and that a woman delivered the official speech, reinforces the observation that women's rights are perceived as worthy of attention in Qatar. More than that, it is an issue in which the Amir has obviously decided to invest time and thought. He is also eager to ensure that the international community is aware of the efforts made in this direction.

Conversely, designating human rights and human rights organizations as within a female sphere of influence may indicate that these issues are not important and not worthy of male time and effort. However, it is unlikely that the Sandhurst-educated Shaykh Hamad is unaware of the international importance of these organizations. It is likely that he is taking advantage of the cultural difference between the West and the Gulf: sending a delegation and a female delegate scores points in the West for open-mindedness and progressiveness; to the home audience, sending a woman to an international event indicates its insignificance and is not threatening in regional eyes.

Of the reforms discussed, the increase in women's rights seems the most concrete. On the other hand, the changes that seem most promising are incremental changes that can only be judged over time. At the same time, as in other spheres discussed above, the Amir is also engineering sweeping "photogenic" reforms in this sphere, in the form of women in the police force and holding public office. However, when it came to popular vote, a woman was elected to the CMC only when unopposed by a man, and there is still opposition to the enfranchisement of women. The Amir may be reaping international acclaim for the larger steps taken toward women's rights, but in this sphere he is also encountering opposition at home.

---

73   *The Peninsula* (Qatar), June 24, 2003.

74   "Statement by Her Excellency Sheikha Hessa bint Khalifa bin Hamad Al-Thani, Vice President of the Supreme Council for Family Affairs, Head of the Delegation of the State of Qatar to the Twenty-Third Session of the General Assembly entitled "Women 2000: Gender Equality, Development and Peace for the Twenty-First Century", New York – June 7, 2000 (http://www.un.org).

Overtures towards human rights organizations. On a more general level, the Amir has demonstrated his willingness to conform to international concepts of human rights. For example, during trials held in 1997 for involvement in the abortive coup of 1996, Shaykh Hamad invited Amnesty International (AI) to observe the trials, and it did so.[75] Although it seems that the Amir attempted to cooperate with AI and it is obvious that the country has made progress concerning human rights, annual AI reports continue to accuse the amirate of torturing suspects, holding people incommunicado for long periods of time, not conducting fair trials, and not complying with international treaties concerning human rights.[76]

In contrast with previous years, after the adoption of the new constitution in 2003, Qatar responded to the *Amnesty International Report 2002*, pointing out changes made by the government in light of some of AI's concerns.[77] In other words, Qatar demonstrated that it was paying attention to what AI thought of its conduct and wished to be seen as making an effort to improve its performance in the sphere of human rights.

Further to this, Qatar signed the UN Convention against Torture in 2000.[78] In May 2003, Qatar established its first national committee on human rights. The committee has thirteen members: eight representatives from government ministries and five human rights experts.[79] In March 2004, it hosted the 12th annual workshop on human rights in Asia and the Indian Ocean.[80] But agreements and committees do not necessarily mean action.

Although it is not included explicitly in the definition of democracy and democratization used here, one cannot ignore the changes in Qatar's education system in the past few years. This is an especially important development since the First Lady has been engineering these transformations. Shaykha Muza founded the Qatar Foundation for Education, Science and

---

75 Teitelbaum, "Qatar," *MECS 1998*, p. 514. For a complete report on the trials held and the activity of Amnesty International, see *Amnesty International Report 1998: Qatar* (http://www.amnesty.org/ailib/aireport/ar98/mde22.htm).

76 See AI reports on Qatar for 1998-2003 (http://www.amnesty.org/ailib/aireport/index.html).

77 *Amnesty International Annual Report 2003: Qatar* (http://web.amnesty.org/report2003/Qat-summary-eng).

78 *Amnesty International Annual Report 2001: Qatar* (http://web.amnesty.org/web/ar2001.nsf/webmepcountries/QATAR?OpenDocument).

79 *Khaleej Times* (Dubai), May 6, 2003. Shaykha Ghalia, a member of the committee, is also the head of the pediatrics section at Hamad Medical Corporation. See *The Peninsula* (Qatar), September 4, 2002 (http://www.thepeninsulaqatar.com).

80 *Al-Watan* (Qatar), March 3, 2004.

Community Development, which sponsors educational institutions[81] and provides scholarships for outstanding students to study at Qatar University free for four years.

After the First Lady traveled abroad to review several institutions of higher education in the West, certain American and French universities were allowed to open branches at Qatar University. For example, Virginia Commonwealth University's School of Arts was selected to develop the Shaqab College of Design Arts in Doha in July 1998.[82] Shaykha Muza was also the force behind the establishment of a medical college in Qatar and the beginning of pre-medical studies there in September 2002.[83]

Business as usual

Although the implementation of many of the changes and reforms listed here will have to be measured over a long period of time, the fact that they have occurred is significant and points to a growing trend on the part of the Qatari leadership. These changes are usually highly publicized and occur in areas that on the one hand seem to be essential to fundamental democratic change (elections, education, human rights); in practice, however, they have had little or no impact. The Amir continues to hold the reigns of government tightly and dominates all aspects of government. For example, in August 2003, Shaykh Hamad surprisingly announced the appointment of a new heir apparent: his fourth son, Tamim.[84] The original heir to the throne, Shaykh Jasim, the Amir's third son, was reported to have renounced the position of heir apparent in favor of his brother. The foreign press speculated that Shaykh Jasim wanted wider powers and Shaykh Tamim complained of not being involved sufficiently in government.[85] Ac-

---

81   See for example the website of the Shaqab Institute for Girls (http://www.qatar.net.qa/sig/).

82   Richard H. Curtiss, "Qatar Selects Virginia Commonwealth University's School of Arts," *The Washington Report* (September 1998). Delegations of Shaykha Muza's advisors were sent to various Western universities to investigate opportunities. For example: "Delegation from Qatar visiting province for post-secondary education opportunities," *News Release: Government of Newfoundland and Labrador*, May 2001(http://www.gov.nf.ca).

83   *The Peninsula* (Qatar), September 4, 2002.

84   For a short biography of the heir apparent, see the front page of *al-Watan*, August 6, 2003.

85   See for example, *Washington Post*, August 5, 2003; *al-Jazeera Satellite Channel*, August 5, 2003 (http://www.aljazeera.net); *Reuters*, August 4, 2003.

cording to rumors in the diplomatic corps in Doha, Shaykh Jasim had also become more religious and this worried the Amir.[86]

Not long afterwards, the Amir appointed two of his ministers as Deputy Prime Ministers: the Foreign Minister, his relative and close ally Shaykh Hamad bin Jasim, and the Minister of Energy and Industry, Shaykh Hamad al-Attiya, also reported to be an ally of the Amir. Deputy Prime Ministers replace the Amir in his absence.[87] Foreign analysts thought this step was another way to consolidate the Amir's administrative power, and perhaps was connected to the change in succession.[88]

Judging from these steps, taken well after the referendum on the constitution, the Amir continues to rule as before without a feeling of accountability toward the Qataris. Moreover, these sudden changes may mean he is trying to manage strife within the ruling family, which is not a promising development if one was expecting more democratic reforms.

Possible causes and motives

If it is true that, as claimed here, the reforms described are primarily window dressing, why bother to go about them? The possible reasons for the democratization campaign described above seem to come from a mixture of regional and global incentives.

Clearly, Shaykh Hamad is trying to build Qatar into a regional power.[89] Qatar has taken steps toward normalization with Israel, even though this attracted criticism from the entire Arab world, especially when Qatar refused to cancel the MENA summit held in Doha in November 1997, to which Israel was invited.[90] In other displays of independent foreign policy and regional leadership, during his service as chairman of the OIC, Shaykh Hamad was involved in attempts to curb the violence in the greater region: attempting to mediate between Iraq and Kuwait before the final crisis, and approaching Afghanistan in March 2001 requesting that it should not

86 Conversation with a foreign diplomat stationed in Doha, May 23, 2004.

87 *The Gulf Times* (Qatar), September 17, 2003.

88 *GulfWire Digest*, no. 215, September 22-8, 2003.

89 Many in the Arab world agree with this idea, stating that Qatar even prefers its connections with the US to its connections to the Arab world in order to further its status as a regional power. See Dina Ezzat, "The Qatari Angle," *al-Ahram* (Egypt), June 12, 2003.

90 For a more detailed description of Qatar's evolving relationship with Israel, as well as the specific occurrences of the Doha MENA Summit, see Elisheva Rosman-Stollman, "Foreign Relations of Weak States: The Gulf States and Israel 1991-1997," unpublished Masters Thesis, Bar Ilan University, Ramat Gan, 2001 (Hebrew).

harm pre-Islamic archaeological relics.[91] Qatar also endeavored to advance a policy of removing sanctions against Iraq during 1999, much to Kuwaiti chagrin.[92] Additionally, Qatar continued to maintain good ties with Iran. These included signing of a number of economic cooperative ventures during the 1990s, as well as reciprocal official visits. During the current round of international opposition to the Iranian nuclear project, Qatar hosted the Iranian President for an official visit[93] in a move that could be seen as an attempt to mediate between Iran and the West.

To balance its pro-Iraq and pro-Iran moves, Qatar upgraded its cooperation with the US during 2000. This upgrading included the hosting of more pre-positioned US forces than in the past.[94] These actions took place after Qatar had purchased much of its arms from France[95] and opposed US steps against Iraq during 1999.[96] Al-Udeid air base has become a major base of US operations in the Gulf region, surpassing Saudi Arabia.[97] The most recent strengthening of its ties with Washington has enabled Doha to portray itself as a better ally than Riyadh, which has been distancing itself from the US. Additionally, after the September 11 attacks, the US itself began to view Saudi Arabia as even less of an ally,[98] and this has boosted Qatar's importance to Washington further.

Clearly, Shaykh Hamad has done his best to play a balancing game in the region and to keep his neighbors on their toes, unable to predict what Qatar will do next. By balancing Iran against Iraq in the pre-2003 era, Israel against the Arab world, and the US against all other regional actors, the Amir kept Qatar safe from aggression and also ensured that it attracted regional attention. True, this *modus operandi* did not find favor in the eyes of the other GCC members, but it was obviously quite satisfying for the

---

91   Qatar MoFA, Nov. 2002 (http://english.mofa.gov.qa).

92   Teitelbaum, "Qatar," *MECS 2000*, p. 487.

93   Iran Republic News Agency, "Ahmadinejad: Iran willing to maintain excellent ties with Qatar," January 23, 2006. (http://www.irna.ir/en/news/view/line-22/0601247418000412.htm).

94   John Duke Anthony, "Qatar's Heightened Profile," *GulfWire Perspectives*, October 27, 2002. (http://www.arabialink.com/GulfWire/GWP_2002_10_27.htm).

95   Teitelbaum, "Qatar," *MECS 1998*, p. 518.

96   Teitelbaum, "Qatar," *MECS 1999*, p. 503.

97   See W. Andrew Terrill, "Regional Fears of Western Primacy and the Future of U.S. Middle Eastern Basing Policy," Strategic Studies Institute, Army War College, Carlisle Barracks, PA, December 2006.

98   *NBC News*, January 30, 2003.

Amir.[99] In this context, projecting a democratic profile in the region contributed to the image Qatar is trying to build for itself in the West: a step that the GCC countries feel threatened by but cannot condemn for fear of offending Western powers.

Arab leaders do not feel comfortable with liberalization in Qatar. Since the Amir has not gone about democratizing in the manner adopted by other countries who portray their regimes as democratic (Egypt and Syria, for example), and since he, his Foreign Minister and the First Lady trumpet these changes as often and as loudly as possible, the Arab world grumbles about the Amir and tends to see him as a troublemaker and a threat to stability. As voices for reform within the Arab world in general grow louder,[100] a leader who actually seems to be listening to these ideas and acting upon them is perceived as a danger. For example, as described above, after the elections for the CMC, Arab countries accused the Amir of trying to build up his internal popularity by advocating democracy in order to compensate for Qatar's isolation in the Arab world, caused by ties with Israel, and its regional isolation, caused by local border disputes. Another popular accusation was that Qatar was only trying to find favor with the West and was therefore trying to project a more democratic image.[101]

If finding favor in the eyes of his regional neighbors or in the eyes of the Arab world was seen by the Amir as a worthy cause, he could have toned down the publicity given to his democratic reforms, as he seems to have done with advances in the overall status of women. Clearly, publicity for democratization is as important to the Amir as the steps themselves. Therefore it might be assumed that part of the motivation to reform is the ability to generate such publicity and the uproar that it causes.

On the other side of the scales, offsetting the regional dismay is the West, which commends the Amir for each step toward democracy. Qatar has tightened its ties with the US over the years since the first Gulf war, especially since Shaykh Hamad came to power. Opening Qatar's air and naval bases to pre-positioned US forces has been one aspect of close relations. Showing a willingness to adopt American values is another. Indeed, the reforms the Amir has chosen to undertake fit in rather comfortably with Western conventional wisdom of the 1990s as to what the desired political

---

99   See: Teitelbaum, "Qatar," *MECS 1999*, p. 513.

100   For a survey of some of these voices in the recent Arab press see American University of Kuwait (AUK) Media and Dialogue Center, *Window of Arab Press*, June 21, 2003.

101   Diab, "Unveiling Democracy."

reform in the Arab world should be.[102] When describing what democracy should consist of, US Assistant Secretary of State William J. Burns offhandedly cited elections, women's rights, a free judiciary and other structures of civil society as the basis for democracy.[103] Although he was addressing the US-Arab Economic Forum, where one might expect comments to be more economy-oriented, Burns still underlined these points as most important, emphasizing the weight the US gives to such steps.

While European and North American countries congratulated Qatar after the elections to the CMC and the vote for the constitution, it seems that none of these countries have been following Qatar's democratic progress closely or paying attention to follow-up elections and the completion of long-term reforms. Evidently, the West is satisfied by the indication of reform and does not actually follow the concrete progress to see if it leads toward viable democracy.

True, not all of the steps taken conform to this model. As Western reports above show, women are creeping towards a better position in society. It seems that the educational project orchestrated by Shaykha Muza is continuing slowly but surely. Higher education is progressing in Qatar, with new academic programs being offered to Qatari students.[104] On the other hand, educational reform has not received the publicity political reforms have received. Perhaps this fact is the clearest indication that the reforms analyzed above seem mostly for window-dressing purposes and are not designed for long-term success.

Concluding observations

Despite the cosmetic quality of most of the Amir's reforms, could it be that Qatar is on its way to becoming a democracy? It would be naïve to expect the Amir to turn over power to his people immediately, and such a move would also be impractical. Considering the form of government throughout the Gulf and regional history, it seems highly unlikely that the Amir will relinquish his authority of his own volition. However, is some form of democracy being constructed, even unintentionally, in Qatar?

---

102   See Rathmell and Schultze, pp. 48-9.

103   Assistant Secretary of State William J. Burns Addresses the U.S.-Arab Economic Forum, 28 September, 2003, as published in *GulfWire.com*.

104   For example, a branch of Texas A & M opened in September 2003 in Doha, offering four undergraduate degree programs (petroleum, chemical, electrical and mechanical engineering). See *The Eagle* (US), September 6, 2003 (http://www.theeagle.com).

The answer to this question is not entirely clear. Participation in political life is growing, elections do occur and they seem to be fair. Apparently there is free and equal political participation and representation. However, these elections are not for a true governing body and Qatar still does not allow freedom of expression and association, regardless of its reputation in the Western media.

In contrast, it seems that some of the Qatari people believe the answer to the above question is yes. Willingness, at least initially, to participate in a democratic political system as active players indicates they believe the Amir's public statements on the matter. As demonstrated above, however, none of the reforms have created substantial changes in the traditional framework of government in Qatar, and all were initiated by the Amir, as opposed to being a response to popular demand. Yes, the Amir, his wife and the Foreign Minister speak out on the ideas of democracy and depict a Qatar that allows for personal freedom and equality, striding confidently toward a democratic tomorrow. Yet various human rights reports claim there is not enough evidence of this in practice.

Another important point to consider in the context of democracy is the issue of foreign labor in Qatar. Of the approximately 650,000 persons living in Qatar, only 150,000 are nationals. Expatriates living in the amirate, even those who have been born in Qatar, have no rights. As stated above, foreign workers will also not be allowed to take part in the new workers' associations. It is difficult to speak of democratization when the majority of the population has no rights and is not entitled to the same freedoms as Qataris.

The traditional frameworks of government in Doha still stand and the royal family and the Amir are very much in control of the country. Nonetheless, some of these changes may prove to take on a life of their own. Just as al-Jazeera is taking advantage of its independence and in the future might choose to deal with Doha as it does with the rest of the Arab world, some of the other frameworks established might decide to test the limits of their authority. The CMC has entered its second term and its members could very well decide to continue to press for more power, as the preceding council did. If indeed a parliament is elected in Qatar in the future, it might take its role seriously. Such a scenario could force Shaykh Hamad to decide just how committed he really is to democracy.

The fact that higher education is coming to Qatar from the West, and that more and more Qataris will be taught by teachers who originate from democratic societies, may also contribute to a change from below that could lead to true reform through the seemingly hollow mechanisms the Amir has constructed. Education, combined with the opening moves the leadership has made, may encourage the emergence of a civil society in Qatar. Taking Shaykh Hamad's rhetoric at face value might one day actually inspire Qataris to challenge their leader to follow through on his promises of reform, instead of merely launching it.

One must also note that the Amir has been in power for only a little over a decade. Many of the reforms are five years old or less. It is difficult, not to say unfair, to judge their true nature in such a short time span.

Clearly the coming years will be most interesting in Qatar. Its neighbors will continue to eye its progress nervously. The West will continue to hope the Amir will practice what he preaches to his neighbors. Time will tell whether, regardless of the Amir's intentions, these changes are real or only ornamental.

9

OMAN:
'SAY YES TO OMAN, SAY NO TO THE TRIBE!'

Uzi Rabi

The Sultanate of Oman held elections to its first Consultative Council in October 2003. But instead of being a departure in the direction of liberalized politics in the country, the newly elected council is designed to co-opt important tribal and business elites and is a continuation of earlier methods of rule. While younger and Western-educated Omanis view the council with skepticism, members of the council have been seen questioning ministers during televised sessions in an unprecedented manner. Ministers are becoming more responsive to members' concerns, but any significant liberalization will be a slow and complex process.

და

On many fronts, Oman has made tremendous progress since the early 1970s. Three decades ago, Oman was known as the hermit kingdom of the Middle East, a "medieval state" lacking even a minimally basic infrastructure. When Sultan Qabus bin Saʻid overthrew his father in July 1970, an event to which most Omanis refer to as the beginning of the "Omani Renaissance" (*al-nahda*),[1] he issued a short proclamation to his people and to the world, attesting to his determination to give the sultanate a new image and make a break with the past. After receiving the oath of loyalty (*bayʻa*) from the armed forces, the new Sultan said: "I have watched with growing dismay and increasing anger the inability of my father to use the new found wealth of this country for the needs of its people. That is why I have taken

---

1   *Al-Watan al-ʻArabi*, June 30, 2000.

control. Now my family and my armed forces have sworn their allegiance to me. The old Sultan has left the country and I promise that the first thing I shall dedicate myself to will be the speedy establishment of a modern government."[2] The coup carried out by Sultan Qabus in July 1970 ended the thirty-eight-year rule of Sultan Saʿid bin Taymur, and ushered in an era of radical transformation of the social structure which, on the whole, had remained intact for ages. During a time-span of more than thirty years the new ruler, Qabus, shook off most of Oman's medieval remnants and began to develop some of the institutions demanded by a modern state.

One of Qabus' first measures was to assume control over the southern Dhofar region, which had been rebelling against his father's rule. Yet, rather than rely on force alone to subdue the rebels, Qabus also employed a policy of economic appeasement, diverting a disproportionate share of government revenues to Dhofar. Another dimension of this widely-used "carrot" policy was the announcement of general amnesty for opponents of his father's regime, enticing them back to the country and providing them with a stake of its welfare. Equally important, the sultanate launched intensive diplomatic activities to develop its international relations. The new regime ended the isolationism imposed on Oman during the reign of Saʿid bin Taymur and the sultanate became a member of the Arab League and the UN. In the process, Oman looked to the Arab world as it had never previously done throughout its history.

Once his rule was consolidated, Qabus designed a government structure. Oil revenues, though more modest than elsewhere in the Gulf, have helped Oman to forge ahead with the physical transformation of its tribal society and prepare the ground for the sociological, psychological and organizational modernity to follow. Following the commercial exploitation of oil in the mid-1970s and a more forward-looking leadership, all walks of life in Oman have been noticeably transformed. Yet, by contrast with the massive development of its social and physical infrastructure, change in Oman's political system progressed much more slowly. The real challenge ahead for the sultanate appears to lie in the area of political power. The October 2003 election in Oman, on which this article focuses, seemed to be a milestone for the sultanate that had previously operated a limited franchise and left the final selection of *Majlis* members to the Sultan. In addition, this chap-

2   Public Record Office, FCO 8/1425, Telegram no. 46, 26 July 1970. From FO (Arabian Department).

ter assesses the nature of the popular participation process in the Sultanate of Oman and to place it in the context of its history and tradition.

Before proceeding to examine the experience that Oman has had with political participation and constitutionalism, it may be valuable to outline some main Omani characteristics that make us aware of the uniqueness of Oman. With a relatively large territory and diverse economy (settled agriculture, fisheries and a long maritime commercial tradition) as well as the Ibadi religious tradition,[3] Oman is more often than not the exception to the rule among the Gulf states. In Oman, though, as in other Arab Gulf states, the reigns of government are tightly held in the hands of a ruling family, the Al Bu Saʻid, which could be perceived as a modern extension of an old tribal tradition. The Sultan, an ultimate authority and absolute ruler, usually makes decisions on every major issue with minimal popular input into the decision-making process.

Oman moved cautiously in the direction of allowing more political participation. What stood out as the most important move in this regard was the inauguration of an appointed *Majlis al-Shura* (Consultative Council, successor to an appointed body created in the 1980s, *al-Majlis al-Istishari lil-Dawla*) in December 1991. As a matter of fact, Sultan Qabus has made his program of political reform a key plank of his rule, remarking time and again that he perceives the council as "a partner with the government in the work to build the Sultanate".[4] The following decade was to witness the initiation of some other constitutional steps that served to continue the slow but steady progress of political liberalization in Oman. Prominent among these was the promulgation of the "Basic Law of the State" (*al-nizam al-asasi lil-dawla*), a constitution-like document defining how the Omani state should function. In 1997 and again in 2000, the government held elections to the *Majlis*, expanding suffrage until by the 2003 elections virtually all adult nationals were eligible to vote.

The 2003 elections constituted a milestone, as the *Majlis* members had never before been elected. These were definitely significant steps forward

3   Oman was brought into the fold of Islam under the banner of the Ibadi sect, the only surviving branch of the *khawarij*, the first schism in Islam that eventually died out as a result of its extremist beliefs. As a result of its moderation and flexibility, Ibadism is the only *khariji* sect that has survived. It constitutes a separate school of law in Islam although it is close to the Maliki school of Sunni Islam.

4   See, by way of illustration, "Speeches of His Majesty Sultan Qabus bin Saʻid on the Occasion of the Opening of the Second Term of the *Majlis al-Shura*," December 1994, *Oman: Political Development & Majlis al-Shura* (Washington, DC: International Republican Institute, July 1995).

for the sultanate, which had previously left the final selection of *Majlis* members to the Sultan. In 1997, for example, the electorate was restricted to some 51,000 Omanis who voted for over 700 male and female candidates. The Sultan then made the final selection from a list of the candidates elected, picking two of the top four candidates in large constituencies and one of the top two in smaller jurisdictions.[5] In September 2000, the delegates were elected by an enlarged electorate of some 175,000, more than three times that of 1997. The top one or two winning candidates in each electoral district were chosen by the Sultan for seats in the *Majlis*.[6] This time the winners were the candidates who topped the poll in each area. With the new decision, voter participation has risen from 25 per cent in each province (*wilaya*) to 100 per cent participation of all eligible citizens in voting for the *Majlis* membership.[7] The October 2003 election was therefore the first poll ever to be held in Oman with a universal franchise. A change in the terminology of the political culture was to follow suit as the process was referred to as *intikhab* (election), not *tarshih wa ikhtiyar* (nomination and choice).[8] The authorities called on voters to "say yes to Oman, no to the tribe" (*na'am li'uman, la lil-qabila*). It was probably thought that the election would result in mass participation in national elections and more political activity across the country.

Oman also moved ahead of most of the other Arab Gulf states in granting women the right to participate in the political process. Women ran for office in 1997 and voted in the election. In September 2000 (where 23 of the 597 candidates were women), women throughout the country also participated in the nomination and election processes, a privilege that had previously been granted only to women in Muscat.[9] In the 2003 election, however, voters failed to add to the two seats already held by women

---

5   *Al-Usbu' al-'Arabi*, September 26, 2000.

6   According to the announcement released by the Interior Ministry all of Oman's 750,000-800,000 citizens of 21 or over were to have the right to vote in the 2003 election. Arrangements were made to set up polling stations for Omani nationals residing in other GCC states or other Arab countries such as Egypt and Jordan. See *Times of Oman*, October 3, 2003.

7   *Al-Bawwaba* (London), October 2003.

8   For more details on the process of political liberalization in the Arab Gulf states see Anoush Ehteshami, "Reforms from Above: the Politics of Participation in the Oil Monarchies," *International Affairs*, Vol. 79, No. 1 (January 2003), pp. 53-75.

9   *Middle East Insight,* June-July 2001, p. 28. See also *Gulf States Newsletter*, September 25, 2000. It was no surprise that more women candidates hailed from the capital area and the prosperous Batina region located along the coast than from the more isolated and tradition-bound regions such as the Musandam Peninsula.

and this time two women, both of whom came from prominent merchant families, won seats in the *Majlis*. Oman has been among regional leaders in promoting the role of women to high-level positions as ambassadors, on commercial boards of directors and as chamber of commerce members.[10] In March 2004, Sultan Qabus appointed Rawya bint Sa'ud Al Bu Sa'idi, an Oxford-educated woman of royal lineage, as the first Omani woman to hold a full ministerial portfolio, as Minister of Higher Education. In recognition of the vital part women play in all areas of life in the Sultanate, the Interior Minister, Sayyid 'Ali bin Hammud Al Bu Sa'idi, confirmed that "there will be no difference in the position of men and women" and "there will be no limit on the number of women who can take part in future elections, either as voters or as candidates."[11]

While women's participation and increased suffrage were indeed signs of greater political liberalization, the *Majlis* elections in 2003 were marked— like the 2000 elections, in which only around one-quarter of the eligible electorate registered to vote—by a lack of enthusiasm on the part of both voters and candidates. Less than a third of Oman's 820,000 eligible voters (262,000) bothered to register for the poll, a highly disappointing performance given that the elections were preceded by a sustained government and media campaign to promote participation.[12]

This voter passivity was coupled with a decrease in the total number of candidates running for office, from 736 in 1997 to 540 in 2000 and 506 in 2003, of whom 15 were women.[13] Conceivably, it seems that the prime reason for the poor election turnout and the spirit of general indifference was that the *Majlis* has been given a narrow mandate and had only a limited scope to influence government decisions. The *Majlis* was primarily restricted to economic and some social matters. As a matter of fact the government, in an attempt to boost the profile of the *Majlis*, tried to broaden its scope of discussions as to include the Omani budget. But even if a voice in fiscal policy would represent a step forward for the *Majlis*, the more contentious issues that politically-aware Omanis would like to see discussed—foreign affairs, or oil policy—were to remain off the *Majlis*'

---

10   *Al-Wasat*, September 25, 2000.

11   *The Middle East,* March 2003.

12   By way of illustration, two of the biggest urban constituencies—Muscat and Matrah— had a very poor voter turnout, with over 5,000 in Muscat and 4,900 in Matrah registering. The truth of the matter is that a similar trend was evident in the 2000 election when only around one-quarter of the eligible electorate registered to vote.

13   *Al-Watan* (Muscat), October 4, 2003.

agenda. While Omanis were pleased to get the vote, widespread skepticism about the effectiveness of the *Majlis* kept many away from the polls. It follows then that the *Majlis* has not evolved into a legislative body, it has highly restricted powers, and rather than leading national debate it acts, in many respects, like a depoliticized local council. Comments made by some of the *Majlis* members could well attest to that. Having been re-elected, a representative from the *wilaya* of Sib, Muhammad al-Ra'isi, explained that his reelection was predictable in view of his effectiveness in dealing with traffic problems in his area.

Moreover, the *Majlis al-Shura* was counterbalanced by the upper house, the State Council (*Majlis al-Dawla*), whose members were appointed by the Sultan. The membership selected by the Sultan—former ministers or under-secretaries, former ambassadors, judges, retired officers—suggested that the *Majlis al-Dawla* would not develop any radical policies, keeping in line with the Sultan's own thinking about the direction and path that the political change should take. The creation of such a bicameral system was therefore in keeping with the Sultan's preference for an arrangement where the elected assembly could be constrained. Thus, the *Majlis al-Shura* held little attraction for would-be members. Significantly, the election reflected Oman's hesitant experimentation with the notion of greater political participation. While the government election campaign called on Omanis to "say yes to Oman, no to the tribe," political rallies were banned during the election run-up and canvassing in public spaces was discouraged. Most electioneering was restricted to door-to-door canvassing for the 540 candidates (519 men and 21 women) who contested 83 seats in the fourth *Majlis* (2001-03).[14]

But at the same time this implies that a significant portion of Omani society, at least those who chose to vote, hoped for greater political liberalization and were therefore disappointed when the *Majlis* did not live up to their expectations. As in other GCC countries, demographic pressures and rising unemployment threaten to alienate certain segments of the Omani society. Despite its remarkable record of economic and social development, Oman confronts a less certain future in light of its diminishing oil reserves. At current production rates, Oman is projected to exhaust its oil reserves within approximately two decades. In contrast to Saudi Arabia and Kuwait,

---

14   This is not to say that there was no campaign. Candidates, especially in the urban areas, made an extensive use of the internet besides utilizing family and tribal links to urge people to vote for them. *Al-Watan* (Muscat), September 15, 2000; *Oman Daily Observer*, September 28, 2000.

where this process is at least a century away, it is estimated as occurring as early as 2020 in Oman. The problem is exacerbated by the growing number of job seekers entering the market annually, forecast as increasing by 212 percent during the coming two decades, with a concurrent sustained growth in Oman's 0-14-year-old population projected beyond 2020.[15] Little wonder, therefore, that socio-economic pressures have appeared to be forcing gradual political change in Oman.

The government's cautious approach to political reform evoked impatience among younger, Western-educated Omanis who were eager for more rapid change. For all the advances made in terms of suffrage, a large proportion of younger Omanis seemed unhappy with the election results. In the final analysis, it seems, the *Majlis* functioned entirely at the discretion of the Sultan. The reappointment by the Sultan of Shaykh 'Abdallah bin 'Ali al-Qatabi as president of the *Majlis al-Shura* and Shaykh Hammud bin 'Abdallah al-Harthy as president of the *Majlis al-Dawla* were a vivid example of control from above.[16] With the *Majlis al-Shura* president hailing from the Dhahira region and the *Majlis al-Dawla* president from the Sharqiyya region—two major *Dakhiliyya* (interior) tribal population centers—the Sultan clearly had in mind that the two would balance out the interests of each of these key areas. For the Omani regime, then, the *Majlis* had the advantage of further co-opting important elites, businessmen and tribal leaders, who were committed to the status quo. The entire exercise, therefore, might easily be perceived as a continuation of traditional policies.

What the new *Majlis* has mostly indicated is the continued salience of tribal interests. Deputies and voters alike have not developed personal networks that cut across family, tribal and other lines to mobilize people on political issues. Countering press criticism that the *Majlis* had lost a number of educated delegates because of tribal favoritism in the election procedure, the Minister of the Interior, Sayyid 'Ali bin Hammud Al Bu Sa'idi, pointed out that "the *majlis* represents varied experiences, abilities and qualifications. Among them are peasants, professionals, fishermen, doctors and engineers. Women also have the right to vote and stand for elections."[17] The charge of tribalism was an insult, he said. "The government does not tell the people to elect anyone because he is of a certain tribe."[18]

---

15   Oman's population has been growing at an estimated 3.5 percent a year, one of the highest rates in the world.

16   *'Uman,* January 4, 2001.

17   *Oman Daily Observer*, September 28, 2000.

18   Ibid.

The growing frustration on the part of younger and Western-educated Omanis notwithstanding, the authority of the *Majlis* was enhanced to a degree by the exercise of its right to monitor government activity and summon ministers to report on the performance of their departments. In effect, such dealings have become one of the main features of the regular sessions of the *Majlis* and are broadcast live on television. In mid-2000, the then Information Minister, 'Abd al-'Aziz Muhammad al-Rawwas, who insisted that Oman was not yet ready for parties, was a target for criticism. Younger deputies made little secret of their view that it was time for him to step down, after more than a decade in office. In fact, the *Majlis* gave al-Rawwas a harsh grilling over the performance of state television, which still enjoys a monopoly of local TV broadcasting: deputies felt the channel was too unadventurous and reliant on the tiresome recitation of bland official news.[19] The *Majlis* also used its opening session of the year 2002 to summon Malik bin Sulayman al-Ma'amri, the Minister of Transport and Telecommunications. As a result, some ministers attempted to establish a dialogue with *Majlis* delegates and deal seriously with their concerns. The government's focus on development policy and several technocratic changes in 2003 also reflected the gradual enhancement of the status of the *Majlis*, particularly in monitoring social policy.

Universal suffrage has increased the *Majlis'* mandate, but the low turnout calls it into question. It is clear that the assembly has not been equipped with full legislative power. But the broadening of the voter base to encompass all adults might strengthen its position as a true representative of Omani society as a whole and a scrutinizer of government policy. Other changes may give members more latitude; term limits have been raised to four years, from three. While the failure of voters to add to the two seats already held by women was the most noticed feature of the election, the poll was also significant for the number of young men elected. Only one-quarter of previous members retained their seats, and half the members of the new *Majlis* were drawn from a younger generation of Omanis.[20] The robust presence of younger Omanis could make for a *Majlis* that is rather open to modernizing economic and social measures.

The real crux of the process is whether the Sultanic system will gradually loosen its control and internalize the new constitutional mechanisms. In recent years, Oman has made some practical moves to answer domes-

---

19   *Gulf States Newsletter*, September 11, 2000.

20   *'Uman*, October 4, 2003.

tic demands, and the Sultan has appeared anxious to balance demands by the younger, urbanized Omanis for greater democracy with the desire of the tribal leaders to maintain the status quo. Political change in the sultanate, therefore, has to be analyzed in light of the paternalistic tradition of tribal and Sultanic rule and its confrontation with contemporary pressures for greater participation in decision-making. This consideration was explicitly reflected in appointment and reappointment by the Sultan of delegates to the *Majlis al-Dawla*, created in 1997. This and the *Majlis al-Shura* together constituted Majlis 'Uman (Council of Oman); both houses functioned as conduits of information between the people and the government ministries.

The second *Majlis al-Dawla*, scheduled to sit for three years starting in January 2001, consisted of 48 members, including five women (two of them newly appointed), appointed in October. The Sultan appeared to have made an effort to keep the membership of the body broadly representative of Oman's various ethnic and religious groups. Still, over half the delegates had served during the previous term. Among those who were reappointed was Khalfan bin Nasir al-Wahibi, who had served in several ministerial positions before being named to the upper house. Many high-ranking ex-military officers were also reappointed for second terms, as were technocrats and members of the tribes close to the royal family. A new appointee to the *Majlis al-Dawla* was Murtada bin Hasan bin 'Ali al-Lawati, of a Shi'i mercantile family, who had headed the economic committee of the *Majlis al-Shura*. Defeated at the polls in the September election, Lawati was now a member of the upper house.[21]

Although the government's election campaign called on Omanis to "say yes to Oman, no to the tribe,"[22] clientelistic arrangements remained an important element of Omani society. Clientelism evolved and persisted along with other forms of participation.[23] The old ways survive to a remarkable degree, in part as the result of official policy and in part because of the tribalized social structure, which was buttressed by Omani Ibadism. Strong bonds of kinship, and religious beliefs and practices, were the two great influences shaping social values.

The October 2007 *Majlis al-Shura* elections reemphasized "the two steps forward, one step back" dynamic of political change in Oman. Voter

---

21   *Gulf States Newsletter*, November 6, 2000.

22   *Al-Watan* (Muscat), September 14, 2000.

23   Turnout was reported to be higher in the provinces of al-Dakhiliyya (the interior), where voters tend to support whoever the local leaders—themselves appointed by the government in Muscat—tell them to support. *'Uman,* October 4, 2003.

turnout was strong; 62 percent of Oman's 388,000 registered voters participated in the elections, maybe because of a modernized campaign of posters, newspaper advertisements, and public banners in the run-up to polling day. However, despite the modern campaign tactics, candidates were not permitted to promote particular policy positions or distribute material outlining any specific political principles. Election banners and advertisements were limited to a candidate's name and photo and a short slogan. Without any substantive information to differentiate one candidate from another, apart from easily identifiable tribal affiliation, voters may have cast their ballots on the basis of traditional loyalties.

Women also voted in large numbers during the 2007 election, but the female candidates failed to win any seats, even though there were 21 women out of a total of 632 candidates competing for 84 seats.[24] This development could be considered a setback for female representation in the Omani political forum, as there had been two female members in the outgoing *Majlis*. Sultan Qabus sought to balance the results of the *Majlis al-Shura* election by appointing six new female members to the *Majlis al-Dawla*, thus raising the number of women to 14 in this consultative body of 70.

Taken as a whole, the process of political liberalization in Oman has occurred without violent opposition. This is not to say that Oman is immune to internal disruption, but that demonstrations and other anti-government activities are relatively rare and appear to be an exception to the stability of Oman's social and political life. However, the Omani regime would not be at all reluctant to make use of the security services when opposition appears. In Oman, no provision for opposition exists within the political framework, which makes the whole issue of political reform a top-down affair.

In the Sultanate of Oman—where political parties are still outlawed[25] and a truly free press is absent—interest groups played an important role in society with tribes providing a dominant social structure. Their role was aptly described in mid-2000 by the then Minister of Information, 'Abd al-'Aziz Muhammad al-Rawwas: "The tribal nature of our society is a civil society establishment, something which Western thinkers often overlook. This tribal establishment is no less influential than political parties. I do not think we are ready yet for political parties. I do not believe personally we could benefit from them. If we had been run by political parties, I do not think we would

---

24   *International Herald Tribune*, October 28, 2007.

25   *Al-Watan al-'Arabi*, September 22, 2000.

have developed so much in the last 30 years. Political infighting would not have allowed this. Our tribal system molds national unity."[26]

In recent years, though, Omani authorities have realized that they need to diversify and privatize the economy and to enhance the Omanization of the labor force in order to increase job opportunities for the expanding young population. They have also allowed, to a limited degree, a public debate on the critical difficulties facing the country. The Omani press has run numerous articles on such topics as the need for Omanization of the labor force, the prospects of unemployment for Omani youths and the role to be taken by the private sector. The Omani regime has actively promoted and instituted a wide-ranging process of economic development while simultaneously seeking to preserve the traditional structure of politics. While the election campaign did not produce any surprises, it helped project a more modern and liberal image for the sultanate. For Oman, like other GCC states, national security will depend not only on the ability of the US to meet the challenge of deep-rooted regional conflicts but also on the ability of the leaders to satisfy the demand of their peoples for genuine social, economic and political change. Clearly, such policies cannot be imposed from outside but need to be built from within and must be fitted into the equation of long-term Omani security.

Oman may serve as an example of how complex the path of liberalization in the Gulf is. What remains to be seen is whether this slow advance will suffice to pacify the restlessness of an expanding Omani middle class that has access to the world through travel, the internet and satellite television. The question is whether economic modernization, the information revolution and expanded education will lead a critical mass of people to thirst for more say in how their government is run. History has shown that the answer is usually yes. Undoubtedly, some of these changes may prove to take on a life of their own. But what the experiment of the 2003 and 2007 elections proves is that Oman's move toward wider public participation is to be a slow and complex process, in which Oman intends to develop a system that reflects the characteristics of Omani society. Oman is working out its own unique balance and mixture of traditional institutions and modern organizations.

A cautionary note made by Sultan Qabus in the mid-1990s still stands: "It is not our intention to import foreign brands of democracy into this

---

26   An interview given by 'Abd al-'Aziz al-Rawwas in *Arabies Trends*, July-August 2000, pp. 16-17.

country; the democratic process that you are witnessing is, and must always be an Omani one, which accords with our people's culture, religion and traditions and particular needs."[27]

27   "Speeches of His Majesty Sultan Qabus bin Sa'id on the Occasion of the Opening of the Second Term of the *Majlis al-Shura*," December 1994, *Oman: Political Development & Majlis al-Shura* (Washington, DC: International Republican Institute, July 1995).

10

THE UNITED ARAB EMIRATES: ECONOMY FIRST, POLITICS SECOND

Christopher M. Davidson

The federation of the United Arab Emirates is justifiably regarded by many as a pioneer of post-oil, sustainable development strategies, with elements of its model already being emulated in Africa, Asia, and Eastern Europe. Comprising hydrocarbon-rich Abu Dhabi, the commercial entrepôt of Dubai, and five other constituent members, the UAE seems to be a contradiction in terms. On the one hand, courtesy of Abu Dhabi's immense wealth, the UAE now operates massive sovereign wealth funds, some of which have assets approaching one trillion dollars,[1] while many have acquired sizeable stakes in first world markets. Moreover, with Dubai's ambitious diversification strategies the UAE is generating strong domestic economic growth[2] and is attracting by far the highest levels of foreign direct investment in the region.[3] With booming real estate, free zones, and tourism industries, the UAE appears to be an unstoppable economic juggernaut.

Yet, confusingly for many observers, this impressive economic development trajectory has been overseen by an assortment of seemingly archaic, traditional leaders heading polities loosely assembled under a cen-

---

1   The assets of the Abu Dhabi Investments Authority are believed to be nearly $900 billion, approximately three times greater than those of Saudi Arabia's sovereign wealth funds. *BBC News*, February 20, 2008.

2   Average GDP growth for the UAE for the period 2000-6 was 8.4 per cent, the highest in the Gulf. Oxford Business Group, "Abu Dhabi Report," 2007.

3   FDI flows into the UAE are thought to be about $3 billion, the bulk of which flows into Dubai. Personal interviews, Dubai, March 2007, and data from the Inter-Arab Investment Guarantee Corporation.

tral, federal government dominated by Abu Dhabi and Dubai. Certainly, the hereditary ruling families of the seven emirates can be considered to be among the world's few remaining absolute monarchs. There has been little evidence of real democratic opening, at least in the Western sense, and far less tangible political reform has taken place in the UAE than in neighboring Gulf states, including even Saudi Arabia.[4] Indeed, international non-governmental organizations regularly rank the UAE as being one of the least free political systems in the world, and consistently place it behind Kuwait, Qatar, Bahrain, and Oman.[5] Viewed through a lens of development scholarship, this is especially significant given that many of the most distinguished proponents of modernization theory writing in the mid-twentieth century predicted that all such traditional political systems would eventually fail: most especially those potentates that were on the cusp of great socio-economic growth afforded by substantial oil revenues.[6]

Economy first, politics second

How then, can one account for this marked lack of political liberalization in the UAE and the noteworthy resilience of its monarchies? Part of the answer lies in the comprehensive and multi-dimensional "ruling bargain" that still obtains between the ruling families and their citizens. As an unwritten pact, this bargain has allowed the UAE's monarchs to trade a package of economic benefits and legitimacy resources in exchange for their national population's political acquiescence. In many ways, the UAE's particular version of the bargain has been stronger than those operating elsewhere in the Gulf. Since the UAE's population of passport-carrying nationals is so small (around 900,000), the government can effortlessly distribute wealth to all, thereby preserving and enriching a distinct elite of rent-receiving or

---

4   In 2005, Saudi Arabia held elections for half the seats in municipal councils. Males over the age of 21 were eligible to vote. *Washington Post*, April 24, 2007.

5   According to Freedom House, the UAE scores 6 for political rights and 5 for civil liberties (on a scale of 1 to 7, with 7 being the worst). This compares unfavourably with other Gulf states, with Kuwait scoring 4 for both categories and with Bahrain scoring 5 for both categories. The UAE's score places it on a par with many African and Asian dictatorships. See Freedom House, "The Worst of the Worst: The World's Most Repressive Societies", Washington, DC, 2007.

6   Examples of such modernization theorists would include Karl W. Deutsch, "Social Mobilization and Political Development", *American Political Science Review*, Vol. 55, No.3 (September 1961), pp. 493-514; Samuel P. Huntington, *Political Order in Changing Societies* (New Haven: Yale University Press, 1968); Daniel Lerner, *The Passing of Traditional Society: Modernizing in the Middle East* (Toronto: Free Press, 1964).

"rentier" citizens.[7] Salaried expatriates, who for many years have made up the vast bulk of the population, can be dismissed as mercenaries—they have come to the UAE to earn higher wages and in most cases remain uninterested in political participation. Furthermore, the relatively small size of the national elite has allowed the UAE's ruling families to more easily maintain old patrimonial and tribal networks under a veneer of seemingly modern governmental institutions. Certainly, the UAE's polity is noteworthy for its ingenious methods of prolonging traditional political practices within what can now be best described as a hybrid, neo-patrimonial government. The UAE's politics remain based on direct lines of communication between citizens and rulers, and recent efforts to expand formal participation through semi-elected councils have yet to amount to much more than window dressing.

The second part of the explanation for monarchical survival, an important one, lies in the belief that *economic* liberalization has come before *political* liberalization in the UAE, in the eyes of both the government and the people, and that any meaningful future political liberalization is more likely to emanate from the needs of investors, entrepreneurs, and the increasing number of other stakeholders in the "UAE corporation." Indeed, many of the economic reforms and the joining of international organizations, which were necessary for the UAE to kick-start its new non-oil sectors and participate in the global economy, have already led to a significant strengthening of civil society, or at least the emergence of relatively independent groups motivated by economic self-interest. Notably, by allowing free zone activity and by joining various international trade and labor organizations, the UAE has been obliged to permit workers' associations and play host to foreign companies with democratically elected boards. By constructing luxury condominiums and inviting foreign investment, the UAE cannot prevent the inevitable formation of residential associations. And while all households and most offices still have their internet services provided by Etisalat (the state-run telecom giant) and remain under a very strict proxy server, almost all of the new property developments run by Emaar and Nakheel, as well as the free zones, have internet services provided by newer, smaller companies such as Sahm Technologies. Sahm does not have any kind of proxy server, so people based in these developments

---

7   A rentier is a citizen in receipt of distributed wealth or other economic privileges afforded by a state that has become enriched through economic rent and that does not normally rely on extractive practices such as direct taxation. See Hazem Beblawi and Giacomo Luciani (eds), *The Rentier State* (New York: Croom Helm, 1987).

enjoy unfettered access. The universities are also beyond the Etisalat proxy. By promoting a knowledge economy that embraces high technology industries and a mushrooming higher education sector, the UAE will have little choice but to further relax some of its controls over domestic media and the internet—the erstwhile blocks on free flowing ideas and information across the country.

The ruling bargain: ensuring acquiescence

Central to the UAE's ruling bargain has been the ability to distribute wealth to the national population.[8] Although the ruling families have enjoyed a number of external sources of income since the early twentieth century, including rent payments for hosting airbases and military barracks, it was only following the first major oil exports of the late 1960s that the scale of economic rent was such that all extractive practices could be curtailed and the state could begin to provide a sweeping range of economic benefits and privileges to its citizens. Free education and healthcare were offered, and continue to be provided. Nationals pay neither medical costs nor school and university tuition fees.

Those nationals who graduated with degrees or other qualifications were normally found jobs within the government or its various parastatals. Although this practice only extended up until the mid-1990s, when the various public sector departments became too bloated, for many years it was entirely possible for a young national to be promoted to the level of deputy director within just a few years of graduation, and as he would often be supported by an expatriate assistant, his job would effectively be "disguised unemployment," with no real need to work a full day or to handle all responsibilities. Similarly, those nationals who preferred private sector work were encouraged to set up businesses by being given free office space and interest free loans by government-backed banks such as the Emirates Industrial Bank.

Another important example of such business-related largesse is the state's provision of free farming equipment and farm workers' subsidies in an effort to build good relations with hinterland communities and to improve the growth of the agricultural sector. Moreover, nationals have always received a number of smaller but no less significant benefits from the state. Notably, nationals do not have to pay for local telephone calls and are

8   Christopher M. Davidson, *The United Arab Emirates: A Study in Survival* (Boulder, CO: Rienner, 2005), pp. 34-7.

exempt from the annual community charges that are normally placed on houses and apartments. Although minor perquisites, these are a constant reminder that the government is a distributor rather than an extractor.

What is important is that this system, it would appear, can be continued indefinitely in the UAE, as the national population is small and the state's resources vast. Indeed, while the GDP per capita for the UAE is now an impressive $55,000, if one considers that some 4.1 million of the total resident population of five million are expatriates, then the wealth has to be distributed only to about 900,000 UAE nationals.[9] It has been estimated that the GDP per capita for nationals could be as high as $100,000, and as high as $120,000 in Dubai and $275,000 in Abu Dhabi.[10] In this respect the UAE is far ahead of all first world countries and appreciably ahead of other Gulf states, especially Saudi Arabia, which although fantastically oil-rich has nevertheless had to spread its rentier wealth far more thinly across a much larger national population of over 22 million.[11] In the long term, with the UAE's numerous sovereign wealth funds channelling excess liquidity into a range of opportunities in "safe bet" countries and emerging markets across the world, the sustainability of such distributive practices seems assured. Even in a future beyond oil, and with an expanding national population, interest payments accruing on these investments could be re-directed back to the UAE in the event of a domestic economic downswing and thereby serve to perpetuate the distribution of wealth.[12]

In addition to providing its citizens with economic benefits, the state's creation of a distinct rentier elite has also conferred numerous other benefits on the national population, not least by effectively placing all "locals" in the highest social class. Few would dispute that for many years even those UAE nationals of the most modest backgrounds have received preferential social and professional treatment by comparison with most Arab and Asian expatriates. Undoubtedly the ruling families have been rewarded by the loyalty of those that they have elevated socially as well as economically.

9   Figures based on the author's estimates; CIA World Factbook, "United Arab Emirates", 2007, online at www.cia.gov/library/publications/the-world-factbook; data supplied by Tedad (including the findings of the official 2005 Dubai census).

10 See Christopher M. Davidson, *Dubai: The Vulnerability of Success* (London: Hurst, 2008), p. 151; and Christopher M. Davidson, "After Sheikh Zayed: The Politics of Succession in Abu Dhabi and the United Arab Emirates", *Middle East Policy*, Volume 13, No. 1 (Spring 2006), pp. 43-5.

11 CIA World Factbook, "Saudi Arabia", 2007.

12 Davidson, *Dubai*, pp. 102-4.

CHRISTOPHER M. DAVIDSON

Hence it has become a key priority for the state to develop mechanisms that aim to preserve the purity and aloofness of the rentier elite. This has been done in part by offering financial benefits to those who keep their families uncontaminated by foreign blood, and in some cases by imposing penalties on those that do not conform to this requirement. Most famously, in 2002, the federal government announced a package of subsidies known as the "Shaykh Zayid Marriage Fund," and set up an office to administer the aid. Ostensibly, this fund was to provide a one-time payment of about $11,000 in order to defray some of the escalating dowry costs faced by young bachelors.[13] More subtly, however, the payment satisfied the twin aims of providing another wealth distribution instrument while also giving men a pecuniary incentive to choose a national bride. The marriage fund cannot be accessed if the man is intending to marry an expatriate. More restrictively, a UAE national woman who chooses to marry an expatriate man effectively has to give up her nationality, as their children will not be entitled to a UAE passport and therefore neither she nor her husband will be entitled to the benefits of the welfare state. Other measures are in place to discourage such relationships. Internet dating websites are routine-ly blocked for fear of encouraging mixed marriages, state-run educational institutions for national females are distanced from society,[14] and separate leisure and beach clubs exist exclusively for national women. Furthermore, unless there are extenuating circumstances, any national woman who in-tends to marry a non-national man is shamed and ostracized from both her family and broader society, even if her fiancé is a fellow Muslim. This is a relatively recent and state-induced mentality and is connected neither to religion nor to local culture. In the pre-oil era it was not uncommon for women from the lower Gulf to marry other Muslim Arabs.

Similarly, it is also important to note how the dress code for the na-tional population has become much stricter over the years: almost all local men now wear a white *dishdasha* while local women will invariably wear a black *abaya* and *shayla*. Again, this is a relatively new phenomenon, with little connection to either religion or culture: such clothes immediately dis-tinguish UAE nationals and the nationals of other Gulf monarchies from expatriate Arabs and thereby serve as a national uniform of privilege for citizens of rentier states. Prior to the 1970s, dress codes were far more var-

13   Personal interviews, Abu Dhabi, March 2002.
14   Most notably the female only Zayed University and the female only branches of the Higher Colleges of Technology.

228

ied and individualistic. By regulating marriage and dress, the state enforces conformity, thereby marking a clear distinction between those who are part of the in-group and those who are not. The in-group is privileged, but the price is conformity.

The UAE's ruling families have also been effective at supplementing the wealth distribution and other rentier elite components of their ruling bargain with a range of ideological, religious, and cultural legitimacy resources. In all cases these resources serve to portray the ruling families in a good light by reminding the national population that their hereditary rulers are merely first among equals, are historically legitimate, and serve as benevolent patriarchs with their people's interests always at heart.

One strategy has been the consistent demonstration of support for other Arab states and pursuit of diplomatic solutions wherever possible. It is no coincidence that over the past 30 years the UAE has intervened in every single regional conflict, either by hosting peace negotiations or by offering some kind of political support. This policy has allowed the ruling families to create public distance from the West, which they awkwardly rely upon for military support, while also being seen as co-operating with Arab nationalist republics or other fellow Sunni Muslim-dominated states.

A telling fact is that the UAE has received a great deal of positive press coverage across the Arab world for its actions. In particular, the UAE's collusion in OPEC's price fixing and supply restrictions of the 1970s and 1980s was regarded as being the most effective way for the militarily feeble state to assist Egypt and Syria in their struggle against Israel.[15] Moreover, during the early 1980s, even when the US was initially supporting Iran, the UAE sided with Iraq,[16] believing that, on the international stage at least, it was important for the UAE to stand shoulder-to-shoulder with an Arab state. Again, in early 1991, the UAE tried to save Iraq by brokering a last-minute deal with the Al Sabah ruling family of Kuwait.[17] Similarly, the UAE hoped to prevent the 2003 Anglo-American invasion of Iraq by offering Saddam Hussayn and his family sanctuary in Abu Dhabi on the condition that he respected George W. Bush's ultimatum and left Iraq voluntarily.[18] The UAE has maintained its peace-brokering momentum by positioning itself as a key intermediary in the looming Iranian nuclear

15   Gavin Brown, *OPEC and the World Energy Market* (London: Longman, 1998), p. 361.

16   Davidson, *United Arab Emirates*, p. 206.

17   Personal interviews, Kuwait, November 2005.

18   Personal interviews, Abu Dhabi, March 2007.

crisis. Thus, in May 2007, the UAE hosted Iran's President Mahmoud Ahmadinejad[19] just hours after US Vice President Dick Cheney had stood on an American aircraft carrier off the coast of Dubai and issued a strongly worded warning to Tehran.[20]

In addition to such high profile political interventions, the UAE has openly supported the Arab cause by providing substantial economic aid, either through various charity organizations or by personnel dispatched as part of larger humanitarian task forces. During the 1973 Arab-Israel war, both the Egyptian President Anwar Sadat and the Syrian President Hafiz al-Asad were informed that the UAE's resources would be at their disposal. Significantly, when the war entered a second week, the UAE backed up its promise by sending medical teams to the battle areas.[21] Following the PLO's ascent in 1974, the ruling families of Abu Dhabi and Dubai oversaw the donation of millions of dollars for the purpose of helping families who had lost members in the Occupied Territories.[22] Dubai's Al Maktum Foundation and the Muhammad bin Rashid Charitable and Humanitarian Establishment continue to support a range of projects in the Palestinian Authority territories, including new schools, clinics, and orphanages,[23] while Abu Dhabi has funded the $62 million Shaykh Zayid Residential City in Gaza.[24] Similarly, the UAE also channelled considerable aid into Lebanon following the outbreak of civil war, and then later sent troops to contribute to Syria's Arab Deterrent Force.[25] In 2006, following Hizbullah's ceasefire with Israel, UAE aid once again began to pour into Lebanon, from both ruling families and government organisations.

Elsewhere in the region, the UAE was heavily involved in Kuwait's reconstruction following its liberation in 1991, and by 1992 attention had been turned to troubled Muslim populations outside the Middle East, with the UAE providing military engineers for the UN-endorsed US intervention force in war-torn Somalia.[26] Perhaps most notably, in 1995, the UAE also began to actively assist European Muslims caught up in the Balkans

---

19   *BBC News*, May 13, 2007.

20   *Reuters*, May 11, 2007.

21   Graeme Wilson, *Rashid's Legacy: The Genesis of the Maktoum Family and the History of Dubai* (Dubai: Media Prima, 2006), pp. 361-2.

22   Wilson, pp. 377-8.

23   Wilson, p. 365.

24   *Khaleej Times*, October 23, 2004.

25   Wilson, p. 424; personal interviews, Beirut, November 2006.

26   Wilson, pp. 511-13.

conflict, providing airlifts for wounded Bosnians.[27] When conflict erupted between Christians and Muslims in Kosovo in 1999, and Serbia chose to intervene, the UAE was the only Arab country to participate in the NATO-led peacekeeping force.[28] In addition to several million dollars of aid, all of the UAE's terrestrial TV stations participated in a charity telethon. The event raised $15 million and then members of the ruling families doubled this. Using this money, over 50 new mosques were built in Kosovo during 2000.[29]

The UAE appears quite committed to this strategy. The estimated share of state revenue assigned to foreign aid is more than triple the contributions of most Western states.[30] The UAE funding of tsunami relief projects in Southeast Asia and earthquake relief in Iran has been enormous,[31] and in the summer of 2007 the ruler of Dubai made what is believed to be the largest gift in history when he donated $10 billion to a new pan-Arab educational foundation.[32] Moreover, Dubai in particular has invested heavily in physical infrastructure for aid operations. In 2003, it set up a processing zone specifically for humanitarian non-governmental organizations, and built huge warehouses close to both ports for the exclusive use of offices based in this new "Dubai Humanitarian City."

The ruling families have been similarly proactive in boosting religious legitimacy resources, regularly sponsoring events relating to the promotion and awareness of Islam. Most famously, the families annually release convicts if they can recite the entire Qur'an, or the prisoners can have their sentences reduced by up to five years if they can remember large sections.[33] Moreover, there is substantial funding and state endorsements for large Islamic conferences that attract scholars and clerics from across the Muslim world.[34] The UAE has also made great efforts to support Islamic banking. Dubai now stages the International Islamic Finance Forum, and one of its sovereign wealth funds has recently acquired a 40 percent stake in the

27   Personal interviews, Dubai, February 2006.

28   *Jane's Defense Weekly*, February 7, 2007.

29   Wilson, p. 516.

30   Personal interviews, Dubai, February 2006.

31   Some $2 million was donated by the Muhammad bin Rashid Charitable and Humanitarian Establishment to Thailand in early 2005. *Gulf News*, February 12, 2005.

32   *BBC News*, May 19, 2007.

33   *Reuters, India Tribune*, October 18, 2002.

34   *Gulf News*, October 27, 2004.

Malaysian-based Bank of Islam—a very strict institution that prohibits any financial activities that derive profits from alcohol, pork, or gambling.[35]

Cultural components of the ruling bargain have also been strengthened over the years. A plethora of museums have been built, several dozen traditional houses have been restored, a number of open air "heritage villages" have been constructed. Most of these celebrate a particular aspect of the UAE's heritage and reinforce both tribal history and the roles of the shaykhs. Crucially, all of these sites host a range of cultural activities such as singing, dancing, pottery making, basket weaving, and cooking. These "live" activities create "living memories" and "imagined communities,"[36] not only for the increasing number of tourists but also for the younger generations of nationals who would otherwise be ignorant of their past. By preserving memories of the UAE's history of traditional activities and the achievements of its most powerful dynasties, it is believed that the hereditary rulers' positions at the head of contemporary, tribal values-based traditional political systems will make more sense to the national population.[37]

In an effort to further reinforce these memories, new activities have been created from reinventions of the past. Notably, members of the ruling families have heavily sponsored camel racing in Abu Dhabi and Dubai. Although camel racing was never really a part of Bedouin lifestyle, except at special occasions such as weddings, this new multi-million dollar industry nevertheless provides another forum for the rulers to greet their nationals in an ostensibly traditional context. Indeed, the opening ceremonies of such race meetings often feature Bedouin dances, poetry in honour of the attending shaykh, and a large banquet of local food.[38]

Patrimonial politics: the case of Dubai

With this small and privileged national population, maintaining a traditional system based on appointing members of certain trusted families to administrative positions is entirely feasible in the UAE. This has led to the development of a "patrimonial network" drawn from the most loyal members of the rentier elite. Although it is no longer common for entire families or sub-tribes to fill whole "lines" of employment in certain govern-

---

35   Personal interviews, Abu Dhabi, March 2007.

36   Sulayman Khalaf, "Poetics and Politics of Newly Invented Traditions in the Gulf: Camel Racing in the United Arab Emirates", *Ethnology*, Vol. 39, No.3 (Summer 2000), pp. 85-106.

37   Khalaf.

38   Khalaf.

ment departments and ministries as they did in the 1970s and 1980s,[39] there nevertheless remain clearly identifiable vertical chains of relationships that extend in a pyramid fashion from the ruling families and their closest associates down through loyal intermediaries, before reaching members of "lesser" national families. A position higher up on the pyramid represents a closer proximity to power. This power pyramid can also work in reverse on those occasions when highly placed individuals abuse their powers or oppose the ruling family: not only are they stripped of their position, their extended family's name is tarnished, and this limits the employment prospects for all others in that family.

In many ways, the government of Dubai provides the strongest example of patrimonial politics in the UAE today. Its number of citizens is small, but it has, perhaps, the greatest number of government departments that need to be staffed, owing to the scale and complexity of its economy.[40] In particular, the ruling Al Maktum family works closely with several prominent families from its parent clan, the Al Bu Falasa section of the Bani Yas tribe. These have included the Al Bu Shamis, which is closely related by marriage to the Al Maktum family. Most notably, members of the Al Tayir have served as Ministers of State for Financial and Industrial Affairs and as directors of the UAE Central Bank, and have assisted Dubai's delegations to the International Monetary Fund. Other members of the Al Tayir family have held influential posts in the Dubai Chamber of Commerce and Industry, in the Jabal 'Ali Free Zone Authority, and in the Dubai Ports World Company.[41] Also derived from the Al Bu Falasa has been the al-Habtur family, which has also held positions in the Chamber in addition to providing many of Dubai's representatives to federal institutions. The Bani Sulayman, another Al Bu Falasa family, have continued to be rewarded with key responsibilities, its members having served in the Chamber and having taken leading roles in the running of the Dubai Department of Tourism and Commerce Marketing, while now, most prominently, they chair two of the government's most important parastatals: the Nakheel

---

39   Most notably the Zawahir controlled dozens of positions in the military; the Mazariyya made up a sizable portion of the Amiri Guard; and the Awamir held many posts in public works and civil defence. See Davidson, "After Sheikh Zayed", pp. 52-3.

40   In 2007, there were about 80,000 Dubai nationals; in 1997, there were only about 40,000. Personal interviews, Dubai, January 2007; Hendrik Van Der Meulen, "The Role of Tribal and Kinship Ties in the Politics of the United Arab Emirates" (PhD thesis, Fletcher School of Law and Diplomacy, 1997), p. 202.

41   Van Der Meulen, pp. 192-3; M.T.G. Pope, *Businessman's Guide to the United Arab Emirates* (Sharjah: Dar al-Fatah, 1996), pp. 204, 273, 297.

property company and the Dubai Ports World Company. Other favoured families from the Al Bu Falasa include the al-Bawardi and a number of smaller families such as the Harib, which have staffed DUBAL, the Dubai Aluminium Company.

Those Bani Yas families outside the Al Bu Falasa section that have proven themselves as capable merchants have often been rewarded with important posts in the administration. In particular, the al-Ghurayr family has held appointments in the Dubai Chamber of Commerce and Industry, the Dubai Municipality, and the Dubai Water and Electricity Authority (DEWA). Similarly, the al-Futtaim merchant family now has many of its members working in the Chamber and DEWA.[42]

Beyond the Bani Yas tribe, the ruling family has been keen to co-opt into its administration many members of Dubai's naturalised immigrant Arab tribes and merchant families, especially the descendants of longstanding residents who moved to Dubai before the early twentieth century. Members of the Al Bu Shamis tribe from Sharjah have been employed in both the Chamber and the police,[43] while many of those families from the Umm al-Quwwayn-based Al 'Ali tribe who chose to move to Dubai now have relatives working in the ruler's office and have represented Dubai in various international organizations. Through the al-'Uways family, the Dubai-based contingent of the Al 'Ali has even provided a former federal Minister for Water and Electricity[44] and the current Minister for Culture, Youth, and Community Development.[45] Moreover, many members of the Manasir tribe who reside in Dubai have also been incorporated into government.[46] A number now work in the police while others work in the ruler's office. From the Sudan (al-Suwaydi) tribe, which also has many Dubai residents, a few families work in the police,[47] while others (including the Balhul family of the Bani Tamim section) have been involved in both Dubai's healthcare administration and the Dubai Ports World Company.

Of those families that arrived in Dubai from Baluchistan following the handover of Makran—an Omani-ruled part of Baluchistan—by Oman to Pakistan in the 1950s, many have become naturalized Dubai nationals and

42   Van Der Meulen, pp. 194-5.

43   Van Der Meulen, pp. 182-3.

44   Van Der Meulen, p. 196.

45   The current Minister for Culture, Youth, and Community Development is 'Abd al-Rahman Muhammad al-'Uways.

46   Van Der Meulen, p. 156.

47   Pope, p. 222.

were offered greater administrative responsibilities following loyal service in the police. Most notably, the al-Balushi and Bin Lutah families have represented Dubai in federal institutions while the al-Nabuda family provided the longstanding chairman of the Dubai Chamber. Also of significance among the Baluchi population has been the al-Majid family, especially Jum'a al-Majid, who quickly emerged as one of Dubai's most prominent businessmen and has served on the boards of many of the emirate's banks, in addition to establishing his own cultural foundation.[48] Similarly, from the highly respected Persian immigrant merchant community many families were also brought into the administration, with the al-Tajir, al-Fardin, al-Sayigh, Galadiri, and al-Ansari families now occupying many positions in the Dubai Municipality, in DEWA, in Etisalat, and in the National Bank of Dubai. Most notably the al-Gurg family has provided the UAE with its long serving ambassador to Britain, while a member of the Gargash family now holds the position of federal Minister of State for Federal National Council Affairs.[49]

It is also important to note the way in which the Al Maktum have carefully expanded their patrimonial network in recent years by bringing in a select number of highly capable young professionals from less well-established families. Indeed, during the 1990s Crown Prince Shaykh Muhammad bin Rashid Al Maktum hand-picked the most able employees from his various organizations and groomed them for higher responsibilities. This strategy led to an expanding contingent of technocrats within Dubai's administration. Many of these relatively young men have now reached the directorial level and, in some cases, have been appointed to high government office. An important point is that the loyalty of these elevated individuals and their families to the ruling family would seem unquestionable. Particularly strong examples of Dubai technocrats include Muhammad 'Ali al-'Abbar, who rose to become director of Dubai's Department of Economic Development and the chairman of Emaar, and who now also serves as vice chairman of both the Dubai World Trade Center and DUBAL, in addition to representing Dubai in the World Economic Forum. Equally prominent among these technocrats has been Muhammad 'Abdallah al-Jarjawi, who was successful in setting up the Dubai Shopping Festival before being appointed chairman of Dubai Holdings and launching Dubai Internet City. Significantly, al-Jarjawi rose to ministerial level with his appointment as

48   Pope, pp. 193, 251, 269.
49   Anwar Muhammad Gargash.

Minister of State for Cabinet Affairs. Similarly powerful has been Muhammad Khalfan bin Kharbash, who for many years balanced his chairmanship
of several Dubai's banks and development-related institutions with his role
as Minister of State for Financial and Industrial Affairs.

Traditional politics, modern institutions

To add greater legitimacy to this patrimonial network, which is little more
than an extended system of cronyism grafted onto a traditional polity, the
ruling families have made great efforts to create and support an outside layer
of more modern "neo-patrimonial" governmental institutions. Indeed, while
the main power clearly rests with established families and prominent individuals, the ruling families have voluntarily transformed the polity[50] by building up various emirate-level councils and departments, most of which are run
along seemingly legal-rational lines with codified regulations and procedures.
Moreover, in cooperation with each other, the hereditary monarchs have ensured that the federal institutions established following British withdrawal in
1971 have been maintained and in some cases upgraded.

At the emirate level, Dubai again provides a strong example of such a
hybrid political system. Modern governmental functions are ostensibly carried out by the Dubai Executive Council which is presided over by Shaykh
Muhammad bin Rashid Al Maktum who became ruler in 2006, and is now
chaired by his second son and the new Crown Prince, Shaykh Hamdan bin
Muhammad Al Maktum. His uncle, Shaykh Ahmad bin Sa'id Al Maktum, serves as deputy chairman, and the above-mentioned Muhammad
'Abdallah al-Jarjawi acts as secretary general. Tellingly, the twelve other
members of the Council include no less than three members of the Bani
Sulayman (two brothers and their nephew),[51] a member of another afore-
mentioned Al Bu Falasah family, the Harib,[52] and a representative from the
Bani Tamim.[53] Also present are Shaykh Hashir bin Maktum Al Maktum,
another member of the ruling family, and the ubiquitous Muhammad 'Ali
al-'Abbar. Effectively in control of the amirate's day-to-day affairs, this dis-
tinctly neo-patrimonial council also acts as an umbrella organisation, with

---

50   For a discussion of voluntary transformation as a means of delaying genuine political
      reform see Manfred Halpern, *The Politics of Social Change in the Middle East and North
      Africa* (Princeton University Press, 1965), p. 42.

51   Sultan Ahmad bin Sulayman, Khalid Ahmad bin Sulayman, and Khalifa Muhammad bin
      Sulayman.

52   Khalfan bin Ahmad Harib.

53   Zahi bin Khalfan Tamim.

several smaller councils operating under its jurisdiction and representatives being fielded from the emirate's various public and private sectors. It is regarded as being dynamic and flexible, with its relatively small core of members often meeting in relaxed settings such as the conference suite of the Emirates Towers Hotel. Interestingly, unlike other emirate-specific councils elsewhere in the UAE, the Dubai Executive Council does not even have to respond to any form of organised consultative council—it simply answers directly to the ruler. This is a testament to Dubai's particularly strong version of the ruling bargain, its merchant heritage, and its more business-focused citizenry that to some extent continues to view government principally as a board of directors.

At the federal level, the UAE's government is run along much the same lines, with the various ruling families and their emirate-specific patrimonial networks contributing a certain quota of representatives to what may appear to be modern institutions, but are in reality the arms of a "monarchical presidency". Most notably, the UAE's highest authority is the Supreme Council of Rulers (SCR), which has the power to initiate policy and to reject laws that have previously been passed. The SCR is simply a forum consisting of the seven hereditary rulers. Its presidency always rests with Abu Dhabi, given its vast oil wealth and immense contributions to the federal budget, and the vice presidency rests with Dubai, given its secondary role in federal contributions.[54] Significantly, while the constitution called for an SCR presidential election every five years,[55] there has only been one such formal occasion, following the end of Shaykh Zayid bin Sultan Al Nuhayan's thirty-three-year presidency in late 2004. The constitution is now without this clause.

Subordinate to the SCR is the federal Council of Ministers (COM). However, since the SCR meets infrequently and often only informally, the COM and its various ministries formulate the bulk of the UAE's policies and it is responsible for much of the day-to-day running of the federation. The COM is dominated by traditional elites and members of patrimonial networks, and, like the SCR, is structured in favour of the wealthiest emirates. Originally, the portfolios in the COM were distributed in such a way that Abu Dhabi controlled six important positions; Dubai controlled

---

54   Abu Dhabi contributes about 70 per cent of the federal budget, with Dubai contributing only about 15 per cent, the remainder coming from various federal parastatals such as Etisalat. Personal interviews, Abu Dhabi, March 2007.

55   See Najat Abdullah Al-Nabeh, "United Arab Emirates: Regional and Global Dimensions" (PhD thesis, Claremont Graduate School, 1984).

the premiership and three other important positions; Sharjah controlled three less important positions; Ra's al-Kha'ima and Fujayra controlled two positions; and 'Ajman and Umm al-Quwwayn held just one position. In reality, however, Abu Dhabi has always controlled more than six positions, given that many of the ministers of state (the deputies of the official ministers) have been members of the ruling family of Abu Dhabi and have been effectively in control of their respective ministries. Dubai's control over the Ministry of Defence is purely nominal since Abu Dhabi controls the amalgamated military (with the Supreme Commander, Deputy Supreme Commander, and Chief of Staff of the UAE Armed Forces all being from Abu Dhabi).[56] In total, there are now 10 members of ruling families sitting on the COM, the highest number there has ever been since its inception in 1971, and the remainder are all either identifiable as members of established families or powerful technocrats with close links to the rulers of their respective emirates.

The federal legislature, or more accurately the UAE's consultative chamber, was originally comprised of forty delegates appointed by the SCR, including an internally elected speaker and two deputies. This *Majlis al-Watani al-Ittihadi*, or Federal National Council (FNC), sits for sessions of two years at a time. Again, this is an institution that is weighted heavily in favour of Abu Dhabi and Dubai, which are eligible to supply eight members each, compared with six members each from Sharjah and Ra's al-Kha'ima (despite these emirates having higher populations of UAE nationals than Dubai) and just four members each from the three smallest emirates.[57] With a broader social profile, the FNC was intended to serve as a forum for debate for members of other established families not represented on the COM, alongside distinguished professionals from less notable backgrounds. In recent years, the FNC's role has been called into question, with many arguing that it is little more than a civilized talking shop that has rarely been able to question the decisions of the COM or the SCR. Indeed, although there are examples of debates in which the FNC has managed to participate in the decision-making process by presenting its suggestions to the SCR, these have normally been over concerns that were already shared by the COM, such as the need for tightening anti-drug legislation and to

---

56   Shaykh Khalifa bin Zayid Al Nuhayan is Supreme Commander, Shaykh Muhammad bin Zayed Al Nuhayan is Deputy Supreme Commander, and Hamad bin Muhammad al-Thai al-Rumaythi is the Chief of Staff. *AFP*, January 1, 2005.

57   S.N. Asad Rizvi, "From Tents to High Rise: Economic Development of the United Arab Emirates", *Middle Eastern Studies*, Vol. 29, No.4 (October 1993), p. 665.

further modify the UAE's property laws.[58] Certainly, on matters where the FNC's views were likely to diverge from the relevant minister's outlook, such as the price of petrol or the cultural content of terrestrial television,[59] the FNC has repeatedly failed to convert its formal recommendations into policy. Remarkably, there have been examples of the FNC's letters to ministers remaining unanswered for several months, and occasions when the FNC has been unable to persuade ministers to attend their sessions and answer basic questions on their policies.[60]

By late 2005, with a series of reforms and elections having expanded the powers of consultative chambers in Bahrain, Qatar and Oman, the comparatively feeble FNC had become something of an embarrassment to the UAE. A consensus emerged that if there was not at least some effort to improve formal political participation, the ruling families and the federal government would risk being branded as backward not only by the international community but also by the nationals of the UAE's closest neighbours. Accordingly, in early 2006, Dubai's Anwar Muhammad Gargash was entrusted with the newly created position of Minister of State for Federal National Council Affairs, and was given a brief to investigate methods of increasing the FNC's powers and its role in political participation.[61] Within months, plans were drawn up to stage limited elections, and in late 2006 the UAE's first ballots were held across the federation. The elections were widely regarded as farcical given that only twenty of the forty positions were to be elected, and only specific "electoral colleges" which had been nominated by the various rulers could vote to fill these "open" positions. Thus, the reforms were seen to be incomplete as all of the FNC members would still be chosen by the SCR, albeit a little more indirectly than before. Moreover, drawing particularly caustic criticism were the rules applied to membership of the electoral colleges: of the 400,000 or so UAE nationals who were above the age of eighteen and therefore eligible to participate, less than 7,000 were selected, many of these being drawn from a small number of families, some electors being under the age of sixteen, while others were even dead. Tellingly, only 60 percent of the eligible vot-

---

58   Shamma bint Muhammad Al-Nahyan. *Political and Social Security in the United Arab Emirates* (Dubai: 2000), pp. 122-3.

59   Al Nahyan, p. 121.

60   Al Nahyan, pp. 178-9, 188.

61   *Khaleej Times*, February 10, 2006.

ers actually cast their ballots; some of the absentees complained about the pointlessness of the exercise.[62]

Nevertheless, although the 2006 reforms were overly cautious and the planners had misjudged the level of political consciousness in the UAE at that time, there is a view that they were still of some use, as they have played an important role in readying a population previously unaccustomed to such formal participation for more extensive reforms in future years. As Gargash has explained, the next round of FNC elections in 2010 will almost certainly involve all 40 positions and the electoral colleges will be greatly expanded.[63] Moreover, as the UAE's President, Shaykh Khalifa bin Zayid Al Nuhayan, has announced, the FNC will be considerably strengthened before then, as he intends it to become a more powerful "bridge between population and government."[64] Indeed, in mid-2007, the FNC began to experiment with a new system of opening its doors to members of the public, in an effort to allow other interested parties to visit and participate in certain debates. Most notably, the FNC held a widely publicized session on the subject of the UAE's education policies, which was well attended by teachers, academics, students, and the Minister of Education.[65]

But by far the most significant development in contemporary UAE politics has been the introduction of a series of measures aimed at actually preserving and strengthening the old informal, patrimonial relationships between the ruling families and their citizens. In some cases, new methods and new technologies have been applied imaginatively in an effort to keep traditional, tribal politics relevant in the minds of a more urbanized twenty-first century national population. Notably, many of the shaykhs who used to hold an informal consultation session or *majlis* have appointed teams of intermediaries to act as agents, thereby increasing the number of grievances that they can hear and to which they can attend. Furthermore, there still exists a school of thought that if details of potentially controversial policies can be gently leaked and allowed to filter through the old patrimonial networks, then any possible public backlash can be determined in advance of promulgation. Most effectively, however, both the federal government

---

62   Personal interviews, London, February 2007. Elections were carried out in a similar manner in parts of the Ottoman Empire in the late nineteenth and early twentieth centuries. See Joshua Teitelbaum, *The Rise and Fall of the Hashimite Kingdom of Arabia* (New York: New York University Press, 2001).

63   Personal interviews, Dubai, January 2007.

64   *Gulf News*, December 21, 2006.

65   *Gulf News*, May 7, 2007.

and the emirate-level governments have invested heavily in e-governance in recent years, with almost all ministries and departments having developed sophisticated websites that not only allow citizens to access government services online but also permit them to record their problems and receive an answer within a few days. Indeed, Dubai has been particularly pioneering in this regard; most of its prominent shaykhs have interactive websites, including the ruler and the Crown Prince,[66] and its various government offices now all provide electronic forums for discussion and feedback. Importantly, most of these appear to work well, with strict quality control and guaranteed response times. Certainly they are far in advance of e-government services in Western democracies and the other Gulf states.

Economic liberalization

With few chinks in the armour of a neo-patrimonial system directed by resilient traditional monarchs and supported and staffed by an enriched and acquiescent rentier elite, the only real pressures for political liberalization in the UAE are those resulting from the extensive economic liberalization that has taken place. In an effort to reduce its dependence on hydrocarbon exports since the 1980s the UAE, and particularly the more oil-scarce Dubai, have attempted to diversify the economy by boosting non-oil sectors such as tourism, while also attracting non-oil-related foreign direct investment into export-processing free zones and real estate projects. Success in all of these sectors has required the UAE to become more integrated into the global economy and to seek and maintain membership of various international organisations, some of which have imposed on the country certain minimum standards of governance and civil liberty. Moreover, while development of the tourism industry has been relatively straightforward, the foreign direct investment strategy has required a number of reforms and relaxations, which are in turn serving to create an increasingly powerful stakeholder community made up of both foreign and expatriate investors, which undoubtedly has a very different mindset from that of the salaried expatriate community. Combined, these new sets of external and internal forces may already be invigorating civil society in the UAE.

In the early 1980s the ruler of Dubai, Shaykh Rashid bin Sa'id Al Maktum, decided that significant levels of foreign direct investment in the UAE would only be possible if foreign companies could circumvent the existing Gulf-wide legislation requiring all businesses to have a local sponsor or *kafil*

---

66   Most notably, Shaykh Muhammad's website has existed since the mid-1990s.

owning at least 51 percent of the stock.[67] The proposed solution was to set up a free zone alongside the new port at Jabal 'Ali. This would allow foreign companies easy access to unloading facilities while also keeping the new authority on the periphery of the city as something of an enclave. Launched in 1985 by the Dubai Department of Industry, the Jabal 'Ali Free Zone Authority guaranteed 100 percent foreign ownership[68] and offered foreign companies the opportunity to move into ready-made "lease office buildings" with additional benefits of streamlined visa processing for their employees, cheap energy, and good transport infrastructure. The zone enjoyed rapid growth, and was soon home to around 300 very diverse companies including textile manufacturers, chocolate factories, and farm machinery exporters. Remarkably, by 2002, the zone had expanded to accommodate over 2,000 companies, and today it employs over 40,000 workers and has generated over $6 billion in investments.[69] About a quarter of these companies are Middle Eastern, while over 30 percent are Asian, and about 45 percent are either Western European or North American.[70] Notably, Jabal 'Ali has proved particularly popular with multinationals hoping to establish a Middle Eastern headquarters, and in some cases has even begun to host companies intent on total relocation. Of this latter category, the most high profile recent entrant has been Halliburton, which in 2007 chose to shift its base from Texas to Jabal 'Ali, citing the UAE's more "conducive business environment."[71]

So successful was this first free zone that many of Dubai's neighbors began to introduce similar enabling legislation and have now proceeded to set up their own authorities. Most notably, Ra's al-Kha'ima has established its RAK Free Trade Zone, Sharjah has launched its Hamriyya Free Zone, and sections of the new Khalifa Port and Industrial Zone in Abu Dhabi will also be operated under a free zone authority.[72] Pushing the boundaries even further, Dubai has since created many other, more specialist free zones in order to attract and accommodate new sectors that require specific infrastructure. In particular, in 1999, Dubai announced that it would be creating two new "cities," one for Internet companies and one for media companies.

67   Personal correspondence, March 2007.

68   Dubai Department of Economic Development, *Statistical Book* (Dubai: 1999), p. 241.

69   Dubai Department of Economic Development, *Statistical Book* (Dubai: 2002), p. 245; personal interviews, Dubai, February 2006.

70   Personal correspondence, March 2007.

71   Personal interviews, Dubai, February 2006.

72   See *Gulf Today*, July 18, 2007.

Set up by Muhammad 'Abdallah al-Jarjawi in partnership with Sun, Cisco, and Siemens, by late 2000, Dubai Internet City was ready to open its doors, providing IT infrastructure to over 100 companies that had been waiting to move in. Incredibly, by 2007, the City had expanded to house nearly 850 companies employing some 10,000 workers, and now it boasts the Middle Eastern headquarters of a number of leading technology firms.[73]

In parallel, and on an adjacent site, Dubai Media City was launched at the same time and operated by a new Media Free Zone Authority. Much like Internet City, Media City also has around 800 companies, and these include many leading regional and international brands. Soon the City's facilities will be expanded further to include a village of studios to facilitate onsite production and to encourage an expanded Dubai-based TV industry. Perhaps the strongest indicator of the project's success to date is that since 2006 almost all international news service reports that are filed in the Middle East are datelined "Dubai," indicating their Dubai Media City location.

More recently, several other zones have been established around Dubai, so many in fact that perhaps one third of the city's land area is now controlled by free zone authorities. These have included the Dubai Airport Free Zone, Dubai Silicon Oasis, Dubai Flower City, Dubai Healthcare City (which will serve as a base for foreign medical companies and services, including a branch of Harvard Medical School),[74] and Dubai Knowledge Village, which, since its launch in 2003, now houses branches of several international universities. Perhaps most significant among these newer free zones have been the Dubai International Financial Centre (DIFC) and its constituent Dubai International Financial Exchange (DIFX). The DIFC has the twin aims of bridging the time zone gap between the financial markets of Europe and Asia while also attracting foreign direct investment from international financial companies. An important factor is that the DIFC is unencumbered by local legislation—the government has decided that the DIFC's regulatory framework should be based on English law.[75] Foreign experts (from Standard Chartered and Julius Bär) were enlisted to assist with the project, and in 2004, the Dubai Financial Services Authority was set up to administer the DIFC. Within months, the new complex was home to a number of well-respected international financial institutions

73   Wilson, p. 551.

74   Wilson, p. 581.

75   *Gulf News*, September 22, 2004; personal interviews, Dubai, June 2006.

including KPMG, Swiss Private, Swiss International Legal, Merrill Lynch, and Credit Suisse.[76]

The UAE's diversification into freehold real estate has encouraged greater foreign and expatriate investment from individuals and required similarly extensive economic reforms. As late as the mid-1990s there was no property market in the UAE. However, by 1997, this began to change following an announcement that the new $200 million Emirates Hills residential complex in Dubai would offer luxury villas to all GCC nationals and, most crucially, to foreigners.[77] The project was managed by Emaar Properties, a company that had been set up in the early 1990s by Muhammad 'Ali al-'Abbar and had pressed the government to liberalize the sector. Following in Emaar's footsteps have been Dubai Properties and Nakheel. Most famously, the latter has constructed two separate "Palm Islands" off the coast of Jumeira and Jabal 'Ali, both of which will feature villas and several luxury hotels. By early 2006, these three big developers were thought to have already provided over 30,000 new homes, most of which were sold to expatriates. Crucially, by this stage, with Dubai claiming over $50 billion in committed property-related projects,[78] the federal government was presented with something of a *fait accompli*, and by the spring of that year the ruler unilaterally announced the Dubai Property Law. This included articles stipulating that foreigners were entitled to own real estate in "some parts of Dubai, as designated by the ruler" and would be entitled to receive residency visas from the Dubai government (previously residency visas were only issued to foreigners subject to proof of employment). Moreover, to settle investors' minds further, the law called for the establishment of a Lands Department that would provide a centralized land registry capable of issuing deeds upon purchase.[79]

With this new legislation in place, demand for Dubai's more recently announced projects soared, and additional developments were soon launched. In some cases, demand was so high that prospective customers for these new off-plan villas and apartments were advised to arrive at sales centers on the morning of the launch in order to get in line to receive a lottery-like ticket that would entitle them to make a purchase. It is noteworthy that many of the other emirates are now seeking to reproduce Du-

---

76   *Khaleej Times*, October 2, 2004.

77   Davidson, *United Arab Emirates*, p. 230.

78   Merchant International Group, "Strategic Research and Corporate Intelligence: Instant Analysis on Dubai", London, 2005.

79   See Law Number 7 of 2006: The Dubai Property Law.

bai's real estate sector, Ra's al-Kha'ima having been the first to jump on the bandwagon, with its own enabling legislation. Sharjah has been a little more cautious than its neighbors, preferring to keep such foreign investment more discreet; however, it would seem that these concerns have now been balanced, since efforts are now being focused on developing the more secluded islands to the east of the city. Most significantly, with similar liberalizing legislation in place, Abu Dhabi now also has several real estate companies, some of which, like Emaar, have opened themselves up to public ownership. Among these, the Crown Prince's Aldar group has been responsible for both the vast Al Raha Beach complex and the exclusive Al Gurm Resort, while Sorouh has been developing al-Rim island by building Shams City.

Liberalization's prospects

With hundreds of branches of foreign companies establishing themselves in the UAE's free zones, and with a number of international NGOs now relocating to the UAE, a critical mass of organizations has emerged in the UAE which subscribe to democratic practices, or at the very least have elected boards and other transparent structures. Many of these foreign entities employ local staff, so that their interaction with the domestic economy and society is considerable. Hence, it is possible that something of a demonstration effect may take place, with domestically incorporated companies and employees undoubtedly being provided with a blueprint for future local organizations, including civil society associations.

Moreover, for the new non-oil sectors to succeed in attracting foreign direct investment and building the necessary global partnerships, the UAE has been compelled to join a number of international economic organizations, including the World Trade Organisation, to which it acceded in 1996. Like all other new member states, the UAE was obliged to agree to a roadmap towards an improved regulatory infrastructure and commit to international standards of good governance.[80] While there has been criticism in the UAE of the WTO requirements for the premature breaking up of some its monopolies, there nevertheless seems to be a consensus that transparency and accountability have increased in both the public and private sectors since accession. Of greatest impact, however, has been the UAE's joining the International Labour Organisation—another implicit

---

80   Gary P. Sampson (ed.), *The Role of the World Trade Organisation in Global Governance* (New York: United Nations University Press, 2001).

requirement of WTO membership. Previously, federal law did not permit workers to engage in any form of collective bargaining.[81] For white collar professions, employee associations were tolerated, and for some years these were allowed to collectively raise work-related issues and to file protests with the government.[82] For blue collar workers, however, any attempt to remonstrate was normally suppressed by the threat of imprisonment or deportation. Significantly, since the federal government's recent adherence to a range of ILO conventions[83] there have been several highly active informal workers' associations that have not been dismantled by the government. In most cases, these associations have been attempting to peacefully redress unfair practices (including deliberate delays in paying salaries and lack of compensation for injured employees),[84] although in some cases there have been violent strikes which have severely delayed the completion of major construction projects. Between 2005 and 2007, more than 20 organized protests took place in Dubai alone,[85] as workers felt emboldened to press claims in a manner that would have been inconceivable for earlier generations of expatriate workers.

Another key feature of civil society that may be emerging is the existence of residential associations. As wealthy investors and residents have been buying luxurious properties across the UAE, they have unsurprisingly begun to express concerns about the opaqueness of town planning, as they fear that their investments and lifestyles may be adversely affected should the government construct new highways or tower blocks in the vicinity of their new possessions. Certainly, in the last few years there have been instances of significant alterations to original blueprints and unannounced new developments being undertaken alongside existing projects.[86] While in some of these cases the initial investors were offered compensation,[87] the system has nevertheless often left buyers feeling vulnerable. By forming associations to which the government cannot reasonably object, since they

---

81   US Department of State, "United Arab Emirates: Country Reports on Human Rights," Bureau of Democracy, Human Rights, and Labor, February 2001.

82   US Department of State.

83   *Khaleej Times*, December 2, 2002, citing the UAE Minister of Labor and Social Affairs speaking at the Dubai Chamber of Commerce and Industry.

84   *Khaleej Times*, October 2, 2004.

85   US Department of State.

86   A prominent example would include Nakheel's decision to squeeze more properties onto Palm Jumeira, thereby reducing the footprint of each villa. In 2005, a new bypass road was constructed close to Emaar's Meadows project, much to the chagrin of residents.

87   Personal interviews, Dubai, June 2006.

are commonplace in real estate developments elsewhere in the world, UAE residents are effectively being allowed to form civil society organizations that may soon be powerful enough to lobby municipalities and other local government departments.

Finally, another major boost for the prospects of meaningful civil society, and perhaps the most important glimmer of hope for political liberalization in the UAE, has been the state's reluctant retreat from the control of information. From the 1970s, a much maligned Ministry of Information and Culture oversaw the censorship of all newspapers, magazines and since the late 1990s the internet, in an effort to curb access to undesirable material including pornography, gambling, magic, and sensitive political information including issues relating to democracy and human rights violations in the Gulf. In 2006, however, the ministry was disbanded, as it was viewed as being anachronistic and incompatible with the UAE's drive for global economic integration. Certainly, it was feared that tourists, investors and other interested parties, especially those involved in the Dubai Media City, would balk at such repressive practices. As a result, there is today a greater feeling of freedom for local media. While journalists continue to self-censor, there is nevertheless a more relaxed atmosphere than before, and a number of critical reports have recently been published that would not have been possible just a few years ago. Most tellingly, a new broadsheet quality English-language newspaper has been launched in Abu Dhabi, *The National.* Funded by a government agency but staffed by Western editors, it has been given a genuine *carte blanche* to provide critical coverage of domestic affairs. Moreover, while there remains an internet proxy server that restricts access to certain websites, many of the new real estate developments, free zones, and universities are operating outside this system and in practice have unfettered access to the internet. Within the next few years, it is likely that this internet freedom will be extended to the entire country as it will become increasingly difficult to justify a two-tier information society in the UAE.

The UAE's combination of traditional, tribally informed monarchy and rapid oil-fuelled economic development represents an important experiment in economically-driven liberalization, which already has had some impact on political liberalization. While it is doubtful that the near term will see any meaningful change in the established way of doing politics in the UAE, since the small population benefits tremendously from the current situation, it remains to be seen if rights extended to the increasingly demanding expatriate population might not have a spillover effect and force the government to extend similar rights to citizens. But they would have to demand them, and the current rentier system treats them so well that doing without these rights might be a small price to pay for a life of luxury.

11

IRAQ: THE BATTLEGROUND
OF REPRESENTATION

Ofra Bengio

The idea of democracy has bedeviled the Middle East for the greater part of the twentieth century. And while at the beginning of that century the very term did not exist even in the Arabic lexicon,[1] by its end, democracy was embraced by all political and ideological trends, be they leftists, Islamists or Pan-Arabists. This across-the-board adoption of the term did not mean that the regimes had really come to terms with the idea itself, or that they were willing to implement it wholeheartedly in the way it was understood and implemented in the West.[2] In fact, the slogan of democracy was adopted as a defensive reflex against an intruding foreign power or as lip service to a popular trend which engulfed the modern world. It might not be surprising, therefore, to find out that the Iraqi Ba'th Party which came to power in 1968 stated in its provisional constitution promulgated in that year that Iraq was "a popular, democratic state that derives its democratic foundations and its popular character from the Arab heritage and the spirit of Islam."[3]

This type of rhetoric, which had become part and parcel of the Ba'thi discourse throughout its 35 years in power, was, as is well known, but a very thin veil covering one of the most totalitarian and undemocratic re-

---

1   For example the dictionary *al-Munjid*, published in 1908, does not contain this term (Jaffa: Dar al-Thaqafa al-'Arabiyya, 1908, fifth edition, 1925).

2   Unlike some other political terms, such as "republic," which was translated into Arabic as *jumhuriyya*, democracy (*dimuqratiyya*) was not—indicating, perhaps, the lack of its real acceptance.

3   *Al-Jumhuriyya* (Iraq), September 22, 1968.

gimes in Iraq and the region as a whole. It was this Iraq which was chosen, by an external power, to be the catalyst for change in the 21st century and become the model of true democracy for the entire Arab world. But as in the first experience of the British in the 1920s, there are different interpretations, models and visions for such a democracy: that of the Americans and their allies, on the one hand, and those of the different trends and groups, with variations within the groups, in Iraq itself, on the other. The need to reconcile the various approaches is indeed the greatest challenge to the building of such a democracy in Iraq.

Competing visions

The American vision of democracy in Iraq. The ambitious American project of democratizing Iraq developed slowly between the 1991 Gulf War and the September 11, 2001 attacks in New York and Washington. It will be remembered that it was the Clinton Administration which in 1993 came up first with the idea of promoting democracy in the Middle East,[4] although it did very little to implement the idea. The 9/11 attacks gave the dormant project urgency and legitimacy. The choice of Iraq was influenced by the facts that the US had already been involved with Iraq for a decade, which kept the country in the mind of policymakers; that Iraq seemed an easier target than Iran, for example (which was also under consideration for a regime change); and that Iraqi exiles had held ongoing contacts with different American administrations throughout the decade and had managed to convince the Bush administration that Iraq was the most suitable candidate for transformation from a dictatorship to democracy. Hence, unlike in the 1991 Gulf War, in that of 2003 "regime change" was part and parcel of the war plan itself and was to become its most important rationale, if not its very raison d'être.

America's own past experience was to be the guide for building the new democracy in Iraq, while the models were to be the successful cases of Germany and Japan in the aftermath of World War II. However, such models could be and indeed were misleading, as they did not take into account the enormous differences between the Iraqi state and society and those of Japan and Germany. Unlike the more or less homogenous society in Japan, the society in Iraq is extremely heterogeneous, and hence divided by competing visions, agendas and goals. Compounding this even further is the

---

4   Martin Indyk, "The Clinton Administration Approach to the Middle East," Washington Institute for Near East Policy, May 18, 1993.

fact that unlike Japan and Germany, religion and tribalism have remained important factors in Iraqi society.[5] The combination of the two made allegiance to religion and blood ties much more important than allegiance to a party, for example. True, there was a strong party in Iraq, the Ba'th Party, but the fact that it managed to stay in power for thirty-five years is the exception which proves the rule. The Ba'th was a mere instrument of power in a one-party state which allowed no room for other parties and political groups.

The Japanese and German models appeared appropriate to those who quoted them because the societies of those countries had also undergone traumatic wars and yet managed to move quickly to the democratic era. However, such a comparison disregards the fact that Iraq has been in a devastating state of war and then under sanctions, not for four or six years but for more than two decades, something which all but destroyed the fragile middle class. This, together with the total lack of civil society and ethos of democracy, made the transformation to a democracy in Iraq much more difficult than in the ideal model. If we add to this that Iraq is not an island like Japan but a country surrounded by neighbors each of which had different aspirations for and expectations from their newly-born neighbor, then we can understand how irrelevant the ideal American vision was, even before the first shot of the war was fired. After the war this conceptual flaw was to be compounded by serious problems of implementation.

The Kurdish vision. Unlike the messianic vision of the Americans, that of the Kurds was solidly grounded in Iraqi realities and experience. For many years the Kurds have raised the slogan of "democracy for Iraq, autonomy for the Kurds," believing that only if there was true democracy in the center could the Kurds enjoy autonomy. Needless to say, this two-part slogan was anathema to the Ba'th. In the Ba'thi view autonomy endangered the unity of the state, and democracy endangered the very foundations of the regime. For various reasons the Ba'th did acquiesce to the principle of autonomy in 1970, but with no intention of implementing it, and this Kurdish "autonomy" therefore lasted no more than four years.[6] For the Ba'th, democracy did not go beyond lip service.

5   See Faleh Abdul Jabar and H. Dawod (eds), *Tribes and Power: Nationalism and Ethnicity in the Middle East* (London: Saqi, 2003).

6   See David McDowall, *A Modern History of the Kurds* (London: I.B. Tauris, 2000), pp. 327-43.

The chance of putting the Kurdish slogan into practice came after the 1991 Gulf War, when the Kurds "disengaged" from the center government, formed an autonomous region—which appeared to many to be a *de facto* state—and began to experiment with small doses of democracy.[7] It is this experience which the Kurds wish to turn into the model of democracy for the entire country. With this model, its representatives went to Washington in an attempt to convince the American administration that democracy was feasible in Iraq. Washington, which stood behind Kurdish autonomy, was quick to adopt the idea. True, "Kurdish democracy" was full of serious mistakes, flaws and problems, such as the two-year war between the Kurdistan Democratic Party (KDP) led by Mas'ud Barzani and the Patriotic Union of Kurdistan (PUK) led by Jalal Talabani; the partition of the Kurdish region into two areas of influence ruled by the KDP and the PUK; and corruption, favoritism, and other non-democratic practices. Yet, comparatively speaking, Iraqi Kurdistan has been better off than other parts of Saddam's Iraq and maybe even some other Arab countries, as far as democratic practices are concerned. Freedom of expression was more widely applied; more or less free elections to a Kurdish parliament took place in 1992; and unlike the lone Ba'th Party in the rest of the country, many parties were active in the Kurdish region and there were signs of the beginning of civil society.

By the beginning of the Iraq war in March 2003, the Kurds had already changed their formula for the model democracy. They no longer spoke of "democracy for Iraq, autonomy for the Kurds," but of a federation for Iraq where the Kurdish part would be a model of democracy for the other part or parts of that federation. Nor did they leave their idea an empty slogan. Preparing the ground for post-war Iraq, they initiated two important moves. First, in 2002, they prepared a draft constitution for the Iraqi Kurdistan region and the Federal Republic of Iraq, in which they foresaw "a multiparty, democratic parliamentarian, republican political system" for the Kurdistan region as well as for the Federal Republic of Iraq.[8] Second, they were reported to have reached an agreement or understanding with the Shi'i opposition groups abroad, with whom they had intensive discussions, that these groups would support a federation in post-Saddam Iraq.

---

7   See Gareth R.V. Stanfield, *Iraqi Kurdistan; Political Development and Emergent Democracy* (London: RoutledgeCurzon, 2003).

8   Michael Gunter, "Kurdish Future in a Post-Saddam Iraq," *Journal of Muslim Minority Affairs*, Vol. 23, No. 1, April 2003.

In return the Kurds apparently agreed to regard Islam as the source of legislation.

Whether there was an agreement or a mere understanding, one thing was clear: the Kurdish vision for democracy was far from being the ideal one for the other partners in the envisioned federation.

The Shi'i/Islamic vision. The idea of democracy, which was part and parcel of regime change in Iraq, surely appealed greatly to the Shi'is.[9] For a group which represented the majority yet was deprived of real power throughout the modern history of Iraq (and before that in the 400 years of Ottoman rule), democracy could be seen as the panacea for all their problems in the Iraqi state. However, the Shi'is differed greatly from the Kurds on the issue of democracy. First, unlike the Kurds, the Shi'is, who suffered from political, social and economic suppression until the very last moment of the Ba'thi regime, have never had the opportunity to experiment with democracy or to develop a vision of such a democracy for post-Saddam Iraq. Another important difference between the Kurds and the Shi'is was that while the Kurds, who supported the US during the war, could expect it to back the Kurdish vision for post-Saddam Iraq, the Shi'is could not hope for wholehearted backing, especially as their ideas and policies collided at times with those of the Americans. Third, unlike the Kurds, who despite internal divisions and rivalries managed to reach consensus with regards to a certain model of regime, the Shi'is were torn apart by different ideas, visions and trends.[10]

One such division is between the secularists represented by Ahmad Chalabi and his rival Iyad 'Allawi who adopted a kind of secular, Westernized model for democracy, and the other religious leaders and organizations who have their own Islamist interpretation of democracy.[11] Another division is among the Shi'i religious groupings themselves. Thus, for example, both of the leading pro-Iranian groups, Sayyid 'Abd al-Aziz al-Hakim's Supreme Islamic Iraqi Council (SIIC) (and their Badr Brigade) and Sayyid

---

9   There are no updated statistics regarding the number of the Shi'is but they are estimated at between 55 and 60 percent. Graham E. Fuller and Rend Rahim Francke, *The Arab Shi'a: The Forgotten Muslims* (New York: Palgrave, 2001), p. 87. After the war, Sunni Arabs began to challenge this received wisdom, claiming that the Sunnis represented the majority in Iraq.

10   The Shi'i Political Council, which was formed in May 2004, included 18 parties and groups. (Al-Jazeera.net, May 19, 2004)

11   The young Shi'i leader Muqtada al-Sadr, for example, spoke about his hopes to become the Khomeyni of Iraq, with all the Islamic connotations involved. (*al-Ahram al-'Arabi*, September 20, 2003).

Muqtada al-Sadr's Sadrist movement (and their Mahdi Army), support a religiously-oriented government.[12] Muqtada al-Sadr even goes as far as to support the Khomeynist ideology of *Velayat-e Faqih* (governance of the jurisconsult—see the chapter by Meir Litvak in this volume). Yet, as we shall see they are also divided on the issue of federation.

Although one cannot speak of one Shiʿi vision for post-Saddam Iraq, one can certainly say that all the trends adopted the slogan of democracy, not as an end in itself but as a vehicle for achieving other ones and because it could serve their interests in the interim period. One of the most important goals is changing the anomaly of a Sunni Arab minority ruling a Shiʿi majority. The time had come for redressing 100 years of Shiʿi deprivation, stated a Shiʿi journal.[13] According to all Shiʿi trends and groupings, this could be achieved through democratic and free elections which would secure for the majority their proper place in the government and the state. In other words, the Shiʿi vision is that of "democracy for the majority." Hence their insistence on "elections now," namely before any other decision was taken with respect to the form of government in Iraq, the division of power between the different parties and groups, the orientation of the state and its relations with the outside world.

The major proponent of this view has been the Shiʿis' spiritual leader, Ayatollah ʿAli al-Sistani, who kept pressing the Americans and the UN to conduct elections even before an interim constitution was adopted.[14] Except for Shiʿi secularists like Chalabi and others with similar views, democracy was also a means for reinforcing Islamic values and traditions in Iraq, as they wished the state to be based on Islamic law.[15]

Analyzing the role and meaning of democracy in post-Saddam Iraq, Diya al-Shaqarji wrote a book on Islam and democracy which differentiated between three aspects or levels of democracy: as a philosophy, as a way of living (*suluk*) and as a ruling mechanism. As for the first, he said that there was inherent contradiction between Islam and democracy because Islam believes in the rule of God and democracy in that of man. Regarding the second aspect, in his opinion Islam itself calls for a "democratic way of living" by virtue of the religion's openness to the opinion of others and

---

12   SIIC was formerly known as the Supreme Council for the Islamic Revolution in Iraq (SCIRI). In May 2007, it decided to drop the term "revolution" since the Baʿth, against whom this revolution had been directed, had already been ousted from power.

13   *Al-Bayan*, December 27, 2003.

14   See for example an interview with him in *Der Spiegel*, February 22, 2004.

15   *Al-Wikala al-Shiʿiyya lil-Anba -- Al-Sharq al-Awsat*, March 13, 2004.

its human and ethical values. As for the third aspect, Shaqarji believes that as a ruling mechanism, democracy can protect and legitimize the *Shari'a*, because he believes that in elections, the majority of Muslims will support this trend. Like other Islamists, then, he adopts the slogan of democracy for achieving the goal of an Islamic state: "The democracy we want is not an ideologized democracy.... We want a vessel without ideological content. Such a democracy will certainly be filled with contents of values and ideas from our own society."[16]

The Sunni vision and veiled anti-democracy trends. If the Kurds and the Shi'is stood to gain from the democratization and liberalization of the system, there were many others who stood to lose from such changes. But since it is not politically correct to speak loudly against democracy, we can rarely find such views expressed in so many words. Instead we must infer them from historical factors, roundabout sayings and declarations, and certain actions and deeds. Generally speaking, on a macro level, the group which lost most from the war and stood to lose even more from democratization were the Sunni Arabs. Not only did they lose their monopoly of power but they also ran the risk of being marginalized if the democratic project were to succeed.

Representing about 20 percent of the population, they could hardly hope to have greater share in power than this percentage. For those who were used to having the lion's share of everything, free expression, free elections, true representation and fair sharing of power were dangerous prospects. But rather than attack democratic norms, some of their spokesmen and leaders came out loudly against sectarianism (*ta'ifiyya*), or the quota system in power-sharing (*hasasiyya* or *muhasasa*).[17] On the face of it, they were protecting in this way the idea of "unity" and "solidarity" of the Iraqi people and the effectiveness of the political system—but in reality they were afraid that giving the Shi'i and Kurdish "sects" their true share of power would jeopardize their own standing in the state. An example of what the future held in store for them was given in the formation of the Governing Council (*majlis al-hukm*) by the Americans in the spring of 2003. Set up according to the quota system, it accorded the Sunnis "just" five seats out of 25.[18] The situation was even worse in the interim cabinet where the Sunnis were given the least important portfolios.

---

16   *Al-Bayan*, April 20, 2004.

17   For an attack on sectarianism and the policy of "uprooting the Ba'th," see Majid Ahmad al-Samarra'i in *al-Zaman*, May 10, 2004. See also Dawud al-Farhan, in *al-Ahram al-'Arabi*, November 1, 2003.

18   For the members' list of names, see *The Middle East*, August-September 2003.

Such a grim prospect for the Sunnis in a future democracy moved the Sunni leadership, now composed mainly of religiously-oriented groupings, to adopt a policy of deferring any move or act for democratizing the system until after the ejection of the Americans and their allies from Iraq, in the hope of frustrating the project altogether.[19] And while the Kurds and the Shi'is pressed, each group in its own way, for a constitution or election "now," the Sunnis' priority was military resistance (*muqawama*) against the Americans and any Iraqi or non-Iraqi elements which might help in stabilizing the situation in Iraq and implementing the democratic project. The Sunnis found ample support for their policy among Arab states which were no less fearful of the success of such a project in Iraq and its spillover effects on them.[20]

While speaking of Sunnis in general, one should not lose sight of specific sub-groups or elites which stood to be severely harmed by democratization. These are the Ba'th Party, the army, the tribes and Islamists. The Ba'th, which had been outlawed, could hardly put up with the existence of other parties playing by the rule of democracy while it remained outside the game itself. The Iraqi army, which was disbanded shortly after the occupation, lost its role as the arbiter of Iraq's fate and became in its own eyes the scape-goat of democratization. The tribes, which gained a lot from the ongoing chaotic situation in Iraq as it enabled them to fill the vacuum in power, were likely to be harmed if political parties managed to become strong enough to start running the country according to the Western multi-party democratic system. Islamist groupings, which were strengthened signifi-cantly in the aftermath of the war, were also extremely hostile to the demo-cratic project because it was identified with the hated Christian West. For them it was a "clash of civilizations" come true. All these sub-groups, which were united by their fear of losing more and more ground as the Western democratic project put down roots, were at the forefront of fighting the Americans and their allies, especially in the proverbial Sunni triangle. The city of Falluja was the symbol of this resistance in the first three years after the occupation.

Democracy in action. If we look on the positive side of the democratization/ liberalization project, we can say that revolutionary changes have indeed

---

19   A Shi'i writer blamed all the Arabs for attempting to deny Iraq democracy, because of their hostility to the Shi'is. (*Al-Bayan*, December 30, 2003)

20   Support for the Sunni agenda (though it was not mentioned in name) was given by Sabah Yasin, a Jordanian university professor in his article, "The Disintegration of the Party System within the American Project," *al-Mustaqbal al-'Arabi*, February 2004, pp. 13-26.

taken place within a short span of time. The most important of these was an end to the anomaly whereby a Sunni minority was ruling the Shi'i majority and a Kurdish minority nearly its own size, as well as other smaller minorities. The shattering of the Sunni monopoly of power, which was the major cause of instability and authoritarian rule in Iraq, gave way to a more representative form of government, and for the first time in Iraq's modern history enabled the disenfranchised groups to regain their identity and participate in power. Thus, for example, the Shi'is could once again, after many years, perform their rituals.

Another no less important move was the dismantling of all the coercive apparatuses in the Ba'thi state, the security apparatuses, the army and the Ba'th Party; all this, together with the collapse of the Sunni center, enabled the flourishing of new and old parties, from the far left to the far right, from Communists to Islamists. Part and parcel of this newfound pluralism, which is at the heart of democratic development, was the flourishing of other social groupings and NGOs. Thus, for example, the one and only Iraqi women's union which acted under the Ba'th, and was a mere vehicle of the government with its one million and a half members, was superseded by many women's organizations representing women from different parts of the country. Women also participated in power for the first time since 1972, sending representatives to the Governing Council and later to the National Assembly and the elected government.[21] Not satisfied with their quota, Iraqi women formed the Women Governing Council to fight for their rights.[22] If emancipation and participation of women are considered a yardstick for evaluating liberalization, then initial moves in post-Saddam look promising.[23]

Another realm in which there were important achievements was that of free expression. As against the six major newspapers under the Ba'th, which were the obedient tools of the regime, there were after the collapse of the Ba'th more than one hundred newspapers,[24] representing all groups and

---

21 Inspite of their participation in these various bodies, however, they were marginalized politically because they did not get any key post in the government. It transpired later that women who were members of parliament did not manage to improve women's lot in the country. *Bint al-Rafidayn*, November 20, 2007.

22 *Yediot Aharonot*, April 23, 2004.

23 It must be pointed out, however, that in December 2003, under the then chairman of the Governing Council, this body voted to scrap secular family laws and place them under Muslim religious jurisdiction. AFP, January 21, 2004. However, this was not ratified by the American governor, Paul Bremer.

24 Al-Jazeera,net, May 19, 2004.

sectors in society. Demonstrations which were not organized from above as in the Ba'thi era also became part of the new game of politics. Another important aspect of liberalization was free enterprise and the free market in an economy which was accustomed to the monopoly of the Ba'th. A flourishing sector of businessmen and entrepreneurs might have had positive impact on the opening of the political system as well.

These achievements were revolutionary indeed, but could just as easily prove ephemeral. For one thing, they were the natural outcome of the collapse of the "Republic of Fear" and the chaotic situation that developed afterwards, and in the longer run this spontaneous reaction has been overtaken by other negative developments.[25] For another, this liberalization seemed to have been conditioned on the presence of the Americans. What will happen when they leave remains an open question. Most important of all, the entire project is punctuated by inherent contradictions and opposing goals of the different players which seem difficult to reconcile.

In his essay on "Democracy and Ethno-Religious Conflict in Iraq" written shortly after the occupation, Andreas Wimmer contends that "democratic politics would very likely lead to a radicalization of...ethno-nationalist parties and lead to an upward spiraling of their demands." Basing his observation on other similar experiences in the world, he reaches the cautious conclusion that "the seeds of democracy may have difficulties [germinating] in the sandy soil of Iraq."[26] Wimmer's observation has proved correct. The United States was not acting in a vacuum where it could dictate its own model of democracy. Instead, local players who had been marginalized for so many years became increasingly active in pushing for their own agenda. What the war and the collapse of the coercive system did was to reinforce primordial loyalties among the different sectors and groups of Iraqi society at the expense of the more recent—and, to an extent,artificial—Iraqi patriotism. The new-found freedom of expression and activity enabled each of the parties to promote its own agenda for post-Saddam Iraq and to interpret democracy according to its own interests and views. Thus, the competing visions of democracy began to clash as each of the parties sought to get the most of it for its own constituency.

---

25   The worst setback was for women who came under severe pressure by Islamists, especially by the Sadrist movement. For a discussion of women's role in post-Saddam Iraq, see Noga Efrati, "Negotiating Rights in Iraq: Women and the Personal Status Law," *Middle East Journal*, Vol. 59, No. 4 (Autumn 2005), pp. 577-95.

26   Andreas Wimmer, "Democracy and Ethno-Religious Conflict in Iraq," *Survival*, Winter 2003.

One test-case was the announcement and endorsement of the interim constitution in March 2004, precisely one year after the beginning of the war.[27] It seemed to be by far the most progressive constitution Iraq has ever had. Article One for example stated that "the regime system in Iraq is republican, federal, democratic and pluralistic and the powers in it will be divided between the federal government and the regional governments, the provinces, the city councils and local government." However, the law's main defect was that it was inspired and written by the Americans and not Iraqis. The fact that this interim constitution was not the result of debates, discussions and compromises among the different local players made it extremely controversial to those parties which felt hurt by it, in this case the Arabs and the small minority of Turkomans.[28]

The two most controversial issues were the federation system and the stated principle that Islam was *a* source and not *the* source of legislation. The endorsement of a federation system meant the acceptance of the Kurds' model of democracy, thus boosting their powers significantly. Moreover, the interim constitution granted them additional power by allowing two-thirds of the inhabitants of three Iraqi provinces to veto the country's future permanent constitution.[29] Although they were not mentioned by name, quite clearly the reference was to the three Kurdish provinces of Dhok, Irbil and Sulaymaniyya. This prerogative meant granting the Kurds the final say on the permanent constitution.

Article Seven, which speaks of Islam as a source of legislation and forbids the promulgation during the interim period of any law which contradicts the basic concepts of Islam and the principles of democracy, was also very troubling to the Sunni and Shi'i Islamists who wanted to give Islam a larger role. As a spokesman of the Sunni Iraqi Islamic Party put it: "To say that Islam should be the main source of legislation does not negate the fact that other sources will have to be used but only in a way that does not violate the Islamic codes…no one can contest the Islamic identity of the Iraqi people." He cautioned, however, against futile discussions about the role of Islam in the future make-up of Iraq since "our battle today is about how to maintain the integrity of Iraq against attempts to divide it."[30]

---

27 For the full text of the interim constitution, see *al-Anba*, March 9, 2004.

28 *Al-Ahram Weekly*, February 26, 2004.

29 Article 61 which includes this point was the main bone of contention in the Iraqi Governing Council which had to ratify the interim constitution.

30 *Al-Ahram Weekly*, February 26, 2004.

The issue of federation was the main bone of contention which pitted the Shi'is against the Kurds before the endorsement of the interim constitution by the Governing Council. In a debate about federalism and democracy held in December 2003, most of the discussants, except for the Kurdish participants, were against federation, maintaining that Iraq was no Switzerland, that it would lead to the secession of the Kurds from the state and that there was no connection between democracy and federalism.[31] The deep differences between these two groups came to the surface on the eve of the signing when the spiritual guide of the Shi'is, Grand Ayatollah 'Ali al-Sistani, directed five Shi'i council members not to sign because of Article Sixty-One which granted the Kurds veto power over the permanent constitution.[32] He finally gave them the green light, but only hours after the signing, while he himself denounced the law, saying that "it sets obstacles in the way of reaching a permanent constitution for the country that preserves its unity and the rights of the different religious communities and members of different ethnic groups."[33] Sistani also started delegitimizing it by demanding that the UN reject it and by inspiring a grassroots Shi'i campaign against it.[34] Other Shi'i leaders and groupings followed suit. Thus the senior Shi'i leader Ayatollah Taqi al-Mudarrisi went as far as to describe the clause that referred to federation as tantamount to a "time bomb" that might cause civil strife in Iraq.[35]

In retrospect, the introduction of the interim constitution caused temporary estrangement between the Kurds and the Shi'is who had formed an ad-hoc alliance abroad and under American aegis for ousting the Ba'th. Initially, Shi'i men of religion were at the forefront of the campaign against federation and other prerogatives given the Kurds (such as keeping their military force, the *peshmerga*) as *they* were now the leaders of the Shi'i community, and not the secular Westernized Shi'is who came from abroad. The estrangement between these two groups was motivated first of all by the clash of visions on democracy.

The Shi'is' leaders, with their vision of "democracy for the majority," were at that stage against anything that might strengthen the "minority," especially the idea of federation and the implied secession of the Kurdish

---

31   *Al-Bayan*, December 30, 2003.

32   *Al-Anba*, March 7, 2004.

33   AFP, March 8, 2004.

34   *New York Times*, March 23, 2004; *Washington Post*, April 29, 2004.

35   UPI, March 12, 2004.

region. Therefore, they demanded all along to conduct elections before any decision was taken on the future government or the shape of the state, or its constitution. Presenting themselves as the real Iraqi patriots, they came out strongly against the federative solution, which in their opinion was likely to divide the Iraqi state. Tasting power for the first time in history, they also regarded any power granted the Kurds as detracting from their own. In addition, the more secular world view of the Kurds looked threatening to them. This estrangement had deeper roots. The Kurds and the Shi'is are divided on both religious and ethnic bases, in contrast to the Arab Sunnis and Kurds who have at least one thing in common, their Sunnism. In addition, in the past, the "Sunni triangle" acted as a kind of buffer between the Kurds and the Shi'is, but with the collapse of the Ba'thi state, the areas of friction, including in the government, increased significantly. Thus, ironically enough but quite expectedly,[36] the democratizing process reinforced the ethno-religious identity of each of the groups, which in turn began to boomerang against the process.

Yet, in spite of this estrangement between Kurds and Shi'is, the marriage of convenience between them continued as they were still united by their common rivalry with the Sunnis. It also transpired soon that the Shi'i camp itself was neither static nor monolithic. Shortly after the introduction of the interim constitution, there began to appear severe cracks within the Shi'i camp regarding the federation issue, and two antagonistic groups developed. The first, led by the Supreme Council of the Islamic Revolution in Iran (SCIRI, which became the Supreme Islamic Iraqi Council in 2007), came out openly and strongly for the federative solution, calling for the formation of one such federative unit out of the nine Shi'i governorates. The second, the Sadr movement, was totally opposed to this notion.[37] As time went by, the gap between the two groups on this and other issues widened significantly, eventually leading to military clashes.

The introduction of the interim constitution also caused cracks in the tacit and tactical cooperation between the Shi'is and the American coalition. The somewhat naive American belief that the US vision of a secular democracy would be accepted wholeheartedly by all Shi'is was shattered on the very day of the endorsement of the interim constitution. Secularism,

---

36 Wimmer, p. 131, quotes a research finding on the basis of a 135-country sample that "democracies are less stable when the country is divided along ethno-religious lines."

37 For example, in October 2007, Sadr came out fiercely against a call by 'Ammar al-Hakim, son of 'Abd al-'Aziz al-Hakim, leader of SIIC, to form self governing regions for the Shi'is. (AFP, October 15, 2007; al-Ahram, October 18-24, 2007)

which was anathema to the radical Shi'i (and Sunni) men of religion, triggered military encounters between the American coalition and the irregular forces, the "Mahdi Army" of the young Shi'i leader Muqtada al-Sadr, which commenced shortly after the endorsement of the interim constitution. The fact that at that time Ayatollah 'Ali al-Sistani came out vehemently against the American version of democracy for Iraq only reinforced the radicals in the Shi'i camp. And even though Sistani was against military escalation, it took him some time before he could move Sadr to stop the fighting.[38]

In this way, the Sunni-led resistance to the coalition, which has been going on intermittently since the beginning of the war, was boosted significantly with the help of the radical Sadrists. True, the Shi'i and the Sunni radicals did not seem to be coordinating their activities. But together, they "robbed" the minimum prerequisite of a democratization process—peace and security. In fact, violence, a main feature of Iraqi politics,[39] reached new peaks in the aftermath of the war. Targets of violence came to include anyone and everything: Iraqis and non-Iraqis, individuals and groups, installations and the infrastructure and even churches and mosques of both Sunnis and Shi'is.[40] This violence was doubly motivated: vengeance for past oppression and killings,[41] and attempts to decide the future shape of the country by force. The competing visions of democracy both increased violence and became its victim as well.

A constitution and a parliament for Iraq: do they matter?

The year 2005 witnessed three important moves which seemed to have elevated Iraq to the level of the leading Arab country in terms of democratic developments. These were the January elections to the interim parliament (which were boycotted by the Sunnis), the drafting of a permanent constitution and the referendum on it in October, and the December elections to the permanent National Assembly. However, closer examination demonstrates that despite the apparent success of these American-orchestrated moves, their long-term implications were far from completely salutary. The

38 Sistani and others kept using the term "peaceful resistance" (*muqawama silmiyya*).

39 A book written by an Iraqi described 5,000 years of history of violence in Iraq. Baqir Yasin, *Ta'rikh al-'Unf al-Damawi fi al-'Iraq: al-Waqa'i', al- Dawafi', al-Hulul* (Beirut: 1999).

40 In February 2006, the Shi'i mosque in Samarra was attacked, and this was followed by attacks on scores of Sunni mosques.

41 *Tha'r*, blood revenge, became rampant because of animosities between Ba'thists and their victims. With no real police and justice system functioning, there was no way to stop them.

birth-pangs of Iraq's new constitution were symptomatic of the deep crisis afflicting the country. And even though it was approved by the majority of Iraqis, it may exacerbate Iraq's problems rather than solve them. The history of Iraqi constitutions may be one such indicator.

In its eighty-five years of existence, Iraq has had no fewer than six constitutions. The first was imposed in 1925 by the British authorities and remained in effect for thirty-three years. But despite—or perhaps because of—the fact that it bore all the hallmarks of Western democracy, that constitution never struck roots in Iraqi society or dictated political processes there, and it was abolished along with the Iraqi monarchy in 1958. The four subsequent constitutions of 1963, 1964, 1968 and 1970 were all defined as temporary instruments and lasted only as long as the regimes that promulgated them.

In fact, no Iraqi constitution ever became the authoritative framework to regulate political processes or determine the country's identity and orientation. Instead, they all served only one purpose: to legitimize the regime in power. And there is no certainty that the sixth constitution will succeed where all of its predecessors have failed. True, this one was not imposed by a foreign power or a local dictator but instead enjoys the apparent advantage of having been negotiated by representatives of the two largest communities in the country—the Shi'is and the Kurds, who together make up about 80 percent of the population. And unlike the interim constitution of a year earlier, the result was the product of lengthy consultations, compromises and mutual concessions. However, the drafting process has left the Sunnis feeling marginalized and further strengthened their opposition to the emerging order. True, the Sunnis did participate in the referendum on the permanent constitution, but this was on condition that they would have the right to debate the constitution again after the elections to the National Assembly. In the meantime they were threatening to torpedo it, either by invoking the right of veto given in the interim constitution to any group of at least three provinces, or by quitting the government, or by sheer violence.

The threat of a procedural veto is only the most visible of the problems. The main stumbling blocks concern the most substantive issues: the identity, character and structure of state and regime, the distribution of resources, and Iraq's political orientation. While Shi'is and Kurds remain divided on these issues, they appear to have reached agreement—at least on paper—if only in order to alter the fundamental balance of power in the state, prevent a Sunni restoration, and correct what they perceive as the injustices done to them in the past. But the Sunnis now see themselves as the main victims of the substantive changes. In fact the same issues which were the bones of contention in the interim constitution remained in the permanent one as well. For example, Article One of the constitution declares that "The Republic of Iraq is a single, independent federal state with full sovereignty. Its system of government is republican, representative (parliamentary) and democratic. This constitution is the guarantor of this unity."[42] This outraged most Sunnis who viewed any reference to federalism as a prescription for the disintegration of a unitary state. Federalism was particularly threatening to them because it might deprive them of the exclusive control they have had since the creation of Iraq over oil and other natural resources, most of which are actually found in the Kurdish north and the Shi'i south.[43]

Another article arousing Sunni fury is Article Three, which defines Iraq as being part of the Islamic world and not part of the Arab world. Those who traditionally depicted Iraq as the incarnation of Arabism and the vanguard of the pan-Arab cause view this article as a trick to erase the state's Arab identity and to elevate Kurdish and Shi'i identities at their expense. Indeed, the Sunni discourse is bitterly resentful of the fourth constitutional provision, that Kurdish be made an official language throughout Iraq and not just in the Kurdish region. And the Shi'is are also viewed with suspicion as a foreign element, not authentically Arab, and linked with Iran.

These issues illustrate a whole host of other problems under discussion. Cardinal questions such as religion and the state, the public role of clergy, sources of law, the status of women, treatment of former Ba'thists, division of power between center and periphery, the role of the army and para-military forces, and the status of Kirkuk suffuse debates over all the articles of the constitution, and almost any one of them could produce an explosive outcome.

In fact, the real test of this constitution, as of all previous constitutions, is not in the drafting of the document but rather in the relations of forces on the ground. Indeed, nation-building and state-building in Iraq have been proceeding in erratic ways. On the one hand, Kurds and Shi'is are pulling in the direction of identity-construction that takes Iraq further and further away from the vision of a unified state. On the other hand, Sunnis

---

42 *Washington Post*, October 12, 2005, *Kull al-'Iraq*, October 15, 2005.

43 President Talabani stated, though, that the Sunni Islamic party was not against the Kurdish federacy but against the "sectarian" one, namely that of the Shi'is. (*Al-'Arabiyya TV*, October 21, 2007)

are waging what looks like a desperate but increasingly futile struggle to restore an Iraq that no longer exists. But the war of the Sunni radicals against the constitution and against stabilization of the situation on the ground may go on for a long time; despite their weakened state since the collapse of the Ba'th regime, they still have considerable capacity to sabotage developments not to their liking. Moreover, there is no functioning center, and social and economic trends do not promise an easy evolution of the new Iraq envisaged by its founders.

The new Iraqi constitution is not the outcome of long-term social and political processes leading to a social contract agreed among large segments of the population. Instead, it is the result of hasty acts, various internal and external pressures, and the constraints of time and place. Hence there is no assurance that it will be a major factor in formulating the character of the country.

Another important landmark on the road to democracy was the elections to the National Assembly held in December 2005. In fact these were considered the crown jewel in American-led efforts to redesign the state of Iraq, for they were intended to provide a strong democratic foundation for the new Iraq. But their success is by no means assured, and many challenges remain.

The American vision of a democratic, unitary Iraq is remarkably similar to the British vision for the country in the early past of the last century, but it has been pursued at a different pace and by different means. The British needed four years (1914-18) to conquer the country and five more years to design its political and geographical map and set up democratic ruling institutions—a constitution, a parliament, a referendum, and elections. The Americans managed all this in only three years, but they took on another and more complicated task—to destroy not only the foundations built by the Ba'th over thirty-five years, but also the political map designed by the British, that is, the anomaly of rule by the Sunni minority. The Sunnis have a vested and abiding interest in preventing any process of democratization that would give expression to the true population balance in the country and permit a fairer distribution of its resources.

The 2005 elections reflect this upheaval and the new political map, whose main characteristics are unprecedented pluralism (about 300 parties contested the 275 seats in parliament) and a fairer representation of the main population groups. Thus, the Shi'i Islamist lists won a plurality—41.2 percent of all votes—but not the two-thirds majority needed to

form a government. The united Kurdish list took second place, with 21.7
percent of the votes, and the leading Sunni Islamist list came in third with
15.1 percent of the votes. By contrast, only 8 percent went to the secular
joint Shi'i -Sunni list led by Iyad 'Allawi. The rest were divided among nine
smaller parties.[44] This outcome could facilitate stabilization and democratization if it were widely accepted, but so far it is not.

In the first place, about 70 parties and organizations boycotted the elections while many others acted underground in the attempt to sabotage the
democratic process.[45] Secondly, some Sunni groups remained highly suspicious of the new political order. True, in contrast to their boycott of the
January 2005 election for the interim parliament, most of the Sunnis did
participate this time in the hope of ending their political marginality and
amending the new constitution that established the federal order so resent-
ed by them. However, they remained divided on their policies vis-à-vis the
elected government. Thus, for example, one party, *al-Hizb al-Islami* (the
Islamic Party), heir to the Iraqi Muslim Brotherhood, has generally participated in the political process.[46] However, the more radical one, *Hay'at
ulama al-muslimin* (the Association of Muslim Scholars), which is said to
include 9,000 Sunni men of religion, continued its violent resistance to the
new political order.[47]

But the Sunnis are not the only obstacle to stabilization and democratization in Iraq. Although the election procedures conformed to those of
established democratic states, the content of the campaign was altogether
different. Rather than elaborating a platform that appealed to the entire
electorate, the parties operated as unabashed ethnic or confessional factions. And voting very much took place along similar lines. As a result,
the election led to further fragmentation rather than national integration.
Moreover, the elections legitimized political Islam, which got its greatest
boost since the elimination of Ba'th rule, and this in turn further intensified inter-confessional tension and conflict.

Finally, there are external elements that complicate the picture even
more. The most prominent of these is al-Qa'ida, which has turned Iraq
into its main base for terror and has gone to great lengths to undermine

44   *Economist*, January 28, 2006.

45   Sayyar Jamil, *"Al-qiwa al-siyasiyya al-'iraqiyya, ru'ya lima ba'd al-taghyir,"* al-Dimuqratiyya,
      July 2007, p. 44.

46   The *Ikhwan* were established in Iraq in the 1950s but for most of the time acted under-
      ground or outside Iraq.

47   *Al-Usbu' Al-'Arab*, August 13, 2007.

processes of stabilization and democratization in order to preserve its new-found sanctuary. A second factor is the United States. The Americans can-not be accused of consciously sabotaging their own program, but their inconsistent policies have nevertheless strengthened internal tensions and inter-factional rivalries. Finally, neighboring states continue to play a role. Each, in its own way and for its own reasons, has been promoting one Iraqi faction at the expense of the others, thereby further undermining prospects for stability.

The conclusion is that while the recent elections were undoubtedly an important step in efforts to institutionalize Iraqi democracy, the deeper processes of liberalization, construction of civil society and national recon-ciliation, so essential to sustainable democracy over the long term, have so far failed to make much headway.[48]

Bent on preventing any stability that might entrench the changes since the overthrow of Saddam Husayn, especially those that have made the Sun-nis a second-rank force, the terrorists and other opposition forces are doing their best to preserve Iraq as "the Republic of Fear" and to turn it into a failed state.

'Iraq First': the right choice?

In embracing the goal of democratizing Iraq, the Americans were following in the footsteps of others before them, like the British and French, who had come to the region to bring the light of "progress, liberalism and democ-racy" or what the French used to call a *mission civilisatrice*. However, not learning from its predecessors' mistakes, the US became embroiled in even more serious ones.[49]

The American democratic project for Iraq was based on several flawed concepts and assumptions. The first of those was that freeing Iraqis from Saddam's hated regime would turn them automatically into supporters of the Americans and their project. However, while this was true for the Kurds, with whom the US has been in a form of tacit alliance since the 1991 Gulf War, it was far from being the case with all Shi'is. Not all of them necessarily supported the vision of secular democracy for Iraq. In

---

48   It must be stressed, however, that in the Kurdish region democratic processes did make important progress in comparison to other parts in Iraq.

49   For the British experimentation with democracy, see Ofra Bengio, "Pitfalls of Instant Democracy," in Michael Eisenstadt and Eric Mathewson, *US Policy in Post Saddam Iraq: Lessons from the British Experience* (Washington, DC: Washington Institute for Near East Policy), pp. 15-26.

fact the Americans, who were led to believe so by Westernized Shiʻis and scholarly well-wishers, began to fathom little by little the depth of Shiʻi religiosity and the ability of some radical leaders like Muqtada al-Sadr to frustrate the democratic project.

Another mistaken assumption was that the democracy-of-sorts which had developed in Iraqi Kurdistan could serve as a model for the entire country. This assumption did not take into account that the type of democracy which developed in Iraqi Kurdistan over twelve years was itself still very fragile; that the Sunnis who lost all their assets would do everything possible to frustrate the project; and that the Shiʻis had different interpretations and agendas from the Kurds' and their new patron. Nor did the Americans take into account the difficulties of reconciling the different visions of democracy and moving all three ethno-religious groupings to act in unison toward one central goal.

But not only in macro-politics were ethno-religious divisions reinforced; in micro-politics as well there were many divisions and rivalries, for example between different tribes or other sub-groupings. Similarly, the most important carriers of democracy—political parties, NGOs and other networks of civil society organizations—were totally lacking in war-torn Saddam's Iraq and its totalitarian regime. In choosing "Iraq first," the Americans disregarded the difficulty of transforming Iraqi society from one extreme to another. If the post-war period was any evidence, there was very little progress toward the development of strong parties, despite the unprecedented freedom given them to organize.[50] Ethno-religious, primordial, tribal and other local loyalties took precedence over loyalty to parties. Indeed, the Americans disregarded the all-powerful forces of continuity which exist in any society, anywhere and any time in the world.

In addition to the flawed models of democracy for Iraq, there were other conceptual problems in the American vision. First, it was not realistic to think that a Muslim society, however abused by its own Muslim ruler, would accept a foreign Christian occupier and adopt its norms in the longer run.[51] Another flawed concept, related to this, was that it was possible to impose democracy from above, in disregard of the fact that such an enterprise required longer, bottom-up processes. In fact, such processes must start from within the society itself and when the economic, social and po-

---

51   Although it is a Muslim country, Turkey's case is different because there the Turkish leadership had decided by its own free will to adopt Western democratic norms.

litical prerequisites are in existence, such as a strong middle class. But even if nothing was wrong with the conceptual basis, the tortuous way in which democracy was being implemented dealt it a severe blow.

What harmed the cause of democracy in Iraq was that its missionaries—the Americans and their allies—were inconsistent in their policies, unheeding of the needs of the population, and were military oriented, which is a contradiction of the project's aim. It was not that plans were lacking for post-Saddam Iraq; the main problem was that such plans did not take into account the inherent difficulties of the Iraqi society and state, and that military people and not civilian administrators were called upon to implement them. It also transpired soon that there was an inherent contradiction between the Americans' lofty ideals and interests and needs on the ground.[52]

An example of a zigzagging policy was the decision to disband the army to help build democracy, and then a counter-decision, a year later, when Iraqi reality forced itself on the American policy-makers. The same approach was adopted toward the Ba'th Party and other Ba'thi apparatuses. This zigzagging policy was doubly harmful. In the first stage, it left the country in a chaotic situation and with a total lack of security, both domestically and along the borders. In the second, it left the impression among those Iraqis who supported the democratic project that the US did not act in earnest, that it did not act in good faith, or that it was unwilling and unable to stand behind its project. The pictures of American soldiers torturing Iraqis which started to come out in mid-2004 dealt a severe blow to the image of Americans as liberators and promoters of democracy. The differences between Saddam's regime and the American occupiers began to be blurred in the eyes of many Iraqis.

The German and Japanese cases which were taken as a model for a democratic Iraq were also misunderstood. If anything, the US, and especially its close ally Britain, should have taken the British experimentation with democracy in Iraq in the monarchical era as a guide. As the earlier episode had proved, a foreign, Christian occupier, even if it posed as a liberator and harbinger of democracy, was bound to clash with the local population. The inherent contradictions between the occupier's interests and those of the population forced it to set aside the ideal of democracy for the sake of promoting its rule and interests in the country. These built-in contradictions between vision and reality, ideals and interests, expectations and disil-

---

52   For a critical view on the American "war of liberation," see Jeffrey C. Isaac, "Thinking about Victory in Iraq", *Dissent* (Summer 2003).

lusions are part and parcel of the new experiment as well, but with much worse results.

As for Iraq, one can no longer speak of a unified Iraqi nation-state. Instead, one should think of a "diffuse" country made of separate and contending entities that have yet to take their final shape. In the past, the contending ethno-religious groups were kept together either by a foreign power, or by a strong army or a strong man, or by all of them together. This institutionalized the politics of violence, so characteristic of this country but also so damaging to any democratizing process.[53]

Yet, this violence does not contradict the fact that on this very soil the most developed culture, art and literature have flourished. In fact, quite often the two went together.[54] Even today, in the most terrible atmosphere of chaos and violence, culture has been prospering as it never did under the Ba'th. Indeed, one should not be tempted to conflate the two levels of human activity and think that rich culture will necessarily prepare the ground for peaceful and democratic political processes.[55]

History has taught us that Iraq needs a strong man, a strong army or a strong party to keep it united and rule it; but in their presence, democracy can hardly develop. Put differently, it is quite difficult to keep the different ethnic groups and entities as one unit and have democracy at one and the same time.[56] Hence the best that can be hoped for, and the most realistic scenario, is that populations previously under-represented, the Shi'is and the Kurds, will now finally come into their own, and the Iraqi government will be more representative of the will of the people than ever before in modern Iraq. This kind of democracy, at least in its Islamist component, might not be to the Americans' liking. Yet this genie, released from the bottle, cannot be returned.

---

53   On violence and "the crisis of the absence of democracy," see 'Abd al-Wahhab Hamid Rashid, *Mustaqbal al-'Iraq* (Nicosia: Al-Mada, 1997), pp. 62-102.

54   In his book on violence in Mesopotamia-Iraq, the Iraqi Baqir Yasin maintained that from time immemorial there were two kind of fires in those lands, a (positive) eternal one and negative one of violence, extremism and bloodletting. (Yasin, p. 5).

55   See, for example Joseph Braude, *The New Iraq* (New York: Basic Books, 2003).

56   Jeremy Greenstock, a British diplomat and special representative for Iraq in 2003-4, suggested the opposite, saying that if terrorism and indiscriminate violence were to be eliminated, then Iraqis would have to develop "the ideology of a unified rather than a communally divided country." *Economist*, May 8, 2004.

12

IRAN: THE CLERICAL DEBATE ON DEMOCRACY AND ISLAM

Meir Litvak

The election of Sayyid Mohammad Khatami as President of Iran on May 23, 1997, launched a lively debate within the Iranian clerical establishment on the compatibility between democracy and Islam. The debate was rooted in the fundamental contradiction in Iran's 1979 Islamic constitution between the two notions of sovereignty embodied within it: the sovereignty of the people, mainly through elections to parliament and municipalities, and sovereignty of the Islamic jurists as God's deputies, manifested in the doctrine of *Velayat-e Faqih*, and the broad authority allotted to the supreme leader of the revolution *(rahbar)*, as well as other appointed juridical bodies, over the elected institutions. Another problem was the conflict between various guarantees of civil liberties and their subordination to, and restriction by, Islamic principles.[1] The debate came to the fore following Khatami's advocacy of Islamic democracy and civil society, as well as in response to popular pressure from below for greater openness, which was clear from the reformist victory in the February 2000 parliamentary elections. It has subsided since 2001, following the conservative backlash and repressive measures against dissident circles.[2]

---

1   For a detailed analysis of the contradictions in Iran's constitutional system, see Asghar Schirazi, *The Constitution of Iran: Politics and the State in the Islamic Republic* (London: I.B. Tauris, 1998), pp. 1, 8-15, 19.

2   Meir Litvak, "Iran," in Bruce Maddy-Weitzman, *Middle East Contemporary Survey 2000* (Tel Aviv: Moshe Dayan Center for Middle Eastern and African Studies, Tel Aviv University, 2002), pp. 206-45.

This chapter proposes to delineate and analyze the contours and argumentation raised in this debate among four schools of thought: (1) a hard-line faction, which unequivocally opposes democracy and denounces it as totally incompatible with Islam; (2) the dominant faction, headed by the Supreme Leader (*rahbar*) of the revolution, Ayatollah Sayyid 'Ali Khamane'i and associated with the conservative Society of Combatant Clergy (*Jame'eh-ye Ruhaniyyat-e Mobarez*, JRM), which adopted the discourse of democracy mainly in its technical aspects, but subordinates it to the ruling doctrine of *Velayat-e Faqih* (governance of the jurisconsult); (3) the reformist advocates of Islamic democracy, headed by Khatami, many of them linked with the Association of Combatant Clerics (*Majma'-e Ruhaniyyun-e Mobarez*, MRM)[3] who seek to reconcile or merge the two concepts; and (4) liberals, who give priority to various democratic principles over the *Velayat-e Faqih* doctrine.

This study examines the differences and similarities among these four trends in relation to three points: (1) the tension between popular sovereignty and *Velayat-e Faqih*, (2) attitudes toward civil liberties and concepts of freedom, and (3) the contrasting of Western democracy with Islamic democracy. Our analysis demonstrates that the debate is a dynamic one which, combined with pressure from below, offers a real chance for significant liberalization and perhaps even democracy.

Popular sovereignty and Velayat-e Faqih

A key question in the Islamic Republic has been whether the political legitimacy and rule (*velayat*) of the clerics is by appointment (*entesab*) by God, since the Prophet and the Imams had designated them as their heirs, or whether it is contingent on popular support through election (*entekhab*).

The debate is not only of crucial importance for the future of the Islamic regime, but relates also to the historical essence of Shi'ism, which, as Talib Aziz noted, was based on the premise of "divine selection" of the ruler and rejected the legitimacy of majorities or communal consensus to decide on such issues.[4]

---

3   On the two clerical groups see Wilfred Buchta, *Who Rules Iran? The Structure of Power in the Islamic Republic* (Washington, DC: Washington Institute for Near Eastern Policy, 2000), pp. 13-15, and David Menashri, *Post Revolutionary Politics in Iran: Religion, Society and Politics* (London: Frank Cass, 2001).

4   Talib M. Aziz, "Popular Sovereignty in Contemporary Shi'i Thought," in Center for the Study of Islam and Democracy Second Annual Conference on Islam, Democracy and the Secular State in the Post-Modern Era, http://www.islam-democracy.org/documents/pdf/CSID_2001_proceedings.pdf, p. 107.

The dominant faction and divine sovereignty. The dominant clerical faction led by Khamane'i and former President Hashemi Rafsanjani adheres to belief in the divinely ordained absolute authority of the supreme jurist, the *Vali-ye Faqih.* Nevertheless, its members employ a democracy discourse, having recognized the need for some popular backing for the government, and possibly also in response to pressure from below. This discourse understands democracy solely as popular support for the government, and as a technical system whereby the people elect government officials, while glossing over such issues as civil liberties and equality before the law. Most importantly, ultimate decision-making remains in the hands of the *'ulama,* led by the *Vali-ye Faqih,* who is the Supreme Leader (*rahbar*) of the revolution.

In his speeches and sermons, Khamene'i described the Iranian system as religious rule of the people (*mardomsalari*). This is not restricted merely to people's votes, "which can be subjected to barter, trade and wheeling and dealing, as is evident in today's world;" it also means "that the people's will, sentiments, faith and love and care for the national interests, are all behind this political system." The country belongs to the people, he said, and, therefore, the people have the right to decide their own fate and elect their favorite legislators through a sound and free election as is envisaged by the law. The Islamic system cannot realize its aims without the will, votes and the inclination of the people. Elections are a symbol of national capability and strength and of realization of people's rights. Both he and Rafsanjani argued that Iran's holding of twenty-one elections for a variety of state institutions in a span of twenty-one years was unprecedented elsewhere in the world, and was the ultimate proof that the Islamic system was based on popular will.[5]

Rafsanjani's view of democracy is formal and technical. He contends that Islamic Iran is the only revolutionary state that sought popular approval by referendum for its system of government within fifty days after the revolution's triumph. The people endorsed the Islamic Constitution, and the presidents and *Majlis* are elected by popular vote, he maintains. Is not the people's vote the essence of democracy, Rafsanjani asked. He also took pride in the fact that in the elections for his first term of presidency and in the *Majlis* over which he presided he received 97 percent of the votes.[6]

5   Islamic Republic News Agency (IRNA), February 15, 2000; Vision of the Islamic Republic of Iran Network 1, August 24, 2000, Federal Broadcast Information Service Daily Report (DR); Voice of the Islamic Republic of Iran Radio 1, August 30, 2000 (DR).

6   *Resalat,* January 24, 2000; Tehran, Voice of the Islamic Republic of Iran Radio, March 31, 2000 (DR). See also *Entekhab* (Internet Version), February 1, 2001.

All *'ulama* affiliated with the dominant faction insist that the doctrine of *Velayat-e Faqih* in the Constitution superseded all other political principles. However, apparently bowing to popular sentiment, Khamene'i contended that *Velayat* has a cordial relationship with the people, and is in touch with their feelings, sentiments, thoughts and intellectual needs. The goal of *Velayat* is to serve the people. Consequently, opponents of *Velayat-e Faqih* are those who consent to the rule of coup-staging military men and of corrupt capitalists.[7]

In a special statement the Assembly of Experts rejected the contention of their opponents that the *rahbar*'s election by the Assembly of Experts, rather than directly by the people, attenuated the institution's democratic essence. It argued that since the people elected the Assembly's members, its choice was therefore a vote by the people.[8]

Proponents of *Velayat-e Faqih* are adamant about its superiority over elected bodies and popular will. Ayatollah 'Abbas Va'ez-Tabasi, custodian of Imam Reza's shrine, charged that no political movement could make policies in a society which was governed by a *Vali-ye Faqih*. Likewise, Ayatollah Abu-l-Qasem Khaz'ali stated that the important task of the *Majlis* was "to obey the eminent leader's orders," and that the very legitimacy of the president and the ministers was subordinated to the *rahbar*'s signature. If 30 million people, instead of 20 million people, voted for the president, Khaz'ali contended, but the leader did not sign his orders, this person would not become president. The basic principle of *Velayat-e Faqih*, Ayatollah Mohammad Reza Mahdavi Kani chided reformists, was "obedience."[9]

Ayatollah Mohammad Emami Kashani distinguishes between the principle of *Velayat-e Faqih*, in which the *Faqih* leads the people and is subject only to God, from the principle of *Vekalat* (delegating authority) in which representatives are elected by and are subordinate to the people. *Velayat-e Faqih*, he said elsewhere, substituted for the role of prophecy in the present era, and without it the Muslims would have been dominated by the "enemies." In order to prevent tensions, he explained, a focal point is needed, and "a single person should be followed so as to maintain social interests

---

7 Tehran Voice of the Islamic Republic of Iran Radio March 1, 25, August 30, 2000 (DR); AFP, January 3, 2001.

8 *Salam*, February 5, 1998; Tehran, Voice of the Islamic Republic of Iran Radio, March 31, 2000 (DR).

9 IRNA, 20 August; *Abrar*, September 5, 2000; *Hayat-e Now*, April 28, 2001. See similar statements by Ayatollah Emami Kashani and Hojjat ul-Islam Mohammadi-Araqi in *Iran*, April 3, 1998 and *Jomhuri-ye Eslami*, January 17, 2000.

and the Constitution and prevent any disorder." He likened this situation to an orchestra, which harmoniously plays to what the singer, namely the *Vali-ye Faqih*, sings. If the singer sings and the orchestra plays a different tune, the music will be only a cacophony of discordant sounds, he concluded.[10]

Hard-line conservatives: dismissing the democracy discourse. The hard-line conservative *'ulama* dismissed the discourse of democracy altogether. Ayatollah Mohammad Taqi Mesbah Yazdi, the most outspoken representative of this trend, compared the demand for a "public mandate" for an Islamic government as tantamount to a claim that the Prophet Muhammad would not have been able to rule without popular consent, and that God himself could not invest His emissary with the power to rule.[11]

Mesbah Yazdi rejected the notion that the term "Islamic Republic" meant a combination of two complementary or opposed concepts, namely Islamism and republicanism, replying to the assertion by reformist circles that republicanism referred to the regime's popular foundation. Those who had the temerity to say that republicanism should take precedence over Islamism whenever the two concepts were in conflict did not understand Islam, he said, since Islamic rule, the Islamic system and the Islamic Republic were all molds inside which Islam manifested itself. Republicanism meant the rejection of monarchy and "not the kind of republic that is understood in the West, namely a democracy under which everything would be subject to the people's whims and votes."[12]

Mesbah Yazdi contended that Islam and democracy were incompatible. In a democracy people can decide to change the rules of their life through elections and parliaments, he said, whereas in Islam "laws should be determined by the Almighty," and "no such change is possible because the rules are fixed for eternity." In Islam, he was quoted as saying, "man has no right to think in any way he wants about anything. Laws govern all human acts and deeds." Rather, "man's mind, heart, and imagination should also be controlled." Not surprisingly, he regards the *Majlis*, the manifestation of popular sovereignty and will, as merely a "consultative body" that "can give its opinion. But its decisions are subject to approval by the Guardian Council," and "the ultimate decision rests with the Supreme Leader."[13]

---

10   *Iran*, April 3, 1998; IRNA, March 30, 2001.

11   *Hambastegi*, January 28, 2001 (DR).

12   *Aftab-e Yazd*, February 1, 2001 (DR).

13   IRNA, April 21, 2000; *al-Sharq al-Awsat*, June 19, 2000; *Hayat-e No*, October 4, 2000.

Ayatollah Kazim Ha'iri, an exiled Iraqi cleric who taught at Qom, was equally blunt when he stated that:

There is no sense in placing legislative power or determination of the type of political system in the hand of the people. They are too ignorant about a great deal concerning even themselves, not to mention their profound ignorance of the world and its mysterious workings. [This is in contrast with] the Wise Creator who has revealed to them laws and commandments that give them happiness and guide them to the right path.... Therefore it is improper for a Muslim to believe in democracy or to practice it, even to elect the executive branch, except if Islam has ordained such a thing.[14]

Hojjat ul-Islam Mohsen Gharavian, Mesbah Yazdi's disciple, argued that if "a dictator is someone who announces that the truth is what I say, and nothing else," then "we must admit that God Almighty is the first dictator of the universe." We must submit to reasonable dictatorship, he continued, but "true dictatorship" was "opposition to God's will." "The people's vote," he stressed, "cannot determine right and wrong. For the same reason, no prophet of God said that right is whatever the people say."[15]

In a similar vein, Hojjat ul-Islam Gholam Reza Hasani, a Friday prayer leader from Urumia, dismissed the significance of a majority decision, and implicitly of popular will. If "6 billion people across the world condemned prayers and fasting and opted for carousing and wanton abandon, and lauded liberty and supported the will of the majority," he would oppose the motion, he stated. Significantly, the same argument was voiced by Ayatollah Mohammad Hosein Beheshti, leader of the Assembly of Experts that wrote the Constitution during the 1979 debate on the Iranian constitution.[16] That members of the dominant faction no longer used such arguments appears to be more a shift of discourse in response to popular feelings than a fundamental change in convictions.

The reformist view: Islamic democracy as a value. Whereas the dominant faction paid lip service to democracy, reformist 'ulama presented it, or rather their version of Islamic democracy, as a value in its own merits. They described it as a system urgently needed in Iran in order to overcome the "destructive effects" which dictatorship had left on the spirits of rulers and people in Iran and as an essential prerequisite for national develop-

---

14   Kazim al-Ha'iri, *Asas al-hukuma al-Islamiyya* (Beirut, 1979), p. 64, cited in Aziz, "Popular Sovereignty," p. 108.

15   *Hayat-e No*, April 28, 2001, citing *Nowruz*, April 21, 2001 (DR).

16   *Bahar*, cited in *Iran News* "Press Review" July 2, 2000. For Beheshti's remarks, see Schirazi, p. 35.

ment. Moreover, Khatami warned, "It's only as a religious democracy in our country that our society will be saved and preserved," implying that the regime's survival hinged on its implementation. He declared his belief on several occasions that the freedom to take part in the political process and the right to decide one's destiny were core values, and not just superficial impressions of religion.[17]

In a similar vein, Hojjat ul-Islam 'Abbas Hoseini Qa'em-Maqami attributed the great appeal of democracy to its respect for the freedom of choice given to humans. Thanks to this trait, he stated, it can be said that after divine inspiration and the prophetic teachings, democracy is the greatest human achievement of all time. According to Khatami, it would not be possible "to have a society whose people do not have the right to rule over themselves." "Democracy is a must in today's world," he told a student rally, and "those who negate pluralism do not understand the spirit of the times." Islamic countries should move toward establishing democratic governments, he told a gathering of the Organization of the Islamic Conference, so that they can maintain their status and power in the international arena.[18]

In contrast to the formalistic representation of the right, Hadi Khamene'i, then editor of *Jahan-e Islam*, sought to produce a more meaningful view of democracy. Democracy, in his view, does not refer merely to the people's rule, but to a system of government that would not impose its authority on social institutions to such an extent that would preclude its removal. Under such circumstances, democracy is a system that prevents mistakes and bloody cruelty. It is a system where there is a lesser possibility for corruption, although some corruption is inevitable. Democracy is a means, he concludes, and does not have a specified goal.

Consequently, the reformist *'ulama* sought some balance between the popular foundation of the government and the *Velayat-e Faqih* doctrine, but without challenging the latter. Both Hojjat ul-Islam Majid Ansari, head of the pro-reform *Majma'-e Hizbollah* in the Fifth *Majlis*, and Khatami maintained that the only reason the *'ulama* held the positions of power in the country was because the people wanted it, and that a suitable Islamic system could only be maintained with the approval of the people. Hojjat ul-Islam 'Ali Akbar Mohtashemi, a former radical turned reformist, argued that the will of the people should be accepted even if the people are wrong.

---

17   IRNA, January 19, 2000; January 6, 21, February 15, 27, May 1, 2001; Reuters, August 22, 2000; Vision of the Islamic Republic of Iran Network September 1, 4, 2000 (DR); *Tehran Times*, May 5, 2001.

18   *Resalat*, June 11, 2000.

The people paved our way to power, and now we claim that they need guidance and control, he admonished the conservatives. The people's voice is highly important, even if the Guardian Council nullifies its choice.[19]

Hojjat ul-Islam Qa'em Maqami distinguished between the need for popular legitimacy for religion *per se* and the need for a religious government. The people have no role in approving the principle of religion, he stated, and it is not for them to decide whether or not Islam is competent to govern. However, in a religious government we consider the people to be involved, and hence the principle of the government being religious must be with the consent of the people, even though religion does not receive its legitimacy from them. If the people accept it, he explained, the government will endure. If they do not, no one, not even the commander of the faithful, can force the people to accept the government. The real legitimacy of religious government and law is beholden to the vote of the people. Qa'em Maqami explained that legitimacy means recognizing the sources and the active parts of the political decision-making system. If the place of the people is merely to accept and follow, one can no longer say that there is popular rule in such a system.

Qa'em Maqami maintained that the Islamic government's source of legitimacy is both divine and populist. The active part of the government is under the people's control and the other part is controlled by religion. Both parts work together to form a religious government. If either of them is absent, religious government does not take shape. In other words, without decision-making by the public and human opinion and reason, one cannot consider a government to be religious. Religious government is a matter of what is right, but the requirement of religious law for achieving this government is that the people must want it, and if they do not, it is a violation of religious law to force them. In religious society, the people are free to make decisions in any way they wish and to choose, even if in some cases their choices are mistaken. The principle of the government being religious, he added, must be with the contentment of the people, even though religion does not get its legitimacy from the people.[20]

Khatami claimed that Iran was "going to introduce to the world the model of religious democracy," in which the people are "the true rulers."

---

19   Deutsche Presse-Agentur, February, 3 1997; *'Asr-e Azadegan*, February14, 2000; IRNA, August 7, 2000; *Khorasan*, May 5, 2001 (British Broadcasting Corporation, Summary of World Broadcasts (SWB). See also Ayatollah Mousavi Kho'iniha in *Time*, June 12, 2000.

20   *Khorasan*, May 5, 2001 (SWB).

In order to ensure that rule by the people was realized, power must be supervised and criticized. The structure should be such that if, within the framework of their system, the people do not like a part or aspect of the government, they should be able to bring about a change without paying a heavy price, he said.[21]

Still, Khatami's position contained some self-contradictions. He maintained that sovereignty belonged to God and "it is the Almighty God who has destined man to be the master of his own fate." Occasionally, he expressed explicit support for the *Velayat-e Faqih* doctrine, and he constantly extolled the Iranian constitution as the foundation of the Islamic system, knowing full well that *Velayat-e Faqih* was its central theme. He stressed that the leader was "the pivot of the Islamic system," but also added that democracy was a principle enshrined in the constitution and the ground should, therefore, be prepared for its enforcement or implementation.[22] Various reformists tried to solve this contradiction saying that the Assembly of Experts, which is elected by the people and which elects the *rahbar*, should exercise greater supervision of his actions.[23]

Ayatollah Montazeri, who had played a key role in framing the 1979 constitution, adopted a critical position toward the dominant concept and implementation of *Velayat-e Faqih* after his demotion in 1989.[24] He argued that according to the Iranian constitution "the basis of government at all levels" was the "voice of the people." He rejected the theory of the absolute authority of the *Faqih* (*Velayat-e Faqih motlaqe*) introduced into the constitution in 1989 (article 57) as being in "clear contradiction" with the intent of the constitution. Accordingly, the official interpretation of the doctrine of the absolute guardianship of the Chief Jurisconsult, the *Faqih*, created "the despotism of the jurisconsult," rendering all responsible institutions

21   IRNA, December 26, 1997; AFP, February10, 2001; *Afarinesh*, February 22, 2001 (DR); Vision of the Islamic Republic of Iran Network, May 2, 28, 2001 (DR).

22   IRNA, December 26, 1997; Islamic Republic of Iran Broadcasting (IRIB) Television, December 30, 1997 (DR); IRNA, May 18, 1998, August 7, 1998; R. Tehran, July 5, 1998; *Tehran Times*, August 23, 2000; AFP, 10 February; *Afarinesh*, January 22, 2001; see also IRNA, June 5, 2000; *Resalat*, June 11, 2000, and *Abrar*, August 17, 2000 for similar views by other reformist *'ulama*.

23   *Hamshahri*, October 13, 1998; R. Tehran, January 28, 2000 (SWB); Mahdi Karubi to *al-Sharq al-Awsat*, February 16, 2000; Tehran Vision of the Islamic Republic of Iran Network 1, May 20, 2000 (DR).

24   Montazeri was officially designated as Khomeini's heir-apparent (*jahneshin*), but demoted after continuously criticizing the Islamic regime's oppressive policies. Politically, he was opposed by the dominant faction, headed by Rafsanjani and Khamene'i. See Menashri, *Post Revolutionary Politics*, pp. 22ff.

"unnecessary and superfluous." The *Faqih*, he stated, was "equal to any other person before the law," and he could never be above the law. Moreover, "the external actualization and legitimacy" of his position was "rooted in its election by the nation," and "in fact [was] a social contract between the nation and the *Vali-ye Faqih*." Consequently, the *rahbar*'s authority and tenure in office could be limited and temporary. In addition, since the *rahbar* was elected to bear a specific responsibility, and since he was not infallible, he should remain open to public criticism and be held accountable with respect to his responsibilities. Montazeri further contended that Islam supported "the separation of powers, rejecting, therefore, electing the *rahbar* by the Assembly of Experts while insisting for his direct election by the people since the will of the people, and not the leader, was supreme."[25]

Montazeri maintained that his interpretation of the concept of *Velayat-e Faqih* was consistent with democracy, since he believed that rule by the people was an integral part of Islamic government. The people were not against Islamic government and the implementation of Islamic principles, he said, but only felt resentment at the "dictatorship practiced by a certain faction that has monopolized Islam."[26]

Declaring himself a disciple of Montazeri, Hojjat-ul Islam 'Abdallah Nuri, a former Interior Minister who was forced out of office, told his judges that according to Iran's constitution and to God's will "sovereignty belongs exclusively to the people." All citizens—the *rahbar* included—regardless of color, race, religion, occupation, wealth or designation, should be fully equal before the law with no discrimination or difference between them.[27] Like Na'ini during the Constitutional Revolution, who advocated equality before the law, Nuri did not specify if he meant the current law in Iran, which in itself institutionalized inequality, or the law as a general concept.[28]

The liberal view: the champions of democracy. A small group of liberal-minded *'ulama* advocated the supremacy of popular sovereignty over major aspects

---

25   For a comprehensive presentation of his position, see Geneive Abdo, "Rethinking the Islamic Republic: A Conversation with Ayatollah Hossein 'Ali Montazeri," *Middle East Journal*, Vol. 55, No. 1 (Winter 2001), especially pp. 14, 16-17. See also his interview with *al-Sharq al-Awsat*, May 25, 2000. For an analysis of his theological view of *Velayat-e Faqih*, see Shahrough Akhavi, "Contending Discourses in Shi'i Law on the Doctrine of Wilayat al-Faqih," *Iranian Studies*, Vol. 29, Nos. 3-4 (Summer-Fall 1996), pp. 253-60.

26   Montazeri to *al-Sharq Awsat*, May 25, 2000.

27   'Abdallah Nuri, *Showkaran-e Eslah* (Tehran: Tarh-e now, 1999), pp. 11-12, 22, 28, 43.

28   For Na'ini's views on this point, see 'Abdul Hadi Hairi, *Shi'ism and Constitutionalism in Iran* (Leiden: Brill, 1977), pp. 221ff.

of the *Velayat-e Faqih* doctrine. Unlike those associated with the two major trends, these clerics held no official positions, nor were they affiliated or linked to any specific association or organization. Grand Ayatollah Yusuf Sane'i of Qom, a former member of the Council of Guardians, came closest to Montazeri's formulation, advocating that the Supreme Leader's right to hold office and his actions "depend on the endorsement by the public as a whole." "Humans can always make mistakes," Sane'i stated, and no leader or group of people was "above the law or 'more equal' than anyone else." Consequently, "power must rest with the people, the majority, not individuals or institutions." He described the precedence given to the will of a single individual or a small group of people over the viewpoint of the majority as the "ugliest manifestation of dictatorship" and stressed that all should keep away from attributing such an idea to Islam. If you "lose popular participation," he told Iran's Interior Minister 'Abd al-Vahed Mousavi Lari, "your divine government will lose its characteristic of being divine even though its laws and regulation are divinely inspired." "Those who do not want the people to be on the scene," he added, are in fact "paving the way for establishment of the sovereignty of arrogance."[29]

Following the trial of Hojjat ul-Islam 'Abdallah Nuri in November 1999, Sane'i alluded to the Qur'anic view of humankind as "the deputies of God" and asked: "How is it possible to give priority to the opinion of one person [the supreme jurist] or a few persons or a small social group [the clerical class] over the opinion and vote of all or the majority of the people? This is the highest form of despotism in its ugliest face."[30]

Hojjat ul-Islam Hasan Yusufi Eshkevari went further in giving precedence to popular sovereignty by arguing that government was not a religious matter or "something dictated by God or by prophets." He praised democracy as "the biggest discovery of humanity," but contended that it was "not exclusive to Western thinking." The Prophet Muhammad ruled by consultation, he claimed, and not from above, nor did he have a theocracy. "If Muhammad had not first of all been accepted by the people of Medina as their leader, he could not have been their ruler." [31]

Hojjat ul-Islam Mohsen Kadivar challenged the very concept of *Velayat-e Faqih* as incompatible with true democracy. In two of his books, Kadivar

29   IRNA, December 1, 1999; *Iran*, January 22, 2000; *Los Angeles Times*, December 29, 2000; IRNA, February 7, 2001.

30   Cited in A.S. Arjomand, "Shi'ism and Constitution in Iran" in W. Ende and R. Brunner (eds), *Twelver Shi'ism in Modern Times* (Brill: Leiden, 2000), p. 328.

31   *Toronto Star*, March 5, 2000.

showed that Shi'ism always entertained conflicting views on government, and therefore the concept of *Velayat-e Faqih* was merely one interpretation among many; and, more importantly, that it lacked any Qur'anic or rational justification. His statement in a subsequent article that "the basic problem of Iran is *Velayat-e Faqih*" was the logical conclusion of his theological endeavor. [32] Reconciliation between democracy and a government based on *Velayat-e Faqih* was impossible, adding that

either we must believe in a religious guardianship of the *Faqih* appointed by God in the capacity of absolute wardship over the people, or believe in the election of leadership as the representative of the people. These two regimes... cannot be reconciled.

Following his 18-month imprisonment for his views, Kadivar intensified his criticism. Pointing to Iran's "2,500-year history of despotism," he explained that it was possible to speak of justice in society only when power was in the hands of the people. He expressed his belief in the compatibility between democracy and Islam, but warned that a religious state was possible only when it was elected and governed by the people, and the governing of the country should not be necessarily in the hands of the clergy. What existed in Iran, he continued, was a system in which one man, Ayatollah 'Ali Khamene'i, had absolute authority under the *Velayat-e Faqih* doctrine, as did the monarchy in the past, and this was against the revolution's goals. As the alternative, Kadivar favored a religious system in which the leader was elected by the people for limited term and did not necessarily have to be trained in Islamic jurisprudence. The *'ulama*'s role in society should be the "role of a father and a fair judge," and as defenders of the people's rights, but not as a political party or as rulers involved in the daily business of government. Kadivar emphasizes that such a system would only be possible on the condition that the people believed in religion. Should the will of the people come into conflict with religion, he said, the people's voice should be given precedence. "People cannot be dragged to paradise in chains," he concluded, and "if we want democracy, *Velayat-e-Faqih* must be abolished."[33]

32   For an analysis of his views see Farzin Vahdat, "Post Revolutionary Discourses of Mohammad Mojtahed Shabestari and Mohsen Kadivar: Reconciling the Terms of Mediated Subjectivity," *Critique*, No. 17 (Fall, 2000), pp. 145-9, and Menashri, pp. 35-6; *Ruzegar-e No*, No. 205 (February-March 1999), pp. 31-3.

33   *Bahar*, July 11, 2000 (DR); Kadivar to *Frankfurter Allgemeine Zeitung*, August 21, 2000 (DR); *New York Times*, September 18, 2000; Kadivar to *Jame'eh-ye Madani* cited in *www.payvand.com*, October 23, 25, 2000.

Freedom in an Islamic system

Civil liberties and freedom—essential elements in any democratic system—loom large in the contemporary Islamist discourse of democracy. By contrast, they never acquired great importance in traditional monotheistic religious thought, because of its central idea of subordinating human beings to God. This is even truer in Islam and Judaism which impose on the believers a system of laws and regulations that aspire to guide their conduct in almost all aspects of life. Conceivably, a major reason might have been the traditional concept of voluntary submission to God ("*islam*"), which regards human beings as God's slaves whose sole purpose is to worship God. In Islamic medieval tradition, therefore, freedom (*hurriyya*) did not refer to political and civil liberties or rights, but was used simply to denote the legal opposite of slavery.[34] Only in the latter part of the nineteenth century did freedom assume its modern meaning, associated with political and civil liberties, alongside traditional meanings.[35]

Civil liberties and freedom loomed prominently in the clerical debate over democracy. Spokesmen of all trends praised the revolution as bringing freedom to Iran, but gave varying interpretations to the meaning of these terms and to their desired scope.

Hard-line conservatives: freedom, but not from God. Discussing the notion of "human rights" from an Islamic point of view, Ayatollah Mesbah Yazdi stated that "right" (*haq*) in Islam meant "true fact" as compared to a false one. Another meaning of "right" was a voluntary act, which brings about a positive result; in other words, any action, which has a just and lofty goal, is called a "right." Thus, any person who is given a right has in turn a duty to society. Consequently, the criteria for human rights should be absolute right, that is, divine laws, rather than the unstable criteria included in the Universal Declaration of Human Rights.

Mesbah Yazdi explained that the slogans of the revolution were about "independence, freedom, Islamic republic," and were inspired by the Qur'an. The desire for an Islamic Republic stemmed from the first two

---

34   For a broad discussion of the meaning of freedom in traditional Islamic thought, see Franz Rosenthal, *The Muslim Concept of Freedom* (Leiden: Brill, 1960), pp. 29ff. For a discussion of freedom in pre-revolutionary Iranian thought, see Farough Jahanbakhsh, *Islam, Democracy and Religious Modernism in Iran (1953-2000): From Bazargan to Soroush* (Leiden: Brill, 2001), pp. 94-8.

35   Bernard Lewis, "The Idea of Freedom in Modern Islamic Political Thought," in B. Lewis, *Islam in History: Ideas, People, and Events in the Middle East* (Chicago: Open Court, 1993), pp. 323-36.

principles. Freedom then meant liberation from the "claws of arrogance"—
that is, the US—and not "from religion, God and common sense." The
scope of freedom in Islam was narrower than in the West, he argued elsewhere, since liberty in Islam was based on the spiritual and material interests of society, whereas in the West only the material interests determined
its boundaries. Thus, freedom of the press granted by the constitution was
possible provided that nothing should be printed that was against the principles of Islam. [36]

Mesbah Yazdi denounced Western liberalism as an idea and culture promoted by Western agents and those enthralled by the West. Its foundations
endangered social issues, he maintained, whereas religion said that whatever God has ordered must be done regardless of whether or not it is in
accordance with the demands of the people. In addition, religion gave priority to social over individual interests. Since the liberal school of thought
preferred the demands of the people to those of God, and required that if
the people so desire, then all religious edicts should be stopped, it could
not be compatible with Islam. The most important cause of cultural and
religious weakness, he concluded, was the influence of the liberal elements
and the spread of the liberal school of thought in society.[37]

The dominant faction: limiting freedom. Members of the dominant faction
consistently took pride in the institutionalization of freedom in the 1979
constitution as a major achievement of the revolution. Ayatollah Rafsanjani, for one, asserted that the principle of freedom came together with the
other principles of Islam and republicanism from the very inception of the
Islamic Republic.[38] He stressed that there are many basic freedoms in the
Islamic system, such as the freedom for people to participate in deciding
their fate and to express their views by various means, and the freedom
of assembly. Freedom, discussion, debate and argument are all good and
constructive, he commented, and society would not progress if it were not
for political reactions and criticism. But he cautioned that such criticism
should respect limits and boundaries so as not to be open to misuse by
"many enemies who are lying in ambush." Thus, while there are no limits
in the Islamic system to people expressing doubts about the basic tenets of
Islam, publicizing such doubts is quite another matter. The problem is that

36 *Iran,* May 6, 1999; IRNA, April 21, 2000; *Resalat,* May 16, 2000; *Aftab-e Yazd,* February 1, 2001 (DR).

37 *Resalat,* May 16, 2000.

38 Voice of the Islamic Republic of Iran Radio 1, March 31, 2000 (DR).

some people think that they can publicize their doubts and thereby infect society and youth with this doubt, commented Rafsanjani.[39]

Rafsanjani contrasted the Islamic perception of freedom with the Western one. The latter emerged as a value after the dark period of the Middle Ages, the Inquisition, and the French Revolution with its killings. In an Islamic society one must "look in the Qur'an and in Islamic teachings for correct, effective, constructive, and harmless freedoms." Such freedoms are different from those of non-religious societies, as there are bounds and limits to dress, social interaction or ownership, and consumption. He maintained that complete personal liberty cannot exist in any country, but there are clearly more restrictions in a religious society adhering to the Qur'an and Islamic traditions, which naturally restrict freedom.[40]

All spokesmen of the dominant faction shared the notion that freedom should be limited by Islamic boundaries. Ayatollah Ibrahim Amini agreed that "freedom and relying on votes will contribute to the increasing sophistication of public opinion and the resolution of society's problems." However, freedom does not mean that everybody can behave or disregard limitations as he pleases. Amini called, therefore, for defining the limits of freedom in an Islamic society, insisting that people "should not write anything they please and they should not insult holy Islamic principles or the holy personality of His Eminence, Imam Khomeini." The limits of freedom as determined by the *rahbar*, he said elsewhere, are when harm is done to the people's beliefs or to the authorities.[41]

The former head of the judiciary Ayatollah Mohammad Yazdi described freedom as "truly a divine gift." God has created mankind to be free and this divine gift must be appreciated without being abused. Before the advent of Islam, he argued, freedom was non-existent. It had been trampled on and destroyed to the extent that men were exploited as slaves. But Islam revived freedom and granted freedom to all strata, particularly to women and children and other weak members of society. Yazdi distinguished between three types of freedom: the first one was the innate freedom in man's soul that enables him to choose between good and evil. Secondly, every person should enjoy personal freedom as long as it did not infringe on other people's freedom; that is, a person may decide his own lifestyle—for

---

39   Voice of the Islamic Republic of Iran, March 20, 1998 (SWB); *Jomhuri-ye Eslami*, June 21, 2000 (DR).

40   *Jomhuri-ye Eslami*, June 21, 2000.

41   IRNA , July 31, 1998, October 4, 1998.

example, he can decide about his place of residence, his profession and the kind of food he likes to eat. The third type of freedom that has been defined in the constitution pertains to political and social freedom. Political freedom means that human beings are free to express their views about the management, and the quality of the management, in their countries. Human beings are free to form political parties or other organizations, and cannot be forced to take part in a particular political party.

However, should such freedoms be without limits or boundaries, Yazdi cautioned, they could bring about chaos, which would be to the detriment of this very freedom, since human beings differ in their views and they have disputes and quarrels with one another. Nowhere in the world did the supporters of freedom demand absolute freedom, which gives free rein to the people to do whatever they wish. This would be tantamount to anarchy and a violation of the boundaries of freedom

Yazdi maintained that the Islamic revolution supported the principle of freedom in accordance with Islamic instructions, and enshrined it in many laws. The government was duty bound to provide political and social freedoms, but it was also obliged to limit and streamline them with certain regulations within the law. Thus, he explains, we can have liberties, such as writing, publishing, holding assemblies, and taking part in demonstrations, as long as they are not contrary to Islamic principles. If they are contrary to Islamic principles, then they cannot exist. In order to avoid unnecessary disputes, Yazdi stressed that the only persons who can decide whether any of these actions conforms to Islamic principles are jurisconsults (*fuqaha*) of the Guardian Council, who are appointed by the *rahbar*.

Yazdi further explains that in the Islamic Republic of Iran freedom, independence, unity and territorial integrity are inseparable. In other words, it is inconceivable to undermine the unity of the people or the country's independence and territorial integrity by exploiting freedom. Freedom is inseparable from these principles, and each one of them restricts another. Freedom is good providing it does not undermine unity among the people or the country's territorial integrity. Therefore, he concluded, no one has the right, under any circumstances, whether through compromise, discussion or influence, to misuse freedom.[42]

---

42   Voice of the Islamic Republic of Iran, September 25, 1998 (SWB), May 5, 2000 (DR); for other *'ulama* who subordinate freedom to Islamic principles as defined by the constitution, see *Kayhan*, May 28, 1998; *Bahar*, July 2, 2000 (DR); *Resalat*, July 11, August 21, 22, October 5, 2000; *Iran*, August 23, 2000; Voice of the Islamic Republic of Iran Radio 1, September 8, 2000 (DR).

Yazdi attacked journalists for interpreting freedom as meaning that they could write about whatever they liked. They considered it their right to resort to sophistry, create doubt, question Islamic principles and mislead our young people, he complained; they even thought they could question the most fundamental Islamic principles, which are set out in the Qur'an and on which there is consensus among Islamic scholars. Yazdi distinguished between legitimate freedom—that is, freedom as defined by the regime, which the judiciary is bound to support—and the anarchic freedom advocated by elements of the press. Both he and Ayatollah Ahmad Jannati, head of the powerful Council of the Guardians (*shura-ye negahban*), threatened journalists that their tongues would be cut out should they continue to write against Islam, the revolution and the people's sacred values.[43]

In a similar vein, Ayatollah Va'ez Tabasi accepted Khatami's view that suppressing freedom of speech might push ideas underground and to opposition against the regime. But he insisted that no one should be allowed to hurt the people's religious feelings. Consequently, he threatened to use force in order to defend the scope of freedoms and liberties as defined by the Islamic regime. Should anyone dare criticize the Prophet or the *Velayat-e Faqih* doctrine, all members of Hizbollah—that is, hardline supporters of the government—and other devotees should respond forcefully. If freedom was kept within the boundaries of the constitution, and the regime dealt properly with those who violated the law, there would be no need to resort to violence.[44]

Most members of the dominant faction dismissed Western notions of freedom and liberty as clearly inferior to the Islamic concepts. Khamene'i, while extolling the freedoms granted by the Iranian constitution, dismissed freedom of expression and of the press in the West as a sham, saying that the only the capitalists are free to do as they wish, and only they can express their own views and can make or destroy anyone they wish. He pointed to the uproar and action taken against the French writer Roger Garaudy, who denied the Jewish Holocaust, as a proof of denial of freedom of expression in the West to anyone who "dares to say something against Zionism." If a person is not affiliated with the capitalists and is not part of the capitalists' power centers, he will not be able to speak, no one will hear his voice and he will be deprived of freedom of speech; this sort of freedom, which the capitalists enjoy, is contrary to human values; they promote a decadent life style and exploit

---

43   Voice of the Islamic Republic of Iran, February 27, 1998 (SWB).

44   *Resalat*, December 3, 1998; January 11, 1999.

the people; they create war anywhere they wish and impose peace anywhere they desire, and they sell their weapons to whomever they choose—this is the meaning of freedom in the West, he concluded.[45] In a similar fashion, the Minister of Intelligence Hojjat ul-Islam 'Ali Yunesi boasted that Iran did not need "to learn from foreigners about consolidating democracy," but was actually in a position to teach them about democracy.[46]

Some 'ulama in Qom, who did not hold official positions, distinguished between freedom of expression for ordinary people and the freedom of thought reserved for 'ulama. Ayatollah Yusuf Sane'i and Mousavi Ardebili defended the rights of Hojjat ul-Islam Kadivar to come out against the Velayat-e Faqih doctrine, claiming that a mojtahed, a cleric qualified to issue independent rulings, was entitled to deal with legal and philosophical question without interruption. A petition of 385 'ulama supporting Montazeri submitted in March 1998 called for recognition of the right of the sources of emulation (maraji' taqlid) to express their views freely in matters of religion. Hojjat ul-Islam Mohammad Taqi Fazel Maybudi insisted on the right of 'ulama to think independently and not follow the crowd, even if their views are unacceptable to the mob. Even the hard-liner Ayatollah Mohammad Yazdi was willing to accept debates in religious or other scholarly circles, where some might eventually deny the existence of God, the Prophet and Imams, but would receive an answer to their questioning. But why, he asked, raise such issues in public and amongst students who had no political experience? [47]

The reformists: liberty as an independent value (almost). As in the question of popular sovereignty, reformist 'ulama praised liberties and freedom as a value in itself. Khatami described freedom as "a divine right of human beings," "the most sacred and most exciting value for humanity throughout history," and as "the greatest element which has always been sought by the human race." Likewise, he praised liberty as the "essence of growth and development," and cautioned that revival and reform were not attainable without liberty. Concurrently, Khatami lamented that "autocracy became second nature" to Iranians, and that they were "a dictatorial people in a certain sense." He criticized those who were using religion as a cover to work against freedom, which they equated with anarchy, and expressed

45   Tehran Voice of the Islamic Republic of Iran Radio May 1, 12, 2000.
46   IRNA, January 13, 2001.
47   *Ettela'at*, December 22, 1998; Voice of the Islamic Republic of Iran Radio May 1, 5, 2000 (DR); *Resalat*, August 21, 2000.

concern over the negative attitudes toward freedom and democracy prevalent among certain groups in Iran which believed that they were defending
Islam. Such views, he asserted, were in fact detrimental to Islam. Iran must
strive for freedom or face the risk of more violence.[48]

Khatami stressed the importance of a plurality of trends and ideas and
of the opportunity to express them, explaining that differences of opinion
or tastes were "natural and the existence of diversity is a necessity of a
dynamic society." Moreover, he favored such pluralism not only out of
necessity—because oppression would not succeed—but also as a positive
value. If we do not allow the expression of other views, he stated, we have
insulted humanity and the free Islamic society. Khatami, therefore, called
for the creation of a desirable milieu in which people could more easily tolerate one another and "come up with an agreed definition of freedom." He
insisted that "limiting and controlling thoughts" was "inhuman and cruel"
for the individual and a "preposterous way to make a society submissive."
No group should impose its opinion on society, he concluded.[49]

Khatami pointed to two aspects of freedom: the first referred to freedom
from within, when the individual gets rid of his domineering passions,
and the second pertained to emancipating oneself from the domination of
hegemonists, that is, the oppressive powers that be. While internal freedom
matures society and makes it rationale, external freedom leads it toward
democracy whereby man can determine his own destiny.[50]

Khatami went further than the dominant faction in advocating freedom
even for those who opposed the regime. "Freedom does not mean freedom
[only] for those who support us," he said. "It means freedom even for those
who oppose us. In an Islamic society, people should have the freedom to
think, and our opponents should be allowed to express their views. We do
not have the right to accuse anyone who criticized us of apostasy and blas-
phemy. Even if we succeeded in stopping criticism for a while, we will not
be able to avoid the consequences of such an action," he warned.[51]

48   Mohammad Khatami, *Mutala'at fi al-din wal-Islam wal-'asr* (Beirut: Dar al-jadid, 1988),
      pp. 190-1; *Time*, January 12, 1998; *Iran News*, May 12, 1998; IRIB Television, May 14,
      1998 (DR); Vision of the Islamic Republic of Iran Network 1, July 25, 1999 (SWB);
      Mideast Mirror, May 24, 1999; IRNA, February 5, 2001.

49   Khatami to *Middle East Insight*, Vol. 13, No. 1 (November-December 1997), p. 27; IRIB
      Television, December 30, 1997, May 14, 1998 (DR); *Time*, January 12, 1998; IRNA,
      March 28, May 18, 1998; Vision of the Islamic Republic of Iran Network 1, July 25,
      1998 (SWB), November 26, 2000 (DR).

50   IRNA, February 5, 2001.

51   Radio Free Europe/Radio Liberty IRAN REPORT, Vol. 2, No. 21, May 24, 1999; IRNA,

Khatami maintained that "religion and freedom should not oppose each other. Freedom should not be held back in the name of religion, or religion in the name of freedom." He therefore criticized Western notions of freedom as too narrow and one-dimensional, because they separated the two. Such notions were incomplete and could not ensure happiness, since freedom without religion was "the reason for the fall of humanity." He argued that there was no contradiction between Islam and individual rights and that the Islamic Republic embodied the ideal combinations of both Islam and freedom. "Religion complies with human rights and civil rights; freedom complies with Islamic cultural values. The Islamic Republic was created for the sake of this combination." Concurrently, he criticized his conservative rivals, noting that the practice of religion without freedom disguised selfish lust for power and bigotry, which are imposed by religious hard-liners on society in the name of God, and therefore pose an obstacle in the path of humanity's progress.[52]

However, this is where Khatami's ideas encounter difficulties. Seeking harmony between religion and freedom, he contends that it is impossible to "have freedom in all its legal, philosophical and political implications without the law." "You cannot endanger security for the sake of freedom, and you cannot endanger freedom for the sake of security.... This is a delicate balance," he admonished impatient students. He emphasized that freedom should come "with responsibility," which is stipulated by the constitution. Freedom in the framework of the law meant the constitution, which defines both the boundaries of people's basic powers and rights and their duties, and the boundaries of the state. Therefore, he said elsewhere, freedom "should not be against the tenets of Islam and the rights of the public." Anyone who accepts the law has rights and such a person's political rights must be defended, but, he warned, those who seek to overthrow the system are a different matter altogether; they must be guided as far as possible, but, if they do not accept logic, they must be addressed with a different language. While Khatami goes further than the dominant 'ulama faction, his views still put major constraints on the meaning and scope of freedom, since the criteria remained those defined by the Islamic regime itself. Thus he stated that freedom should not violate public rights and the fundamentals of Islam, and that "no person is at liberty to endanger the

October 17, 2000.

52   Khatami, *Mutala'at*, pp. 190-91; Vision of the Islamic Republic of Iran Network 1, Tehran, July 25, 1998 (SWB); AFP, February 10, 2001; *al-Hayat*, May 1, 2, 2001.

security of the society, the interests of the country...and scar the fundaments of Islam."[53]

In a similar fashion, Hojjat ul-Islam Qa'em-Maqami contended that although the basic element of democracy is free will, it is a relative concept. After all, even in Western democracies, people may exert their will and their liberty only within a certain framework. Even John Stuart Mill, who was extremely liberal in his views, considered a framework of social benefit and national interests to be vital for realizing democracy and freedom. Mill said people are free, Qa'em-Maqami explained, but society can never give individuals the liberty to destroy society itself. Therefore, even in Western democracy, we can see that people exert their will and their opinion within a framework of national interests. The national interests of each society are defined according to its particular culture. This notion also exists in Islamic society. After all, no religious society can allow the expansion of liberty and freedom to an extent that would damage its social and historical identity. One of the factors that limit freedom in a liberal society is the need to safeguard social identity. When a society has a secular, non-religious identity, it will never allow this identity to be jeopardized in the name of freedom, just as a religious society will not allow its identity to be damaged by irreligious behavior.[54]

Khatami praised the Iranian constitution, which after the "oppression" of the Shah "brought us freedom." "My pivotal slogan is that the foundation of the society should be based on the Constitution," he declared, "so that any movement or reform or any other process should be specified within the Constitution." There is a theoretical discussion about freedom of expression, but "we as the government officials, try to do our job on the basis of law," he added, hinting perhaps at some difference between his personal views and the limitations imposed upon him by his office. Khatami argued that the constitution defined the scope of rights of individuals and granted the people the freedom they deserved. At the same time, it also put the limits of this freedom and established the authority and responsibility of the government, so that the Islamic Republic was an integrated and coordinated system. By invoking the constitution, Khatami may have wanted to stress his interpretation that the "state, too, has boundaries."[55]

53 IRIB Television First Program Network, December 30, 1997 (DR); IRNA, August 7, 2000; *Tehran Times*, August 23, 2000; *New York Times*, September 8, 2000; AFP, February 12, 2001; Vision of the Islamic Republic of Iran Network May 2, 28, June 2, 2001 (DR).

54 *Resalat*, June 11, 2000.

55 IRNA, May 18, 1998, February 5, 2001; Iran Weekly Press Digest (IWPD), July 25-31,

Other *'ulama* of the reformist trend followed Khatami's argumentation. Mahdi Karubi, then secretary general of the MRM, spoke in glowing terms of the age in which "nobody can annihilate thoughts and ideas by resorting to excommunication or wielding truncheons." Reform, he told foreign journalists, meant freedom of thought, participation and the rule of law. Like Khatami, he contended that religion and freedom were not opposed to each other and deplored those who believed the revolution could be protected only if some of the people's rights were denied. Yet he also insisted that the principles of democracy and freedom of political action could be practiced only within the framework of the constitution. "Freedom does not mean irresponsibility and lack of discipline," he explained. It meant respecting the people, as well as Islamic values and sanctities, and acting within the framework provided by the constitution. Those who took undue advantage of freedom, he added, and insulted and exhibited disrespect for Islamic sanctities, must be dealt with within the framework provided by Islamic rules and regulations. Thus when Khamene'i forbade the *Majlis* on August 6, 2000 to debate the liberalization of Iran's harsh press law, Karubi as the *Majlis* Speaker adjourned the session forthwith, saying that "the constitution emphasizes the absolute rule of the Jurisconsult [*Velayat-e Motlaqe*] and this is how it is. We are all duty-bound to abide by it."[56]

Other reformist *'ulama* sought a compromise between liberties and their interpretation of Islamic values. Hojjat ul-Islam Mohammad Javad Hojjati-Kermani criticized members of Hizbollah for disrupting the assemblies of their political rivals. Yet he conceded that whenever the scope of freedom in Iran became too broad, it led to chaos, as was the case during the Mosaddeq period of the early 1950s. The result of this loss of restraint under the guise of "freedom" always resulted in the return of harsh rule.[57]

The insistence of the reformist *'ulama*, headed by Khatami, on adherence to the 1979 constitution when discussing their attitude toward freedom and liberties suggests that they are not fundamentally different from the mainstream *'ulama* of the dominant faction. Both groups see freedom as subordinate to and restricted by Islamic values and both deny the validity of freedom *from* religion. The difference between them is more a matter

---

1998; *Tehran Times*, August 23, 2000; AFP, February 10, 2001.

56   *Ettela'at*, November 21, 1998; Vision of the Islamic Republic of Iran Network 1, September 26, 1999 (SWB); *al-Sharq al-Awsat*, February 16, 2000; *Washington Post*, May 31, 2000; IRNA, August 6, 2000, February 5, 2001.

57   *Ettela'at*, April 8, 1998.

of degree rather than of essence, as they only differ as to the meaning and scope of the Islamic framework in which freedoms are allowed.

The liberals: freedom is not limited by government or Islam. Unlike the reformists, liberal *'ulama* are willing to consider liberties and freedoms which actually challenge the regime's ideology as well as basic Islamic precepts. 'Abdallah Nuri's position on freedom presented at his trial served as a bridge between the reformists and the more liberal *'ulama*. Facing his judges in a political trial, he argued that the revolution led by Khomeini constituted a golden opportunity for liberating the people from suppression, tyranny and despotism. Although this had not been attained, he added, Iranians now had another opportunity to achieve this sacred goal. Only by acknowledging and preserving the rights of our opponents, he said, can we help to ensure the longevity and independence of our regime. The abrogation of freedom by the government, he warned them, was a sign of its feebleness, not of its power and strength.[58]

Nuri cited the late Ayatollah Mortaza Mottahari's statement that the Qur'an sought to liberate humans from enslavement and subjugation by others, and added that this social freedom was one of the greatest epics of the Qur'an. Reciting verse 58 of Surat al-'Imran, which calls the People of the Book to "worship none but God," he told his judges that there could not be a "more lively and more exciting passage, neither in the 18th nor the 19th centuries when the philosophers' ideas of human liberty were realized, and when freedom evolved from mere expressions of faith to reality."[59] Taking into consideration the constraints which Nuri faced when he made this statement, it implies that he regards the freedom to worship God and the spiritual unity of the believers as the greatest liberty possible, but apparently he cannot fathom, or cannot bring himself to say, that freedom *from* worship is also a possibility.

According to Kadivar, autocratic regimes, by their nature, prevent freedom. A society that does not respect social and political rights, and international principles of human rights, is by definition undemocratic. People have the right to experience freedom, and there is nothing in Islam to prevent such a sacred right.[60] The one red line for freedom of thought in Islam, he stated, "is violating and invading the freedom of other people"—

---

58   Nuri, *Showkaran-e Eslah*, p. 197; *Iran News*, November 14, 1999.

59   Nuri, *Showkaran-e Eslah*, p. 159.

60   Debate with Shabestari on *"Din, modara va-khoshunat"* [Religion, tolerance and violence], *Kiyan* Vol. 8, No. 45 (January-March 1999), cited in Menashri, p. 35.

a statement which puts him closer to the classical liberal position than to traditional Islamic ones.[61]

Hojjat ul-Islam Mohammad Mojtahed Shabestari argues that Islam subscribes to the notion of freedom and basic human rights, but as mentioned before, he laments the fact that these ideas were never implemented. Moreover, in his attempt to reconcile between religion and modernity, Mojtahed Shabestari insists that critical attitudes and the concept of critique are of central importance. In this type of society, even external critiques of religion, such as those by Marx and Feuerbach, are not only tolerated, but can help the faithful refine their conceptions of religion and thus achieve purer forms of religiosity. In this type of society, if books against religion are not published and critique of religion is not allowed, faith loses its main characteristic and will no longer be a conscious act of choosing. Furthermore, "in the society of the faithful there are no 'red lines' to demarcate the limits of critique. The critics must have all the space to engage in critique without any red lines."[62]

Islamic vs. Western democracy

All Islamist movements in the Middle East—Sunni as well as Shi'i—reject Western democracy as a flawed system that put human law above God's laws, and as an essentially unjust system. The association of the term "democracy" with Western practices was among the major reasons for Ayatollah Khomeini's refusal to include the terms "democratic" or "Islamic democratic" in Iran's name, while he was willing to accept the less charged term "republic."

Hardliners: Western democracy is a charade. Contrasting the two systems, Ayatollah Mesbah-Yazdi maintained that Western democracy resulted from separating religion from politics when Western intellectuals realized that Christianity was unable to offer firm guidance in every aspect of human life, especially social life, and therefore concluded that it should not interfere in the fields of government and politics. Consequently, they were obliged to transfer government to the people, in order to avoid dictatorship. The situation in Islam was different since Islam was not distorted like Christianity and the text of the Qur'an as well as the traditions of the

61   *Hamshahri*, July 31, 2000.
62   Farzin Vahdat, "Post Revolutionary Discourses of Mohammad Mojtahed Shabestari and Mohsen Kadivar: Reconciling the Terms of Mediated Subjectivity," *Critique*, No. 16 (Spring, 2000), pp. 52-3.

Prophet and Imams were full of instructions applicable to social and governmental questions. In a Western-type democracy "everything would be subject to the people's whims and votes" and people could decide to change the rules of their life through elections and parliaments. "In Islam no such change is possible because the rules are fixed for eternity."[63]

Khamene'i made a clear distinction between the people's rule in Iran and Western democracy. He dismissed liberal Western democracy as a charade disguising the total dependence of political parties and leaders on "major capitalists," who played "a very decisive role" in determining the outcome of elections. Western democracy was superficial as it was devoid of justice and coincided with "oppression, colonialism, genocide and propagation of all kinds of corruption among various nations." Islam, he says, is more people-oriented than Western democracy, and "religious democracy is preferable to liberalism or Marxism."[64]

Dominant faction: religious democracy as an organic bond between people and state. Emami Kashani, too, contrasts Islamic democracy with "national democracy." He agrees that democracy represents the people's will, but he argues that in practice Western democracy became an instrument of politicians, who ignored the people's true will. Moreover, religious democracy, which holds all individuals responsible, creates an organic bond between people and state. The public participation is not limited to the forms accepted in standard democracy, such as casting votes in general elections. Rather, in an Islamic democracy all individuals in the community consider themselves to be just as responsible as state officials for state and administrative affairs, according to the religious obligation of promoting virtue and prohibiting vice (*amr be ma'ruf va nahy az munker*). Besides, in Islam voting is regarded as proof of a divine pact of allegiance and devotion.

He criticizes the individualism inherent in Western democracy. In such democracies, people are indifferent to issues other than their own prescribed duties and responsibilities and do not consider themselves obliged to step in and fulfill obligations that the government fails to handle. A sense of responsibility about others is regarded as something undesirable, like meddling and interference. In a religious democracy, on the other hand, members of society are never estranged from each other, because this type of regime is one of

---

63　*Abrar*, September 8, 1999 (DR); *Mideast Mirror*, June 19, 2000; *Aftab-e Yazd*, February 1, 2001 (DR).

64　Vision of the Islamic Republic of Iran Network August 1, 24, 2000 (DR); Voice of the Islamic Republic of Iran Radio 1, February 15, 2001 (DR).

unity, based on the notion that believers do good to each other and sympathize with and comfort each other, like the parts of a single body.[65]

The source of authority, according to Ayatollah Mohammad Yazdi, was the core difference between Western and Islamic democracies. In Western democracy, the authority to govern was given by the people, whereas in Islam it is God who bestows the authority to govern and the people help its implementation.[66]

In the Islamic system, according to Yazdi and Hojjat ul-Islam Mohammadi-Araqi, the people's true will and demands can be expressed or implemented only within the principles of Islam, after they voted for an Islamic government during the revolution. This is clearly different from Western democracy where the people's ideas and thoughts may change from time to time. In order to attain the aims of an Islamic society, Mohammadi-Araqi maintains, the Guardian Council plays a decisive role, similar but not identical to constitutional courts or senates in other countries. [67] He fails to mention, however, that the Guardian Council is appointed by the leader, whereas in other democracies such bodies are usually elected or appointed by elected parliaments.

Hojjat ul-Islam Ruhollah Hoseinian drew a distinction between Western republics and the Islamic Republic. But at the same time he argued for some similarities between the Islamic system and the Western system of Christian democracy, which also qualified democracy to some extent because of religious considerations. Hoseinian described the Iranian system as a "guided republic" based on indirect democratic rule, in keeping with Islam. Like other members of the dominant faction he described the Islamic system as having two dimensions: an Islamic one manifested by the indirect elections of the *rahbar,* and a populist one expressed by the direct election of the *Majlis* and president. But, he added, "the nature of our system requires supervision so it does not deviate from the Islamic framework, and for that purpose the Constitution has provided for the guardianship of the *Vali-ye Faqih* and the Council of Guardians."[68]

---

65   *Iran,* April 3, 1998; Voice of the Islamic Republic of Iran Radio, September 1, 8, 2000 (DR).

66   Voice of the Islamic Republic of Iran Radio 1, 22 June 2001 (DR).

67   *Jomhuri-ye Eslami,* January 17, 2000; IRNA, June 30, 2000.

68   "Iran's clerics defend the guided republic," *Guardian,* September 4, 2000. For other criticism of Western democracy, see Intelligence Minister Hojjat 'Ali Yunesi in IRNA, January 13, 2001.

Khatami was the leading proponent of Islamic democracy as an alternative to Western liberal democracy, not just for Iran but as a new model for the Islamic world that would serve as a "new pole in the new world order." He criticized contemporary Western democracy as lacking "moral values" and spirituality. While Western democracies "had their advantages for the westerners themselves, their outward manifestation was colonialism," and therefore, he implied, they were unsuitable for Muslims. The Muslim world, he concluded, should show that it could establish an intrinsic, that is an Islamic, democracy.[69]

However, unlike the dominant faction, Khatami did acknowledge some positive elements in Western democracy. He spoke in almost glowing terms of the Puritans in 17th and 18th century America whose "vision and characteristics, in addition to worshipping God, was in harmony with a form of republicanism, democracy, and freedom." The Puritans, according to Khatami, "desired a system that combined the worship of God with human dignity and freedom," an ideal that served as basis for American civilization. He cited approvingly Alexis de Tocqueville's *Democracy in America* as saying that the "significance of this civilization lies in the fact that liberty found religion a cradle for its growth, and religion found protection of liberty its divine calling." That was the model that was suitable for Iran, in his view.[70]

Khatami did not elaborate on the actual characteristics of Islamic democracy usually, speaking in general terms. Yet he maintained that Islamic democracy, like the Puritan model, should have a "religious identity," meaning that it should be "ethical and humane," based on a "respect for Islam's values," and "harmonious" with "our cultural value systems." An important aspect of this democracy was that "power should be criticized" since—he said echoing Lord Acton—"too much power leads to corruption, even if those who hold power are good people." Since Iran's religious democracy was an "innovative" and a "special type" of democracy, he admitted that Iran has "a long way to achieve full democracy" and envisaged great obstacles in realizing it. Yet, he was confident that Iran's "journey for democracy [was] irreversible." At the same time, he argued that the Islamic revolution brought more than a measure of democracy to Iran, and claimed, probably to appease hard-liners, that Khomeini too "preached the

---

69   IRNA, July 31, August 7, 2000, January 14, 21, May 1, 2001; Vision of the Islamic Republic of Iran Network, September 1, 4, 2000, 28 May 2001 (DR); AFP, February 10, 2001.

70   Khatami to CNN, broadcasted by IRIB TV, January 8, 1998 (DR).

establishment of a democratic regime" in which "the wishes of the people" were the criteria by which the regime should lead. There was no other way but to accept the democratic religious regime of the people. He conceded, however, that a gap existed between the ideal and the reality when he spoke of "a missing link" in Iran, due to the "separation between the people and power." A revolutionary must try to fill that deficiency, and it is in doing so that we will serve the republican character of our regime, he stressed.[71]

Reformists: limited tolerance. Khatami's notion of Islamic democracy implies the exclusion of non-Muslims or at least a distinction between them and the Muslim majority. Equally important, the distinction he made between tolerating those who oppose government policies and suppressing those who seek to remove the Islamic system altogether, restricts this democracy only to those who accept Islamic principles and deprives those outside of the rights and benefits of democracy. In this sense, Khatami is not fundamentally different from members of the dominant faction in rejecting the legitimacy of secularists to be part of Iranian democracy. Again, the difference is more in the scope of pluralism and tolerance within the Islamic system.

Another such problem is Khatami's discussion of the status of women in his Islamic democracy. Khatami says that Islam attaches great importance to the role of women in society. Concurrently, he conceded that "many of the rights of our women have been infringed and they face discrimination," but he does not mention the source of this discrimination. Nor does he address the possibility that Islamic laws and cultural attitudes in themselves may have a negative impact on the status of women. Likewise, he too stressed the importance of the women's role in the house and family, an argument often used in order to preserve women's traditional roles.[72]

Other reformist *'ulama* have views similar to Khatami's. Ayatollah Montazeri, for instance, agrees that the legal bases of Islamic government are different from those of democracy, but both rely on acceptance by the people. Yet in discussing his notion of democracy, he added that "we are of course assuming at this point that all the people abide by the teachings of Islam, they call for the establishment of Islamic government and implementation of Islamic decrees, and respect Islam and its teachings." He did not address the problem of those who do not fit into these assumptions. He also insists that the democratic system which he envisions must remain Islamic, since

---

71   AFP, July 31, 2000; IRNA, August 7, 2000, May 1, 28, June 21, 2001; *al-Hayat*, May 1, 2, 2001.

72   Tehran Vision of the Islamic Republic of Iran Network, May 3, 25 2001 (DR).

the "Islamic nature of the legislation in the *Majlis* is guaranteed by the supervision of the jurists of the Guardian Council."[73]

The liberals: the people's voice comes first. Even Kadivar, in his earlier writings, spoke of a "social contract" based on collective logic and on public interest, although not in violation of the fundamentals of religion. Later, however, he spoke of a religious system based only on popular consent. "Should the will of the people come into conflict with religion," he says, the people's voice should be given precedence. And he asserted: "The people cannot be dragged to paradise in chains."[74]

Iranian 'ulama and Sunni Islamists: democracy has a better chance in Iran

The majority of Islamist leaders and thinkers, both Sunni and Shi'i, have adopted the discourse of democracy and promote the idea of Islamic democracy or the argument that Islam is essentially more democratic than liberal democracy.[75] Only radicals, Ayatollah Mesbah Yazdi and his supporters among the Shi'is and the radical Sunni Islamic groups which adhere to Sayyid Qutb's ideology, totally reject the discourse of democracy as an alien idea tantamount to heresy. This is a proof of the power of the idea of democracy, even though its interpretation and implementation may be wide in scope.

The debate in Iran assumed new momentum after two decades of Islamic rule, in response to popular pressure from below for effective democratization and to dissident views among some *'ulama*. Sunni Islamists most often discuss the compatibility between Islam and democracy in order to allay fears of non-Islamist circles, as part of their effort to win broader support or pave their way through coalition building, as was the case with the FIS in Algeria in the 1990s. They also employ the discourse of democracy as a challenge to unpopular military-authoritarian regimes. In other words, the Sunni debate is more theoretical whereas the Iranian discourse has to

---

73   Montazeri to *al-Sharq al-Awsat*, cited in *Mideast Mirror*, May 25, 2000; Montazeri to *Middle East Journal*, p. 15.

74   Menashri, p. 35; Kadivar to *Frankfurter Allgemeine Zeitung*.

75   For an overview of the Islamist discourse on democracy among Sunni movements, see Aziz Al-Azmeh, *Islams and Modernities* (London: Verso, 1995); Robert W. Hefner (ed.), *Remaking Muslim Politics: Pluralism, Contestation, Democratization* (Princeton University Press, 2005); David Odell-Scott (ed.), *Democracy and Religion: Free Exercise and Diverse Visions* (Kent, Ohio: Kent State University Press, 2004).

take into account the very real 1979 constitution and established governmental practices.

Both the Shiʻi *ulama* and Sunni Islamists reject Western liberal democracy as inferior to the Islamic system, citing the same reason—that it regards fallible human beings rather than God as the sovereign and, therefore, the source of legislation is seen as human and not divine. Both argue that a majority is not a proof of the validity of truths, since the truth is eternal whereas majorities are based on the changing whims of the people. Therefore, the *shariʻa*, whose sources are the word of God, is always superior to human systems of law. Both groups maintain that Western democracy lacks moral foundations or values and is unable to promote a moral society. Both agree that the Islamic system, on the other hand, is essentially a moral system and will guarantee the evolution of a moral society.

The mainstream Shiʻi *ulama* and Sunni Islamists regard the people as clearly subordinate to the leaders and rulers; they can advise the rulers but in reality have to abide by their decision. Thus the Sunni Sudanese leader and thinker, Hasan al-Turabi, who glorified the principle of *shura* or consultation, states that whenever there is a disagreement between the Islamist ruler and the community, the ruler's opinion must prevail. The mainstream Shiʻi *ulama* make the same statement. The reformist Shiʻi *ulama* seek greater balance between the *rahbar* and the community, and liberals such as Kadivar go even further in recognizing the superiority of the people over the unelected leader.

Both types of Islamists claim that liberal democracy is essentially fake and does not guarantee real liberties or prevent exploitation and oppression, since it is dominated by capital and capitalists. Islamic democracy, or the *shura* system, they argue, secures both, as it based on a perfect system of legislation and it shapes a moral society.

Both types also restrict their democracy to Islamic groups, and deny the legitimacy of secularist or non-Islamic movements or groups taking part in the democratic game and enjoying its benefits. It is possible to see similarities between the reformist trend in Iran and Sunni thinkers like Shaykh Yusuf al-Qaradhawi and Rachid Ghannouchi, who accept pluralism and a multi-party system, but only within an Islamic framework. Similarly, there is a resemblance between the mainstream *ulama* in Iran and Sunni Islamists, such as Hasan al-Turabi, who frown at such a possibility even within an Islamic system.

The exclusionary nature of the Islamists' notion of democracy pertains to non-Muslims as well. The Iranian constitution allows non-Muslims to vote and guarantees them some seats in the *Majlis*. However, senior governmental positions are reserved for Muslims only, not to mention the dominant role of the Muslim *'ulama*, headed by the *rahbar*, that precludes any possibility of genuine equality for non-Muslims.

Both groups reject civil liberties if they are opposed to Islamic teachings and values. They insist that freedom of speech should not violate the fundamentals of Islam. It appears, however, that Khatami is willing to give these liberties wider latitude than many Sunni thinkers allow. Similarly, it seems that there is greater pluralism and a more intensive debate among the Shi'i *'ulama* on these issues than among Sunni Islamists.

In assessing the relative readiness for democracy amongst Shi'i as opposed to Sunni Islamists, it is clear that the debate amongst the former carries with it a greater potential to advance toward genuine democracy. This impression is strengthened by the fact that the debate in Iran is largely a response to pressures from below for greater democratization, whereas among the Sunni Islamists it evolved largely to allay fears of non-Islamists. Overall, the fact that the Iranian system created legal and constitutional mechanisms which resemble democracy, even while depriving it of its meaning, leaves some hope that pressures from below, combined with the institutional setup, a certain pluralism and flexibility within the Iranian clergy, and genuine religious voices seeking to reconcile Islam and democracy, will eventually help produce an effective and genuine democratic system in Iran.

INDEX

Association of Combatant Clerics (Majma'-e Ruhaniyyun-e Moba-rez, MRM) (Iran), 272
Association of Muslim Scholars (Hay'at ulama al-muslimin), 266
al-Attiya, Hamad, 204

Ba'th Party (Iraq), 249, 251, 256, 269
Badr Brigade, 253
Bahrain, 14, 22; abolishment of State Security Court, 163, 170; constitution, 175, 183; constitutional monarchy, 176; discrimination against the Shi's, 179; economic liberalization, 42; expatriates, 49; foreign labor, 80; government corruption, 179; National Charter, 161, 174–5, 176; naturalization policy, 180; New Year's Eve riots, 2002, 179; parliament, 166, 176–8; political liberalization, 38–9, 157–85; political parties, 164–5, 178, 181; security services, 178; tourism, 77; women's suffrage, 160, 184
Balkans conflict, 230
Bandargate affair (Bahrain), 167, 169
Bani Sulayman family, 233, 236
Bani Yas tribe, 233, 234
al-Barrak Musallim, 119
Barzani, Mas'ud, 252
Basic Law of the State (Oman), 39, 84, 213
Bin 'Abd al-Wahhab, Muhammad, 94, 95, 99
Bin Baz, 'Abd al-'Aziz 90–8, 103, 104
Bin Jibrin, 'Abdallah, 101
Bin Khalifa, Muhammad 182

Bin Ladin, Usama, 122, 197
Birth Spacing Services Program (Oman), 79
Board of Senior 'Ulama (Hay'at Kibar al-'Ulama) (BSU), 89, 101, 104
Bughayth, Sulayman, 114
Burns, William J., 207
Bush, George W., 2, 3, 122, 229
Bushahri, Jinan 112
business community, 44–5

Catholic Church, 9
censorship, 247; see also individual states
Central Municipal Council (CMC) (Qatar), 190–2, 208
Chalabi, Ahmad, 253, 254
Cheney, Dick, 230
Christianity, 102
citizenship, 60; see also individual states
CNN, 127
Commanding Good and Forbidding Wrong (al-amr bil-ma'ruf wal-nahi 'an al-munkar), 103
Committee for the Defense of Legitimate Rights (CDLR), 100, 104
constitutional monarchy, 134; see also individual states
Consultative Council (Saudi Arabia), 39, 42, 84
contraception, 79
Convention against Torture (UN, 2000), 202
Convention on the Elimination of All Forms of Discrimination against Women (UN, 1979), 198
Council of Ministers (COM) (UAE), 237–8